David Yallop's l... *the Earth*, is abo... the Jackal, the wo... ...ous terrorist. His other books are *To Encourage the Others*, which has twice forced the British Government to reopen the Craig/Bentley murder case; *The Day the Laughter Stopped*, a biography of Fatty Arbuckle that posthumously rehabilitated him and solved a 50-year-old murder mystery; *Deliver Us From Evil*, an investigation that established the truth about the Yorkshire Ripper seven months before Peter Sutcliffe was arrested; and *In God's Name,* an investigation into the death of Pope John Paul I which was translated into nearly forty languages, sold more than 5 million copies worldwide, and won the Crime Writers' Gold Dagger Award for the best non-fiction book of the year in 1984.

Also by David Yallop

TO ENCOURAGE THE OTHERS
THE DAY THE LAUGHTER STOPPED
IN GOD'S NAME
DELIVER US FROM EVIL
TO THE ENDS OF THE EARTH

and published by Corgi Books

BEYOND
REASONABLE
DOUBT?

David Yallop

CORGI BOOKS

BEYOND REASONABLE DOUBT?
A CORGI BOOK : 0 552 13453 8

Originally published in Great Britain by
Hodder & Stoughton Ltd

PRINTING HISTORY
Hodder & Stoughton edition published 1978
Corgi edition published 1995

Copyright © David A. Yallop 1978, 1995

The right of David Yallop to be identified as the author of this
work has been asserted in accordance with sections 77 and 78
of the Copyright Designs and Patents Act 1988.

Conditions of Sale
1. This book is sold subject to the condition that it shall not,
by way of trade or otherwise, be lent, re-sold, hired out or
otherwise circulated in any form of binding or cover other than
that in which it is published and without a similar condition
including this condition being imposed on the subsequent
purchaser.
2. This book is sold subject to the Standard Conditions of Sale
of Net Books and may not be re-sold in the UK below the net
price fixed by the publishers for the book.

Set in 10/11pt Linotype Times by Kestrel Data, Exeter.

Corgi Books are published by Transworld Publishers Ltd,
61–63 Uxbridge Road, Ealing, London W5 5SA,
in Australia by Transworld Publishers (Australia) Pty Ltd,
15–25 Helles Avenue, Moorebank, NSW 2170,
and in New Zealand by Transworld Publishers (NZ) Ltd,
3 William Pickering Drive, Albany, Auckland.

Reproduced, printed and bound in Great Britain by
Cox & Wyman Ltd, Reading, Berks.

FOR ANNA
STILL MY BEST FRIEND

CONTENTS

Appendices:

Photo credits
We would like to thank the following for permission to reproduce photographs as listed below:

Auckland Star: 3, 9, 24; *New Zealand Herald:* 23, 30, 35, 36; Police Department: 5-8, 10-20, 22, 26-29, 31, 32; Doig Photography: 1, 2, 21; Vivien Thomas: 4

AUTHOR'S ACKNOWLEDGEMENTS

To the many people who assisted me in seeking the truth I would like to express my gratitude. Some only agreed to help on the strict understanding that their names were not made public. I have respected their wishes. I am grateful to them and to the following:

Ernie Alexander; Mrs Alexander; John Barr; Beverley Batkin; Pat Booth; Arnold Brooks; Richard Brough; Michael Bungay; the late Mrs Dorothy Cathcart; Mervyn Cathcart; Cherry Cathcart; Ron Chitty; Mrs Chitty; Keith Christie; June Donachie; Bill Earl, producer of the TV1 programme 'Dateline'; William Eggleton; Dr Martyn Finlay; Ross Fleming; Jocelyn Fleming; Peter Garratt; Mrs Garratt; Robin Garratt; Bernard Heath; Sir Trevor Henry; Grace Hessell; Graham Hewson; Lyrice Hills; Robert Hills; Mr Hobson, Mr Ward and the staff of Paremoremo Prison; Kenneth Hooton; Lynette Hooton; Bruce Hutton; Alan Jameson; Edith Judge; Odette Leather; Claire MacGee; Queenie McConachie; Ella McGuire; George McGuire; Des Monaghan, Controller of Programmes TV1 New Zealand; David Morris; George Morrison; Brian Murray; Dr Donald Nelson; Sir Alfred North; G. S. Orr, Secretary for Justice; David Payne, Julie Priest; Owen Priest; Bob Rock; Mr Roddick; Mrs Roddick; Bruce Roddick; Kevin Ryan; Rory Shanahan; Margaret Smith; Ted Smith; Ian Spratt; Peggy Spratt; Dr James Sprott; Janet Sutherland; Lyall Sutton; Paul Temm; Allan Thomas; Arthur Thomas; Ivy Thomas; Jean Thomas; Laura Thomas; Mary Thomas; Peter Thomas; Ray Thomas; Richard Thomas; Robyn Thomas; Vivien Thomas; Pat Vesey; Peter Walter; Robert Walton, Assistant Commissioner of Police; Peter Williams; the staff of the Auckland Supreme Court; the librarian and staff of the Government Library, Wellington, particularly Cheryl Watts; the staff of the Court of Appeal at Wellington, particularly the Registrar, Douglas Jenkin.

For her help with the research for this latest edition, I would like yet again to thank Cheryl Watts, now of Radio New Zealand.

INTRODUCTION

After this book's initial publication in New Zealand in 1978 a great deal of nonsense and fantasy was written and reported by that country's news media concerning the circumstances and the reasons surrounding my initial involvement in what since 1970 has always been referred to as 'the Thomas case'.

It was said that I had been paid a huge amount of money to come to New Zealand and investigate this case. The amount would vary, as would my benefactor, depending on who was telling the tale, but the thrust was always the same. I was commissioned, so it was confidently asserted, to investigate then write a book that concluded that Arthur Thomas was innocent of the murders of Harvey and Jeannette Crewe.

That this book exists and that as a result of it Thomas is a free man is solely because of two love affairs. The first, with my wife Anna, continues. The second, with New Zealand, well, that is another story.

In late 1976 I flew with Anna from London to Wellington to meet my future wife's parents for the first time. For Anna this was a return to her homeland, for me a first visit. Some months before our departure I casually mentioned this intended trip to colleagues at my then British publisher, Hodder and Stoughton. They had recently published my second book, *The Day The Laughter Stopped*, not only in the United Kingdom, but also in what publishers still identify as 'The Commonwealth'. To the Sales Director at Hodders it was an opportunity to exploit. To this particular author it was a moment when I wished I had kept my mouth shut. This was intended to be a holiday and a strictly private trip. There are undoubtedly times when reporters are invaluable to an author. The first meeting with prospective in-laws is not one of them. We reached a compromise. Two weeks of anonymity before any interviews.

During those two weeks that second love affair began. How could it fail not to? A country more or less the same size as my own but with only some three million people. That amount of space ensured less aggression, less stress, less violence, less crime; a greater degree of gentleness, of tranquillity and of something that was called when I was young a caring Christian community.

I had read before this first trip to New Zealand that it was 'a country in a time warp, some thirty years behind England'. In some respects that is exactly what I found in December 1976 and I revelled in it.

During the third week the first of a series of interviews took place. The interviewer, Margaret Hayward, had in another existence been the personal and private secretary of Prime Minister Norman Kirk. At the time of our meeting Kirk had been dead for a number of years. I recall being particularly struck by the fact that notwithstanding her close professional relationship with the ex-Premier and despite the fact that he could only be referred to in the past tense, whenever she spoke of him it was always 'Mr Kirk'. There was something else about that interview that I also very clearly recall.

'Of course many people in New Zealand are wondering why you are here.'

'Really? I'm surprised that anyone knows that I'm here.'

'Oh, it's a small country.'

It isn't, but over the years I came to know exactly what she meant. On one occasion two years on I fell down a flight of stairs inside Noah's Hotel in Christchurch. Twenty minutes later I had a telephone call from a lawyer friend in Auckland. His opening observation, 'I hear you were pissed in Noah's this afternoon,' was slightly wide of the mark, but it indicated that Margaret Hayward had a point. I told her that the trip was merely an extended holiday. She smiled and shook her head.

'The Press think you're here to investigate the Thomas case.'

'Thomas who?'

'Arthur Thomas.'

'Margaret, until this moment I have never heard of Arthur Thomas. Who is he and why would the Press think I'm here to investigate his case?'

Thus I learned a little of the farmer from Pukekawa.

At every subsequent interview much the same scene occurred. After questions about a teenager named Derek Bentley[1], who had been taken out one cold January day in 1953 and, courtesy of the British Government, murdered, and questions about sweet, talented, funny Roscoe Arbuckle[2], who had been murdered in quite a different way at the bar of American public opinion, the assertion that I was in New Zealand to write about Thomas would be made, to be followed by my denial and a request for information. I would listen while the reporters outlined the case from their own knowledge and perspective. Putting to one side the variable quality of the information, one fact shone out like a beacon. If these reporters were representative of the country as a whole then the nation was split right down the middle when it came to consider the guilt or innocence of Arthur Allan Thomas.

After the interviews Anna and I continued our holiday and I rapidly saw the truth of Margaret Hayward's 'small country' observation. I concluded that I was shortly going to marry into a family with three million members, certainly everyone seemed to know

[1] *To Encourage The Others*
[2] *The Day The Laughter Stopped*

everyone. I was enthralled with the country and my desire for knowledge of it was insatiable. The fact that it was high summer helped, but there was an easy-going 'she'll be right' philosophy that was quite new to me. Nobody in England went around saying 'she'll be right'. Looking back now, seventeen years later, it is obvious that even an extended holiday of six weeks is no way to come to terms with a country, but hindsight always has twenty-twenty vision.

After Christmas in Lower Hutt we began to drive North to visit other members of this, by my only-child experiences, vast family. From time to time at a barbecue or dinner party I would raise the Thomas case, then sit back and listen. Opinions always divided: a wife disagreeing with her husband; a sister with her brother. These experiences stimulated within me a memory of another warm summer's evening in London, more than three years earlier.

As a result of the publication of *To Encourage The Others* and my television play of the same name, the then British Government had been forced to re-open what is known as the Craig–Bentley murder case. Their secret inquiries concluded that all was well, that justice had been done. Many remained unconvinced, among their number the Lords Arran and Goodman. In June 1973 they provoked a full-scale debate on the case in the House of Lords. Speaking without recourse to notes for some forty minutes, Lord Goodman made a speech that for lucidity and clarity of thought surpassed anything I have ever heard in my life. Sitting in a variety of New Zealand homes nearly four years later a particular part of that speech kept resounding in my mind:

'Very occasionally, as I have said, cases occur in our criminal courts in which, although they have been concluded, and concluded with the finality with which these cases were concluded, that is to say, by a capital sentence, there nevertheless remains a stir of public anxiety and concern. Where this happens and where that stir of public anxiety and concern fails to be allayed by the passage of time, it appears to be a pretty historic certainty that there is something that needs to be looked into. If you examine the occasional cases where this has happened, public concern is a pretty good index of the need for examination and re-examination. This has happened with very great rarity. It is difficult to put a finger on any number of cases of which this observation could be made; but where it has happened – as in the case of Oscar Slater, the case of Evans and a few others – *time does not enable one to bury the situation.*'

In early February 1977 our visit to New Zealand was coming to a close. We had returned to Auckland. I was recounting to Neil Robinson, my editor, my feelings about his country. My love affair with 'God's Own Country' was now in full flower. Neil smiled at me tolerantly.

'Hodders would like you to come back here and write a book for them.'

'Would they now.'

'Yes, very much. We can't afford to pay you much. The advance would be two thousand dollars.' [At that time a little over one thousand pounds Sterling.]

'Any particular subject that you have in mind?'

'Yes, David, there is. Have you ever heard of a man called Arthur Thomas?'

AUTHOR'S NOTE

The reader will see that from time to time I refer within the book to 'this country' and to 'now, eight years later in 1978'. The Introduction and the Epilogue are of now. The main text is of a time when Arthur Thomas was still serving a life imprisonment inside New Zealand's maximum security prison.

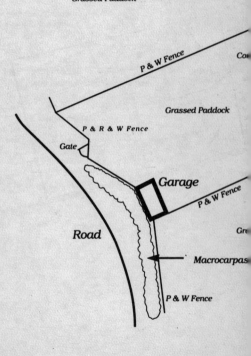

Plan of Surround of
Mr and Mrs Crewe's Home at Pukekawa

Surveyed by B.K. Sly Registered Surveyor on 24th June 1970

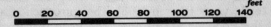

```
                                    feet
0   20   40   60   80   100  120  140
```

TC 104/80

Grassed Paddock

P & W Fence   Co

Grassed Paddock

P & R & W Fence

Gate

Garage

P & W Fence

Road

Gre

Macrocarpas

P & W Fence

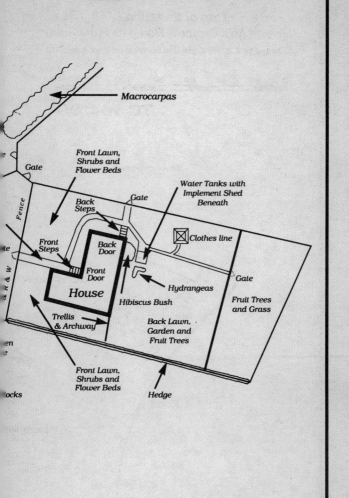

Macrocarpas

Front Lawn,
Shrubs and
Flower Beds

Gate

Back
Steps

Gate

Water Tanks with
Implement Shed
Beneath

Fence

Clothes line

Front
Steps

Back
Door

Front
Door

House

Hydrangeas

Gate

Hibiscus Bush

Fruit Trees
and Grass

Trellis
& Archway

Back Lawn,
Garden and
Fruit Trees

Front Lawn,
Shrubs and
Flower Beds

Hedge

'Throughout the web of the English Criminal Law one golden thread is always to be seen, that it is the duty of the prosecution to prove the prisoner's guilt . . . If, at the end of and on the whole of the case, there is reasonable doubt, created by the evidence given by either the prosecution or the prisoner . . . the prosecution has not made out the case and the prisoner is entitled to an acquittal.' —*Viscount Sankey L.C. expressing the unanimous opinion of the House of Lords in the case of Woolmington v. D.P.P.*

'It is no business of the defence to prove innocence or even prove reasonable doubt. The defence, if it can show any weakness in the Crown case, if it can bring you to the stage where you have a reasonable doubt, then, of course, you ought to acquit, but that is only argument on the evidence. The burden of proof, as we call it, to prove the crime and to prove who was the criminal, rests and rests always upon the Crown.' —*Mr Justice Henry (now Sir Trevor Henry). From his summing-up to the first jury. The Queen v. Arthur Allan Thomas March 1971.*

'Now the words "beyond reasonable doubt" mean exactly what they say. It means you should not be deterred by a fanciful or frivolous doubt. But that you must feel sure. If guilt of the accused is not established beyond reasonable doubt, then the accused is entitled to be acquitted.' —*Mr Justice Perry (now Sir Clifford Perry). From his summing-up to the second jury. The Queen v. Arthur Allan Thomas April 1973.*

Prologue

Pukekawa, 17 June 1970. Night-time. The gusting south-westerly wind buffeted the car as it sped along the deserted country roads. The strange collection of items in the trailer behind bounced and rattled as one of the wheels hit a pothole. At the wheel of the Hillman, Arthur Thomas turned his head at the sound, anxiously checking that none of the items had been thrown into the road. Satisfied, he turned back to peer through the moving windscreen wipers at the road ahead. Still staring in front, his left hand reached out to the front passenger seat and came into contact with his .22 rifle. The feel of the wooden butt gave him that measure of reassurance he had been seeking. He glanced at his gold wristwatch. It was a few minutes after 11 p.m. At this time of the night if his luck was in he would get to his destination without meeting another car. As it transpired his luck was indeed in.

Switching off ignition and lights he stared out of the window at his ultimate destination. The farmhouse of Harvey and Jeannette Crewe. The lounge and kitchen lights were still on, indicating that at least one of the Crewes was still not in bed. Good, that would make the task he had set himself that much easier. That left hand went out again and reached for the Browning. Quietly getting out of his car, he moved unseen and unheard on to the Crewe farm. The dogs were kennelled well away from the house and the rain and the wind were proving useful allies as he approached the house. Opening the garden gate, he moved cautiously from the path that led to the front door on to the front lawn. Pausing, he stared with unblinking eyes into the lounge a short distance away. Thoughtful of them not to draw the curtains. Harvey was sitting in one of the armchairs, his back towards Arthur Thomas, the smoke from his cigarette curling up into the air. On the sofa facing him sat Jeannette, the knitting needles in her hands moving quickly as she talked to her husband.

Thomas began to walk across the lawn to the side of the house. At the kitchen window and the back door he paused with a frown of concentration on his face. Harvey was in profile to him now and Jeannette completely masked. The frown was replaced with a smile at the sight of the open louvre windows. It was all going to be so easy. Moving to the back door, he quickly climbed onto the small wall. Familiar with the house and its layout he knew that the sliding kitchen door was never closed. He could see right through into the lounge. Harvey was still chatting to his wife. Thomas flicked the safety catch and pushing the rifle through the open louvre windows aimed at the side of Harvey's head. Thomas held his breath then squeezed the trigger. The impact of the shot jerked Harvey's head to the right arm of his chair. As Thomas jumped from the small wall he quickly reloaded. Bursting into the house through the back door he was down the short passage across the kitchen and into the lounge within a few seconds. Jeannette was on her feet staring in shock at the dying body of her husband. The shock turned to fear at the sight of Harvey's murderer standing there smiling. With equal rapidity the fear switched to anger. She swung her arm to bang that smile from his face but Thomas was quicker. He parried the blow with his rifle then smashed the butt of the gun into her face. Screaming with pain she fell back. Then, standing over her, he shot her in the head. As with Harvey, it required only a single shot.

He stood still, looking at the two bodies. Harvey's sprawled grotesquely in the armchair, the six feet two, sixteen stone man appeared to be sleeping – only the blood running from the head to the arm of the chair then the base of the chair and finally to the carpet indicated that he would never again rise from that chair. He glanced down at Jeannette's body. For the first time he realized that the blow he had struck with the rifle butt had broken her nose and smashed a number of her teeth. Her face was covered with blood. Her black hair was fast turning red. This was not the image that he had carried in his mind for so many years. The image that had driven him with an ever tightening jealousy to destroy her husband and then her. The passion within him was now spent. Picking a cushion up from the couch he placed it over her face to hide the reality. As he did he became aware for the first time of somebody calling and crying out.

'Mama. Mama. Want you, Mama.' How long the child had been calling out he had no idea. Time had frozen from the moment that he had got Harvey in the sights of his rifle. Walking through the lounge and the front hallway he entered the bedroom of Rochelle Crewe, the eighteen-month-old daughter, now orphaned. She was standing up in her cot.

The sobs turned to frightened screams as the young child saw not the comforting face of her mother but that of a stranger. For a moment Thomas stood staring at her; then, speaking softly, reassuringly, he laid her down in her cot. She clutched at the teddy bear he handed her. The comfort of the familiar toy soon stifled the tears. Wrapping the blankets around her Thomas patted her on the head and, retracing his steps, closed her bedroom door.

Back in the lounge it occurred to him the shots and the sounds that had disturbed Rochelle might have been heard by others. From the lounge windows he anxiously scanned Highway 22, some sixty yards away. No sign of activity there. The Chitty farm on the other side of the road was just a sea of blackness, their farmhouse was out of sight. He waited for a few minutes to see if there were any car lights approaching. There were none. Pulling the lounge curtains, he discovered to his annoyance that the wealthy Crewes did not possess a complete set of drapes.

Ahead of Arthur Thomas lay many hours' work. He returned to his car and drove it up the paddock to the garden gate. Taking some lengths of wire from his trailer he re-entered the house. He had no intention of leaving the bodies there to be found. Dead men do tell tales, particularly when they have traceable bullets in their heads. Stripping blankets and bedspreads from a couple of the bedrooms he tied them around the bodies with the wire brought from his own farm. A nearby wheelbarrow was utilized to serve as a macabre vehicle to move the remains of what such a short while ago had been a happily married young couple. First Jeannette then Harvey was put into the car trailer. Sheets of black polythene that would later be destroyed ensured that no blood dripped on to the trailer itself. Weights were attached to the two bodies to ensure that when they were dumped into the Waikato river the bodies would stay down until they had disintegrated. For Jeannette a piece of scrap metal served as a grisly ballast. For Harvey an old car axle.

The carpet that had served as Jeannette's last resting place within her own home and the cushion that he had placed over her face were burned in the fireplace. Thomas began to clean the bloodstains that abounded throughout the kitchen and lounge. Eventually he realized the impossibility of completing the task successfully. The wheelbarrow presented an easier problem and he was able to wash it out before replacing it by the water tank.

Once more he returned to the lounge. Picking up his .22 rifle he idly flicked on the safety catch as he surveyed his efforts to hide, at least for a little while, his double murder. As his hand flicked the catch a sudden thought struck him. He had reloaded immediately after killing Harvey. That reflex action would have ejected a .22 cartridge case. He searched in vain for minute after desperate minute in the garden. Despite the light from the kitchen and an outside light that small case was nowhere to be seen. Perhaps if he could not find it the police would not be able to either? Leaving the louvre windows open and the back light on, Thomas walked to his car. Minutes later he was on his way to the Waikato river. As a local boy he had an intimate knowledge of the area and knew a dozen places where the two bodies could go into the river. If his luck was in he could get to the Waikato, dump the bodies, and return to his own farm without being seen. As it transpired his luck, yet again, was indeed in.

The above account of the murders of Harvey and Jeannette Crewe is based entirely on the Crown prosecution case that was subsequently and successfully brought against Arthur Allan Thomas. The case for the Crown has triumphed not once, but twice. It has convinced two juries. It has survived two Courts of Appeal. It has withstood an official examination by a senior retired judge. Even a further referral to the Court of Appeal has left the Crown's case persuasive enough to ensure that Arthur Thomas remained in New Zealand's only maximum security prison.

Yet that above account of the deaths of the Crewes is demonstrably inaccurate, riddled with error and palpably false. I do not claim that this book contains all the evidence or all the facts pertaining to what has become known as 'The Thomas Case'. I do claim that it contains new facts and new evidence that have never been laid before a jury. The question is at once both simple and complex: 'When all the evidence contained in this book is duly considered, has Arthur Thomas been proved guilty, beyond reasonable doubt?'

1

It Begins

Pukekawa, 17 June 1970. Daytime. The day that preceded the events I have just described held no hint of
the horror that was about to burst upon this small and
friendly farming community. Situated twenty-five crow-
flying miles south of Auckland, its population of six
hundred people undoubtedly regarded it as just a
run-of-the-mill day when they rose from their beds. The
weather was as typical as the tasks that lay ahead of
them. A cold wet windy wintry New Zealand day.
Something largely to be endured rather than enjoyed.
They little knew then that two gunshots that would
be fired that evening at 8.30 p.m. would still be
reverberating throughout the district nearly eight years
later.

Opinions differ as to the meaning of the Maori name
Pukekawa. Some believe it means 'Bitter Hill', others
'Fertile Hill', still others 'the Hill of the Kawa Tree'.
Whatever its origin the district has a history that belies
its quiet rolling hills. Where sheep and cattle now graze
in peace violence has erupted on a number of occasions.
In 1820 the local Maoris were confronted by the
Ngapuhi warriors from the Bay of Islands armed with
muskets obtained from early Europeans. The Maoris
of Pukekawa died in great numbers.

In 1863 Governor George Grey found he had a
full-scale war on his hands in the Waikato. Killing was
again in the air of Pukekawa.

In 1920 it returned yet again, this time in sensational

1

form, when a Pukekawa farmer, Sidney Seymour Eyre, was murdered in his bed on the night of 24 August. That murder has some extraordinary parallels with the investigation of the deaths of the Crewes and the subsequent trials of Arthur Thomas. Those parallels will be examined later in this book.

In 1932, just fourteen miles from Pukekawa, farmer Sam Lakey and his wife were murdered in what was to become the most sensational murder case in New Zealand's history. The most sensational, that is, until the night of 17 June 1970. Like the murder of Eyre this double murder also has strange counterparts to the deaths of Harvey and Jeannette Crewe. It will also be the subject of comment within this book.

On 17 June 1970 it is unlikely that any of this violent heritage was the subject of conversation in Pukekawa. Cows and sheep do not wait while a farmer considers his heritage.

Down at the Mercer Ferry end of the township, Ted Smith, having completed the morning's milking and checking of stock, returned to his house to wrestle with that bane of all farmers' lives, forms. His wife Margaret, although suffering from an influenza attack, told him of her determination to play indoor bowls at Glen Murray that evening.

David Payne sat in his farm studying the minutes of the last ratepayers' meeting, and wondering who had not been contacted and advised that there was a meeting in the local hall that evening. As secretary of the association he had more than a passing interest in a good attendance. Glancing out of a window at gusting wind and rain, he opined to his wife that they would be lucky to get twenty.

Arthur Thomas and his young English wife, Vivien, mulled over a problem of their own. A lunchtime appointment with their dentist in Tuakau plus a garage check-up on their car in the same town would keep them away from their farm for a number of hours. The

2

problem was cow No. 4. It was due to calve but a recent heavy fall had left the animal partly paralysed. Slings and supports acquired from local veterinary surgeon Henry Collett had taken the weight off the cow's rear. The first fight was to keep it alive until it calved, the second to see if its survival could be sustained beyond that time.

Len Demler stayed close to his farm most of the day. He for one would not be going to any ratepayers' meeting that evening, but then he never went. Having spent the previous evening at his daughter Jeannette's farm he decided to catch up on some letters that needed writing.

Up at the Crewe farm there was greater activity. While next door his father-in-law merely pottered about, Harvey was sitting in his lounge discussing the potential purchase of a bull with stock agent John Gracie. The stock agent had arranged for Harvey to accompany him to Glen Murray to check on a particular animal. Meanwhile Jeannette was preparing for a visit from an old friend, Thirryl Pirrett. Harvey told his wife that if he didn't like the look of the bull at Glen Murray then they would both drive to a clearing sale at Bombay and check the stock there.

These, then, were the kind of events that were going on in the community of Pukekawa, that day. Plebeian, mundane and so ordinary. The 'Hill' of Pukekawa, rising over nine hundred feet above sea level, had looked down on such events for many years. In a district noted for its prime lambs, beef and excellent dairy produce, life had a settled stable quality. Farms tended to pass from father to son. A considerable number in the area could trace their families' first involvement in Pukekawa back to the late nineteenth century. Roads, some still little more than dust tracks, bear names that recall early settlers – men whose descendants still farm there: Marshalls, Brewsters, Logans. By big city standards, the work is hard and the pleasures simple.

3

Even now, the community relies on a single store, the focal centre for exchanging gossip. In 1970, the quickest route across the Waikato river was by boat at the end of Mercer Ferry Road. Pukekawa still awaited the bridge it had been promised for over one hundred years.

Even after the end of the Second World War children could still be seen riding ponies to the primary school although by that time the school bus had been operating for a number of years.

The occasional dance at the Pukekawa Hall, attended not merely by the teenagers but by entire families. The mobile library with a membership that dwindled from a mid-1930s high of fifty-nine to a total of twenty by 1970. A tennis club which had opened and closed over the years so many times that to chart its exact history would drive a historian mad. A rugby football club that from early Spartan times when the players rode on horseback to the field, used a manure shed to change in and a cattle trough for a shower had, by 1954, finally admitted reality and amalgamated with nearby Onewhero. A thriving golf club with an ever-growing membership. An equally popular bowling club complete with a pavilion erected piece by piece by the local people. Indoor bowls, table tennis matches. Talk of lambing or the current price of a bull. Talk of fruit preserves or of taking a trip to Tuakau to look at the latest fashions. Of a rabbit shot or some whitebait caught. People who stopped, not merely to pass the time of day but also to take a genuine interest in each other. Like all small communities it had its groups, its cliques. It had its class structure. It still does. It had its scandals, its extra-marital sex. A little bit of rustling. The odd piece of poaching. But any big skeletons were securely locked away in the back of older minds.

Curious, now, how many can recall the plebeian, mundane, ordinary things that they were doing on 17 June 1970. If it had not been for what occurred at

4

the Crewe farm that evening it is extremely doubtful if those everyday things would have stayed within the recall and memories of the individuals concerned for more than a few weeks at most. In the event, nearly eight years later, most of those remaining in the area who were there on 17 June 1970, can tell you, if they care to talk about that day, exactly and precisely what they were doing and where they were doing it.

The first indication that something dreadful had occurred on the Crewe farm did not come until Monday 22 June. For five days various people had phoned the Crewes without success, yet no-one became alarmed. Until the Monday Emmett Shirley had continued to deliver milk, bread, newspapers and mail to the Crewe box. Despite the fact that he could clearly see that none of the deliveries for Thursday, Friday and Saturday had been collected, he did not become alarmed. He merely considered they might have gone away without telling him, something they had never done before, and refrained from leaving any further deliveries on the Monday.

Jeannette's father, Len Demler, having dined with his daughter and son-in-law on the eve of their deaths, was apparently not perturbed when he heard no more from them. He did not become alarmed when his son-in-law, a good footballer and a keen follower of the game, failed to put in an appearance at the Onewhero Jubilee match on Saturday 20 June. He equally did not consider it was cause for concern when the young Crewes did not appear at the dinner and dance that followed the match.

I believe that the fact that these people and others did not show concern in those five days is as much a comment on Harvey and Jeannette as upon those who others, with the wisdom of hindsight (always a valuable weapon when conducting an armchair investigation), have criticized. The fact that no-one had any social contact with the Crewes for those five days, that none saw them or spoke to them is, for me, confirmation of a fact that I have established from countless sources. Harvey and Jeannette Crewe were antisocial people. I am sure that if the stock agents who phoned without success, the delivery man who allowed provisions to pile up, and the father who ignored their absence for five days had experienced the same lack of contact with any of their other clients or relations then their reaction would have been markedly different. It has been said that those reactions were not normal. I contend it was the Crewes who were abnormal, at least by social definitions.

On Monday 22 June Len Demler received a telephone call from stock agent Ron Wright. He wanted to send trucks to pick up sheep from the Crewe farm but despite continuous phoning had not been able to contact Harvey. Earlier, Demler had received a call from another stock agent advising him that he, too, was unable to contact either of the Crewes on the phone. This earlier call at about 8 a.m. from Jerry Moore had been to the effect that Moore and another agent had actually called at the Crewe farm and could find no sign of either Harvey or Jeannette. As a result of the call from Ron Wright, shortly before 1 p.m., Demler finally decided that he should take a drive up to his daughter and son-in-law and see what was going on. If Demler's actions to this point are explicable, from this moment on, try as I might, and I have tried very very hard, I cannot find an explanation for what he did and for what he did not do. Neither for that matter can the police, the Crown prosecutor or any of the other eighty people I have interviewed. I let Demler speak for himself:

'I went up there about one o'clock. I went up in the car and left the car at the gate and walked in. The road gate was shut when I got there. There were ten sheep in the paddock between the gate and the house. When I got up towards the house, I went in the front gate, I heard the baby talking to herself in there and I went round to the back door and I saw the light was on at the back and the light was on in the kitchen, and the key was in the door. That was on the outside of the door. Harvey had a wheelbarrow to use on the farm and that was normally kept down at the back door down by the fence there. On this Monday it was there, it was in its normal place, not far away from where it was generally kept. I did not touch it at all. I went into the house and first of all the dishes on the table with all the flounder on it, just eaten, were all just there and then I walked on and I could see there was blood on the carpet and went in and had a look at the baby and then I looked into the bedroom and the bed was still made and there was no-one in there and I didn't know what to do for the best and thought I would have to find somewhere for the baby. The blood that I mentioned I saw along the carpet mainly at the time, towards the bedroom, towards the passage. At that time I noticed no other blood. I didn't look anywhere else. Rochelle looked very thin. She had been crying a lot and her eyes were sunk in but she wasn't crying at the time. She had a pyjama top on and napkins and she had no blankets on her at all. The napkins were dirty. At that point I didn't know what to do exactly so thought I had better go home to stop those trucks coming for the sheep, then I thought I would pick up Owen Priest on the way back and have a good look around to see if they were perhaps about the farm somewhere. I left the house and went down home and rang Ron Wright . . .'

That extract comes from Len Demler's sworn deposition, made in November 1970. Some five months after his daughter and son-in-law had vanished off the face of the earth. Five months in which he had had time to consider his actions. Lights on in the middle of the day, bloodstains on the carpet, blood drag marks clearly in evidence, a distressed child in her cot, yet the grandfather comes to the conclusion that above all else, he

7

must drive back to his farm and phone a stock agent to cancel trucks that were due to come out for sheep. Why leave little Rochelle in her cot? Why not immediately phone the police? Why not immediately phone a neighbour? Or go to the Chitty farm, immediately opposite? Why not look over the entire house? Having returned to his own house and phoned the stock agent, he discovered that Ron Wright was not there. Instead of merely leaving a message about the trucks, he waited until Wright came back into his office and returned the phone call. Then, and only then, did he drive to the Priest farm and ask Owen Priest to accompany him to the deserted, bloodstained farm that contained a young distressed child.

During the course of my interviews with Owen and Julie Priest, Owen described to me that June afternoon when Len Demler called:

'I was working in a paddock between my house and the hatchery. Heard a car pull up on the road. When I got to the gate I recognized it as Len's red Cortina. He asked me to go up to the Crewe farm with him and said, "I don't know what the hell's happened up there. But there's a terrible bloody mess." With that Len turned and walked back to his car. On the way up Len turned to me and said, "They're not there. I wonder where the bloody hell they've gone to." He made no mention of any bloodstains. Then when I went in and saw all this blood, it stopped me stone dead. Len was behind me. I recall him saying, "I want to know what's happened. But I don't want to find them." I moved forward to search the farm not knowing what to expect. I comforted myself with the thought that if there was any funny business going on Len was right there behind me. Although I was pretty composed and my mind was working clearly I was nevertheless apprehensive. I found Rochelle and then continued to explore the house. When I got to the bathroom and toilet I looked around to make some comment to Len. He was

8

standing by the back door! I realized that I had gone over the entire house on my own. With perhaps some joker waiting to attack me. That rocked me a bit. Initially when we had entered the house Len kept saying, "The bugger's killed her and done himself in. I tell you Harvey's killed her." It began to play on my nerves after he'd come out with this two or three times. I turned to him. "Look Len, we don't know what's happened. It could have been a third party." He was silent after that.'

They searched the outbuildings and surrounding area for about twenty minutes and found nothing. Returning to the farmhouse, they took Rochelle from her cot. Of her parents, apart from the ominous bloodstains, there was not a trace. Back at his own farm Owen Priest phoned the local police. Len Demler meanwhile had taken the little girl to the house of a friend. The news that would shock a nation had finally become known. Soon, apart from Constable Wyllie who had come from Tuakau, well-meaning neighbours were pouring on to the Crewe farm. Now they had something far more important than stock prices or last night's bowls results to concern themselves with. They little knew it then, but for many of them their lives were about to be changed irrevocably. As the news flew around Pukekawa it was also reaching places further afield.

In another ten minutes Inspector Hutton would have been out of the building that houses Auckland CIB. But waiting for him when he emerged out of the lift on the ground floor was his superior, Mr Ross, with an offer that Hutton could not refuse: 'Would you pop down to Pukekawa?' At that time Bruce Hutton had behind him some thirty homicide investigations that he had either led or been involved with. Forty-one-year-old Hutton was in many ways the ideal man to head the Pukekawa investigation, one of the few senior officers in Auckland who had intimate knowledge of farmers and a way of life totally different from that of

9

the average Auckland sophisticate. Born in a small country community, he had been a farmer before turning policeman in 1948. After two years in the force he returned once more to the land having married a farmer's daughter. In 1956 he went back to a career in the police force. Now in June 1970 he was returning once more to the land, but this time as a detective inspector in charge of a potential homicide inquiry.

When I interviewed him in the summer of 1977, that first marriage and his career in the police force were over. He had remarried, yet again a farmer's daughter, and was master of a superb farm. He left the force early, very early, and many breathed a sigh of relief when he resigned, not least I suspect the criminal fraternity of New Zealand. Still only forty-seven, his mind is as sharp as a pin. It is not only a highly organized mind, it is a very controlled one.

'I vividly remember going out there. It was late afternoon. Never been to Pukekawa in my life. I arrived at the farm and was immediately horrified. My first reaction was, "If this is a homicide what are all those vehicles doing parked on the farm?" I got the vehicles and the people out, but by that time the damage had been done. Irrevocably. Now this is no criticism of the local people. They had rushed in to help. The most natural thing on earth to do.'

Having taken his first look over the farm with some of his men, Bruce Hutton was deeply troubled. Despite the bloodstains he held the view initially that 'there were no obvious signs that it was a homicide'. Within a few days he was even more deeply disturbed.

'It became apparent as information was assimilated that we were dealing with something very unusual. Something very, very, complex. It bore no relationship to the many other investigations that I had undertaken. Or any that I had read or studied. To New Zealand, this was something very odd indeed. Even by the standards of the Bayly murders, it was still unique. Not just one but two persons missing and a child alive in a cot.'

It is easy to understand the bemusement of the man who led the police investigation. The Crewe farmhouse was a landlocked *Marie Celeste*. The remains of a flounder fish meal on the dining-table set for two. A third flounder virtually untouched in the middle of the table. No signs of forced entry. Rochelle in her cot, unfed, from who knew when. The furniture clearly not in its correct place and some of it heavily bloodstained. More bloodstains on the carpet and lino. More bloodstains spattered in the kitchen, still more on the wall outside the front door. There the trail stopped abruptly. Dirty nappies on top of the refrigerator. The clothes drier still on, as were the kitchen and outside lights. Television still switched on but disconnected at a double plug on an extension lead in the hall and also turned off at a bedroom switch. Attempts to clear up the carnage were clearly indicated by the diluted bloodstains on the kitchen lino and saucepans in the sink that contained diluted blood. Bedclothes missing. Knitting lay on the couch but one of the needles lay bent on the floor. A woman's slipper in the vicinity of a fireplace that contained the remnants of a fire. No fingerprints within the house other than the Crewes'. They had last been seen on Wednesday 17 June at the stock clearing sale at Bombay. That had been at about 1.30 in the afternoon. Later that day Beverly Batkin, a friend of Jeannette's, had seen their car drive through Tuakau. Later still at about 4.30 in the afternoon their car had been seen parked alongside their fields. But in terms of actual positive sightings of Harvey and Jeannette there were none after they had been seen with Rochelle at that cattle sale.

The experts descended upon the farm. Men like Dr Donald Nelson and Rory Shanahan of the DSIR, a Government forensic unit that the police always use. Men like pathologist Dr Francis John Cairns.

11

Nelson and Shanahan and their colleagues from the DSIR put in their initial appearance at the farm on the morning of day two – that is, the day after Len Demler walked in and found the scene previously described. The first question they had to answer was, 'In view of the fact that two people are missing do the bloodstains represent one or two people?' At least, Dr Nelson told me that was the first question they determined to answer. My interview with him made it clear that they never considered the possibility that the bloodstains could have represented three people. Having taken blood samples they were able to advise the police as early as day three that the blood was from at least two people and that they were either dead or seriously injured. The reasons that they were able to come up with those conclusions so quickly are very simple. Harvey's blood group, it was quickly ascertained from previous blood tests, was Rhesus-positive, Jeannette's was Rhesus-negative. Both types were present in the lounge. On what was to be subsequently known as 'Harvey's chair' they found brain tissue which almost certainly meant that Harvey was dead.

Unable to obtain access to such information, a number of the newspapers in New Zealand thrashed around in search of copy that would sell copies. Bruce Hutton, reluctant to release information that might alert the third party involved – and within forty-eight hours it was established beyond any doubt that a third party was involved – played his cards close to his chest. The press, or at least some sections of it, were determined not to be thwarted by lack of facts. On Sunday 28 June the *Sunday News* ran a front page headline that screamed 'He's Alive'. Underneath the story told of a 'rumoured sighting' of Harvey Crewe at a Taupo motel. According to the *Sunday News*, Harvey had been accompanied by a woman.

Anyone reading that paper and also the *Sunday*

Times of the same date must have been very confused. The front page of the latter paper told its readers 'Double Death: Blood Clue They are Both Dead'. It was bang on target. It quoted its source as Inspector Hutton, much to his chagrin. He'd made no such statement.

According to the *Sunday News*, their source advising that Harvey was alive was also the CIB. Accurate and responsible coverage of the deaths and the subsequent trials has not been, over the past eight years, a highlight of the saga. There are numerous examples that could be quoted from press, television and radio. Even after the first trial in 1971, ridiculous errors were still occurring.

The *New Zealand Herald* published a booklet entitled 'The Crewe Murders' written by one of their crime reporters, Evan Swain. Demonstrably Swain had police co-operation when compiling his booklet which makes the following passage even more remarkable:

'Dr John Cairns, an experienced Auckland pathologist, had been taken to the Crewes' house on the day their disappearance had been noticed. From knowledge assimilated over many years of practice, he was able, by careful examination of the bloodstains and the position of the furniture, to suggest how the pair might have been killed. Months later a senior detective was to say privately that Dr Cairns's theory was amazingly accurate.'

In fact, a study of the evidence given at the first trial by Dr Cairns suggests that the initial theory put forward by him was amazingly inaccurate.

Having studied the condition of the entire house, Dr Cairns discussed with Hutton and his fellow-officers his view of how the Crewes had been killed. He considered death had been caused by a blunt instrument, a heavy piece of wood that had been subsequently burned on the fire, an axe or a tomahawk. There was some discussion about the possibility of bullet wounds but Dr

Cairns ruled this out on the grounds that no weapon was in evidence and there was no indication in the room that bullets had been fired. I find great difficulty in following his reasoning. That a man of the undoubted experience of Dr Cairns could rule out bullet wounds after a 'brief mention' is hard to understand. I invited the pathologist to discuss this and other aspects with me. He was one of the very few people who declined to be interviewed. I pointed out to him that there were a number of questions that should have been put to him during the trials that had not been put. He observed, 'There were a great many questions that should have been put that were not.'

While the police searchers combed the countryside looking not only for Harvey and Jeannette but for a non-existent axe or tomahawk, Inspector Hutton quickly moved into the national investigation pattern for homicide. The CIB concentrated on the house and its immediate surroundings while the uniformed men were responsible for the wider search. This aspect of the investigation was controlled by Inspector Pat Gaines. The magnitude of his task can only be fully appreciated by touring the area. To begin with there was the 365-acre farm of the Crewes. There were streams, the Waikato river, steep hills, valleys, gorges, volcanic holes, some of them hundreds of feet deep and full of water. Apart from the local residents, Gaines had the assistance of soldiers, Navy frogmen and Air Force helicopters. The search was conducted for the most part in appalling weather conditions, heavy winter fog that did not lift sometimes until well into the afternoon. A few minutes in that and a man was soaked through.

While this systematic search was covering an ever wider area the CIB were making progress, but it was progress of a most mystifying kind. On the one hand not a single report reached them of any activity, be it usual or unusual, occurring on or around the Crewe farm on that fateful Wednesday evening. But on the morning of Friday 19 June, a young man had been working on the farm directly opposite, owned by Ron Chitty. His name was Bruce Roddick. He didn't know it that Friday morning, but he was soon to become one of the many casualties in New Zealand's most famous murder case. Roddick's evidence had direct bearing on one of the most important questions to arise out of the deaths of Harvey and Jeannette Crewe, a question that has remained unanswered for nearly eight years: 'If eighteen-month-old Rochelle Crewe was fed between Wednesday 17 June and Monday 22 June, who fed her?'

In view of the massive controversy that has surrounded that question it cannot be examined too closely. Here published for the first time is Bruce Roddick's original statement to the police. This is not evidence given months or years later. This statement was made within twenty-four hours of Len Demler's discovery of that bloodstained farm and the crying child.

After giving details of his date of birth and address and stating that he is a self-employed casual labourer in the area who works for whoever needs a workman, it continues:

'Last Friday morning at about 7.30 a.m. I was at home when Mr Chitty telephoned me. He asked me if I could come up and help him to feed out hay. He was going to be busy at 10 a.m. with some buyers from Gisborne. I said "All right. I could work for a couple of hours in the morning." I left home at about 8.15 a.m. so it would have been about 8.30 a.m. when I passed the Crewe house. I did not notice anything. Later I was feeding out hay just behind Ron Chitty's old cottage where the police are now. This would be just after 9 a.m. The car was just parked on the grass outside the small front gate. I have seen the car before, it is a green Hillman, the modern shape, bigger than the Imp. It was facing north. There was a woman standing just inside the fence from the gateway. She seemed to be looking in my

15

direction. She would be in her thirties, and about 5ft 10ins to 5ft 11ins. I am 5ft 10ins and she looked very tall to me. Her hair was not blond, but light brown, her hair was cut short but curled up at the bottom. I was about seventy-five yards away, and she looked quite good-looking to me. She was wearing dark slacks but I don't know about the rest. It was a dull day, no sunshine at all.

'I was there for about two or three minutes and I did not see anybody else. I don't know Mrs Crewe and I have never worked for them. I don't know whether the woman I saw was Mrs Crewe or not.

'If I saw this woman again I think I could recognize her. I have just remembered she would be about medium build, I would not say she was slim.'

Having made this statement the roof fell in on Bruce Roddick. He had heard on the previous evening's radio news of the discovery of the bloodstained farm and that the police thought that whatever had happened had happened on Wednesday 17th. In view of what he had seen on the Friday, he turned to his parents and said, 'The police have got it wrong. I saw Mrs Crewe on Friday morning.' Now, of course, as his statement makes clear, he did not know Jeannette Crewe and had never worked for either her or Harvey; but seeing a woman standing by their gate on a Friday he reasonably assumed that it must be Jeannette. The thought process leading to that assumption is easy to see. If one took a man who had never seen a photograph of the Queen of England and stood him outside Buckingham Palace and told him the Queen lived there, and a short while later he saw a woman being driven out in a Rolls-Royce and waving to the crowd, he might reasonably assume he had seen the Queen, when he might well have seen Princess Margaret. All of that might seem rather obvious but in view of subsequent developments and the present attitude of Bruce Hutton it has become essential to state the obvious.

When he told his parents, they advised him to go to the police. Unsolved murders like that of Jennifer Beard were very much on their minds. It occurred to them that the same maniac might have paid a visit to Pukekawa. Bruce, like many country people, was reluctant to get involved with the police, an attitude that ex-farmer Bruce Hutton explained to me:

'Something that I was reminded of again and again during that particular investigation at Pukekawa were remarks made many years ago by a very great New Zealand detective, Frank Aplin. He used to say, "When you are dealing with farmers or cow cockies you are dealing with a totally different breed of human being. You don't just see a farmer once. You see him many times before you pop the old question. You have a look at his stock. Go over his best cow." And I think what became apparent to me in those early stages was that my field detectives were city detectives, dealing almost with foreigners. They were just not getting out of those farmers what they should have been getting. The farmer is very much like the canny Scot. He only tells you so much when he first meets you. But if you call back a few times . . . Oh, this has been proved so very many times with such an investigation. It was proved true again in Pukekawa. You know, there is a great tendency with farmers and folk that live in the countryside not to want to get involved in such an inquiry. I feel they consider that it is in some way shameful that this has happened in their neighbourhood. In my view town dwellers do not feel the same way at all.'

Having spent many weeks in Pukekawa I would endorse every single word of that. The great pity is that neither Bruce Hutton nor the men working under him in the CIB adopted such an approach in Pukekawa.

The same week that Roddick made his statement, the police asked him to come up to the Chitty farm. One of the places they were using as a control base was

the cottage that Roddick refers to in his statement.
Situated on the edge of the Chitty property and virtually
opposite the Crewe farm with Highway 22 bisecting
the two farms, it was ideal. It was a measure of the
goodwill that the local farmers felt that men like Ron
Chitty and Ian Spratt happily gave the police use of
such buildings. Perhaps if these men had witnessed the
treatment handed out to Bruce Roddick during his
second interview they might have thought twice. They
took specimens of his fingerprints. They asked him to
account for his movements, minute by minute from the
Wednesday of the previous week. They asked him what
girlfriends he had. When he told them that he did not
have a current girlfriend they asked him if he was
homosexual. They thought it odd that having reached
the ripe old age of twenty-four he was still unmarried.
They asked him if he had ever slept with a girl. It
was not just the questions, it was the heavy manner of
the interrogation that shook Roddick. It also shook
his parents when they saw their distressed, disturbed
and distraught son return home. What they felt then
was still clearly evident when I interviewed them. Mr
Roddick recalled:

'When Bruce came back home the police descended
on our farm. They stripped his car, a Standard Ten. I
told them, "Don't be bloody silly, the lad can hardly
get into it himself. Where do you think he put the
bodies, in the glove compartment?" There was an old
blanket on the passenger seat. Mum used it to protect
her clothing when she was in the car. They got very
excited about that, didn't they, Mum?

' "Oh yes," one of them started shouting, "it's got a
bloodstain on it. Look, it's covered in blood." I said to
him, "Don't be silly, that's raspberry ice cream. I
dropped it on the blanket some time ago." You could
tell just by smelling the stain. No, they were sure it was
blood. Took it away for forensic tests. When they
eventually brought it back I asked them what the DSIR

18

had made of the stain. "Oh, it's raspberry ice cream" I was told.'

While Bruce had been getting a verbal third degree up on the Chitty farm Myra Lindbergh, a local woman that Bruce also worked for, walked in with tea for the police. Seeing Roddick there she exchanged a greeting, then smilingly remarked, 'Oh, they've finally caught up with you have they, Bruce?' This led to Myra and another woman being taken home by the police and subjected to heavy questioning along the lines of, 'Has he ever attempted to sexually assault you?'

I can see a logic in treating the young man who came forward to help the police as a suspect. As Bruce Hutton said to me:

'Oh, you've got to. When there is no apparent motive. When there is no apparent suspect. At that stage you treat these sorts of people as suspects. That type of murder can just be something out of the blue. Something happening at the gate. You know, farmer telling some car wreckers to get on their way and all of a sudden it's on. That can happen.'

Indeed it can and does, but what is not justifiable is to alienate in this way the people who are being questioned. In many respects the CIB investigation in Pukekawa resembled Apaches running wild. Nevertheless, despite police methods rather than because of them, the police had been given by Roddick a vital and crucial piece of evidence as they considered the puzzle of Rochelle Crewe. The second piece of crucial evidence was not long in coming.

As a result of Bruce Roddick's statement, Bruce Hutton, while putting Roddick on his list of suspects, moved very quickly on the information that the young farmworker gave him. At 2 p.m. the same day, Rochelle was entering the consulting rooms of Dr Thomas Fox. Dr Fox at that time had had some thirty years in the medical profession. His speciality is childcare. Accompanying Rochelle was Mrs Willis, the woman who had been looking after the child since she had been found the previous day. With them was Detective Sergeant Mike Charles. This particular policeman, like Bruce Roddick, has ample cause to rue his involvement with this case. But that was in the future. On 23 June 1970 the purpose of the visit was to seek Dr Fox's opinion on two questions:

1. 'Had Rochelle been left unattended from Wednesday 17 June 1970?'
2. 'Could she have survived unattended during this period?'

I have deliberately broken off from my narrative of the investigation in Pukekawa because I consider and have considered from the outset of my research that those two questions are absolutely central to 'The Thomas Case'. For nearly eight years now this case has been debated and argued in homes, offices, farms, hotels, bars, and the Courts of this country.

Accusations of police malpractice have been countered with accusations of intimidation of Crown witnesses. There have been accusations about the planting of evidence. Accusations of phone bugging. Accusations of perjury – both sides have levelled that one at each other. Bruce Hutton has been accused of virtually every crime except starting the Second World War. The DSIR has been attacked. Lawyers, Judges, even the former Minister of Justice Martyn Finlay, all have been the subject of enormous attack. Protest meetings throughout the country. Vivien Thomas talking to a crowded university campus or a packed Auckland Town Hall. Enquiries on television conducted by, among others, Brian Edwards. Enquiries in the press conducted by, among others, Pat Booth. Discussion of cartridge case categories by forensic experts for the defence, like Dr Jim Sprott and for the prosecution by Dr Donald Nelson. Two things have been largely if not totally forgotten. The first is the flesh and blood that today languishes in prison, the man called Arthur Thomas. The second is Rochelle Crewe. These two human beings are linked in a strange, bizarre, awful way. One stands condemned of killing the other's mother and father. While one flicks through his scrapbooks of press cuttings in Paremoremo Prison, the other has been told that her parents 'were murdered by a very sick man'. Perhaps they were, but which 'very sick man'?

What shocked this country about the Crewe deaths was not that two adults were dead, but that a young innocent defenceless baby girl of eighteen months of age had been left in a Kafkaesque situation. Abandoned in a bloodspattered farm in Pukekawa. It shook the country rigid. It was, to use a word I hear frequently in New Zealand, 'unreal'. It was this aspect, and this aspect alone, that freaked a nation.

Every mother, every father could relate to that little girl. She touched something deep in the psyche of New Zealand. Metal traces of wire. Corrosion of cartridge cases that may or may not have been planted. Ballistic tests on rifles. The history of axles. Trips to Australia by defence and prosecution witnesses to determine how ICI make bullets and cartridge cases. Talk of a bullet called 1964/2. Switching of exhibits in the Supreme Court of Auckland. How circumstantial evidence should be considered by a jury. Does the burden of proof always rest with the Crown? All of this and a great deal more were as nothing and are as nothing to the average member of this good and gentle country. But talk to a farmer in the Waikato. Or a housewife in Remuera. Or a bridge-playing lady in Lower Hutt. Talk to any of these as I have done. It will soon become clear what disturbs them about 'The Thomas Case'. Again and again it comes back to the same question: 'Who fed that little baby?'

I have heard many noble and distinguished judges talk to juries about common sense. Judges prize, above all else, the common sense of what they are pleased to call in my country 'The man on the Clapham Omnibus'. Or what they might refer to here as 'The housewife in Mount Albert'. That common sense, so rightly prized, is aware that not a single piece of evidence has been adduced that links Arthur Thomas with feeding Rochelle Crewe. The Crown office is equally aware of that fact. As is the man who led the police investigation, Bruce Hutton. That public common sense then rightly deduces, 'If that baby was fed by someone other than Thomas, that means an accessory after the fact of murder is walking free in this land.' It is an inescapable conclusion. For the police, the politicians, the retrial committee, investigating journalists it has become something they would rather not consider. I find that a nonsense. Because of that I determined that if I resolved nothing else I would resolve this issue:

1. 'Had Rochelle been left unattended from Wednesday, 17 June 1970 until 1.30 p.m. on Monday 22 June?'
2. 'Could she have survived unattended during this period?'

What follows is Dr Fox's report, verbatim:

PREVIOUS HISTORY OF ILLNESS:
No information was available.

BIRTH HISTORY:
Rochelle was thought to have been her mother's first pregnancy. She had been born at Pukekohe. No details were available as to her birth weight and general development of childhood skills.

According to a verbal report from the maternal grandfather, she had been 'walking' for three months (possibly from March 1970).

FAMILY HISTORY:
No details available, although as far as was known, the parents were healthy.

The history was that Rochelle had been found by her maternal grandfather Mr Demler in her cot at 13.30 hours on 22 June 1970. She was said to have been crying and whimpering as the grandfather approached the house, but to have stopped as he went to the cot side. Her eyes were said to have been 'sunken back'. Mr Demler took her by car to the home of Mrs Willis at 14.30 hours.

On arrival at the residence of Mrs Willis, she was sitting on a blanket in the car. Mrs Willis noted 'a dreadful smell, that the child was very cold and shaking, that Rochelle just clung to her for the following two hours, that her eyes seemed sunken, that the whites of her eyes were bloodshot, that she was frightened and shocked, that she did not seem sick and that she was not desperately ill.'

The odour was dreadful and due to bowel motion.

The child was dressed in a woollen singlet and winceyette pyjama top. She was wearing two napkins, covered by domed plastic pants. The napkins were soaking wet, while the bowel motion was foul, dry and dark brown. The area of skin covered by the napkins was inflamed and blistered in parts. In answer to questions, Mrs Willis suggested that the napkins may not have been changed since Friday 19 June 1970.

Mrs Willis gave her a meal of lightly boiled egg, one finger of bread, one tablespoon of ice cream, one slice of peach and a 'marmite jar' of milk (4–6oz). Rochelle seemed ravenous and repeatedly indicated her desire for more milk, which Mrs Willis withheld. The child then vomited what seemed to be all the meal.

From the time of arrival at the residence of Mrs Willis at 14.30 hours until 18.30 hours Rochelle may have taken one pint of milk (20oz). At 18.30 hours she was put down to sleep with a bottle containing 8oz milk which she drank and retained.

At 22.00 hours she was changed and her napkins were soaking wet.

As far as can be ascertained, the child may have taken and retained approximately 24–26oz of fluid. She had no further fluids during the night.

At 07.00 hours, Tuesday 23 June 1970 she was picked up. She took 4oz of milk with one teaspoonful of added glucose, but refused toast. Between the hours of 07.00 hours and 14.00 hours, the time of interview, she took 5–6oz of milk on five occasions – a total of 25–30oz. During this same period she clung to Mrs Willis and was unwilling to be left alone.

During the interview, Rochelle appeared to be very apprehensive. She moved little, preferring to cling to Mrs Willis.

On physical examination Rochelle was of good build and well covered. The tone of her skin and muscles suggested that she had recently lost one to two pounds in weight. A marked napkin rash with some blistering was evident. This rash was in marked contrast to her general standard of care. No bruising or other abnormalities were found. Her weight was 27lb 5oz.

COMMENT:

1. At the time of this first examination, the child had been in the care of Mrs Willis for twenty-four hours (14.30 hours Monday 22 June 1970 to 14.00 hours Tuesday 23 June 1970).
2. Mrs Willis appealed as a very intelligent, experienced, observant, affectionate person.
3. The details of the child's intake of food and liquids given by Mrs Willis and the fact that the child had not been regarded as ill suggested that Rochelle had been without normal care for a maximum of seventy-two hours, the more likely period being forty-eight hours.
4. The description of the contents of the napkins and the napkin rash were consistent with the child being left unchanged for forty-eight hours and possibly seventy-two hours.

5. On the basis of these assessments, the child had been unattended and without food or drink from either:

14.00 hours Friday 19 June 1970.

14.00 hours Saturday 20 June 1970.

The latter date, 20 June 1970 is the more likely.

After further consideration, the writer approached Detective Charles at 08.30 hours on Friday 28 June 1970 regarding a *further examination* (sic) of Rochelle in the company of Mrs Willis. It seemed possible that any improvement or otherwise in the child's general condition, weight and napkin rash might assist in assessing the duration of the period she was without attention, food or fluid.

At the time of this second interview and examination at 11.00 hours on 26 June 1970 a period of sixty-nine hours had elapsed (approximately three days).

Mrs Willis was able to itemize the child's intake of 'solids' and fluids and without giving the detail, the totals were somewhat less than average for her size and age.

The napkin rash had almost completely healed. Her weight had increased by 12oz from 27lb 5oz (on 23 June 1970) to 28lb 1oz. Her general muscle tone was comparable with that at the first examination and this may well be normal for Rochelle. She was a happier child in every way.

The improvement in her condition was regarded as consistent with the previously expressed view that Rochelle had been unattended for approximately forty-eight hours with a maximum of seventy-two hours prior to 14.30 hours on Monday 22 June 1970.

The search of literature for further information is to continue. Any relevant material will be brought to your notice.

In considering the period of survival without food or liquids in a *well* (sic) child of eighteen months, the following factors are relevant:

1. No literature on this subject has yet been found, despite a diligent search.
2. The situation has not been encountered previously in an otherwise normal child.
3. Rochelle was probably a robust child.
4. She probably spent a great deal of the time sleeping and thus conserving her resources of fluid and calories (energy).
5. Being confined to the cot, her activity would be less than usual with reduced losses in energy and perspiration.
6. She was moderately well clothed in an average cot inside a house.
7. The colder atmospheric temperatures would reduce fluid losses by perspiration to a minimum while her good nutrition could withstand a substantial period of deprivation of energy intake in food.

In the absence of previous experience of similar cases and informative literature on the subject, it is difficult to assess the likely period of survival of an otherwise well child of eighteen months of age, deprived of *both* (sic) calories (energy) and fluid.

A child such as Rochelle, living under the conditions outlined above might survive five days, but she would be seriously ill at the end of that time. (MY ITALICS)

T. G. FOX

Doctor Fox was in no doubt, in his very experienced mind, that Rochelle had been fed in that five-day period. Among other factors that he had borne in mind was that the child Rochelle had remained in her cot throughout that period.

If he had been given access at the time of his examinations to the statement that was already in police hands from another Pukekawa resident I believe that his opinion would have been even more assertive. The resident in question was Queenie McConachie.

26

On the day after Bruce Roddick had seen a woman, Queenie McConachie saw a child. This was at 1.30 p.m. on Saturday afternoon. Forty-eight hours before Len Demler walked into that farmhouse. The child that Mrs McConachie saw was wearing identical clothes to those worn by Rochelle on the Wednesday morning when Thirryl Pirrett visited her parents. The child was down by the front gate near Highway 22, when Mr and Mrs McConachie drove by. Mrs McConachie was at that time pregnant and had more than a passing interest in young children. She turned as the car went by and watched the child toddle up the path to the Crewe farmhouse.

While Inspector Hutton delegated various officers to specific tasks, one to search the house and make a full inventory, another to take charge of all exhibits, the search for more information on Rochelle continued. A second specialist was consulted, Dr Ronald Caughey, but this man's examination of the young girl did not take place until Dr Fox had seen her twice. Indeed Dr Caughey's examination did not take place until 1 July 1970 – *nine days after Rochelle had been found*. The police promptly suppressed Dr Caughey's report. The Crown Office in Auckland also suppressed his report or any knowledge that such a report existed throughout the whole period of lower Court hearing, first trial and appeal. Those who naively consider that Arthur Thomas had been accorded two fair trials might ponder on that suppression. It was one of a great many. In due course during the second trial in 1973, *nearly three years later the fact that Dr Caughey had examined the child became known*. His conclusions will be examined when the second trial is discussed in this book. Suffice to say here that Dr Caughey disagreed with his eminent colleague. He felt Rochelle had not been fed.

In September 1970 the police consulted Professor Elliot for his view and opinion on whether or not Rochelle had been without food or fluid for a five-day period. Like Dr Caughey's report that too was suppressed. In the case of Professor Elliot's report the suppression continued until *Auckland Star* deputy-editor Pat Booth came upon it by accident in December 1976 and drew the public's attention to it in 1977. *Seven years later*.

Professor Robert Elliot is a world authority on paediatrics. Why suppress the considered opinion of such an eminent man? The answer is very simple. The prosecution of Arthur Thomas was not a search for the truth. It was a game where evidence was put in and taken out to serve one particular purpose: that Thomas was convicted and stayed convicted. One would think that when Detective Inspector Hutton consulted Professor Elliot he would have made the professor aware of all the evidence that existed on Rochelle. One might think that and one would be wrong. The first lines of Professor Elliot's report make it quite clear that he was not shown Dr Caughey's report. It read as follows:

I have perused the report of Dr T. G. Fox and spoken with Detective Inspector Hutton, and viewed the former residence of Rochelle Crewe.

I have been asked to make comment on this information to determine the possible time which Rochelle Crewe was without food and water prior to 13.30 hrs on 22nd June 1970.

There is little doubt that Rochelle could have survived without food or fluid for approximately five days, as I have personal knowledge of even younger children surviving for greater periods under similar circumstances. However, for the reasons outlined below, I am of the opinion that she was without intake for a period less than 48 hours before 14.40 hours on the 22nd June.

The child was weighed at 30lb approximately two weeks before the time it is thought her parents were killed.

Assuming this was her minimum weight at about the

time her parents were killed, her weight after a period of about five days without food and water would be lessened by loss of tissue solids and water.

1. Tissue solids lost in five days (assuming a minimum activity and room environment, and a calory equivalent of 6 Cals/gm tissue solid, a generous estimate) would have approximated (at minimum) 1lb 14oz.

2. Fluid losses during the same time: (calculated from minimum obligatory losses by insensible sweating, and minimum faecal loss) would have been *at least* (sic) 3lb 2oz.

This amount represents approximately 10 per cent of the child's body weight and, as such, is known to be consistent with an extremely ill child – ill to the degree where spontaneous activity such as sitting and clinging would have been impossible.

It should be emphasized that these minimum losses *were* (sic) exceeded – the cot mattress, bedding and napkins were soaked with fluid, and large amounts of faecal material were noted.

The maximum weight that the child would have been at 13.30 hrs on the 22nd June was 25lb – if no food and water had been given for about five days. On the following day she weighed 27lb 5oz. If this 'weight gain' had been due to retention of fluid (54oz were given) again, a state of at least 8 per cent dehydration would have existed. This is again inconsistent with the child's stated activity on the 22nd June.

The child passed a large quantity of urine between 18.30 hours and 22.00 hours after receiving about 23oz of fluid. This, again, is not likely to have occurred if serious dehydration (i.e. five per cent of body weight) existed at 14.30 hours. On this basis (of degree of dehydration) it seems likely that the child was less than 48 hours without fluid.

Weight gain noted between the 1st and 2nd examination of the child by Dr Fox, together with his observation of apparent tissue loss, suggests that the child's food intake may have been inadequate for a period exceeding 48 hours before 14.30 hours 22nd June.

R. B. Elliot
Professor in Paediatrics.

Thus two men, both highly qualified, both with a lifetime's experience and knowledge of childcare had come to the same inescapable conclusion. Rochelle had been fed during that five-day period and fed possibly as late as the Saturday. Add to their considered opinions the sighting of the woman and the car by Roddick on the Friday morning. Add to that the sighting of a young child by the gate and a light-coloured car parked outside the house by Queenie McConachie on Saturday. Add to that what detective Sergeant Jeffries found when he compiled an inventory of the house. 'I made an examination of the cot and found that it contained a mattress, an underblanket, 2 cot sheets, and a cot blanket, a pair of pink baby's pyjama pants and *a soiled nappy.*' (MY ITALICS) Then further on in his deposition: 'On top of the refrigerator, I found 2 sets of soiled nappies, one pair of nappies were contained in a plastic bag and the other pair of nappies were not covered in any way. On the lid of the washing machine I found another soiled nappy, a soiled pair of plastic pants and a soiled pair of baby pants. To the side of the washing machine I saw a bucket containing a solution of Nappisan.'

Although some of the photographs in this book clearly show that Jeannette Crewe was not the world's most successful housewife, it is surely unreal to believe that she would leave soiled foul-smelling nappies on top of the refrigerator that contained food for the family. It is even more unreal to believe *that she would leave a soiled nappy in Rochelle's cot.*

Add to that the opinion of Mrs Barbara Willis, the woman who made such a favourable impression upon

Dr Fox. Mrs Willis, a woman with her own children, received Rochelle directly from Len Demler after the discovery of the child. Apart from phoning the local doctor and obtaining cream for the nappy rash, Mrs Willis did not consider Rochelle was in need of medical attention.

Add to that the description given by Mrs Willis of the nappies the child was actually wearing. 'There were two. The outer napkin was folded in a triangle and there was another nappy folded lengthways which went between the legs, done with a single pin.' Such a complex dressing as this clearly shows the hand of a woman. Would Arthur Thomas, a man without any children, have dressed the child in such an experienced manner?

Add to that the opinion of the public health nurse who brought that cream out to Mrs Willis on the afternoon of Monday 22 June. Upon delivering the cream Mrs Crawford examined the child. This was at 4.30 p.m., only three hours after the discovery. Having completed her examination Mrs Crawford 'did not consider that her condition required the services of hospital or doctor'.

Add to that the view expressed to me by Owen Priest, the married man with four children of his own who with Len Demler picked Rochelle from her cot and took her away from the nightmare that had been her existence for the previous five days and four nights:

'Her cries were not those of a child who had been five days without food or drink. I do not believe that she would have been able to utter a sound if she had been that long without fluid. Her nappies were soaking wet, indicating that fluid had recently passed through her system. When I walked in and saw her, she was propped up on one elbow. She clung to Len with a strength that belied five days without sustenance. It was like picking up a child of my own after a night's sleep. She was not in a weakened condition. The cries I had heard were those of a normal healthy child. That child had been fed. I thought that at the time. I still think that.'

Owen Priest, as can be seen by the last few pages, is not alone in holding that view. Every single person that I have spoken to about this case, with one notable exception, holds the same view. The exception? First a quote from Inspector Bruce Hutton:

'The child was obviously fed during the time between the killings and when she was found. The file on this aspect of the inquiry is not closed.'

Hutton made that statement on 8 August 1971 – nearly two months after Arthur Thomas had unsuccessfully appealed against his conviction.

The following quote, also from Hutton, was made to me when I interviewed him in late 1977:

'I personally believe, and have always believed, that the baby was never fed and could not have been fed.'

If I were obliged to make a short list of the ten most astonishing statements made to me during my twelve-month investigation into 'The Thomas Case' that would have to be among them.

Ex-Inspector Hutton talked at great length on this subject to justify his belief. He talked of medical experts disagreeing; of the scant amount of research material that existed on the subject; of the nappy sores; the dishevelled hair; the deep sunken eyes. He dismissed the evidence of Roddick, indeed he developed a scathing attack on that young man. He dismissed the evidence of Queenie McConachie. He was at that stage of my interview with him extremely dismissive. As an insight into aspects of Bruce Hutton, it was an illuminating experience. I can only deduce that this unsolved aspect of the case is a source of constant irritation to Bruce Hutton. He is a very orderly man, a man who still works by system. It must offend his sense of order that nearly eight years later this entire nation is still asking, 'Who fed the baby?'

As I have said previously, I began my research with the belief that the answer to that question would resolve many things. Not least of them the question of Arthur Thomas's guilt or innocence.

I know who fed Rochelle Crewe. I know the identity of the woman that Bruce Roddick saw on that Friday morning. The information concerning this aspect has been placed in the hands of the Prime Minister of this country with certain recommendations. At the time of writing it would be injudicious to reveal her identity until the due process of law has taken place.

To return now to Pukekawa in the June of 1970.

While Detective Sergeant Murray Jeffries, a former New Zealand high-jump champion, checked and double-checked his inventory of every item in the Crewe farmhouse, while Detective Graham Abbot, who had been placed in charge of the collection and retention of exhibits, carefully numbered every bloodstain in the lounge and the kitchen, the man in charge, Detective Inspector Bruce Hutton, was deeply troubled. There is a common expression amongst experienced, well-trained detectives, 'If there's no motive, boy, you're in trouble. You are in trouble.' Hutton was in trouble. He, already, in those first few days had Len Demler top of his list of suspects. But motive for Len Demler? He began to dig into the background of Harvey and Jeannette Crewe.

2

The Farmer's Daughter
and the Shepherd

Sheep farmer Len Demler moved on to his Pukekawa
farm in 1937. An extremely hardworking man and a
good farmer, he most certainly needed both of those
assets to cope with nearly 470 acres. Known from his
schooldays by the nickname 'Merry' because whatever
happened to him he always laughed, there would have
been little time for merriment in those prewar days.

He acquired from Pukekawa not only a farm but also
a wife, May Chennell, a member of the family that
farmed alongside his own property. In February 1940,
their first child was born, Jeannette Lenore Demler.
Two years later they had a second daughter, Heather.
In May 1950, Howard Chennell, the brother of May or
Maisie, as she was generally known, died in a tractor
accident on his farm. A bachelor, Howard left his farm
to his two young nieces, Jeannette and Heather. They
were each to receive a half share when they respectively
attained the age of twenty-five. In the interim period,
the farm was looked after by a series of managers with
the profits going into trust for the two girls.

Although destined to be wealthy young women, the
two Demler girls had little indication during their
childhoods of this fact. Beverly Batkin, a friend of both
in those early days, explained:

'We knew, as children, that the Demler girls had a
half share each in that farm. Probably knew before they

34

did. Apart from five or ten pounds at Christmas and the fact that they were both taught ballet and music privately, there was little external indication of their wealth.'

Initially both girls attended the small local school in Pukekawa, along with the other daughters and sons of the farming community. As with many families, the parents had their particular favourite. Len's was the outgoing, attractive and strikingly tall Heather. Maisie's was the quieter Jeannette. But the shy elder daughter was not without admirers amidst the simple school life of calf clubs and lamb clubs. Years later, one such admirer, Malcolm McArthur, was able to recall how he gave up the pleasure of riding to school on a horse and subjected himself to an additional journey of some twelve miles on the school bus, merely to sit alongside Jeannette.

Both girls continued their education at the exclusive Auckland college of St Cuthbert's. As boarders who made only infrequent visits home it was inevitable that they would grow away from many of those early friends and that a feeling of superiority should develop. Certainly, Jeannette considered the young men of Pukekawa her social inferiors. She determined on a teaching career and attended Ardmore Teachers' College in 1957/58. This was followed by a year teaching at Pukekohe North School. One of her friends who was with her at both establishments was Edith Judge. Speaking of 1959, when both women were teaching at Pukekohe, she recalled:

'Jeannette went home most weekends to Pukekawa. She was unimpressed with the social life and the male company of Pukekawa at that time. Social life which she was involved in stemmed largely from her member-ship of the local tennis club. The only times I ever recall her mentioning Arthur Thomas's name was among others whom she listed as attending tennis club dance/socials that year. She also mentioned him, I vaguely recall, as somewhat of a nuisance in that he kept pestering her to go to "this and that" with him. She really thought the "local yokels" the absolute "last word", but nevertheless her references to them were still made with a goodnatured tolerance . . . Her thoughts were chiefly occupied with planning her overseas trip.'

After a year of teaching at Pukekohe North School she took up a teaching position at Mangatangi, in February 1960. During her year at that school she lived at a teachers' hostel in Maramarua. In view of certain allegations that were later made both by the Crown Prosecutor David Morris and also by Len Demler it was clearly a period of her life that required careful research. I have spoken to a number of those women who worked and lived with Jeannette during 1960. At no time were there more than eight of them. With such a small number living in such close proximity their statements are revealing. Here, for example, are some of the statements that Mrs Grace Hessell made to me. Although called as a Crown witness three times, virtually all of what follows was never elicited from Mrs Hessell in front of a jury.

'During that year that I lived with Jeannette at the hostel, February 1960 to the end of January 1961, we lived in and out of each other's pockets. It was a very friendly atmosphere. Took turns in doing the chores, eating together. Everyone knew what everyone else was doing, it was that sort of environment. If any of the girls was going out the rest of us knew exactly where and exactly who they were going with. If someone called for one of them we would all know. *As far as Jeannette was concerned there was no Arthur Thomas in the picture at all*. I am sure that if she had any personal problems, in that environment she would have discussed them. It would have been inevitable. At no time did she appear to have any such problems. The girls there that had boyfriends or boyfriend trouble, would naturally mention them ... She was a very self-confident girl, typical of her age and generation. Very capable, very domesticated. A good cook, indeed the best cook amongst us. She had less contact with people in the locality than most of us mainly because she preferred to do extra preparation for her classes. She was very conscientious. She wasn't anti-social, just very occupied with her teaching, it consumed a great deal of her time. Men were allowed to call at the hostel and visit. *I never saw Arthur Thomas there.*

'She would go home every weekend to Pukekawa. I know she went to local dances at the weekend, she would talk about them. *She never mentioned Thomas when discussing those dances.* We all knew that she was going abroad. She planned to spend one year teaching at Mangatangi and then go to Europe, which is precisely what she did.'

Another of the women who lived with Jeannette throughout that year was Mrs Janet Sutherland.

'Yes, boyfriends were allowed to visit us. My husband and I were courting at the time and he would often call on me. Arthur Thomas? No, neither my husband nor I saw him during the entire time Jeannette was there. I do recall on a couple of occasions when she had been home and had attended a local dance she would casually say the following week, "Oh he was at that dance again"; or "He came round home again." She did mention a name. It could have been Arthur Thomas. It could have been another name. It obviously did not have any particular significance to Jeannette. It was just a fairly typical remark of a young woman. There was no deep meaning to it. There was no question of her being driven to go to England. Such a suggestion is nonsense. She had been looking forward to going from the time that I met her. We corresponded regularly while she was away. There were no problems then either. Nor were there any when she returned at the end of 1962.'

If Jeannette was not experiencing any problems in her life during that period the same can certainly not be said for her father. He had been fined £10,000 for tax offences. In August 1962, Maisie Demler paid her husband £9,540 and received, by way of return, a half share in the 464 acres. Demler swore on oath during the second trial of Arthur Thomas that he did not receive this money from his wife. Yet there was a Memorandum of Transfer, a copy of which will be found in the Appendices of this book, which may well interest the reader.

Jeannette's stay in Europe with friends Diane Ambler and Beverly Willis was undoubtedly a happy one. Her eighteen-month trip also took her to North America. She returned to New Zealand in mid-November 1962.

After a brief spell teaching at Maramarua District High School from February to April 1963 she moved several hundred miles south to Wanganui. Much was to be made of this move south. Later it would be alleged that she had been driven to leave Maramarua, a district near her Pukekawa home, by Arthur Thomas. Crown Prosecutor David Morris would make such allegations, as would Len Demler. Those allegations make the comments that follow particularly significant. Firstly Mrs Grace Hessell:

'When Jeannette returned from abroad and came back to work in this area she was not working on any particular course. She equally was not on permanent staff. She was merely doing relief teaching. It's absurd, that point the Crown tried to make, that she was driven out of Maramarua by Thomas. When she returned she was at a bit of a loose end and took this relief teacher position at Maramarua District High. The headmaster tried to persuade her to stay on because he liked her and she was a good teacher. She told him that she wanted to join her friend Beverly in Wanganui. It's absolute nonsense for anyone to suggest Thomas was

38

pestering her and forced her to leave. There was nothing timid or shrinking about Jeannette. She was quite capable of defending herself against anyone or anything. I have always thought that the so-called "motive" presented by the prosecution was ridiculous.'

Several other women who knew Jeannette during that period confirmed Mrs Hessell's view of the situation. But rather than quote them, I prefer to quote the woman whom Jeannette lived with when in Wanganui for three years. Following in the steps of the farmer's daughter from Pukekawa I went south and interviewed Mrs Claire MacGee in the house that had been Jeannette's home during those three years in Wanganui.

'The only reason she came down here was to be with Beverly. She had no friends in Pukekawa. Going to St Cuthbert's had cut her off from girls of her own age at home who, having gone to different schools, had established different friendships. Beverly was a close friend of hers from St Cuthbert days onwards. Jeannette stayed with her for a while then came to live with me.'

The two women became very close friends. Mrs MacGee, a young widow of similar age to Jeannette, was during this period receiving the unwelcome attentions of an aspiring suitor. Jeannette reassured her and told her of a similar experience she had had in her past. Of how she had been 'chatted up' at dances and how the same young man had given her a Christmas present of a brush and comb. When I questioned Mrs MacGee about her subsequent trial evidence on these aspects I reminded her directly from verbatim transcript precisely how she had recalled this conversation with Jeannette. During the trial she had clearly conveyed the impression that Jeannette had spoken of her unwanted suitor, Arthur Thomas, with distaste. Her reaction was revealing:

'The police came and took a statement from me within a couple of weeks of their disappearance.

Subsequently, before the second trial, they told me exactly what questions they wanted me to answer. I didn't know I could qualify my answers if I wished. I'm aware of the impression the answers I gave may have left in the minds of the jury. I assumed that the defence counsel would ask me a great deal more than he did. If he had, I could have corrected that business of distaste. You see, on the occasion that Jeannette mentioned these incidents, it was not with distaste, it was not even with amusement. It was just ordinary, everyday conversation. *I didn't know until the police came and told me, that the man she had been referring to was Arthur Thomas. I don't recall her mentioning him by name.* He certainly never got in touch with her during the entire time she was living with me. In my view the motive is no motive at all.'

The pattern of life led by Jeannette during her stay at the hostel in Maramarua was re-established in Wanganui. Jeannette preferred to stay at home, checking her school work, spending quiet evenings, to going out. Apart from Beverly and Tony Willis who was at that time courting her friend, Jeannette drew upon Claire MacGee's friends for companionship. She was content, she told Claire, to stay in Wanganui for the rest of her life. She told her friend that she 'did not get on very well with her father' and that apart from her mother whom she obviously loved very deeply, there was nothing to take her back to Pukekawa. The half share in the farm that was soon to be hers was, at that time, presumably a minor consideration. In Claire's view, her young friend had at that time all the makings of a spinster for life. Even when a local man named Alex tried to woo her, the response from the young woman was half-hearted.

Her life was enlivened by visits from her ex-teacher, then air hostess sister Heather and trips that she made to Pukekawa. And if those aspects were for her enlivening as they clearly were, it just underlines how very ordinary her life was. It was soon to take on a more significant meaning. She was bridesmaid at Beverly's wedding, the groomsman was Harvey Crewe. Their meeting quickly blossomed into full romance, most of it conducted at Mrs MacGee's home. Jeannette, the former pupil of St Cuthbert's, Auckland, and Harvey, the former pupil of Scots College, Wellington had, it seemed, a great deal in common. Just how much in common can only be realized when one looks at their lives retrospectively. The Demler family were shortly destined to be involved in family discussion, debate and argument about who would get what from the mother's will. That was in the future. In Harvey's past, the same wrangling had taken place over his father's will. In brief the facts are as follows:

At the time of his father's death in August 1952, Harvey's parents were separated. The mother had filed for judicial separation, the father for a restitution of conjugal rights. A few months before his death both of these actions were abandoned and a separation agreement was entered into. Mr Crewe agreed to pay during their joint lifetimes £450 a year out of which the mother was to maintain Harvey and his sister Beverly as well as herself. He also agreed to pay his wife the sum of £3,000 so that she could purchase a house. These payments were duly made and indeed continued to be made after his death. At the time of his death Mr Crewe's estate was worth in excess of £26,000. He willed the bulk to his sister and some to his cousin. With regard to his wife and children he said:

'I declare that the reason I am making no provision in my will for the benefit of my wife and children is that I do not wish them to participate in my estate by reason of the fact that I have been deserted by them and that they have made statements concerning me which are untrue and harmful to me.'

In 1954, in the Palmerston North Supreme Court Mrs Crewe took legal issue with that statement and also the manner in which her late husband had disposed of his assets. She was awarded £1,000 for herself plus an annual sum of £416, reducible to £208 pounds per annum in the event of her remarriage. Her daughter Beverly was awarded £3,000. Her son Harvey was awarded £3,000.

The judgment was a clear and startling indication that in this world you cannot leave your money or assets as you please but only as the Court pleases.

Mrs Crewe was obviously dissatisfied. She wanted more. The following year she appealed against the judgment. The appeal was heard by a full court of five judges, three of whom, North, Turner and Henry, little knew then in 1955 as they dispensed monies to the Crewe family that in the 1970s they would be deeply involved in the judicial inquiries into the death of the young boy to whom they sought to give security and a good education. Apart from increasing the amount awarded to the two children to £4,500 each, the judges increased the amount allocated to Mrs Crewe to £500 a year. Consequently over £20,000 at the time of writing has gone to people whom Mr Crewe cut out of his will.

His schoolfriends at Scots College whom I have interviewed do not recall Harvey as the most brilliant of students. His main distinction appears to have been his size. His ambition was to be a sheepfarmer like his father before him. It was while learning some of the rudiments of this profession during his late teens that he first met Graham Hewson in the Turakina Valley. They became close friends. Graham would accompany him when Harvey turned out for a local rugby team at Marton. He recalls him as 'a good forward who always went in hard'. Another aspect of the big young man showed during this period. He had a temper, a violent one. Whilst working in the Woodville area he lost it while having an argument with the farmer who employed him. Graham subsequently employed him for

42

about two years as a shepherd on farms in the Kumeroa area.

Someone else who personally observed Harvey's temper was Jeannette's friend and landlady at Wanganui. She recalled Harvey and Jeannette with great fondness, thought they were terrific people and liked them very much, but:

'I think Harvey had a pretty violent temper. He got on the booze one night. She had cooked a meal for him and he was late back for it. When he came in she had words with him. He got very snaky indeed. Eventually he stormed off. But of course they resolved it happily.'

The farmer's daughter and the shepherd were married in an Auckland church in June 1966. Before the wedding, Harvey had bought Heather's half of the Chennell farm from her, paying forty-five thousand dollars; nine thousand dollars were paid in cash, the rest by way of a mortgage that he raised with State Advances. Thus it was that in mid-1966, the estate became known as 'The Crewe Farm'. For both of them the farm was a second choice. They would have preferred a farm in the Wairarapa but the cost precluded it. In the event the farm in Pukekawa was to cost them everything.

As he traced the course of their lives Inspector Bruce Hutton must have experienced considerable bemusement, not only over some of the details that I have already given, which he may or may not have discovered, but over some aspects covering the next four years; which were to be the last four years of their young lives.

First, in a country rightly famed for the hospitality its citizens extend not merely to one another but to strangers, Harvey and Jeannette Crewe were curiously unique. Close friends like Claire MacGee never went to the farm during that four-year period. Neighbours like the Chittys, living immediately opposite, entertained the Crewes to dinner several times and they were also among the guests at a Christmas party on the Chitty farm. It was hospitality that was never returned.

Neighbours like the Priests and the Spratts, good friendly sociable people, were others who never sampled the Crewe hospitality. Ron Chitty said to me: 'One could never say that you got to know them very well. It's hard to explain. They were good neighbours, it was an ideal neighbour relationship. We felt you could borrow a bottle of gin or as Carolyn my wife did on one occasion a bag of potatoes. Harvey would come over and help me with the lambs or loan me a piece of equipment. But basically they kept themselves to themselves.'

Of the Demler family, only Len had mixed freely in the area, his abiding passion for bowls bringing him into contact with many. The rest of the family basically remained aloof from the day-to-day affairs of the small community. The Crewes would make arrangements to go to local meetings; then, again and again, cancel them at the last minute.

Some attribute this lack of socializing to the determination of the young couple to work extremely hard on their farm and bring it up to peak efficiency.

'No, the Crewes did not socialize,' said Mr Spratt. 'The impression that I got right from the start was that Harvey, having married a wealthy young girl, was not going to live the life of a playboy. He was determined to prove himself by his own hard work. To justify his presence there by his own efforts.'

Beverly Batkin: 'Harvey was very conscious of the opportunity he was being given to start up on his own farm because of Jeannette's circumstances. When we first visited them he remarked, "Well, you won't see me for a few years. I'm going to get this farm into shape the way I want it."'

Work hard he certainly did, and so did Jeannette, and yet four years later no-one in Pukekawa could claim to be intimate friends of the Crewes. The awareness

44

that some were saying he had only married Jeannette for her money was certainly a driving force in the young shepherd from Wanganui. Jeannette confided during one of her visits to Claire MacGee:

'She told me that it would have been better if she had not had any money. Better for the marriage if they had had to rely on Harvey's income. He resented the fact that she was wealthy. That's why he worked so hard to justify himself. There were quite a number of people, I know for a fact, who thought he had married her for her money.'

The marriage therefore of the woman whom Beverly Batkin described as 'a bit of an ugly duckling who as she matured became an elegant lady' and the man whom Claire MacGee thought 'had a pretty violent temper' was not without its serious pressures.

That 'violent temper' exploded a number of times during those four years. On one occasion Harvey had arranged for two stock agents to drive out to see him. The appointment was for 8.30 a.m. The two men arrived at 8.20 a.m. Harvey burst out of his house in his stockinged feet in a rage. He told the men that they were early, that they had interrupted his breakfast. That they could sit and stew in their car until he was good and ready to talk to them.

In March 1967, the aerial top-dressing firm of Barr Brothers arrived on the property, making one of their regular bi-annual visits to top-dress. They were just getting the cover off their equipment when Harvey Crewe appeared. Pilot Keith Christie recalled:

'He came roaring across the farm. He went absolutely bonkers. Started screaming at me, "Get off my farm. I don't want you on here. You're not going to top-dress for me. Clear off. I don't want Barr Brothers on my property. You cheat on your prices. I don't believe you can do it as cheaply as you do and still do it properly." I tried to explain that we had been topdressing the area for so long that we knew the short cuts around the corners. At first he just would not listen. He was very unstable for a time, then he settled down and invited us to have a cup of tea. We did, but we still didn't get to top-dress the Crewe farm that day, or ever again.'

Ernie Alexander, ex-farmer, now a local newspaper editor in the area had, with his wife, known the Demler family for many years. They had watched the girls grow up, had attended Jeannette's wedding. He observed:

'Harvey was a stern sort of man. He was a bit abrupt. If anybody was shooting on his property he would simply order them off and tell them not to come back, whereas many farmers would not be bothered. He was rather tactless, brusque.'

Did that instability, so clearly demonstrated in the above statements, finally culminate in a lethal explosion one June night in 1970?

Adding fuel to the fire of Harvey's temper were a number of curious and still unresolved incidents that occurred on the property.

On the evening of 29 July 1967, while Harvey and Jeannette were at the Demler farm, their house was broken into. Much was to be made later about a brush and comb set that were stolen. Too much. It has always been assumed that this brush and comb set were of the High Street chemist's variety, but in fact they were sterling silver. Also stolen at the same time was Jeannette's handbag, her engagement ring, a string of real pearls, her watch and two brooches. All of these items were taken from her dressing table. The police were later to make the point that money and other valuables in another dressing table were not taken; the implication being that it was not a genuine robbery, that all the thief really wanted was the brush and comb set that had been given to her by Harvey Crewe, presumably obliging her to use the one that Arthur Thomas had given her years before. An extraordinary innuendo. One of the other valuable items that was not stolen, an item that no-one before now has officially admitted to exist, was *Harvey's gun*.

When discussing the robbery with me Beverly Batkin listed a number of the valuable items that were not touched:

'Harvey's gun was also there. In the lounge. I don't know much about guns, but apparently it was quite a good one. That was not taken.'

The robbery was never solved. None of the stolen items has ever been recovered.

Maisie Demler asked local editor Ernie Alexander not to publish details of the robbery in the local paper. He duly obliged.

In December 1968, Rochelle Crewe was born in Pukekohe Hospital. Harvey returned from visiting his wife one evening to find the spare bedroom ablaze. The cause of that fire, like the identity of the burglar, remains a mystery. Adding to this particular mystery are the alleged remarks of Harvey Crewe. According to a fire officer and an insurance assessor Harvey was emphatic that the fire had been caused by faulty wiring. Yet an electrician calling a few days after the fire could find no fault in the wiring or in the electrical installation that could have caused the fire. Len Demler was later to say that his son-in-law was equally emphatic that the fire had been started deliberately.

Equally odd was the occurrence in June 1969, when a haybarn on the farm went up in flames.

Apologists for Arthur Thomas have gone to some lengths to dismiss these incidents. In view of the fact that there is not a single shred that links Thomas with any of them I feel they have fallen into a trap set by the Crown. Undoubtedly all three incidents did happen. There was a robbery and there were two fires. Clearly if either of the Crewes had had the slightest reason to suspect Arthur Thomas he would have been subjected to police questioning at the time. He wasn't. As with the robbery so with the fire inside the house. Maisie

Demler again asked the local editor to suppress details, again he obliged. Amongst other items destroyed in the house fire were a pile of new baby clothes that had apparently been used to start the inferno. What price an accidental fire?

These incidents undoubtedly affected the Crewes. They also upset Maisie Demler who remarked to her neighbour Peggy Spratt, 'What are they going to do next?' She did not elaborate on who 'they' were.

On the day after the haybarn fire in June 1969, Owen Priest called at the Crewe farm to see if he could help clear up the mess. 'Jeannette refused to open the door to me. She would not even open the fly-screen door even though she knew it was me. She was scared for some reason.'

Jeannette became very nervous. She refused to stay in the house on her own. She would rather sit in the car with Rochelle in the fields waiting for Harvey to finish his work.

The Priests, who had received visits from the police three times in three years concerning the incidents on the Crewe farm, were destined within the year to be visited yet again in connection with happenings on the property. But that lay in the future in mid-1969. At that time Jeannette was not the only member of the Demler family coping with problems.

Maisie Demler was a very high-principled woman who, unlike many, apparently lived by her principles and expected her children to do the same. In July 1969 she changed her will, cutting her daughter Heather off from every single cent. Not even an item of her jewellery was to go to her younger daughter. The reason? Heather had married a divorced man named Robert Souter. As a father of three and an undischarged bankrupt, Maisie did not consider him the ideal husband for one of her children. The favouring of children that was such an aspect of this family burst into bitter acrimony. Len subsequently changed his will cutting Jeannette out and leaving his half of their property to Heather. So once again the two sisters were destined to have a half-share each in a superb farm, Len and Maisie Demler's. But destiny or fate were about to take a hand. Jeannette would never live to enjoy the fruits of her mother's generosity.

Maisie Demler died of a brain tumour on 26 February 1970. Her will, a copy of which is at the back of this book, was probated on 16 March. She had appointed Len Demler and Jeannette Crewe as her joint trustees.

Shortly before their deaths the Crewes visited Claire MacGee. Jeannette told her friend:

'It seems that the farm has got a jinx on it. So many things have happened there.'

On 16 June, Jeannette visited her solicitors. She signed the estate accounts and was given a copy of the provisional balance-sheet of her mother's estate. It was her first knowledge of just how much her mother's estate was worth, of the detailed assets of the estate.

The following day, she and her husband were last seen at a stock sale about 1.30 p.m. After that the farmer's daughter and the shepherd vanished from the face of the earth.

Her estate was worth at least one hundred and fifty thousand dollars. In her three personal bank accounts were sums totalling 4,640 dollars, in a joint account with her husband was a further 1,667 dollars.

His two bank accounts totalled 34 dollars.

As Inspector Bruce Hutton pondered these facts, he and the men serving under him made no secret of the man who they suspected was responsible for what they quickly, perhaps too quickly, were calling a double homicide. The man in the target sights of Hutton's gun was Len Demler.

3

The Hunt

A curious feature of this whole episode was the fact that, whilst hundreds of men made a shoulder-to-shoulder search of his property, Demler at no time took any part in the search for two members of his family. In fact he actively discouraged neighbours like Ian Spratt from assisting the police.

'Let the buggers get on with it on their own. It's their job,' he said. While David Payne and the other farmers of Pukekawa were being told by Inspector Gaines: 'Give us a body and we will make the arrest. Give us a body and we will arrest him.' While other police officers were saying to the Priests and the Spratts: 'How does it feel to have a murderer as a neighbour?' Len Demler, the object of all of these remarks, could be seen riding a horse over his land and casually checking his stock. The land that he had farmed since 1937 and the stock upon it took precedence over the search for his elder daughter and her husband.

Perhaps it was remarks like those made to him by Inspector Hutton less than twenty-four hours after it was known that the Crewes had vanished – 'You did it. Come on, you old bugger, you did it. You know you did it. Where have you put the bodies?' – that caused Demler to ignore the search. Or were there perhaps other reasons for his attitude?

On 6 July while the countryside was alive with Army, Navy and Air Force search parties augmenting the police and volunteer search parties, Len Demler, his daughter Heather and her husband drove to Pukekohe and had a party to celebrate Demler's birthday.

Five days later Detective Sergeant John Hughes yet again accused Demler of murdering Harvey and Jeannette. The police officer confronted him with: 'We have got you now. You've had it.'

Among the evidence that the police had been compiling against Demler was a bloodstain found in the passenger seat of his car. He had previously told the police that Jeannette had not used his car or been in it for some time. The police told him that the bloodstains they had found on the seat were fresh ones. They also told him that they were Jeannette's.

They were critical of the fact that he had left his granddaughter in her cot when he had discovered her. They were critical of the fact that he was taking no part in the search.

The full case, the complete dossier that the police built up against Len Demler, has never been revealed. Here are just a few items from it:

1. Opportunity. He lived on his own and lived immediately next door to the Crewes.
2. Availability. Harvey and Jeannette would have freely let him enter their home. For a long time the police were convinced that both murders had been committed *inside* the Crewe farmhouse.
3. Financial and psychological pressure on the suspect. Maisie Demler's will, which had only recently been probated, made it clear that not only had she cut Heather Demler off without a cent but she had also ensured that the entire farm would no longer be her husband's. He would only retain a life interest in her half of the farm which would then pass to Jeannette. Her will stripped him of his mana, and it would ultimately strip him of half the land that he had worked and owned since before the Second World War. The police were also in possession of a number of statements that made it clear that before

his death Harvey Crewe had wanted to buy his father-in-law out. Ian Spratt was one whom Len discussed this with prior to the deaths of the Crewes. Demler had commented that if he sold out to Harvey his son-in-law would kick him out and he would have nowhere to live. Len had treated it all as a big joke when discussing it with Spratt, and yet . . .

4. The fact that whoever committed the murders must have been a local. Someone had been back to clean up. A local could get away with that. Like the postman in the story of *The Invisible Man*, his presence would go unnoticed.

When the above factors are added to Jeannette's bloodstains in his car, the fact that he had not been observed by Owen Priest when he allegedly went to the farm on his own and discovered it empty, this despite the fact that Priest had been in precisely the same position that he was in when he saw Demler pulling up at his gate to ask him to accompany him on a *return* visit to the farm; the fact of his strange behaviour when he and Priest had gone to the farm; the fact of his even stranger behaviour during the massive search; when all of these factors are taken into account it can be clearly seen that the police built a powerful if largely circumstantial case against Len Demler. When he assured them that he was on the best of terms with the dead couple they dismissed the assurance. When he told them how Harvey had dined with Len and his wife virtually every night during the period of Jeannette's confinement with Rochelle; how he had lately dined with the couple at least once a week since his wife's death, they brushed such facts to one side.

Demler, the man who never showed emotion, the man who laughed the day he was told that Maisie had died but cried on the day of her funeral, most certainly showed emotion to his friends in Pukekawa at this time. The Priests, like the Spratts, also had the constant enquiries from the police of 'What does it feel like living next door to a double murderer?' Julia Priest said to me:

'Two days after their disappearance, Len told me he was the number one suspect and with tears running down his face said: "I honestly did not do it." What upset him so much was that nobody would believe him.'

Peggy Spratt recalled:

'I remember going up to the Demler farm during the search for the bodies. Len and Heather were there, both were very upset. Len was going around the house saying, "I didn't do it." Heather pulled me to one side and asked, "Do you think Dad did it?" Even if I had doubts myself, I felt obliged to console her with an assurance that I did not think he had.'

This had been the second such ordeal for Peggy Spratt. One of the men who took part in the land search was local vicar Gerry Hadlow. He succeeded in vanishing down a large hole one foggy day. It took a number of men several hours to get him out. The vicar also succeeded in electrifying the atmosphere of the Pukekawa Church shortly after the Crewes vanished. In his sermon he talked about the Crewes, he talked about 'Justice being done'. He also talked less directly about the fact that Len Demler was the prime suspect. After the service he asked Peggy Spratt for her views. She told me that at that moment she acquired an absolute conviction that Len was innocent. The question could not have been an easy one for her to answer. Standing next to her and her husband were Len and Heather Demler. It was obviously clear to Demler that he was in need of the kind of guidance that is not readily obtained from a church pulpit.

Having consulted his solicitors, Demler obviously considered it was high time to take out some insurance. A top Auckland QC, Lloyd Brown, a renowned and talented defence lawyer, was instructed on behalf of Demler.

Mr Brown was not the first member of the Auckland

Bar to take an active professional interest in the bizarre mystery at Pukekawa.

David Morris, the Crown Prosecutor in Auckland, told me that he had been down to the Crewe farm and taken his initial look around it within the first week. He also subsequently attended many of the police conferences. As Crown Prosecutor it was an unusual devotion to duty. He was destined to have closer involvement with this case than with any other in his career.

In the same week that Lloyd Brown was being retained to defend Demler against a potential double murder charge one of the police conferences just referred to took place. It was by any standards a high-powered conference.

Present were Inspector Hutton and several of the men acting under him. Also present were Detective Superintendent Ross, Assistant Commissioner Rob Walton, police pathologist Dr Cairns and one of the DSIR's top men, Dr Donald Nelson. There was just one item on the agenda: 'The recommendation from Hutton and his men that Len Demler be arrested and charged with the murders of Jeannette and Harvey Crewe.' Debate, discussion and argument raged for a considerable period of time; eventually it was decided to wait until the bodies had been found.

At this time, Len Demler was not alone in having to cope, with or without legal assistance, with the police. Gerry Willis, his friend of many years standing and near neighbour, the man to whose home the frightened Rochelle was initially taken, felt the heat of their 'subtle' tactics. One police officer declared to him that it was known that he had assisted Len Demler in moving the bodies and the sooner he confessed the better it would be for him. It was not phrased quite as delicately as that, but that was the general drift.

As already recorded, the history of both the Crewe and Demler families is marked by squabbles and infighting about property and money, people cut out of wills, people contesting wills. Less than one month after Harvey and Jeannette vanished the two families were at loggerheads. At the centre of their dispute was little Rochelle Crewe. Both families wanted custody of the child. Heather Souter *née* Demler wanted to take the child to America. Mrs Marie Crewe wanted Rochelle to remain with the Crewe family. The issue went to an Auckland court.

Mrs Marie Crewe was successful and the child went to live with members of her family. The police meanwhile were still trying to find out what had happened to her parents.

On 2 July, Detective Sergeant Hughes had called at the Thomas farm. He was making what he later described as a 'routine inquiry, the kind that is made when there is no obvious suspect'. He stayed about thirty minutes, chatting to Arthur Thomas in one of his fields. The subject of their conversation was Jeannette Crewe. Thomas told the police officer that he had been quite keen on her many years before, that he had phoned her during her schoolteaching days, written her letters but that Jeannette had kept the relationship on a platonic level. Thomas told him of working on that farm when it had been the Chennell estate, top-dressing. When Thomas was asked to account for his movements between 17 and 22 June, the police officer was later to say: 'He was not able to give me anything specific, and I asked him to think back to the night of 17 June. He said that he would have been home with his wife. He said he couldn't say why he was certain of this, but knew he had been.'

Hughes examined the Thomas car but 'found nothing in it to connect with the inquiry'. What the two men actually said to each other will be the subject of further comment. After arranging for Thomas to call at the police headquarters on the Chitty farm to have his fingerprints taken, Hughes left.

On 12 August, Detective Sergeant Parkes was following up yet another possible lead when he called on the farm of Arthur Thomas. The link they had found with him was a tenuous one. But even tenuous links must be followed up. Parkes, while searching the Crewe farm, had discovered a brush and comb set. Obviously a present, it was still wrapped up in Christmas gift paper and there was a card attached that indicated the giver was 'Arthur'. The present had been found stuck away in one of the spare bedrooms. Showing it to Arthur Thomas, the young farmer agreed that years before his marriage to his wife Vivien he had given the set to Jeannette when he was 'trying to court her'. The message on the card told Parkes about as much as he gleaned from that interview with Thomas: 'To Jeannette. Best Wishes for a Happy New Year. From Arthur.' Having established that the Arthur in question was Thomas, Parkes left.

Five days earlier, on 7 August, the massive search was called off. Inspector Gaines and the hundreds of men working under him had been obliged to admit defeat. Despite searching an area that ranged from Glen Murray and Rangiriri to Port Waikato and covered nearly 400 square miles no trace of the missing couple had been discovered.

On the evening of 8 August, Ian and Peggy Spratt chanced to look out of their farm in the direction of the deserted Crewe property. Aware that the police had been pulled out of the area they were startled to see a light moving around. Knowing that Len Demler was the No. 1 suspect they considered that he might be searching on the Crewe property. Frightened, they deliberated about what they should do. Unfortunately, but understandably, they decided to do nothing. Some seven years later when they discussed this incident with me they regretted that decision. One phone call to the police on that night would have resolved who the intruder was.

The CIB investigation had also reached a stalemate. Despite the thousands of hours spent interviewing, despite the hundreds of statements taken, despite the many potentially promising leads that had been followed up, despite the belief that Hutton and most of his men held that Len Demler was their man, the inquiry looked like slipping into that macabre area of unsolved crimes, along with such unresolved murders as those of Walker, McKay and Beard – three that at the time of the investigation were unsolved; three that in 1978 are still unsolved.

The CIB working with Inspector Hutton was reduced to just four men, based on Otahuhu police station. As the days ticked by with these men working deep into the night each piece of evidence already acquired was checked and rechecked. Yet again all unsolved crimes in the area were re-examined in an attempt to find a link. One such crime, midnight prowling, had in fact been solved during the initial investigations in Pukekawa. For one exuberant moment the detectives had thought they had their man, but although he admitted the offence, committed years before, he was quickly eliminated from their investigations into the Crewe deaths.

For hours the police stared at the photographs taken in the days that followed the discovery of the blood-stained farm. Odd, strange photographs. Some of them are in this book. Photographs of the home of a wealthy young middle-class couple that show to my mind not a settled, comfortable, happy home. Where is the personality of that couple? A baby's bedroom, barren as a prison cell, not one colourful poster or painting on Rochelle's walls. A lounge equally devoid of those little things that make the statement 'Harvey and Jeannette live here'; no paintings, ornaments, those little nicknacks that we all clutter our homes with, none are in evidence. Windows that are curtainless. Floors that are bare. I have seen more homeliness in a motel room than I can find in those photographs of the Crewe farmhouse. Clothes slung everywhere. A woman's dressing table devoid of any femininity. In the lounge a child's playpen, no longer used by the now walking Rochelle, not put away in one of the spare rooms, but left propped against the wall; cartons that contained fluorescent tubes, wool, pelmets. The place – I cannot refer to it as a home – reeks of apathy. It reeks not only of the deaths that undoubtedly occurred there but also of a dead relationship, dead long before 17 June 1970. The fact that the sofa and armchairs do not match is of little concern when one knows they were a present from Harvey's mother. One hardly rejects a gift from one's mother-in-law. The fact that some of the windows are curtainless was rationalized to me by a number of their friends. It was because of the fire that had destroyed the original curtains. *But the fire was in 1968*. A curious postscript to the missing curtains is the fact that Jeannette did, in fact, have material for new ones on order from two stores in Auckland. On 15 June Harvey Crewe rang up one of the stores and cancelled the order. If he intended to do the same with the other order he never got the chance – two days later he was dead.

A discussion about money, bills, their budget, had clearly been in progress shortly before they died. On the dining table were accounts, bills and receipts.

Another curious factor is that, if the Crown contention is correct that the murders happened after television closed down at 11 p.m., and the remnants on the table represent the evening meal, then why were they reading the mail during the evening meal? The mail that had been delivered that morning at 9.30 a.m? It could be that the uncleared table represents not an evening meal, but a mid-day lunch, eaten before they went to the stock sales. It had been a busy morning with a stock agent and a friend Mrs Pirrett calling, and early lunch may well have been the first time they had to go through their mail. I cannot believe they left it in the box until evening. That dining table could easily represent a mid-day meal. The fact that it was left uncleared is consistent with the untidiness and mess that abounds throughout the house. Such a possibility plays havoc with the theory of a killing after 11 p.m. *It would put their deaths after their return to the farm at approximately 4 p.m. and before their evening meal.*

It is a well-known and established fact that between sixty and seventy per cent of all murders come under the category of 'domestic murders', that is murders committed by the spouse or a near relative. Exhaustive research in Great Britain has established this as a fact. Dr Nelson of the DSIR advised me that the percentage is the same for New Zealand. When one realizes that not a single piece of evidence has ever been produced to refute the theory that one of the Crewes killed the other and then turned the gun on themselves, who can deny the possibility of murder/suicide being the explanation of the deaths of Harvey and Jeannette Crewe? If that is the solution, it would of course mean that a third party moved the bodies, cleaned up, and fed Rochelle. Without doubt the little girl was fed. Without doubt someone did clear up and move the bodies. It does not follow – indeed the evidence in my possession directly contradicts it – that the person responsible for those acts is at this moment in Paremoremo Prison.

Much was to be made later of the fact that the Crewes died on the eve of their fourth wedding anniversary. It was to be held that this was all part of a pattern along with the fires and the burglary. It has been stated, quite incorrectly, that each of these events occurred on their wedding anniversary. The dates of these incidents previously given, demonstrate the fallacy of that statement. What has never been the subject of comment, as far as I know, is the absence of presents. Surely a happily married couple, devoted to each other, would exchange gifts on the fourth anniversary of their marriage?

Edith Judge, a close friend of the Crewes, movingly described to me a good marriage:

'Harvey and Jeannette were always open with each other, completely honest. They had a very real appreciation of each other and a deep respect for each other . . . A well-suited, wonderfully happy, strong and mature couple, completely capable of working out life in a harmonious, positive manner. Both intelligent, witty, fun to be with if they knew you well, otherwise reserved, but not awkward. Jeannette had a very hearty, deep-throated laugh which lives on always in one's memory. Good as parents. Could be described as a very private couple.'

Fully conscious that Rochelle Crewe is alive I would normally be reluctant to question that view of the relationship; yet the equally honest views of Clare MacGee, Keith Christie and others inevitably pose such a questioning. The condition of the Crewe farm when it was discovered raises a myriad of questions about their relationship. Is that really the home of a happily married couple?

As Bruce Hutton pondered these and other aspects, his research took him into strange areas. The case was attracting tremendous publicity. Reporters, television teams, radio units roamed all over Pukekawa. Members of the public descended at weekends and drove up and down Highway 22 to get a look at the murder farm. It was 'somewhere to take the children at the weekend'. Letters by the thousand poured into the police all telling them to look here or arrest this person. Anonymous phone calls, each caller knowing 'for a fact' who was responsible. Clairvoyants, mystics, water diviners, psychics, all claimed they knew the answer. Bruce Hutton recalled one clairvoyant who told him she was an expert:

'This particular woman wanted to come out to the

farm and hold something belonging to Harvey and just walk around the house. The day she came out there was a bit of a lull in the local inquiries so I went with her over the house. She then drew a massive plan of the area and said that the bodies had gone down the Waikato river and out to sea. On her plan she drew a cross just where they were out at sea, one was about six and a half miles outside the Waikato Heads, the other was about ten miles north of that. According to her both were drifting at a steady rate of knots. She wanted me to call up one of the helicopters and take her out to sea so that she could more accurately pinpoint the positions. A few days later Jeannette's body was found. Five miles west of Pukekohe, in the Waikato river.'

It would be more accurate to say that Jeannette's body found them. It was floating in an area known as Devil's Elbow, by two men whitebait fishing. This was on 16 August 1970. The body was wrapped in bed-clothes and tied with wire. She had been shot in the head with one .22 bullet; there were also serious facial injuries.

So after a search running into millions of manhours and utilizing local knowledge, police expertise, frog-men, divers, potholers, the Army, Navy and Air Force, a body had been found by two men out fishing.

Bruce Hutton moved. He moved fast.

'I'll tell you what swung me away from Demler and I've never revealed this before. I wasn't making a great deal of headway and then I found Jeannette. At that time I made a decision. I still had my options open, Demler No. 1. Thomas No. 2. Then the others. I then decided, there is only one way. The way I'd been trained by Bob Walton. Whether you are right or wrong, take hold of one of your suspects, you've got something tangible now, you can prove a murder. She's been shot. I just took Demler down and showed him her body when we brought it out of the water, and I was there watching him like a damn hawk, looking for any glimmer of reaction. Then I put him through a very tough interview, immediately on top of that. He didn't break. I felt then that he wasn't my man. Bear in mind we were dealing with a totally different kind of murder here. We were almost going around and around in circles. Couldn't see anything tangible.'

As an insight into the way that Inspector Hutton worked, his thought processes, I find that statement revealing. Some might criticize such techniques, condemning them as overly brutal. I do not. He was absolutely right when he referred to 'a totally different kind of murder', if murder it was. Somewhere stalking the land was a double murderer who might at any moment strike again. If putting Len Demler through that ordeal had established his guilt and removed him from society, all would have applauded Hutton. The fact that he did not break Demler does not justify a criticism of the method used, but I would seriously question the quality of the thought processes used by the inspector.

Len Demler was taken to the river without being told the reason for the journey, the premise being that the sudden shock of the sight of his daughter's dead body would catch him in an unguarded moment. Now this man had farmed in the area since before the Second World War. It would be obvious to him, very quickly, that he was being driven to the river. If he was guilty he would immediately realize why he was being taken there. He would have at the very least thirty minutes to compose himself, to steady his nerves for the ordeal that he would know lay ahead. What price the tactics of shock and surprise then?

I also found his comment about Thomas being No. 2 curious, very curious. He maintained throughout the interview that Thomas was always his No. 2. I do not believe it. A No. 2 suspect in a double murder who is left entirely to his own devices for nearly two months, apart from two brief interviews? Interviews conducted not by the inspector but by two of his detective sergeants who leave after brief discussions with this No. 2 suspect about an abortive courting and a present given to the dead woman many years before? A No. 2 suspect who is then left again entirely to his own devices for over a month?

As for Hutton feeling that Demler was 'not my man' after that torrid interrogation, it will be shown in a little while that Bruce Hutton most certainly did not strike Len Demler from the top of his list after that interrogation on 16 August 1970.

Among others that came to the banks of the Waikato to view the body of Jeannette Crewe was pathologist Dr Francis John Cairns. He carried out a detailed post mortem examination the same day. While the blanket, bedspread and wire that held those items around the body were rushed to the DSIR for analysis, Dr Cairns made a careful examination of the fully dressed body.

'There were two small injuries in the right temple, injuries about the right eye and the nose, and some small injuries to the face which appeared to have been caused after death. Apart from the last injuries, I made a detailed examination of the injuries later, and considered that the injuries to the eye, nose and the right side of the head were probably caused before death.'

Of the clothing on the body which included a cardigan, a check skirt, a singlet, bra, pantyhose and panties:

The clothing had not received any prior cuts or tears before I cut them off.

As a result of his examination he was able to determine that a .22 bullet had entered her head on the right-hand side, in front of the ear and about one and a quarter inches above it, and there was an exit wound in front of the left ear. Further on in his deposition he considered the manner in which she had died:

'The line of fire of the bullet was from right to left and slightly forwards, and that path and the injuries I saw would be a possibility (sic) that the weapon had been fired from behind her right shoulder whilst seated, that is one possibility but I think it more likely that the weapon was fired when she was lying on the floor with the left side of her face to the floor. From the reconstruction of the bloodstains and from the other injuries she showed, that is to say, the injury to the tissue about the right eye, the injury to the nose and the fracture to the nose, these all suggested to me that she had received a blow to the face with a blunt weapon and that this had knocked her to the ground and while on the ground the shot had been fired. The bloodstain on the carpet suggested that she had been bleeding on the floor, there was a clear area in front of the fire where there were no bloodstains, and this suggested that she had been lying partly on a mat which could have been in front of the fire.'

He went on to suggest that the injuries to the face could have been caused by a rifle butt. The bruising to her left armpit he could offer no explanation for. Her six lower front teeth were missing, also possibly as a result of a blow to the face, but Dr Cairns makes no mention of these in his deposition. Perhaps the omission is because this aspect was covered by a deposition from Jeannette's dentist.

Apart from having clear and tragic proof that Jeannette Crewe was dead, the police now had invaluable evidence: the bullet fragments recovered from her body and the wire that had been used to bind the blanket and bedspread.

Inspector Gaines and his searchers were pulled back into the area, certain now that the heavy rain that had flooded into the Waikato and caused the body of the thirty-year-old farmer's wife to surface, could also discover the body of the husband. The CIB moved back with a vengeance. Detective Sergeants John Hughes and Murray Jeffries collected wire samples from the Crewe farm and the Demler farm. From the farm of

Arthur Thomas, the No. 2 suspect? Nothing. A curious omission, particularly when one realizes that Thomas's .22 Browning pump-action rifle was collected. It was one of sixty-four collected. 'All .22 rifles within a five-mile radius of the Crewe farm, rifles from relatives of the dead couple, from friends, acquaintances and other persons who had become involved in the inquiry into their deaths' was the brief that Detective Sergeant Mike Charles was given. It was a brief that was to be and still is subjected to scathing criticism. Why merely five miles? Are they sure they obtained all the .22 rifles within that radius? What of the rifles of men like farmer Ted Smith, admittedly as Arthur's neighbour outside the five-mile radius, but a man who was not only out on the night of the murder but one who went past the Crewe farm twice that night? Another rifle that did not interest the police was that of David Payne, again like Ted Smith a man who lived outside that arbitrary five-mile line, but again like Smith a man who was out on the night of the murders, out at a ratepayers' meeting about three miles from the Crewe farm, a meeting that finished at 10.40 p.m. The Crown were later to state that the murders took place late in the evening, that the 'television had been switched off'. Closedown time for television was 11 p.m. That put not only David Payne but the other thirty people who attended that meeting within three miles of the Crewe farm at exactly the right time after the meeting closed, to drive to the Crewe farm and commit a double murder. Yet the police displayed a total indifference not only to David Payne's rifle but to a number of others belonging to people who had been at that meeting. McGuire, the farmer next door to Payne and like him a man at that meeting, is yet another whose rifle to this day remains unchecked. There are others. Yet Detective Sergeant Charles was later to say that rifles belonging to people such as Smith, Payne and McGuire 'would have been collected if the police had known they were out that night'. Demonstrably the police, having questioned at least two of these men, did know they were out that night.

In view of the fact that several of the rifles collected were not five or nine miles but nearly fifty miles away from the Crewe farm, the omissions became even more inexplicable.

The rifle owned by Heather's father-in-law was collected from the Auckland North Shore. The rifle owned by the brother of Bruce Roddick was also collected from the Auckland area.

The rifle belonging to Graham Hewson, one of Harvey Crewe's closest friends, was another that the police requested. In view of the fact that Hewson was living at Woodville this means that the five-mile radius search had in that particular instance been extended to about three hundred miles.

The sixty-four rifles that were collected after Jeannette's body had been found went to the DSIR. The object of the exercise was to establish if any of them could have fired the .22 bullet, fragments of which had been recovered, that killed the young woman.

A fired bullet has upon it marks as unique as human fingerprints. Just as the whirls and ridges of skin on the fingers leave prints that are traceable to one hand and one hand alone, so do the grooves, twists and marks in the metal of a gun barrel leave impressions that can come from one gun and one gun alone. On the base of the bullet that had killed Jeannette was the figure 8. Initially all that meant was that the bullet was one of 158 million rounds manufactured by one of the subsidiaries of the I.C.I. company between 1948 and 1963. Ultimately that small figure 8 was to have a significance that still reverberates, nearly eight years later.

Having test fired the sixty-four rifles the DSIR concluded that the fatal bullet could have been fired from one of two rifles. Or to put it exactly in Dr Nelson's words: 'I was able to exclude all but two rifles.'

One of these rifles belonged to Arthur Thomas. The other had been collected from a family in Pukekawa named Eyre, though it in fact belonged to a family friend named Brewster.

To say that the bullet that killed Jeannette could have been fired from either of those rifles is over simplistic. Given a complete bullet in a reasonable condition one of those two rifles must, by all the laws of science, have been eliminated from the inquiry. It is clear that the DSIR did not have a complete bullet in a reasonable condition, but incomplete fragments. It is equally clear that the Crown conclusions that were subsequently drawn are dangerously misleading. There is no doubt in my mind, neither is there any in the mind of Dr Donald Nelson, that if he had been handed another sixty-four rifles of .22 calibre he would have discovered at least another two that could not be excluded. Yet another sixty-four would have produced yet another two and so it goes on. There is no doubt whatsoever that in New Zealand today, in Pukekawa this minute, are rifles that could have been and could be directly linked with those bullet fragments. The number of rifles that could be so linked runs into hundreds. Such a slender link in the chain of evidence led ultimately to a man being imprisoned for life.

While Dr Nelson was busily engaged establishing a negative, the Crewe house and the surrounding gardens were a hive of activity.

Detective Jeffries had, in the days that followed 22 June, gone through the house and gardens not with the proverbial fine toothcomb but in the case of the interior, with a Hoover, collecting even the fragments of dust. The gardens and paddocks were subjected to a marked-out pattern search. Photographs demonstrate just how detailed that pattern search was.

Now, in the sure knowledge of the weapon that had killed Jeannette Crewe, Detective Sergeant Jeffries returned to the Crewe farm. The first search, thorough and exhaustive as it had been, had not revealed a .22 cartridge case. In June, of course, with pathologist Dr Cairns talking about blocks of wood, tomahawks and axes, a .22 case would not have been uppermost in the minds of the police. Now on 17 August it was the one object, the only object that they were seeking. Amongst those assisting Jeffries on that search was Graham Hewson, the close friend of Harvey, who had previously employed him, watched him play rugby, had both Harvey and Jeannette to stay at his Woodville home, had stayed at theirs, had attended their wedding . . . In case the reader should wonder why I itemize the obvious involvements of two close friends, I should perhaps explain that certain members of the police and certain people in Pukekawa freely asserted to me: 'Hewson hardly knew Harvey; they had only met a few times.'

Graham Hewson, this man who 'hardly knew Harvey', drove from Woodville to Pukekawa, on 23 June, the morning after it was known the Crewes were missing, and with him was Harvey's uncle. Upon arriving at the farm, the police, realizing that in Hewson they had an invaluable mine of information concerning the missing David Harvey Crewe, questioned him for some time.

The man 'who hardly knew Harvey' then stayed at Demler's farm, at Demler's request. When Heather and her husband arrived from the United States Hewson moved to a nearby hotel, staying with Harvey's mother and brother-in-law. This man who 'hardly knew Harvey' was then asked by Len Demler, Mrs Crewe senior and Harvey's brother-in-law to manage the Crewe farm until a farm manager could be appointed. I could go on for many pages demonstrating that not only was Graham Hewson a close friend, but also a man much liked and highly regarded by those closest to Harvey and Jeannette. The point has to be made if only because of the way his character was smeared later by the police and the Crown Prosecutor. There are many obnoxious aspects of 'The Thomas Case'. The attack that was mounted on Hewson is one of them.

When Graham Hewson arrived at the Crewe property on 23 June, he had two basic aims: to give whatever assistance he could to the Crewe and Demler families and to find out what had happened to Harvey and Jeannette. His view about their deaths has remained unchanged: 'If someone murdered them I don't want that person in prison for life, I want them hung.' As a shepherd with a lifelong experience of dog-breeding one of the first curious things he noticed was the condition of the three dogs on the farm. After five days, during which, in theory, they had not been fed, they were 'as fat as seals'. The cattle, too, were in good condition and took only a normal interest in the hay that he fed out to them.

As the days went by, he was drawn more and more into the police investigation. He rapidly became not merely a trusted confidant of the police but someone they used again and again during the course of their investigation. One of the ways they used him was as a weapon in their attempts to break Len Demler. Ron Chitty recalled this aspect when talking to me:

'The police used Hewson a great deal. They used him to interrogate Len a fair bit. One thing I could never understand was why they set a member of the public to intimidate another man. And intimidate him he did. I think Hewson thought he had become a detective. He started to act like a policeman.'

Hewson's recall of that situation is equally clear:

'Hutton and Hughes continuously spoke of Demler in terms that he was without doubt the murderer. They both said to me: "As soon as we find a body we'll turn the key on Len Demler." They were absolutely certain it was Len. Every morning when I came up to the farm from Len's house, they would ask me what he had said during the previous evening. What his manner was like.

69

If he phoned anyone. Then when Heather and her husband came to stay I would be asked to report on the family conversations. Gates would be deliberately wired up so that when Len came home he would be subjected to the aggravation of having to mess about on a cold winter's night trying to open them. I came back from Tuakau one day a bit late. "Where the bloody hell have you been?" Demler asked me. I told him that I'd been to see Rochelle, which I had. Then at a suggestion from the police I added a bit, told him there was a policewoman with her and a child specialist and that they were teaching the child to talk. He went white. Harvey was a hell of a good mate of mine and anything I could do in any way, to help catch whoever murdered him and Jeannette I would do.'

In early August, with the investigation at a stalemate and a manager appointed on the farm, Hewson returned to Woodville. On the 16th of that month when he heard of the discovery of Jeannette's body, he immediately returned to Pukekawa, driving Mrs Crewe back to what was now known as 'murder country'.

In view of the fact that a manager had been appointed, Hewson offered to assist the police in any way that he could. His offer was accepted and he was invited to join the search party in the gardens of the Crewe farmhouse.

In their search for .22 cartridge shells, they sieve-searched the flower beds, mowed the lawns and carefully examined the grass clippings. On their knees they made a careful inch-by-inch search of the mown lawns, they gave the paddocks outside the enclosed gardens the same treatment; the guttering of the house, even the water tank was searched. The only item found was a complete bullet discovered by Hewson, but that had been deliberately planted by one of the police officers as a joke on their civilian colleague. Of fired cases there was no sign.

Having been advised that the search for a .22

cartridge case on the Crewe property had produced negative results Inspector Bruce Hutton reconsidered the information that had been furnished to him by the DSIR.

The psychological warfare on Len Demler was stepped up by rumours deliberately circulated through Pukekawa that he was a voluntary patient at a nearby mental institution and that his daughter Heather was firmly convinced of his guilt. Neither rumour had even a vestige of truth, but the Demler family were powerless against the mischief within the community. In the light of subsequent events it was perhaps fortunate that Demler did not own a .22 rifle. After the discovery of Jeannette's body her father's friends and acquaintances were closely questioned as to whether any of them had loaned Demler a .22 rifle before 17 June. In the event, none had. What was unfortunate for the man at the centre of the storm was that a gun that had been part of the Chennell estate could not be found. Despite intensive and desperate searches of both the Crewe and Demler farms that missing gun remained missing.

Bruce Hutton turned his attention back to the guns that he did have – the two that the DSIR had been unable to exclude. One from the Thomas farm, one from the Eyre farm. The latter one linked to the tragedy a family who were no strangers to violent death. For the Eyres it must have seemed like the replay of a nightmare from the past – from the night of 24 August 1920. That was the night that Sidney Seymour Eyre had the top of his head blown off as he lay sleeping in his bed. His wife's lover, Samuel Thorne, was charged with the murder and after two trials was found guilty. Protesting his innocence to the last he was hanged at Mt Eden prison. For fifty years the Eyre family had been living with that case. In 1970 it was brought out, dusted over and closely examined by first the police and subsequently by the press. The similarities were uncanny but at this stage of the investigation into the

71

deaths of the Crewes, not readily apparent. In August 1970, Inspector Hutton's prime concern was not a solved murder from the past but two unsolved murders on his desk. Looking at the Eyre family his attention centred on Mickey Eyre. A man in his late twenties, Eyre had a reputation in some quarters that left a bit to be desired. Police collected statements from residents who gave specific instances of cruelty that the handicapped, deaf young man had perpetrated on animals. Other statements mentioned Eyre being discovered late at night outside a farmhouse with a rifle. Again, there was talk of the time when he had worked for Harvey Crewe and of how Crewe had exploded into rage when he discovered that Eyre had cut the grass in the wrong paddock.

With the exception of the Thomas and Eyre rifles all the guns were returned to their owners. On 7 September, Arthur Thomas got a taste of what Demler had been experiencing since mid-June. Detective Sergeants Seaman and Parkes called at his farm. Parkes was later to say that they asked Thomas to accompany them to Tuakau police station. Thomas was later to say that he did not know where they were taking him until the police car was heading towards Tuakau. There is also considerable disagreement about exactly what occurred once the group arrived at the police station. What is quite clear is that, if Thomas was not given the third-degree treatment, he most certainly received something approaching it.

He was asked to account for his movements on the night of 17 June; it was 'pointed out to him that was the night the Crewes were killed.' That was how Parkes later referred to the opening moments of that interview. In fact, the opening question was: 'Arthur, it was your rifle that was used to kill the Crewes. What do you say to that?' The two police officers were anxious to trap or bluff Thomas into confessing to the murders. They accused him of hating Harvey Crewe. They questioned him about his friendship with the dead woman going back to schooldays. They asked him for details covering his working life up to 1970, of his various meetings with Jeannette. Of the presents that he had given her. Of his reaction when rejected by the woman. Of his knowledge of the Crewe farm. They attacked him for not taking part in the search. They probed into his financial position. Throughout the interview, Thomas protested his innocence. He denied any knowledge of the murders. He offered to help the police in any way possible to establish his innocence. With regard to his rifle being the murder weapon, he accepted their lie as the truth: 'If you say it was my gun, it must have been, but I didn't do it.' When they continued to accuse him of the murders he asked to be given a lie-detector test. They threatened to take him to Auckland and charge him with the murders. When he vehemently protested yet again that he was innocent, the police officers dropped their bluff and told him that they had just been 'trying you out'. He was driven back to his farm.

The following day, Detective Sergeant Mike Charles called at the Thomas farm. He returned the rifle and advised the Thomases that it 'was not the one we are looking for'.

On 9 September, the day after Thomas received his rifle back from the police, Pukekawa farmer David Payne was in nearby Tuakau. By the river he saw Inspector Pat Gaines still looking for that second body. They discussed the case. Payne asked the policeman how they could be so sure that Demler was their man. Pat Gaines replied:

'It's like this. We assemble all the evidence that we've got. We put it together piece by piece and we get one answer. In the event that we may have made a mistake, we dismantle it and attack it from another angle. Then we put it all together again and we come up with precisely the same answer. What would you think?'

One week later, on 16 September, the body of

Harvey Crewe was found floating in the Waikato. Like Jeannette's, it had only surfaced because of a heavy freak flooding of the river producing a sudden tidal surge. Like Jeannette's there was a .22 bullet in the head. Like Jeannette's it had been discovered at a time when the police investigations had reached an impasse.

The man who found Harvey's body was Constable Wyllie, the local officer who had been called to the Crewe farm by Owen Priest. Now nearly three months later he had discovered the second body that Bruce Hutton told me he 'had dreamed of finding the night before'. Would that second body give the inspector the answers he was seeking or would it merely pose more unanswered questions?

Harvey's body had been found four miles upstream from where the first gruesome discovery had been made exactly one month earlier. The snagged body was badly decomposed and Bruce Hutton feared that it might break up and vanish before they could get it on shore. A body cradle was rushed to the scene as police frogmen encircled the corpse. Inspector Hutton recalled the scene in his deposition:

'Whilst a police party in my boat pulled in on the downstream side of the snag and the body, efforts were made on the upstream side of the body by two members of the diving team to slide the cradle under the body. Despite frequent attempts to do this it just wasn't possible and on pulling my own boat closer in, I was able to observe a thin wire around the body, firstly travelling under the left armpit, across the back and over the right shoulder. A further piece of wire could be seen around the stomach of the body. Whilst Constable Spence was endeavouring to force the cradle under the body, I reached over and placed one hand under the shoulder of the body nearest to me in an attempt to free the body as at that stage we either thought it was weighted or deeply entrenched on numerous snags that were present. At that precise moment, I felt an object under the body and close to it and at the same moment, Constable Spence forced the cradle and tugged at the body itself. The body came free all of a sudden and the object slipped from my grasp. The body itself became more buoyant and surprisingly moved into the cradle with little further effort needed.

'The object I felt, felt to me like iron or something very solid but the weight was such that I had no chance to pull it towards me. Following the recovery of the body itself, I directed the police diving team to carry out an extensive search immediately below the body for the weight or weights that may have been attached. After searching for a short time Constable Spence surfaced with a car axle which he handed to me and which I immediately had photographed whilst in my possession.

'That is the axle previously produced as Exhibit 293. I examined the axle immediately and what could be described as the kingpin end of the axle was consistent with what I had felt prior to the wire breaking. I examined the axle further and it was obvious to me that at one point on the axle, wire or some similar substance had been very recently fastened to it.'

If that axle was indeed originally attached to the body of Harvey Crewe as it lay in six feet of water then the police placed a very important aspect of their subsequent case in serious jeopardy by not ensuring that body and axle were recovered together. The fact that it was brought ashore as a separate entity raised the first question of many that were to be subsequently raised with regard to an exhibit that I consider to be the most important in the entire case.

With the aid of a vintage-car enthusiast the police quickly established that the axle recovered from the bed of the Waikato had originally been part of a 1929 Nash motorcar; at least that was the origin of the axle that was shown to the car enthusiast. Whether one accepts that he was shown the same axle that came ashore with Harvey Crewe's body is another matter. Amongst the men of Pukekawa who were shown an axle was Peter Garratt. Apart from farming and assisting with the running of the local school buses, Peter Garratt, like Mickey Eyre's father Joff, was a man much in demand in the area because of his expertise at repairing cars and building car-trailers. The police, working on the premise that the axle they had discovered might at some time in its life have been part of a trailer, showed it to this man. At least they showed him *an* axle. Mr Garratt, now a justice of the peace on Auckland's North Shore, said to me:

'Within a day of taking the axle out of the river they brought it to me at the garage in Pukekawa. I was standing by the school bus ready to take off. It was between 3 and 3.15 p.m. when I was shown this axle. There were two police officers, I think one was Parkes. The other was a very tall, slightly built man (I believe this man to have been Detective Sergeant Jeffries). The axle had obviously had welding work done on it at some time. They wanted to know if I could identify the welding as mine; if I could identify the axle as one that I had worked on or handled at any time, that sort of thing. The axle weld was bright and shiny, a different composition to the cast steel of the stubs.'

Mr Garratt asked the police officers what material had been used for the welding, in order to ascertain if it was a metal that he was accustomed to using. At that stage the police had no idea and were advised by Peter Garratt to take the axle to the DSIR for metal trace tests. They never brought the axle back to him. A few months ago Mr Garratt was shown Exhibit 293 at the laboratory of Auckland forensic scientist, Dr James Sprott. He said:

'The axle I have recently seen at Dr Sprott's was not the same axle. I can't swear to it, but I'm pretty sure that was not the one that the police brought to me after they had recovered the body of Harvey Crewe from the river. The one that I saw at the laboratory has got one stub on and the other missing. The axle they showed me that afternoon at Pukekawa either had two stubs or none at all. In either event the ends were uniform.'

I showed Mr Garratt a number of the official police photographs of the axle that was Court Exhibit 293. He studied them carefully then said:

'That is not the axle I was shown at Pukekawa by those police officers. These photographs are of a different axle.'

As I have already observed Mr Garratt is now a justice of the peace, a man who sits on the bench administering the laws of New Zealand. Bearing in mind the character assassinations that have been perpetrated in this case on a number of people I shall be interested to see police reaction to this particular piece of evidence, now made public for the first time.

I found Mr Garratt's views about police behaviour in the case equally illuminating. He said:

'I see a lot of the police in my capacity as a JP and I think they are a fine bunch of people. But in the Crewe murder investigations they were inclined to treat many of the people in the most appalling manner. For instance, they treated young Bruce Roddick as though he was a Greys Avenue dropout. They were using entirely the wrong tactics and techniques. Instead of getting the local people to co-operate by the use of tact they alienated and upset. Despite their methods, rather than because of them, the locals still attempted to help.'

An example of the police using the correct methods was the gesture they made in September. A large party of local schoolchildren were taken to Auckland and shown over Auckland CIB. It was while the children were actually at police headquarters that Harvey Crewe's body was found.

While the police utilized the press and television in an attempt to obtain information about the Nash axle,

Bruce Hutton turned his attention back to Len Demler, who yet again had been obliged to identify the dead body of a member of his family.

'Then I got that axle and I said to myself, "I don't believe that Demler is involved, but don't let's do it that way, let's prove with this axle that he's the murderer, and we'll hang it on his bloody haystack or somewhere where it's obviously been used around his farm." So we set out, just as a team. I brought this team down to a very small group of top-class men and we went into it. It didn't take long to prove the bloody opposite to what we were trying to prove. To satisfy ourselves, we proved him innocent. That's what created the wider search. The search of that dump on the Thomas farm again.'

One part of proving Len Demler innocent that Bruce Hutton did not mention during my interview with him was an interrogation of Demler lasting between six and seven hours, an aspect I uncovered months after my interview with Mr Hutton. Another extraordinary fact that I have subsequently discovered is the police conference that took place just a day before Harvey's body was found. At that conference it was finally decided to arrest Len Demler and charge him with murder. Before that decision could be implemented the second body was found, at which point the police obviously decided to bide their time in the hope that the axle would give them further evidence. It did, against Arthur Thomas.

Less than two weeks after a photograph of the axle had appeared in the national press, the police officer who had been given the task of tracing the owner of the axle received a phone call. For Detective Len Johnston, the officer in question, it was the breakthrough that he and his colleagues had been so urgently seeking. The caller, a Mr Shirtcliffe, informed him that he had once owned a trailer with a 1929 Nash axle on it, but he had sold it in 1958. He did, however, have an old photograph of the trailer. Within two weeks the trail of ownership and re-sale led the police directly back to the Thomas farm. Arthur's father was the last known owner of the trailer.

On 12 October, Johnston interviewed an engineer, Roderick Rasmussen. He too had a story to tell about the trailer and even more particularly about the axle. It transpired that in the mid-1960s Rasmussen had worked on the trailer for Mr Thomas senior. Part of the work had involved replacing the Nash axle with a new tubular drop axle. According to Rasmussen the original axle and its stubs had been collected by his customer with the modified trailer.

The following day, 13 October, Detective Johnston called on Arthur Thomas. He showed him the axle. Thomas did not recognize it and told him he had never seen it before and that the only axle on his farm was one with two wheels attached to it. This, he and the police officer found near the farm dump. Shown the photograph of the trailer Arthur Thomas told the police officer that it was similar to one that his father had had on the farm at one time, which if he remembered correctly had been painted blue. He advised the policeman to get in touch with his father and gave him his address and instructions on how to get to the father's farm in Matakana, a township north of Auckland.

Detective Johnston asked for permission to take some wire samples and Thomas told him to take what he wanted. He also gave the officer upon request his entire current stock of .22 ammunition.

During their discussion the brush and comb set that Thomas had given to Jeannette seven years earlier was mentioned. He was asked if he knew whether or not she had used it. His reply according to the police officer was: 'I don't know. It could still be wrapped up for all I know.'

Asked why he had not contacted the police when the photograph of the trailer had appeared in the papers two days earlier, Thomas said that he wasn't sure just how similar it was to the one owned by his father and that he also thought his father might have contacted the police.

The following day found Detectives Johnston and Parkes at the father's farm in Matakana. Like his son, Mr Thomas gave them all the help he could. He dug out the certificate of ownership for the trailer, showed the police the trailer itself, found his cheque-book stub that covered the purchase of the trailer and also advised the police officers where to look for the other parts of the axle on the Pukekawa farm that he leased to his son.

On 15 October Johnston was back on the Pukekawa Thomas farm. He and Arthur searched in a variety of places including the farm dump for components that might have been part of the trailer before the axle conversion. They were unsuccessful.

That same week also found Detective Johnston with a .22 rifle in his hand, crouched outside the kitchen window at the Crewe property. This was late on the evening of 13 October. Among others that were present that evening were Dr Donald Nelson and Inspector Bruce Hutton. Johnston was responsible for this bizarre scene.

A recent addition to the police investigation team, Johnston had been reading his way into the case. While studying the police file that now stood six feet high he also examined the initial police photographs, including the one that showed that the louvre kitchen windows were open at the time the police were first called to the property. It occurred to the detective that perhaps one of the Crewes had been shot by a rifle aimed through those open louvres.

On the evening of 13 October, the theory was put to the test. Items of furniture were placed exactly where the police had found them. A target at head height was put into Harvey's chair which could be seen clearly when a marksman crouched on the window ledge outside. Shots fired by both Johnston and Nelson convinced the team of the feasibility of the theory. It was possible. Dr Nelson went further:

'In fact it was relatively easy to shoot accurately at a target in the armchair using the room lighting in the sitting-room from the position where I was.'

The following morning Dr Nelson received the last of the sixty-four rifles referred to earlier. Again the DSIR were 'unable to exclude' both the Thomas and Eyre rifles when they compared test bullets with the fragments that pathologist Dr Cairns recovered from Harvey Crewe's head.

In my view the questions and criticisms already raised in this book concerning this piece of forensic evidence are doubled by that second failure to exclude one of the two rifles. As with the death of Jeannette Crewe, so now with the death of Harvey; collection of another sixty-four .22 rifles would have produced on average at least two more guns that could not have been excluded. This aspect of evidence, therefore, is highly suspect when considering the question of who killed Harvey and Jeannette Crewe.

The post mortem that Dr Cairns performed on this second body established yet again that just one bullet had caused death. The bullet had entered behind and above the left ear. The exit wound was in front of the right ear.

Dr Cairns considered that Harvey Crewe had probably been sitting in his armchair, that the chair would not have been in the position it was found in but would have been around facing the fire and that he was hit in the back of the head by a shot fired from the direction of the kitchen.

On 20 October Johnston paid yet another visit to the Thomas farm, this time accompanied by Detective Sergeant Parkes. The two officers told Thomas that they would like to take some more wire samples. Again Thomas told them to help themselves and they collected another eleven pieces for the DSIR. The Thomas farm was the eighth from which such samples were taken.

When Parkes told Vivien Thomas that they would also like to take the Thomas .22 rifle back in again she produced it from the wash-house. Exactly why did they need the gun again? It certainly was not to assist the DSIR in arriving at any conclusions about the bullet samples recovered from either of the two bodies. They had already arrived at their conclusions and advised Bruce Hutton of them.

Having collected the wire samples and the rifle the two police officers searched the farm dump and Johnston found two stub axles and various other scrap metal parts. No photographs were taken of the find *in situ*. The two men left the farm without advising either Arthur or Vivien of the items they had removed from the dump, then drove nine miles to the Crewe farm and there washed the stub axles. It was subsequently established that the stub axles were from the axle that had been found in the Waikato river.

On the following day, 21 October, while his car was being photographed by the police, a team of detectives armed with a search warrant took the Thomas farm apart. From the tip they removed old number plates and a variety of scrap-metal parts and from other parts of the farm and its buildings they took an equally bewildering array of items; a memo book that contained engineer Rasmussen's phone number, pieces of wood, split rims. From the scullery, fourteen old .22 bullets were sorted out from a jar that also contained screws, nuts and bolts. From a drawer old letters written many years before his marriage to Vivien were taken. These letters from former girlfriends were to vanish without trace, only reappearing when the fate of Arthur Thomas had been determined.

One of the detectives taking part in the search, Stanley Keith, was working his way along the shelves in the garage. Through the cracks and holes in the old building he could see Thomas working in a vegetable garden. As he watched, Arthur was joined by an unhappy Vivien who by now was more than a little annoyed at the passage of policemen through the farmhouse. She and Arthur commenced to talk. Keith strained to hear the conversation but could make out only one remark from Arthur Thomas. There is some confusion about exactly what he overheard, simply because it later became apparent that there was some confusion in Keith's mind. Initially, at least, Keith recalled the remark as: 'If they think I am guilty, I am and that's that.' The onlooker may well see the best of the game but judging from Detective Keith he certainly did not hear the best of it. What preceded the alleged remark and what followed it were unfortunately lost in the wind.

Still in the garage, he had better luck with his search of an old apple box. Among the nuts and bolts he found a single .22 bullet, unfired. Later that day, Keith was present when that bullet was separated from its cartridge case. On the base of the bullet was the figure 8 that had also been discovered on both fatal bullets. To remove any powder that might have remained within the cartridge case it was fired in a single-shot .22. That simple, effective and totally correct action was later to assume massive significance.

The following day, 22 October, the man controlling the hunt for a double murderer met for the first time the man destined to be his final quarry. Exactly four months had passed before Bruce Hutton decided he should take a look at Arthur Thomas; four months in which he had tried desperately hard to establish that Len Demler had murdered the Crewes. Now four months on, still with no arrest, Arthur Thomas was clearly in his sights.

Their initial meeting was only a short one, about twenty minutes. The official reason why Hutton had called was to ask for authority to inspect Arthur's legal papers held by his Tuakau solicitors covering various transactions. Thomas happily gave him the authority. After a brief discussion about his father's trailer, the inspector left.

On 23 October, the Thomas farm was again visited by the police; this time it was Detective Sergeant Mike Charles. Having previously, with the aid of a search warrant, obtained access to Thomas's bank account and statements, and having also uplifted from the Tuakau solicitors all the private and personal documents that he considered relevant, he now held in his hand yet another search warrant and removed from the farm numerous accounts, documents and letters.

Saturday 24 October fell in Labour Day weekend. That evening Arthur and Vivien went to a local football club dance. It was a fancy-dress affair and judging from the photographs the Thomases were blithely unaware of the net that was closing around them. Despite the fact that they made a late night of it, they were up early the following morning milking cows when the police called yet again.

It is an interesting insight into Inspector Hutton's psychological approach that he deliberately chose that Sunday morning to pull both Vivien and Arthur Thomas in for intensive and lengthy questioning. He had through several of his officers previously ascertained that the Thomases would be going to the football dance and would not be coming back to the farm until very late. As an ex-farmer he knew better than most that they would have to be up early to milk. He shrewdly deduced that a couple of bleary-eyed people might well be vulnerable, might let their guard slip. Turning the screw another notch he had them driven on a twenty-five mile journey to Otahuhu police station rather than interview them locally at, for example, Tuakau police station.

The premise clearly was that a journey of that

duration would make them more apprehensive, more likely to make the confessions he sought.

Bruce Hutton has been heavily criticized for this action, just as he has been taken to task for his treatment of Len Demler. I find such criticism naive and quaint. The inspector was hunting a fox. It requires the hunter to have the cunning of the hunted in such a situation. His visit to the Thomas farm on 22 October was obviously to gain a little personal knowledge of the two people he was stalking. If he had shown throughout the entire investigation such flair, I for one would be delighted. Regrettably, as has already been demonstrated, he did not. Many aspects of the CIB at Pukekawa have about as much subtlety and finesse as a Sherman tank without a driver careering down Queen Street, Auckland. Spreading lies about a main suspect like Demler, for example – and this was done by a number of police officers – is a banal technique when compared with the way Hutton approached this particular interrogation of the Thomases.

Hutton designated Detective Johnston to question Vivien; her husband he saved for himself. During the course of the interrogations both were shown the impressive array of potential exhibits that the police had acquired. The axle, complete with its matching stubs; the wire, the rifle, with a packet of Arthur's bullets neatly tied to the trigger; the Christmas present of the brush and comb set with the card; these and other items were put on display for the benefit of Thomas and his wife. They were the fruits of four hard months' work by Hutton and the men under him. Now he wanted just one thing more, he wanted Thomas to 'cough', to confess that he had murdered Harvey and Jeannette.

Hutton got down to business at 10.10 a.m.

'Is your marriage a happy one, Arthur?'

'Yes, I think so, but it'd be better if we were able to have children, but that's my fault.'

Hutton was relaxed, totally in control of himself and the situation. He was very aware that in September, Detectives Parkes and Seaman had given Thomas a heavy time and failed to break him. The inspector had decided to use directly the opposite approach – gentle, friendly, dropping in the Christian name frequently.

'Tell me Arthur, how long had you known Jeannette?'

'Oh, I've known her for ages, Mr Hutton. Known her since we went to primary school together.'

'Is that a fact? Did you know her well?'

Thomas grinned at him. 'When we were at school together, I had a real schoolboy crush on her. I remember later on I became quite fond of her.'

'Did you see much of her then? Later on?'

Arthur Thomas was relaxing now. This policeman was different, not like those others. This was a man you could trust.

'Well, I lost contact with her once she went to St Cuthbert's.'

'Like a cup of tea, Arthur?'

'Yes please, Mr Hutton.'

The inspector smiled at him as he picked up a phone and requested some tea.

'So I don't suppose you saw her after that then?'

'Oh yeh. While I was working in the Forestry Department out at Maramarua. Jeannette was teaching out there. I visited her a couple of times at the hostel where she lived with the other teachers.'

'You've got a good memory. When would that have been?'

Arthur frowned for a moment as he concentrated, then his face brightened. 'It would be some time in 1960, Mr Hutton.'

The door opened and a policewoman brought in a tray of tea and biscuits. The inspector handed him a cup.

'Help yourself to sugar. Do you remember when Jeannette went to England?'

'Oh, thanks very much. Um, yes, can't remember the date she went though. I remember calling on her mum and dad, I wanted to keep in touch with her. They gave me her address in England.'

'Did you write to her?'

'Yes, a couple of times.' He reached into an inside pocket. 'I've got something for you.' He took out a dog-eared envelope and handed it to the inspector who, trying hard not to show his eagerness, glanced at it casually.

'What's this then, Arthur?'

'It's a letter she wrote to me while she was abroad. I dug it out this morning when the police said you wanted to see me. Thought it might be useful.'

'Useful' was an understatement. What worried the inspector was why his men hadn't found it during their many searches of the Thomas property. If Arthur had not in all naivety and innocence produced it, the police would never have known of its existence. They had been looking specifically for this, they had found quite a number from other women, but none from Jeannette. Bruce Hutton smiled at him again.

'Did you keep this hidden away then?'

'No, it was in one of the kitchen drawers. Don't suppose it's of any use, otherwise your men would have taken it, wouldn't they?'

The inspector was reassuring.

'I'm sure it will be of great use, Arthur. May I read it?'

'Sure, keep it.'

It had a London postmark, dated 14 February 1961. In the letter Jeannette thanked Arthur for 'the beautiful writing compendium which I have just received'.

'I see you sent her presents while she was in London.'

Arthur grinned sheepishly and sipped his tea as the inspector replaced the letter in its envelope and put it

87

carefully in a drawer. That was a bonus, a beautiful, unlooked for, unexpected bonus. An important link in the chain he was forging that would link this man inextricably to the dead woman.

'Talking of presents, I understand you gave Jeannette a brush and comb set. When was that?'

'That was after she came back to New Zealand, a few months after she returned. Can't remember what year, it was a Christmas present. I popped round to the Demler farm and gave it to her.'

'With a little card?'

'Yes.'

'What did she think of it? Was she pleased?'

Arthur looked at the inspector ruefully. 'I think she got the idea I was trying to hang around.'

The two men smiled at each other, a silent agreement that men often experience such rebuffs. Encouraged, Arthur continued:

'She told me she was going out with a steady boyfriend; well, later I realized that she must have been talking about Harvey Crewe.'

'Were you very fond of her at this stage?'

'Yes, I was very struck on her.'

'When was the next time you saw her?'

'Didn't see her again. Not to court her anyway. I was married to Vivien and she was married to Harvey, the next time I saw her. That was years later.'

'I wonder how you'd be today if you'd married Jeannette.'

'Well, of course, if that had happened, I would have been a wealthy man today.'

And so it continued for hour after hour with Inspector Hutton moving gently around his prey. Drawing him out. Getting from Arthur statements, words, phrases that would become significant, important and incriminating in the hands of a clever Crown Prosecutor. They talked about a wide range of subjects, but they all had one common denominator, the deaths of the Crewes. The above reconstruction of just a small part of an 'interview' that lasted over five hours is based on the sworn deposition of Inspector Hutton. At 2.20 in the afternoon Bruce Hutton took down from Thomas the following statement:

I am a married man 32 years of age. I reside with my wife Vivien Thomas on my father's farm at Mercer Ferry Road, Pukekawa. The phone number is Pukekawa 838. I lease the farm from my father Allan Thomas who is living at Pt Wells, Matakana.

I am being spoken to by Detective Inspector Hutton about the deaths of Jeannette and Harvey Crewe in June of this year. I have been warned that I am not obliged to say anything more about this matter or to answer any further questions unless I wish to do so and that anything that I might say will be taken down and may be used in evidence.

I was brought up on the farm that I am now leasing from my father. In 1966 my father agreed to lease the farm to me for $2000 a year. I have been on the farm ever since. My marriage is quite a happy one. We do not have children but that is my fault.

I remember going to Pukekawa Primary School with Jeannette Crewe. We were both in the same class right through primary school. On second thoughts I was a class ahead of her until she caught up when I failed a year in standard one. I had quite a schoolboy crush on Jeannette at school. When I finished primary school I went and started work on the farm with my father. Jeannette carried on her education by going to St Cuthbert's. After this she became a schoolteacher at Maramarua. At this time I was working in the Forestry at Maramarua. I met Heather Demler one night at a dance at Pukekawa and she mentioned that Jeannette was a schoolteacher at Maramarua. She told me that I should look Jeannette up. On my return to Maramarua I went and looked Jeannette up. I actually visited her a couple of times but I never took her out. Not very long later I heard Jeannette had gone overseas to England. I went round and saw Len Demler and asked him for Jeannette's address so I could write to her. I think I wrote to her twice whilst she was away. She was away for about two years. She replied to my letters. I now hand one of the letters from her to the police. Later when Jeannette returned I took her round a Christmas present. The brush and comb set I have just looked at is the one I gave her. The card has my handwriting on it. I did not take Jeannette out.

She did mention at the time I gave her the present that she had a boyfriend.

I have been asked about my movements on the night of the ratepayers' meeting of 17 June 1970. I remember soon after Jeannette and Harvey were missing Vivien and I discussed what we were doing that night. I recall remembering that we were home attending a sick cow. Peter Thomas was home also. The cow had been sick for some time and I think Peter helped me the previous night but I am not sure. This cow was in a sling in the tractor shed and was sick for some time. I finally had to shoot this cow with my .22 rifle. I also remember that day as I think both Vivien and I went to our dentist in Pukekohe. We arrived back home at about 4 p.m. We attended to the cow between 5 p.m. and 6 p.m. I think I intended going to the ratepayers' meeting but by the time we had tea it was too late to go.

I have been shown the axle which was found with Harvey Crewe's body together with the two stub axles found by the police on my farm tip. After looking closely at these and also some photographs I agree that the axle and stub axles belong together. I cannot recall any of these articles being on my farm. I cannot explain how the axle got with Harvey Crewe's body. After looking at the axles I think they must belong to the old trailer.

I faintly recall the old trailer and the fact that there

was some blue on it. I do not know what happened to that old trailer. Seems like the axle must have been on my farm but I cannot help any further.

I have been asked about my .22 rifle and where it was on the night of 17 June 1970. I am almost certain that this rifle could not have been taken out of my house without me knowing. I certainly did not lend it to anyone round that time. I remember using this rifle to shoot the sick cow I have mentioned, about two weeks after Jeannette and Harvey went missing. That dead cow is now on the tip on the farm where the stub axles were found. I also used the same rifle about a month ago to shoot a blind dog. I also put the carcass of this dog down at the farm dump. I also used to use this rifle to shoot rabbits with. Vivien does not shoot and Peter Thomas has never used this rifle to my knowledge.

I have been told that samples of wire found on my farm are similar to wire found on Harvey Crewe's body. I can only say that someone must have come on to my farm and taken the wire and axle. I have been told that the .22 bullets in Harvey and Jeannette's body had the figure 8 stamped on them and that similar ammunition with this number has been found at my farm. I cannot explain this. I was aware however that ammunition does have numbers stamped on the bullet.

I have viewed the brush and comb set I gave to Jeannette. I think this present cost me about four or five pounds. This was in 1962. I know Len Demler quite well but he has never been to visit me at my farm.

I have been told that a detective overheard me say to Vivien when I was planting seeds on Friday something to the effect that if the police thought I was guilty then I must be guilty. I cannot remember saying anything like this to Vivien.

I have been told about a pair of overalls found in the boot of my car having blood on them. I do not remember any blood getting on these. I use these overalls to fix a puncture or other repairs to the car when I am in good clothes.

The rubbish tip on my farm is used by me when necessary. I use it regularly and take all sorts of things to it. I remember a few weeks ago taking some stuff out of the horse stable to the farm dump. I also remember some time ago cleaning stuff out of a stable to put the Dodge truck inside. This was about two years ago. I remember seeing one of the wheel rims found by the police on my farm dump but I have not seen the axles there.

I did not help the police and local farmers with the search for Jeannette and Harvey Crewe but by the time I finished my daily chores by 1 p.m. I thought it would be too late to go. I thought that unless you could get to the Crewe farm by 9 a.m. you would not be able to assist. I was busy at that time of the year as my cows start calving on 10 June. I do not know how many cows I had in when the search started. I suppose I could of helped for a few hours but I was fairly busy.

I know I have been a suspect all along in this case. I suppose I did use to chase Jeannette along a bit and used to write to her.

I have read this through and it is true and correct. I have nothing to add.

A. A. Thomas.
25 October 1970.

Hutton finished taking down that statement at 3.41 p.m. He had tried hard, very hard, to obtain from Arthur Thomas the confession he needed. He had failed.

An indication of just how hard he had tried and just how well he realized that the case he had built against Arthur Thomas did not even justify arrest let alone trial can be gauged by the remark contained in Thomas's statement about bloodstained overalls being found in the boot of his car. Those 'bloodstains' presumably come into the same category as the raspberry ice cream bloodstains on Mrs Roddick's blanket. Nothing has been heard of those bloodstained overalls since that afternoon of 25 October 1970.

Thomas was also told, while at the police station, that the axle came from his farm. In fact, he was asked how the axle had got off his farm and had become wired to the body of Harvey Crewe. Bruce Hutton told him that he had traced the axle back to the Thomas farm. The inspector had done no such thing; the tracing came to a halt in 1965 at Rasmussen's engineering works.

Likewise with the wire. Hutton informed him that it had 'been traced back to your farm'. It had not. I believe the techniques that Inspector Hutton used are perfectly proper but they clearly indicate Hutton's acknowledgement of the paucity of evidence against Thomas on that Sunday in October 1970. If Hutton had considered that the case he had assembled against Thomas could be made to stick, Arthur Thomas would not have walked out of Otahuhu police station that afternoon.

Thomas's recollections of that interrogation make a fascinating counterpoint to Hutton's. The following is from a handwritten account by Arthur Thomas originally published by a man who has been deeply involved in the case for a number of years, Pat Booth. In his book *Trial By Ambush* he quotes Arthur Thomas's version:

'Hutton showed me in his room, my rifle in the corner with a packet of bullets tied to the trigger, beside the rifle was the Christmas present and copper and galvanized wire. We went into the next room and he showed me the axle with the stubs on each side. He said what did I think of that. I said they must go together. We went back into his office and he said to me: "Arthur did you go for a quiet drive?" I said: "No, Mr Hutton, I never left the farm." He said: "What about this homemade wine you make?" I said: "I never touch the drink. Supposing I did I need to get pretty rotten

93

to do a thing like this. How am I going to get there with all the power poles and corners on the road? Supposing I was lucky and got there and did the job what was I going to do?" Mr Hutton never answered me. Then he said: "Well, Arthur, the rifle, bullets, wire and axle all came off your farm, what do you say about that?" I was standing up at this time behind his bench. I walked up and down twice thinking what could have happened. I said: "It looks like someone has come on the farm at night or the weekend before and taken what they needed and if anything blows up like all murders they all make mistakes there is only one man to blame." He said: "Do you mean you have been framed?" I said if that's the word you used that's what I mean, I have been framed. He said: "One other thing, Arthur. I have one other piece of evidence up my sleeve. I'm not going to tell anyone. I've got a good mind to lock you up but, Arthur, I'm going to give you a chance." '

Thomas then says that the taking of the statement was then begun.

During my interviews with Arthur Thomas inside the maximum security prison of Paremoremo we discussed that account. He confirmed that it was accurate, particularly the remark from Inspector Hutton about 'another piece of evidence up my sleeve'. Thomas said to me: 'I couldn't understand why he wouldn't show me this other piece of evidence or tell me about it. After all he'd shown me everything else they had.'

Careful analysis of the police investigation shows that Thomas was indeed shown or told about all the important aspects of the evidence that had been assembled against him on Sunday 25 October 1970.

Whether Inspector Hutton made the remark or not there is no doubt that within forty-eight hours he did indeed have another piece of evidence, not up his sleeve, but right in the palm of his hand. It was to become the most important piece of evidence in the case against Arthur Thomas.

The inspector asked many other questions that afternoon which are not revealed in that statement of Thomas's. Questions about rape. Questions about spermatozoon. Whether Thomas knew that seminal fluid could be traced. When I interviewed Bruce Hutton, the reason for those questions was made clear:

Hutton: I'm convinced in my own mind that she was raped.

Yallop: But she had all her clothes on when you found the body. Even her pantyhose were intact.

Hutton: Oh yes, but look at the injuries she had, though.

Yallop: The broken nose, the lacerations?

Hutton: Yes. Now you tell me why that mat was burnt then? Decent-sized mat in front of the hearth. Why burn it?

It was a good question. I pointed out to Bruce Hutton that clearly attempts had been made to clear up. Scrubbing of bloodstains on the fitted carpet. Mopping up in the kitchen. In view of the fact that pathologist Dr Cairns believed that Jeannette had been shot after being knocked to the floor, could it be that the carpet by the hearth would have been so bloodstained that whoever cleaned up considered it was beyond salvaging and had therefore burned it in the grate? Hutton held to the view that Jeannette had been raped on the carpet and the carpet was then burned to destroy any seminal fluid stains upon it. It is a theory, unsupported by any evidence; indeed what evidence there is refutes it. The condition of Jeannette's clothes for example, even two months after death, showed no tell-tale tears or rips indicating a sexual attack. Nevertheless, the Crown Prosecutor was to make devastating use of this theory that was unsupported by an atom of evidence.

Meanwhile, on that Sunday afternoon, Vivien Thomas was being questioned by Detective Johnston. Again the technique was the soft approach. Full of 'Now you are telling us the truth, aren't you, Vivien?' And

'You wouldn't lie to protect Arthur, would you, Vivien?' The purpose of questioning Vivien was not merely to obtain confirmation, or more hopefully contradiction of her husband's statement. What the police were anxious to get from Vivien was another confession. A confession that would state that her husband had murdered the Crewes, that she had assisted him, either at the time or subsequently, with the clearing up and disposal of the bodies and that she was the woman that Bruce Roddick had seen on the Friday morning when she had returned to feed Rochelle.

Totally convinced by October that the child had indeed been fed during those five days before discovery, the police believed that Arthur and Vivien fitted their requirements to the last letter. One or both had murdered. One or both had cleared up. Vivien had fed Rochelle. Fitting police requirements and fitting the actual facts are, however, two quite different things.

Detective Johnston asked for a detailed account of what the two Thomases had done and where they had gone over the five days from 17 June to 22 June. Prior to their interrogation of 25 October, both of the Thomases had been asked to account for their movements over this crucial period. On that warm Sunday they yet again recounted the details.

The whole aspect of the sick cow that Arthur Thomas had referred to in his statement was again discussed. It was because of his sick cow No. 4 that he was able to pinpoint his movements on 17 June. Vivien's statements to Johnston agreed with those that her husband was at that time making in another part of the police station, but the information she gave the police went even further. The sick cow that her husband had been fighting to keep alive was in calf and that was the main reason they had tried so hard to help the animal survive; if it died before giving birth, they lost two animals. Vivien told Johnston how, when they had returned from their dentist's at nearby Pukekohe at about 4.30 p.m.,

Arthur had discovered that Cow 4 was about to calve, was in fact beginning to calve. She had gone down to the sheds and helped her husband. After the cow had calved successfully she had come back up to the farmhouse. This was sometime between six and seven in the evening. By this time Peter Thomas, the seventeen-year-old cousin of Arthur who was living with them at the time, was home. While preparing the evening meal Vivien received a telephone call from Arthur's aunt inviting them to accompany her to the local ratepayers' meeting. Vivien explained to her that because of the sick cow dinner was running late and they would not be going to the meeting. During the course of this phone conversation Arthur returned from the sheds and confirmed that he did not feel like attending the meeting. This was at 7.30 p.m.

The three of them – Arthur, Vivien and Peter – had dinner, bathed, watched a little television and went to bed between 9 and 9.30 p.m. Neither she nor Arthur left the house that night. She was adamant that once they had retired, Arthur did not get out of bed. As a light sleeper she was sure that had he got up she would have known.

Vivien Thomas then covered with the police officers the events of the next few days. Thursday was a normal farm day. More calves were born and they were also occupied with the commencement of the milking season.

On Friday, the only time that either of them left the farm was in the evening to attend a 21st birthday party. Peter Thomas, who worked at a nearby engineering works in Mercer, was also at the party.

On Saturday their movements off the farm consisted of Vivien attending a cat show in Auckland in the morning and returning to the farm about 11 a.m. In the evening she and her husband, in company with most of the district, attended a local dinner and dance.

Other than these everyday events there was, Vivien

asserted, nothing of note that happened in those five days.

Asked if either she or Arthur or Peter had during that time used the .22 rifle, Vivien recalled that her husband had been obliged to put Cow 4 out of her misery two days after she had calved.

The police were therefore confronted with a situation where three people insisted that on the night of the murder none of them had moved off the Thomas farm. With regard to Peter Thomas, when the police showed him their array of axle, stub axles, rifle, bullets, etc and told him there was no doubt that his cousin had murdered the Crewes, the seventeen-year-old broke down and cried, but through his tears he insisted that Arthur had not left the farm that evening or night.

When I interviewed Peter Thomas he recalled that he had been taken in for questioning three times:

'On the first occasion Hutton and Johnston picked me up from my place of work, Roose Shipping. They took me into Tuakau police station. Before they asked me any questions, a copy of my finger and palm prints was taken. They were all very friendly. I remember Johnston went out and bought pies for all of us. While Hutton was questioning me Johnston was busy writing it all down. They were very interested to learn from me what Arthur's reaction had been when news of the murders came out. I told them it was a shock to Arthur as it was to everyone else in Pukekawa. I told them there was no way Arthur could have left that farm without me knowing.

'The third time they took me in they showed me the axle and the stubs. They said it had come off Arthur's farm. I was very upset. Both Hutton and Johnston insisted that I had seen it on the farm. I insisted I had not, because I hadn't. They went on and on insisting that I had, and that I should say I had, that I must say I had. I couldn't understand why they were so desperate to get me to tell a lie, it didn't make sense. Hutton said:

"We've got enough evidence to arrest Arthur, anything you say will help Arthur out." '

Having interviewed not only Bruce Hutton and Peter Thomas but many others who were deeply involved in this case, there is no doubt in my mind that not only is that above description of the pressure applied to Peter Thomas accurate, if anything it understates the desperation of the police to get a witness, any witness, who would state that he had seen the axle on the Thomas farm at some short time before the deaths of the Crewes. The police failed with Peter Thomas. They failed with everyone else on whom pressure was applied. They have continued to fail. Even though the police state that the Thomas case or the Crewe case, call it what you will, is closed, it is not closed. They are still seeking proof that the axle was on that farm in mid-1970. They will never find such proof. It was not there.

The Thomas trio were not the only people to find themselves talking to the police over that particular Labour weekend. Quite a number of the farmers in Pukekawa received visits from the police.

On Saturday 24 October, David Payne received a visit from Detective Toothill. The police officer wanted to know if Arthur Thomas had been at that ratepayers' meeting on 17 June. It is yet another clear indication of the police anxiety to break the alibi. The thinking is clear. Get Thomas to that meeting and you have him within three miles of the Crewe farm. David Payne showed him the list of those who had attended; there was no Arthur Thomas on it. He then made a written statement to Toothill confirming that Thomas was not there.

On Sunday 25 October, while Vivien and Arthur were at Otahuhu police station, David Payne received yet another visit from the police. This time it was Detective Parkes. He wanted to know where David Payne was on the night of 17 June.

That was not the end. Parkes then called on another farmer, L. F. McGuire, who had also been at that ratepayers' meeting. Mrs McGuire opened the door and Parkes advised her that he wished to talk to her husband in order to check his movements on the night of the double murder. He was told that Mr McGuire was in the piggery, some 150 yards from the house. Parkes thanked her and departed, not to the piggery but to his car. Now this investigation even at that time had cost New Zealand several million dollars, yet a detective could not walk 150 yards to interview a man for the purpose of eliminating him from the police hunt for a double murderer. Mr McGuire, who had clearly been out that night, within three miles of the Crewe farm, is still waiting for Detective Parkes to call back.

The Robinson family of Pukekawa are others who have kept the teapot warmed for the return of Detective Parkes:

Parkes: Excuse me, Mrs Robinson, but where were you on the night of 17 June?

Mrs Robinson: I was playing indoor bowls at Glen Murray.

Parkes: How did you get to Glen Murray?

Mrs Robinson: My husband drove the car.

Parkes: Where is he today?

Mrs Robinson: He's not at home.

Parkes: Oh, all right. I'll come back and see him.

He didn't come.

Brian Murray, who also attended that ratepayers' meeting, had stood and chatted outside the hall with David Payne when it finished at 10.40. He was another Pukekawa farmer to be visited by the tireless Parkes on that Sunday. This near neighbour of Thomas was asked the same questions: 'Where were you on the night of 17 June? Was Arthur Thomas at the meeting?' Presumably Parkes felt that if he asked enough people he might find someone who would give him the answers he was seeking. Again he drew a blank. Like so many others in Pukekawa, Brian Murray had a .22 rifle. Like so many others in Pukekawa, his rifle has yet to be checked. Like so many others in Pukekawa he comes, by Detective Sergeant Mike Charles's terms of reference, within the category of people whose rifles should have been collected and tested by the DSIR.

Ignore all talk of a five-mile radius; these were people who were within *three* miles of the Crewe farm.

If the visit of Parkes to the Murray farm did little for the police officer it did a great deal for Brian Murray, a highly respected man in the district, riding member for the county. While Detective Parkes continued on his way, presumably to interview at least the sixty-one people who I know were out in Pukekawa that night, Murray considered the implications of that police visit, not for himself but for the young farmer he had watched grow from boyhood. He paid a call on Arthur and Vivien.

When he arrived they were sitting unconcernedly watching television. He told them of the visit he had had from the police and the questions about Thomas that had been asked. He'd expected this would be a bombshell to them both. It wasn't. They told him where they had been that day, virtually all day; of the visits, the searches, the items that had been removed from the farm. Unlike Len Demler, Thomas had not even considered talking to a lawyer, let alone instructing one to represent him.

Murray was appalled. 'My God, Arthur, they're trying to pin this on you,' he exclaimed.

Arthur Thomas's reply perhaps sums up the man more succinctly than an entire book can: 'It's all right, Brian. I've got nothing to worry about. I've done nothing wrong. Inspector Hutton knows that, he's helping me to find out who's trying to frame me.'

Brian Murray sat for hours attempting to persuade Thomas to go to a solicitor. Thomas couldn't see the point. He felt sure that 'Mr Hutton will find out who's at the bottom of this.'

Speaking of Thomas, Brian Murray was later to remark: 'He was too trusting, too honest, too naive to take care of himself.'

Murray sat there and told them that he was not going to leave the living-room until they promised that the following day they would contact a solicitor. Eventually, with great reluctance, they agreed.

The following day, unfortunately for the Thomases, was the bank holiday Monday of Labour Day weekend, and members of the legal profession have always shown a marked reluctance to work on bank holidays, unlike the police force who work every day of the year. On that bank holiday, Inspector Hutton called yet another conference, a major one. The purpose of all the previous major conferences had been to establish whether the case against Len Demler was strong enough to arrest him and charge him with the murders of Jeannette and Harvey Crewe. This one had as its first item on the agenda:

'Was the amount of evidence assembled against Arthur Thomas enough to arrest him and charge him with two murders?'

The conclusion reached was 'No'.

Having arrived at that conclusion, the police present at that conference reviewed the entire course of their investigations. The fact that the Crewes' outside light was on when the police had arrived at the farm on the afternoon of 22 June was mentioned. Recalling the conference at a Court of Appeal hearing in early 1973, a hearing that was secret, Inspector Hutton said:

'Mention was made of the fact that the electric light could have been on for the purpose of a desperate attempt by the offender to find a shell or shells which may have ejected from a rifle. Arising from this conference on the same evening, I instructed Detective Sergeants Charles and Parkes to carry out a further search the following day. This was done. At the same conference it was discovered that part of the beds of the Crewe section had not been sieve-searched. This was one facet of the inquiry that was conducted the following day by these two men.'

There had of course been at least two, possibly more, extensive searches of the gardens already carried out. One search took place in the first week of the police inquiry. Another search that involved sieving the beds took place in the days immediately following the discovery of Jeannette's body, when it was known for a certainty that she had been shot by a .22 bullet. If one accepts as accurate the conclusions of the police conference held on 26 October, one small flowerbed inside the fence had not been sieve-searched at that time *though the paddock beyond this bed had been subjected to minute examination, including a careful hand search of the mown clippings of grass.*

With regard to the outside light and the reason for it being on, it could be equally reasoned that as the Crewes died after dark it would not be unreasonable to find lights on. The kitchen light was also on when the farm was discovered; was that also to help the offender in the desperate search for cartridge cases?

The following morning, 27 October, Charles and Parkes set out for Pukekawa to make their own urgent search for cartridge cases.

At about the same time as Charles and Parkes called initially at the Priest farm, presumably to pass the time of day, Inspector Hutton arrived at the Thomas farm, nine miles away.

The fact that the two officers engaged on a crucial search did not drive direct to the Crewe farm is odd. This exercise of searching the flowerbed was top secret. Hutton was later to say that only he and the two men involved in the actual search were aware that it was going to take place. That is clearly contradicted by Hutton himself who on another occasion said that

Detective Sergeant Murray Jeffries was present when he gave the order for the flowerbed to be sieve-searched, and in view of the fact that the whole aspect was discussed during the conference, it would be reasonable to assume that all present were aware that this particular search was going to be made. Nevertheless, I am certain that the police were extremely anxious and careful to keep knowledge of this search within their ranks. That makes the casual visit of Charles and Parkes even odder.

Mrs Priest said: 'Mike Charles and Bruce Parkes came here that day at about 11 a.m. They said they had some work to do up on the Crewe farm but would be back later for a cup of tea.'

Having, it seems, made their presence in the district deliberately known, the two men departed.

Bruce Hutton, meanwhile, was collecting more invoices from the Thomases who, like most farmers that year, were attempting to fight off the effects of the previous season's drought. Clearly any debts outstanding, recent bills demanding payment and an overdraft situation were items of acute interest to Hutton, who felt such aspects could be used in a courtroom to demonstrate an accused person under considerable financial pressure at the time of the murders. He was also still curious about that sick Cow 4.

'How,' he asked Thomas, 'can you prove to me that Cow 4 calved on 17 June?'

Thomas replied, 'There is no way of actually proving this. The cow had trouble calving and about 7 p.m. I returned to the house after I had helped it calve.'

Hutton, still anxious to establish that his suspect was at the ratepayers' meeting, observed that there would have been time for Thomas to have attended the meeting. Thomas pointed out to him that after a meal and a bath, there would not have been time. When again asked what time he had gone to bed his reply, according to Bruce Hutton, was: 'It was about 9 p.m.

but it could have been a lot later.' As the police had previously taken possession of the shed sheets covering the Thomas herd, the conversation was rather superfluous. The sheets showed Cow 4 had calved on the 17th, Vivien had even ringed it when handing the sheet to Detective Toothill. To the Thomases there was nothing they could add.

While the inspector was engaged in a Kafkaesque conversation about cows his men a few miles away were having a much more rewarding morning. They had first weeded the bed without finding anything significant. Parkes then loosened the soil with a fork. Charles then came along behind him searching to a depth of six inches. Whether this was merely a hand search or whether he actually sieved as well, depends on which version of his subsequent evidence one accepts. In either event, Charles was handling a lump of soil when suddenly, there in the palm of his hand was a .22 cartridge case. After four months and ten days, after at least two previous pattern searches, Mike Charles had succeeded where all before him had failed. Excitedly he called Parkes over. As Charles examined it, bone dry earth ran out of the case.

Mr Priest: 'They arrived back here about one o'clock. They had their cup of tea and with that Mr Hutton, and Mr Toothill arrived. Mike Charles put on one of my daughter's hats and a pair of sun glasses and was dancing around the room like a kid. That was the kind of atmosphere. I said to Julie (his wife): "Those jokers have found something." The air was electric. It's hard to describe. They were happy, they were pleased, as though there had been a breakthrough. They didn't tell us what it was of course but Julie heard one of them say "I.C.I.". I knew what that meant all right.'

Ironic, that 'I.C.I.'. Over the years that followed that moment, a great many other people would come to know what that meant.

While Inspector Hutton was discussing cows with the

Thomases and Detective Sergeant Charles was finding a cartridge case at the Crewes, a police diving team was settling in on the banks of the Waikato. Their purpose was to search the river for the murder weapon and the weight that had been used to sink the body of Jeannette Crewe. Their subsequent search was fruitless with regard to finding anything that would incriminate Arthur Thomas. If they found any weight that incriminated anyone else, and undoubtedly they brought up a considerable number of metal objects, it has never been revealed.

The following morning, 28 October, Mike Charles took the case that he had found to the DSIR in Auckland. The specific task was to compare it with test cases fired from the Thomas and Eyre rifles. In the absence of Dr Donald Nelson, the task was undertaken by Rory Shanahan. While Charles, trying to contain his excitement, gave evidence at Auckland Magistrates' Court on another case, forensic science was attempting to establish the exact significance of his find.

While Shanahan was peering down his microscope, Detective Toothill was once more on the Thomas farm, looking at records of the herd. Vivien Thomas, having found the book in which she recorded the deaths of any animals, had realized that her statement made at Otahuhu three days earlier contained an error. The cow had not been shot two days after but six days after calving. She pointed this out to the detective who took possession of the book to add to the ever-growing list of items removed from the Thomas farm.

At lunch-time, as Mike Charles left the Magistrates' Court he was advised that Shanahan, after initial examination of the brass cartridge case and comparing it to copper cases previously fired from the Thomas rifle, was fairly certain the case that Charles had found had been fired from the Thomas rifle.

The test firings he performed the next day with brass cases removed any element of doubt in the scientist's mind. The case was from the Thomas rifle. Finally the police had a fragment of evidence that put Thomas on the Crewe farm. It was the first fragment they had discovered that achieved that object. It was to remain the only fragment within the entire history of the case that achieved that object. The Charles case, as it was destined to be called, was to become the most discredited court exhibit in New Zealand's history, but that lay in the future. In late October 1970 Inspector Hutton, confident that he had successfully hunted and trapped the fox, turned his attention to the vixen.

On 30 October, an identification parade took place at Pukekohe police station. There were eight women in the line up. Seven of them worked in a factory in Pukekohe, the eighth was Vivien Thomas. All were dressed in slacks, as was the woman that Bruce Roddick had seen on the morning of Friday 19 June at the Crewe farm.

As the women stood in line three feet apart, the police entered with Bruce Roddick. He walked slowly up and down the line several times. He then told the police that the woman he had seen on that Friday morning was not in the line up. It is clear that they were hoping he would pick out Vivien Thomas although why they should think he would is beyond my comprehension. *They had previously asked him many weeks before if the woman he had seen was Vivien Thomas. Roddick was able to tell them categorically that in view of the fact that he knew Vivien by sight, and knew her by sight prior to 19 June, she was not the woman he had seen on the Crewe farm.*

Why indulge in meaningless charades? Was this an attempt to break both the Thomases down? It failed to achieve that purpose as had all previous attempts.

That same day the police drove Bruce Roddick around the town of Pukekohe. The purpose was to see if he could spot a car resembling the one that he had seen by the side of the mystery woman. The police had Arthur's car parked in one of the streets. Every time they drew level with it the police driver almost stopped. Again the ploy failed. As with Vivien, so with the Thomas car; Bruce Roddick knew it well by sight. When he pointed out another car and remarked: 'That's not the make, but that's the colour,' they gave up. The colour was different from the Thomas car.

Also on the same day Arthur and Vivien finally got around to talking to a solicitor. They spoke to a member of the firm of Sturrock and Monteith who normally handled all their business transactions. Having told the solicitors some of the recent events they were then advised that the firm could not help them because 'we are already handling Len Demler's problems over the same matter'. Indeed they were, having instructed Lloyd Brown QC to defend Demler in the event of his arrest. Arthur and Vivien were put in touch with another firm of solicitors, Grierson and Jackson of Pukekohe. Fortunately that firm was not already acting for any of the suspects on Hutton's list. A number of barristers were discussed including Paul Temm, Peter Williams and Kevin Ryan, all extremely talented advocates. Messages were left for Kevin Ryan to call the solicitor on behalf of a client called Thomas. At that time Ryan had had a previous unfortunate experience with a different client called Thomas. He studiously ignored the phone calls. Peter Williams was discussed. The Thomases were advised that he was out of their price range, far too dear for their pocket. In this country the quality of the barrister you get to defend you directly relates to the size of your bank account. That's part of the judicial system that we are all supposed to be so proud of. Paul Temm was neither ducking phone calls nor pricing himself out of the market. As he said to me:

'I was minding my own business one Friday morning in my chambers when I had a ring from these Pukekohe solicitors. They asked me if I could take a case for them.

I asked them what date had been fixed for the hearing. They told me that no date had been fixed. Their client had not been arrested yet. It was in connection with the Crewe murders. I said: "I have a feeling I know who your client is." Then they told me his name was Thomas. It didn't mean anything to me at all, never heard of the man. After further discussion I agreed to take the case.'

Paul Temm, like many another person, has lived to regret his involvement in 'The Thomas Case'. He subsequently spoke to Arthur Thomas and advised him that on no account was he to answer any more police questions and equally he was not to leave his farm accompanied by the police, unless of course he was arrested.

The Thomas couple, happier now that they had not only Inspector Hutton but also Paul Temm to help them, went blithely on their way.

In early November they attended a big country-and-western show in Auckland. It was to be the last such outing they would ever make together. Those early days in November were to be the last days of their marriage. Two bullets had already totally destroyed one marriage. Now that destruction was spreading to a second relationship.

Looked at objectively, the first ten days of November 1970 are not unlike the phony period at the start of the Second World War. The police ceased their visits to the Thomas farm, life appeared to be returning to some form of normality. Why the police left the Thomases alone for two weeks after the identification parade is curious. Could it be that they were still uncertain, still unsure that the case they had built against the Thomases would stick? Perhaps they were waiting for the return of Dr Donald Nelson of the DSIR. He had been in Sydney since before the Charles cartridge case had been found. He returned on 6 November and two days later his colleague Rory Shanahan asked him to

109

check his conclusions. He duly did; his findings were the same as Shanahan's.

On 11 November Inspector Hutton and Detective Johnston called at the Thomas farm. It was late morning. Vivien was on her way out with a cat, her destination the local vet. They asked her where Arthur was and were informed he was working in one of the fields. Unconcernedly Vivien drove away. The two police officers asked Arthur if he would accompany them to Otahuhu police station for further questioning. Ignoring the instructions given to him by Paul Temm, he readily agreed to go.

This was to be the final attempt by the police to obtain the confession. Arriving at the police station, Detective Johnston went into bat first of all. He went over the whole case point by point with Thomas. He told him how all the evidence pointed to him being the murderer. His 'relationship' with Jeannette was discussed. If he had been framed, then who had framed him? Who had taken his gun? How had 'they' obtained the gun? 'What about the murder on that particular night?' whatever that question might mean. Like the police force Thomas was a little short on ready solutions. Perhaps if he had asked for the kind of task force that Hutton had had at his disposal for the period of nearly five months that the inspector had taken to get this far: the facilities of the DSIR; the power of the search warrant; the right to question anyone and everyone at whim and at random; the financial commitment that had been made to this investigation running into millions of dollars – perhaps if he had asked for and been granted all these things he might have been better placed to answer Detective Johnston's rhetorical questions. As it was, he stumbled blindly from one answer to another. Answers that revealed no guilt, but answers that would be fashioned at his trial into powerful assertions of guilt by the Crown Prosecutor. That was the best that Johnston could extract from him.

Inspector Hutton took over. He repeated all that his colleague had said, then elaborated. He wanted to know why Thomas had not told police officers during the earlier stages of the investigation about the sick Cow 4 and the fact that it had calved on 17 June. Regarding his initial interview with Hughes, Thomas explained that the officer had been concerned with what he had been doing during the *night*. The calving had occurred during late afternoon and was completed by early evening. He was asked why, then, had he not told Seaman and Parkes when they had interrogated him. His reply was: 'They didn't mention it, so I didn't tell them.' If that reply can be held up as a sign of guilt I would point out that police officer after police officer, when asked at judicial hearings that followed the initial magistrates' court hearing why their evidence on particular aspects now contained new aspects, gave as justification precisely the same answer that Thomas gave on 11 November to Bruce Hutton.

During Paul Temm's initial interview with Arthur Thomas, the farmer from Pukekawa, having discussed with his barrister all the evidence that Hutton had assembled against him, then talked of Hutton's remark about 'having another piece of evidence up my sleeve that nobody knows about'. The comment intrigued Paul Temm. He remembers clearly today how Thomas talked of this before 11 November. If Thomas is right in his recollection of that remark made by Hutton at Otahuhu on 25 October, the inspector's final remark to him at the same police station on 11 November solved the puzzle.

'Look, Arthur, a .22 shell was found near the rear door of the Crewe house by the police. Scientists say that that shell was fired by your rifle.'

According to Hutton the reply from the man he had been hunting was: 'The murderer must have got hold of my rifle out of the house somehow. I'm not a fortune teller, I can't help you with that one. I wouldn't leave

111

it there if I had shot them as I know shells can be identified by the firing-pin markings. I have been framed and that's all there is to it.'

At that point Inspector Bruce Hutton realized that there was not going to be any confession. He told Thomas that he was under arrest for the murder of Jeannette and Harvey Crewe on or about 17 June 1970.

The vixen was still running free. The fox had been cornered.

That afternoon a newsflash on the wireless told the nation that a 33-year-old Pukekawa man had been arrested and charged with the Crewe murders. Margaret Smith, neighbour of the Thomases, rang Vivien in great excitement. 'You won't have to worry about the police any more, Vivien, they've arrested someone and charged them with the murders.'

Vivien, still in shock, replied: 'I know, it's Arthur they've arrested.'

Margaret Smith's reaction was one that was echoed in many Pukekawa homes that day: 'It's unreal. It's impossible.'

Later Inspector Hutton phoned Vivien to see if she needed help with the milking but by that time the Thomas farm was crowded with neighbours who had come to help. They reassured Vivien, told her of how they had watched him grow up. They talked of earlier happier times.

4

The Farmer's Son
and the Typist

Arthur Thomas, the second eldest of a family of ten, the son of a farmer, was born on a farm and destined like a number of his brothers to become a farmer himself. The Thomas family, like the land they farmed, were poor. Raising the nine children that survived would have been a struggle for any couple but Allan Thomas and his wife Ivy gave their children qualities that are lacking in many wealthier families.

There is about the Thomas family a fierce mutual loyalty that quickly becomes evident as one gets to know them. The children were also taught other qualities. Peter Garratt recalled:

'The Thomas children were the most respected children in the whole of Pukekawa. They were civil, they were polite, they were friendly. I cannot speak for the younger two, Lloyd and Desmond, they were younger and I have little knowledge of them. Arthur went to school with our children. He was best man for one of my sons and my wife and I attended a number of Thomas family weddings. As a family they were highly regarded in the district.'

These were sentiments that I heard expressed again and again from people who knew the Thomas family from pre-war days onwards. I heard the other side, too. But, again and again, when I checked these statements they simply did not stand up to cold fact. Mischief had been afoot in the land for many years when those latter opinions were expressed and it had taken many courses. As will become clear during the course of this chapter I have no desire to sanctify either Arthur Thomas or his family, but a man and his family deserve to be judged on fact, not unsubstantiated rumour.

'I wasn't very brilliant at school,' Arthur Thomas remarked one day in 1973 while giving evidence at Auckland's Supreme Court. It was an accurate statement. When author Pat Booth, writing of Thomas in 1965, quoted the Revd William Vercoe's description of the farmer from Pukekawa: 'He's a simple, honest man,' Arthur Thomas was deeply upset. He wrongly equated simplicity with stupidity. Simple he is. Stupid he is not.

He attended Pukekawa Primary School as did the Demler sisters and all other local children, and left in 1952, when he was between fourteen and fifteen years of age. Popular with his schoolfriends he clearly was not destined to set the groves of academe alight. After a period of work on his father's farm and another local farm he went to work for a local company, Roose Shipping at nearby Mercer. I can find no-one who worked with him over the five to six years he was at Roose Shipping who speaks other than highly of the quiet, rather shy young man they remember. The men he worked with recall him as 'someone who was always cheerful. He never complained. No matter how dirty the job he was given, he worked hard and was cheerful.' These are not, of course, people who can swear where Arthur Thomas was on the night of 17 June 1970. They are, however, people who worked side by side with him in the boiler-making department of Roose Shipping for nearly six years.

I have spoken to many people who knew Arthur Thomas during those six years as he grew to manhood. I have also been fortunate in obtaining access to many private diaries covering this period – entries made at a time of innocence as opposed to recollections years later when men and women stood in the witness box and evaluated a man charged with a double murder.

Pukekawa life and the life of Arthur Thomas at that time emerge very clearly from those diaries. These are the years when if one believes the case for the Crown, the schoolboy crush that Thomas had for Jeannette Demler, as she then was, grew to a deep overriding passion.

No-one speaking of that period can recall a single instance of Thomas displaying such passion. No-one writing of that period makes mention of Arthur's interest in Jeannette.

His closest friend during those years was a young man from a neighbouring farm, Mervyn Cathcart, whose mother's diaries over a six-year period are full of details of everyday life. Clearly the two young men shared a number of interests. Both were deeply involved in this period not only with helping on the farms owned by their parents but also on neighbours' farms. References abound in the diaries to haymaking and milking, to rotary hoeing and ploughing. The two young men went to the local cinemas frequently. They attended meetings of the young farmers' club. Apart from going regularly to the church services they also joined the choir. They played tennis, shared an interest in country-and-western music, particularly the songs of Johnny Cash. In view of subsequent allegations that were to be made by one Crown witness, an entry in the diaries of Mrs Cathcart is of particular interest. Part of the entry for 19 March 1959 reads:

'Merv milked some cows and then he and Arthur went to Pukekohe and left car at garage and went to Auckland by 7.40 a.m. bus from Tuakau. Went to ballroom dancing for first two lessons, 10.30–11.30 a.m. and 2 to 3. Arrived home about 8 o'clock . . .'

An apparently insignificant piece of information, but it has a direct bearing on later comments by Crown witnesses. Mrs Cathcart's diary for that year records every dancing lesson that the two young men had, also the subsequent dances they attended.

One Crown witness would later swear on oath that three years prior to those first dancing lessons, Thomas was regularly attending dances, regularly dancing with Jeannette and regularly pestering her. I find it impossible to reconcile that particular witness's recall of alleged events that occurred some fourteen years previously, with the day-to-day diary entries of a woman writing without a vested interest other than the normal interest of a mother in her son's activities. March 17 1959, for example. There was that evening a big St Patrick's night dance at the Pukekawa Hall. One would expect Thomas who, according to the Crown, had been dancing for some four years, to be at the dance. In fact he was babysitting for Ted and Margaret Smith while they went to the dance. That was forty-eight hours before Thomas and Cathcart went to Auckland for their dancing lesson.

Small fragments perhaps, but when one is dealing with a man serving a life sentence for a double murder after having been found twice guilty on evidence as suspect as this, small fragments become important aspects.

In early 1960, Thomas went to work for the Forest Service at Maramarua, some twenty miles from Pukekawa. He had previously, in August 1959 when driving through the area with Mervyn Cathcart, expressed a desire to work for the service. He lived near his place of work, making frequent trips home to see his family and attend local functions in Pukekawa. At one of these functions he met Heather Demler and casually remarked what he was doing for a living. She told him that Jeannette was working in the same area as a teacher and urged him to call on her sister. Arthur Thomas duly did. During the ten months that he was working in Maramarua he called on Jeannette twice at the teachers' hostel where she lived. Much was to made of this later by Crown Prosecutor David Morris. He saw it as part of the passionate tapestry that he alleged Thomas had woven around Jeannette. Morris contended that Arthur Thomas had followed the object of his affection to Maramarua and that the sole reason he had given up his job at Roose Shipping was to be near Jeannette.

The incontrovertible facts are that Thomas had obtained his job at Maramarua and was already working there *before* Heather told him that her sister was working in the same area.

He only called on her twice. The only record of those visits comes from Thomas himself. None of the women who were at that time living with Jeannette has any recall whatsoever of Thomas being seen at the hostel. Jeannette, who was at that time commenting to at least one of her fellow-boarders about 'a man' who would call around to the Demler farm or would appear at local Pukekawa dances, made no mention of Thomas appearing at the hostel. If his love was so ardent for Jeannette Demler one would expect Arthur Thomas to have been a frequent and noticed visitor at the teachers' hostel. He was not. Undoubtedly he was attracted to Jeannette. Undoubtedly he did attempt, to use an old-fashioned word, to court her, but two visits in the space of ten months is hardly indicative of overriding passion, even from a member of a so-called passionless nation. *The final absurd point in this picture of an eager unrequited lover is that during this time Arthur Thomas began an intimate relationship with another woman, one that lasted for over a year.* This, like so much else, was known to the police. This, like so much else, has been suppressed until now.

In October 1960, with Jeannette still at the hostel in Maramarua, Thomas went north to Dargaville. Again one would expect this young Lothario to stay near his loved one, but no; he moved 150 miles north to work for a top-dressing company. An interesting footnote to the Maramarua period of the lives of Arthur Thomas and Jeannette Crewe is that if this man was making such a pest of himself in the late 1950s to Jeannette at local Pukekawa dances then why would her sister urge him to call upon her at Maramarua? That allegation about pestering was one to emerge from the Crown's case.

At Dargaville, Thomas once again acquired a reputation for being a good worker. He also acquired one or two other things. At a farewell party for one of the workers, the guest showed the gathered males a small box. It contained, he said, his prize collection of pubic hairs. Thomas was intrigued; before the end of the evening he was the proud owner of the box.

Subsequently Thomas would with some prompting from his workmates produce the box for them to see. Previously, while at Maramarua, he secretly tape-recorded a conversation in a car with one of his girlfriends. The conversation consisted of 'love talk'. From time to time he would play this tape to his friends at the top-dressing company. The girl in question had discovered the tape running and had taken it, only to return it after she had listened to it. Whether such behaviour as that described above is normal I do not know. I am still waiting at the age of forty-one for someone to define 'normal sexual attitudes' to me. Some undoubtedly would consider such behaviour abnormal or kinky; equally there are some who consider any deviation from the standard missionary position to be abnormal. Oral sex, for example, which is freely practised in this country by many married couples, is considered a criminal act in some of the States of America.

Pubic hairs and a tape-recording were not all that Thomas acquired. Letters from girlfriends were also kept. The love affair that he had begun while working in the Forest Service at Maramarua was with a girl named Lorna. Her letters to him would not give

118

Elizabeth Barrett Browning any competition but Arthur carefully tucked them away. Great significance was to be made of the fact that he had kept a letter from Jeannette written years before. It was held that this was a clear indication of his burning passion for the woman. The police were equally aware that he had kept other letters from other women. They removed them from the farm during one of their searches. Then they suppressed them until after the fate of Thomas had been resolved. After all, to have admitted they existed or to have given them to defence counsel who were ignorant of their existence would have put the letter that he had kept from Jeannette into its proper perspective. The significant would have become insignificant. Suppression was clearly the order of the day when Thomas came to trial. In fact, apart from Jeannette's letter that the police had failed to find and which he in total innocence had given to them, there was also a Christmas card and another letter from Jeannette. There were also letters like this one from Lorna; this is merely an extract:

'Would you like to go to a 21st dance with me on Friday 30th September in the Mangatawhiri hall? I got an invitation on Monday, "Lorna & Partner". If you have nothing arranged? If you have it doesn't matter I might get someone else to go or go on my own . . .'

That one is postmarked 13 September 1960.

As a gay young bachelor Arthur Thomas certainly did not let the grass grow under his feet. Another letter he kept, this one dated 4 November 1961, begins with the proclamation: 'Love you with all my heart.' Apart from telling Arthur that she had been busy doing the silage and asking him to send her a photograph of himself, it invites him to spend a weekend with her at Hamilton. That one is signed 'Gert'.

Other girlfriends included a Diane, a Margaret and a young lady I do not intend to name. This last relationship produced a baby, now in its teens. By early

1964 that relationship, like the collection of pubic hairs and the tape-recording, was a thing of the past. The last two items had been thrown away some years before, the letters I have quoted were stuck in a kitchen drawer on the Pukekawa farm. The attempts to court Jeannette had failed. During her stay in Europe between February 1961 and November 1962 Thomas had written several times to her. He had sent her a writing set, beads, stockings, and upon her return had given her in December 1962 a final present, a brush and comb set.

Thomas then accepted his romantic defeat and retired from the field. If Jeannette was not interested there were plenty of others who were. His job with Barr Brothers' aviation took him top-dressing all over the North Island, giving him ample opportunity to develop new relationships. There was also the bonus of having a couple of sisters nursing in Hamilton. They ensured that he met plenty of young, unattached females. He little thought, as he turned to leave the Demler farm that Christmas evening in 1962, that the brush and comb set purchased in a High Street chemist's would become a time bomb gently ticking away for eight years before it exploded in his face.

The pilot that Thomas regularly worked with lived in the small town of Wellsford. One day they both called on a sign-writing friend of the pilot, Pat Vesey. The pilot wanted an insignia painted on the side of his plane. While they discussed the job, Vesey introduced the two men to his niece who had recently arrived from England, twenty-one-year-old Vivien Carter. As she and Arthur talked they discovered a common interest, dancing. That was in January 1964. In November of the same year they were married in Wellsford. That chance meeting leading to marriage was to ensure that the list of people permanently damaged by the deaths of Harvey and Jeannette Crewe grew considerably. None was to be more damaged than Vivien Thomas.

I have one of the wedding cards that the Thomases received. In the light of subsequent events, the joke card has a bitterly ironical flavour: 'Congratulations. Well, Buddy, you'll soon find that marriage is not just a word . . . It's a sentence.'

Vivien was born in Farnham, Surrey in 1942. Life in a dormitory town in England holds little excitement. After leaving school at the age of fifteen, Vivien worked initially in a chemist's shop, then a hairdresser's. The only child of working-class parents (her father was a lorry-driver), her overriding ambition was to earn the princely sum of ten pounds a week. A nightschool course of typing and English opened the door to secretarial work and at the age of twenty she achieved her monetary ambition. Like most such ambitions, once realized, it paled. She watched her contemporaries 'get married like flies' and decided there was more to life than that. 'I just decided I would like to travel and New Zealand was the only place in the world where I had relations. I didn't have much courage to go somewhere and live on my own. So I emigrated here.'

So having travelled some 13,000 miles to avoid the trap of a young marriage she found herself within one year of arrival happily accepting that fate.

Talking to the pair of them now, as I have done, it would be easy to consider them a strangely assorted couple. But I met them first in 1977, when Vivien was attempting to build a new life for herself and Arthur was hopelessly caught in the limbo world of a maximum security prison and clinging to a life that had been with Vivien. A life that can never be again. The Vivien I met appeared initially supremely confident, articulate, intelligent and also rather self-centred. The Arthur I met appeared initially to be shy, inarticulate and bemused. Those elements are there in both people but as I got to know them, as I peeled away the layers that seven years' damage plus what television, press and radio have put on these two people, one was able to

121

glimpse them as they must have been at the outset of their love for each other.

Their marriage was an ordinary one, like their interests. While he listened to his Johnny Cash recordings, she would read a Georgette Heyer book. While he fiddled with an old car engine, she would cook the latest recipe in a woman's magazine.

After their marriage Thomas worked on three farms. In Farnham, England, the only cows that Vivien had seen were those hanging in butchers' shops. Now for the first time she experienced farm life. When in mid-1966 Arthur's father offered to lease the Pukekawa farm to the young couple they jumped at the chance. The farmer's son and the typist moved into Pukekawa in June 1966. At virtually the same time some nine miles away Harvey and Jeannette Crewe were doing exactly the same. Both marriages had four years to run. While the Crewes generally maintained their privacy, the Thomases had open house. While the former were making a success of their 650-acre spread, the latter were struggling on their 272 acres.

Arthur introduced his English wife to his Pukekawa friends, people like Ted and Margaret Smith. Ted knew Arthur from early schooldays. In 1966 when Arthur and Vivien moved on to the Pukekawa farm, their immediate neighbours were the Smiths who over the next few years got to know them very well. Ted Smith said to me:

'Looking at their marriage, superficially, it was easy to get the impression that Vivien was the dominating factor. It was not like that at all. I recall inviting her to come bowling with me on one occasion and she remarked, "I'd better ask the boss." They were two young people working hard to make a success of that farm. Yet they functioned as individuals more than as a joint unit.'

They were an odd combination, the Thomases: the straitlaced, rather old-fashioned girl who was more intelligent than her happy-go-lucky, 'she'll be right' husband. As a farmer Arthur was good. He worked hard; like many farmers he had a loathing for paper work and that side of the business was left to Vivien. Their work life was unsophisticated; socially the same pattern emerges. Not for the Thomases the golf and tennis set; bowling and sampling homemade wine was their forte. Sexually, their relationship was the same as in many marriages, though few would have the candour of Vivien Thomas:

'There was some difficulty in maintaining a sexual balance. I just didn't know much about it and he wasn't the person to teach me or to learn with. I just wasn't particularly interested in turning on. It didn't do anything for me to get that way. So therefore I found other things in life. I went into breeding cats. I had no children and I had to find something else apart from the farm or I would have gone potty. I got a lot of pleasure from the cat breeding and Arthur has always been fond of animals. We would work so hard on that farm that we would just go to bed and sleep. With regard to the sexual side of our marriage it did sometimes come to a situation of him wanting to make love and me not being prepared to co-operate. He never made any unusual demands. He was very straightforward sexually.'

The picture that emerged quite clearly to me is of a humdrum marriage that while it was not setting the Waikato on fire would have endured for life.

I asked Vivien about children, whether she and Arthur had wanted to have a family. They had, and had tried but without success. Vivien Thomas elaborated:

'At the time of the murders we were in the process of seeing a gynaecologist at Grafton. We had tried to have a family for three years; we had tests and Arthur's sperm count had gone right down and was nil by the time we got to the gynaecologist. He advised us that there was no way we could have a family and recommended adoption or artificial insemination for me. I

123

said we had better start off on the same footing and adoption seemed the more logical thing. That was in August 1970. At that time we decided that perhaps close to Christmas when things were a bit better financially we could approach the adoption authorities but we never got that far. He was arrested in November.'

Though they were childless and obliged to count the pennies the marriage was a stable one in those four years. There would come a time when gossip and rumour would say that both of them were indulging in extramarital relationships during that four-year period of 1966 to 1970. I have traced every rumour, checked every piece of gossip. I am still awaiting a single shred of evidence or one fact to indicate that either of the Thomases strayed from the marital bed during the six years that their marriage was a reality.

Neither is there any evidence of violence within the marriage. The nearest would be Arthur playfully turning the hose on his wife one day in the cowshed! By 1970, Arthur Thomas, the man whom his closest friend Mervyn Cathcart remembers as 'a quiet shy boy', was fighting the effects of a severe drought as was every farmer in the district. By the middle of that year the overdraft figure in his local bank account stood at a little over 900 dollars and like many of his neighbours he was sweating on a loan from the State Advances Corporation. He was already repaying to the corporation a loan of some 6,000 dollars that had been used to build a herring-bone cowshed. But the Thomases, like their neighbours, were confident that 'she'll be right'. Financially this view was justified; they received later that same year the maximum amount that the State Advances were offering drought-hit farmers – 1,000 dollars. By then, however, the net was already closing around Arthur and Vivien.

Late in 1969 Arthur's cousin Peter Thomas came to live with them. Working in nearby Mercer, the Thomas farm made an ideal temporary home for him. He enjoyed living with them, recalls it now as 'a lot of fun; Arthur had a great sense of humour.' Apart from his work Peter would lend a hand on the farm, an aspect that was to be the subject of much debate in the subsequent trials.

In common with most farmers in the district, the Thomases never locked up when they went out. Consequently on 17 June, with Peter at work and Arthur and Vivien in Pukekohe, the farm was deserted and unsecured for over four hours, a period when anyone could have walked on to the property and taken what they wanted, including a rifle, wire and an axle. I can find no mention of this possibility during the hearing of the case.

On 22 June 1970, when the news spread through Pukekawa of the bloodstained farm, Arthur, Vivien and Peter, like everyone else, were shocked.

Vivien recalls how they discussed the events and how Arthur looked at his wife and said: 'She was too nice a girl to end like that.'

In the weeks and months that followed that discovery Pukekawa became New Zealand's Peyton Place. Vicious rumour and gossip, those twin enemies of truth, swept through the district. The phones were hot with the latest titbit of misinformation. In the first forty-eight hours it was 'known for a certainty' that Harvey had killed Jeannette and had taken off into the bush and was hiding.

On the first Friday of the search dozens of local women appeared at the farm with food for the searchers. Among them was Vivien Thomas. She had gone to the Crewe farm with Margaret Smith because she was 'not too sure of the way'.

Margaret recalls going to the Thomas farm to collect her. Arthur was there having a late lunch, no different in manner or in conversation from usual. Apart from talking about the missing couple, Margaret recalls how both of the Thomases were concerned with their sick cow No. 4. They told her of the trouble it had had calving.

In the months that followed, sick cows were not the only subject of conversation in that small community of about two hundred adults. Some of the old-timers were able to speak firsthand of a night in 1920 when violence had been abroad. The scene of that particular murder was but a mile from the Crewe farm, at the Eyre property. Now in 1970, fifty years later, the details that began to unfold when the police presented their case against Arthur Thomas in the Magistrates' Court in Otahuhu, in December 1970, bore a strange resemblance to that murder in 1920.

It was not of course just the odd similarities between the two cases that made Pukekawa re-examine a lurid part of its past. The name Eyre was the link. It was widely known in mid-1970 that Mickey Eyre was on Inspector Hutton's list of suspects.

In 1970, the police asserted that Thomas's motive had been his love and passion for Jeannette Crewe.

In 1920, the police asserted that Samuel Thorne's motive had been his love and passion for Dora Eyre.

In 1920, the police asserted that Thorne had crept up to the Eyre farm at night and, having climbed up on to a board, held on to the windowsill with his right hand and fired left-handed into a bedroom window, killing Sydney Eyre with a shot to the head.

In 1970, the police asserted that Thomas had crept up to the Crewe farm at night and having climbed up to a kitchen window and put his rifle through the open louvre windows, had killed Harvey Crewe with a shot to the head.

In 1920, no-one saw Thorne at the Eyre farm on the night of the murder but there was strong circumstantial evidence. Distinctive hoofprints found at the scene of the murder were said to match those of a particular horse found on the farm where Thorne worked some eighteen miles away. The fragments recovered from the head of Eyre were said to match cartridges that Thorne had. Days after the initial police search of the Eyre farm further ballistic evidence in the shape of a wad blown from the end of a cartridge case had been found by a member of the Eyre family.

In 1970, no-one saw Thomas at the Crewe farm on the night of the murder but there was strong circumstantial evidence. Wire found on the bodies was said to be similar to wire found on the Thomas farm some nine miles away. The bullet fragments recovered from the heads of the Crewes were said to match with the Thomas rifle. Months after the initial police search further ballistic evidence in the shape of a cartridge case had been found by police.

There are many more such 'coincidences', including the fact that both Thorne and Thomas stood trial twice. Thorne ended on the gallows and there is little doubt that if New Zealand had been practising capital punishment in 1970, Thomas would have suffered the same fate. Thorne died protesting his innocence. Thomas still protests his.

Sydney Eyre was the grandfather of Mickey, the young man on Bruce Hutton's list in 1970. The name of the horse with the distinctive hoofprints that had, according to the police, carried Thorne away from the Eyre farm was Mickey.

In 1934, William Bayly stood in the same courtroom where Thorne had twice been tried and where ultimately Arthur Thomas would face two trials. Bayly was accused of the double murder of farmer Samuel Lakey and his wife Christabel. The scene of the Lakey murders was at Ruawaro, a small farming community less than fifteen miles from the Crewe farm. Bayly followed Thorne to the same Mt Eden gallows. His case again has many remarkable similarities with the Thomas case. But whether those similarities occupied the minds of the citizens of Pukekawa in late 1970 is a moot point. What primarily disturbed them was that the Lakey murders had always been widely regarded as New Zealand's most sensational murder case. Now that dubious title had passed to a double death that had occurred in Pukekawa. They didn't like it. They liked it even less after nearly five months of police investigation which left them bemused and frightened. When the press, television and radio turned their attention to the small community they began to hate it.

In the years that have followed many of them have learned to be a little evasive when asked by a stranger where they come from. To mention Pukekawa is to reactivate 'The Thomas Case', something that most of them would rather forget.

But the damage suffered in Pukekawa has been partly self-inflicted. When the news of the arrest of Arthur Thomas ripped through the country lanes it was only seconds before some began to recall odd events, strange occurrences that had at their centre the man who now stood accused of murdering Harvey and Jeannette Crewe. The 'I always knew he was a bad lot' syndrome got under way with a vengeance. It was said that Thomas had phoned a young woman named Karen Piper and asked her to go out with him. It was said that he had been seen prowling around the Piper farm on the Friday after the murders. The Piper farm is relatively close to the Crewe property. The busy tongues suggested that of course he had been hanging around the Piper girl's home after going to the Crewe farm to clean up. This was just one of the tales I was confronted with in mid-1977. I was told to seek out Pete Garratt, then a farmer, now a JP. I was told that Garratt, who in 1970 lived opposite the Piper farm, could confirm this story. The Thomas car had a very distinctive whine in its differential. Garratt, I was told, had heard the car on that Friday night as Thomas, having been spotted, roared away.

The truth?

Thomas freely admitted to me that he had on one

occasion phoned this girl, that he had asked her if she would like to go out with his cousin Peter. She had declined. He had not, he insisted, been anywhere near the Piper farm on the Friday in question.

Peter Thomas confirmed this account to me. Cynics, I am sure, are immediately leaping up and saying: 'His cousin, of course he would.' Then what of Peter Garratt? I finally located him on Auckland's North Shore. The first he had ever heard of these events, he assured me, was when I interviewed him. He had not heard a car. He had not seen Arthur.

When I returned to Pukekawa and, during the course of a discussion with one of the instigators of this rumour, quoted Mr Garratt's reaction, the response was very typical: 'He's lying.' Karen Piper? She declined to be interviewed, though in 1970, when confronted by Vivien Thomas she had freely admitted that Arthur's phone call had been on behalf of his cousin. The police spent several hours interviewing Karen Piper when this story first circulated through the district. Perhaps the most pertinent comment I can make is to observe that at no time did Karen Piper give evidence. If the rumour had any basis whatsoever, Miss Piper, as she then was, would undoubtedly have found herself in a witness box.

Others insisted at the time, and insisted to me, that the story of the sick cow was a concoction, borrowed from Arthur's friend Mervyn Cathcart who did in fact have a sick animal. The fact that Thomas had purchased harness equipment from a local veterinary surgeon to lift the paralysed animal, the fact that it was subsequently shot, the fact that Mr Cathcart has categorically stated to me that he did not have a sick cow at that time: these points are brushed aside by some of the closed minds of Pukekawa. Like Mr Garratt before him, Mervyn Cathcart is, according to those closed minds, lying.

Again the information had been given eagerly to the police, once Thomas had been arrested. Again it was checked by the police. Again one looks in vain for any mention of it in the trial transcripts.

The battle lines were drawn in Pukekawa before the Lower Court hearing. Those battle lines are still clearly discernible. Two of its community died sudden brutal deaths. A third is serving a life sentence for having been found guilty of causing those deaths. In a country that stubbornly refuses to admit that it has a class structure, when demonstrably it has, class can be seen to be operating in its usual destructive manner in this farming community. Up near the hill are the older, more settled, richer farms. In that area the anti-Thomas feeling is strong. Down towards Mercer are the poorer farms; there can be found many of the people who are convinced that Thomas is innocent. There are, of course, exceptions on both sides of that division. The place saddens me. Perhaps it is time that the Revd Mr Hadlow got up in that Pukekawa pulpit again and reminded the community of some of the Christian concepts that so many of them pay only lip service to. Personally I believe that as far as Pukekawa is concerned, 'she will never be right'.

The locals often refer to it as a ghost town, because now, in 1978, so much of the land is owned by market gardeners who live elsewhere and merely grow their produce on the land. The fact is that it is a ghost town haunted by a living man named Arthur Thomas. The man who shortly before his arrest met Mrs Garratt one day in Pukekohe. Discussing the situation with her, he remarked: 'Oh, I'll be all right. I've got the police on my side.'

5

The Kill

Four days after Arthur Thomas had been arrested and charged with the two murders, his mother was making arrangements for a Christmas party. Ivy Thomas felt sure some foolish mistake had been made and she was confident that her son would be home for Christmas. The party was to celebrate the end of the nightmare.

Mrs Thomas might have felt less confident if she had been aware of the difficulties that Paul Temm, the man briefed to defend Thomas, was experiencing. He told me:

'The defence were obstructed at every turn. Facts were withheld. Information was suppressed. Incorrect evidence was offered. I could not get access to the wills or any of the official records of the Crewe estate. In particular we could not get access to the paid cheques of the estate, which is what I wanted to get at.

'We were not allowed to see any of the personal accounts of either Harvey Crewe or his wife, we had no way of getting this information unless it was to be freely given. It was not. There was no procedure by which we could get discovery from the Crown. We made special application to the trial judge, which I had never had occasion to do before. We asked that the police files be examined; that we be given the right to examine them or alternatively that the judge himself examine them. We believed that there were statements from witnesses on those files that we could have found useful. We were refused permission because "there is no authority for it". The Crown can, of course, and did, get access to Arthur's bank account and his official records.

'When I inspected furniture that had been removed from the Crewe house and was being held by the police I noticed a fingerprint that the police had isolated on a table. I asked Hutton whose print it was. He refused to say.

'At the DSIR while inspecting other exhibits I asked Detective Sergeant Mike Charles about the cartridge case he had found. He refused to answer and stated that he had been told not to give me any information.

'During the course of our enquiries in Pukekawa I asked specifically for some information about what part of the carpet had been removed from the living-room. The information that I was given by a detective sergeant turned out to be wrong and I cannot believe he was mistaken; he was the man responsible for cutting out the piece of carpet.'

Paul Temm cited many more such instances. Now, this is not a case of a lawyer attempting to twist evidence, attempting to pervert the course of justice. This highly respected and conservative member of the Auckland bar was attempting to establish facts. If the case against Thomas was so strong, so overpowering, if the police were so confident that they had finally got their man, why this obstruction? Society does indeed need to be protected from those who commit crimes. In some instances it also needs to be protected from those we pay to detect the criminals.

While Paul Temm and the man assisting him with the Thomas defence, Brian Webb, did their own door-by-door tour of Pukekawa, the Thomas family were trying to grasp the reality of the situation that confronted them. For the Thomas family, loyalty is something that should be expressed in practical ways. When Detective Mike Charles advised Vivien Thomas on the afternoon of 11 November that her husband had been arrested, her response was 'What for?' When she was told: 'For the murder of Harvey and Jeannette Crewe,' she exclaimed: 'You must be bloody mad.' After further conversation Mike Charles observed: 'I admire your loyalty.' Vivien still clearly recalls her reaction to that particular remark.

'Loyalty be damned. You're wrong and we'll prove you wrong.'

Lloyd Thomas, Arthur's nineteen-year-old brother, arrived on the farm the following day. Lyrice, one of his sisters, flew in from Australia 'to help out for a short time'. Nearly eight years later, Lyrice, now married, is still there.

Vivien's first conversation with her husband after his arrest was at Mount Eden prison.

'I went there with my brother-in-law, Ray, and my mother-in-law. I can remember Mum was sobbing in her throat. We were all in some kind of shock. So was Arthur when we saw him. He asked how I was. Asked if the farm was all right. He was groping for words. He told me about the baby that he had fathered long before we met. It rocked me but I told him that there were more important things to worry about. He'd wanted to let me know himself as he felt it would come out in the hearing. No, I did not ask Arthur if he had done it. I knew he hadn't. Ray asked him, for his own peace of mind. Arthur said: "No, I did not do it. If I had I would expect to be punished. I would expect to be where I am." '

The routine of farm work and prison visiting was to become a grim treadmill over the years. But in November 1970 the Thomas family were supremely confident. When the Lower Court hearings opened at Otahuhu in December 1970, Vivien had a suitcase in the family car. In it were Arthur's clothes for him to wear when he was released a free man from the Magistrates' Court.

The desire for conviction, so readily demonstrated

by the wall of obstruction presented to the defence lawyers during their early investigations can, I believe, be clearly seen to reach to the Crown prosecutors, David Morris, the man who had taken such an active interest from the first week of the police investigation in June and his colleague David Baragwanath. It is, in the view of Paul Temm, rare for the Crown not to open when presenting depositions for a murder trial in the Magistrates' Court. Normal procedure would be for the Crown Prosecutor to give a summary to the Court followed by witnesses. In the case of The Queen v Arthur Thomas, the opening speech was dispensed with. When I talked to him, Paul Temm elaborated:

'We were in a terrible difficulty at deposition stage. We were placed in a position quite deliberately by the prosecution where they did not open on the case at all. We had no way of knowing how each of the witnesses coming forward fitted into the story. What we did have was the mass of information that we had obtained ourselves. The results of our inquiries over the preceding month. Of course if the Crown calls witnesses in succession without first putting the Court into the picture, the story unfolds gradually and you might find that witness 10 did something that you would have asked witness 4 about, if only you had known what witness 10 was going to say.'

I do not know whether events like that described above are indeed rare, as Paul Temm considers. I do feel that the laws of evidence should be changed, so that the prosecution is obliged to give, at the depositions stage, an opening summary of their evidence. It's something to do with justice being seen to be done. While such a situation can occur as occurred at this particular Lower Court hearing, the courtroom remains a playground rather than an arena where truth is sought by all parties.

It is certainly rare for a defence counsel to cross-examine to any great degree at a Lower Court hearing. Normal procedure is to quietly listen to the entire Crown case and attack that case at the subsequent Supreme Court hearing. Because there had been no opening speech outlining the Crown case, Paul Temm abandoned this strategy. He attacked from the outset in a remarkably effective manner.

The very first witness, for example, Brian Sly: as a surveyor, his evidence could not have been more plebeian. He had been brought to the house by the police to draw an interior and exterior plan of the Crewe property; a copy of that plan can be found on pages xii-xiii. Such an item would be crucial in a case of this nature; many witnesses would have need to refer to it. Under cross-examination Mr Sly admitted that the three-seater sofa had been moved by the police before the drawings were made. He had 'been given to understand by the police that, apart from the sofa nothing had been moved'. Without any cross-examination not even the movement of the sofa by the police would have been recorded. Undoubtedly other items were moved during the initial police search. Whether they were replaced in exactly their original positions before Mr Sly did his drawings is a moot point.

An illustration of the difficulties that Paul Temm was labouring under can be gauged from his cross-examination of police photographer Alan Arnold. He was the second police photographer to depose evidence; the first had not been cross-examined by Temm. During his research in Pukekawa, Temm had overheard in a crowded saloon bar a fragment of conversation: 'Demler's car had bloodstains, they took photos.' The first police photographer had produced as an exhibit a booklet containing sixty photographs. Nowhere was there a photograph of a bloodstained car. Arnold also produced a booklet. In his were forty-four photographs, but again there was no photograph of a bloodstained car. Paul Temm rose to question him:

Temm: Are these all the photographs which you took?

Arnold: No, sir.

Temm: Did you take any photographs of Mr Demler's motorcar?

Arnold: No, sir.

Temm: Are you aware of any photographs taken of Mr Demler's car?

Arnold: I am not aware . . . Constable Stevens, police photographer at Auckland, may have taken photographs of that car. I am not aware if he did or not.

Temm: Are you swearing on your oath, Mr Arnold, that you don't know whether Stevens photographed Demler's car?

Arnold: I have already given that evidence.

Temm: You do not know whether he did or didn't?

Arnold: I have already given that evidence.

Temm: I didn't ask you whether you have given this evidence, I am asking you on oath whether you know if any photographs were taken of Demler's car?

Arnold: I don't know.

In fact, Stevens had taken photographs of the bloodstains in Demler's car. In view of the fact that Arnold was attached to the police investigation as early as 16 August 1970, he must have been the only member of the investigating team who did not know that his colleague had taken these photos, photographs of the then main suspect's car. It was clearly going to be a long uphill battle for Paul Temm and Brian Webb.

The story began to gradually unfold in the Otahuhu courtroom. Of how Jeannette had worked and lived at Maramarua, of the close proximity of Thomas at the same time. Previous resident of what had then been the Chennell estate, manager's wife Moira Handcock, told how on three occasions Thomas had assisted with top-dressing activities on what was to become the Crewe farm. How Thomas would have the odd meal or cup of tea or use the toilet. This evidence was to justify the Crown's subsequent contention that Thomas knew the layout and the run of the Crewe house. It was a contention that was rather dented when Paul Temm established that these visits had been made 'about 1961/1962'. Some eight years before the deaths.

Diane Ambler, one of the women who had enjoyed that working holiday in Europe with Jeannette, was only one of many whose evidence would fluctuate and vary through the various hearings. In December 1970 she testified about a visit she had made to the Crewe farm in August or September 1966, how on the day of her visit 'There was a fire burning in the fireplace (of the lounge). The temperature inside the room with the fire going was very cold and we had to keep our coats on most of the afternoon. Subsequently, after a burglary had occurred at the Crewe house, Jeannette visited my home. Her state of mind about the burglary was that she was petrified to stay in the house on her own afterwards.'

What price open louvre windows on a cold wet windy winter's night? It was obviously a thought that struck someone connected with the prosecution as will be subsequently demonstrated.

The first element approaching sensational evidence came from Beverly Batkin. She told of attending local dances in 1956/57, of meeting her old friend Jeannette at these dances, of how Arthur Thomas would pester Jeannette and of how the dead woman was not 'particularly flattered by his attentions'. She described Arthur Thomas's appearance on these occasions: 'Usually rather untidy in general appearance and his shoes usually were particularly dirty.'

The image of her lifelong friendship with Jeannette took a bit of a dent when under cross-examination she admitted that before the deaths of the Crewes the last time she had visited them had been eighteen months earlier. The lapse was because 'my children had hepatitis and we didn't do any visiting.' When she talked of Thomas's 'odd behaviour towards Jeannette' at the dances Paul Temm attempted to clarify that remark:

Temm: And when you speak of odd behaviour do you mean he had a crush on Jeannette which she would not reciprocate?

Batkin: I would not call it a crush. I would call it a passion for Jeannette.

Temm: Do you tell us that this sixteen- or seventeen-year-old-boy had a passion for her that was apparent to all?

Batkin: His passion for her was apparent to me and I would think it would be apparent to others.

Temm: If this sixteen-year-old boy at a country dance had such a passion for a girl as you convey wouldn't you expect it to be the talk of the countryside?

Batkin: I wouldn't really know as I had not had a great deal to do with the general run of people. I was only home at weekends and holidays.

Temm: And do you say that this passion of which you speak might not have been seen by other people at the dances you attended?

Batkin: No, I don't say that at all.

Temm: Well, if you saw it at dances, would you not expect others to have noticed it too?

Batkin: I am quite sure other people did notice it.

I have tried very hard to find some of these other people. These dances were attended, according to Mrs Batkin, by between 100 and 250 people. I have located nearly 50 of those people. Many of them recall seeing Jeannette at those 1956/57 dances, frequently in the company of her mother. All of them are prepared to swear on oath that Arthur Thomas did not attend these dances. That makes the odds against Mrs Batkin's version fifty-to-one. With regard to her recollection about the appearance of Arthur Thomas, the odds are also against Mrs Batkin to the same degree.

Neighbour Ted Smith encapsulated what many others said to me:

'He was a man who never went into town without a clean white shirt. He was very concerned about his appearance. Rarely, if ever, did you see him in need of a shave. When he worked for Barr Brothers if he ever came home for a weekend he always brought his own sheets and blankets.'

Despite the fact that Mrs Batkin (who 'throughout my childhood knew Jeannette. I have known her all my life,') did not attend the same primary school as Jeannette, one would have expected her to know that this man who plagued her close friend had been in the same class as Jeannette. It is an expectation that is not realized. She did not know. She had, however, given the *Auckland Star* a circulation-boosting headline for 14 December:

VICTIM 'PESTERED AT DANCES'
WITNESS TELLS OF MAN'S 'PASSION'

Tucked away down in the article that Mrs Batkin's outburst about passion had provoked was the significant fact that the information about the 'pestering' and about 'the passion' had not been given to the police when they had first interviewed Mrs Batkin in June 1970. She had 'volunteered' these additional pieces of information only after she had heard 'that parts of the trailer had been traced to the Thomas property; that is, at the end of October or the beginning of November'. Over four months later. Yet if I am to believe Mrs Batkin, 'Arthur Thomas's attitude toward Jeannette was the unhappiest thing that happened to me in those years'. Equally revealing were Mrs Batkin's comments to me about those later police interviews with her in November 1970:

'They asked me if I had any knowledge of Thomas visiting Jeannette after she returned from overseas. I did not know if he had ever given her presents. I didn't know the significance of those questions until the trial was under way.'

Near the end of my three-hour interview with Mrs Batkin came perhaps her most significant comment. It was with regard to this pestering at dances. The pestering that had 'marred her entire adolescence'. She has sworn on oath three times that these events occurred either in 1956 or 1957. This, despite the irrefutable evidence that Thomas did not learn to dance until 1959. She said to me: 'It could have been 1959. Thomas would still have been around.'

Len Demler's testimony introduced one element of confusion. For nearly half a page of the printed deposition, evidence that would take some ten to fifteen minutes to hear, Len Demler placed himself at the Crewe farm on the day the Crewes died. He said he had a meal with them on the *Tuesday*; that was the last night according to his evidence that he saw them alive. They were in good spirits. He told the Court that since the death of his wife he had 'made it a habit to have a meal at Harvey and Jeannette's just about once a week. The times would change – it depended on the programme, it varied, but mostly on *Tuesdays*. I would go when Jeannette asked me, if I wasn't doing anything else. The last visit I made was on the *Tuesday* night, the *Tuesday* 16 June, before her death.'

Having told the Court of how he and Harvey and Jeannette had finished dinner 'just after 7 and I left about 10 o'clock', he gave a description of the arrangement of the lounge furniture on that '*Tuesday* night'. He continued:

'When I left the house on *Tuesday* night, I noticed nothing unusual whatsoever about Jeannette and Harvey at all, they were talking about buying something for my birthday and wanted to know what I wanted. *On the following day, Wednesday 17 June*, after getting a ring in the morning about eight o'clock from Jerry Moore who said he didn't get any answer from up there,

140

he had some wool valuations to give him and then I didn't take much notice, thought he must have been around the farm perhaps, so I let that go, then about quarter to one I think Ron Wright rang, and then he said he had some sheep to go from that place and he couldn't get hold of Harvey. So I said I would go up and see what was wrong up there, I wasn't getting any answer. I rang too, but it didn't make any difference. On the *Wednesday* I went down to Harvey's farm to see if they were home. Apart from going down to Harvey's farm on the *Wednesday*, I didn't go anywhere, and on *Wednesday* evening, I just looked at TV. The next time that I visited Jeannette and Harvey's farm I was up there the next day, the Thursday, the 17th. Oh, I have got that date wrong, I never went up there on the 17th. I never went there until Monday the 22nd.'

It had been by any standards an extraordinary performance under oath. We are not talking here about a slip of the tongue, a single error. It went on and on and on. Yet one looks in vain in the press of New Zealand for any comment, then or later, about this aspect. Why bother with the father of the dead woman placing himself, under oath, on the Crewe farm on the day of the murders? 'Passion' is presumably what sells papers.

Evidence of the early intensive police searches of the Crewe property was given by Detective Sergeant Murray Jeffries. It had been a very detailed, very careful, meticulous search. Surprisingly, his deposition revealed that not only were members of the investigation team allowed to enter the house while it remained in police control, also at least six of Harvey and Jeannette's friends and relations were allowed access. I find that extraordinary. A number of those people, if not all of them, would have been suspects, yet they were allowed access to the Crewe farm. *This was within the first week of the police investigation.*

Evidence was given by Dr Fox that clearly showed he had no doubt that Rochelle had been fed during the five-day period before she was discovered. Professor Elliot and his confirming opinion were suppressed. Dr Caughey and his conflicting opinion were suppressed.

The evidence of Harvey's mother Mrs Marie Crewe drew a picture of Jeannette the perfect mother, the perfect housewife. If that was an accurate picture, then either Jeannette Crewe had a complete nervous breakdown in the days that preceded her death or her house was subsequently ravaged by an army of sluts.

Evidence was given about the burglary at the Crewe farm in July 1967, the house fire in December 1968 and the barn fire in June 1969. No evidence was given linking any of these occurrences with the accused but it is clear that in an effort to build up a motive for Thomas, the Crown felt it essential to throw in these three events. Eight years later there is still not a single fragment of evidence that links Arthur Thomas with these happenings on the Crewe farm. The events may well have significance. They may well be linked with the deaths of Harvey and Jeannette. They have yet to be linked to the man found guilty of those deaths.

The premise that the Crown was functioning on was now beginning to take shape. Arthur Thomas, harbouring a deep unfulfilled passion for Jeannette, had pestered her at local dances, had pursued her to Maramarua, had written to her and then hoarded her replies, had given her presents. Then after he had married Vivien, and Jeannette had married Harvey, Thomas had brooded on his lost love and gone to the Crewe farm and removed Jeannette's brush and comb set, obviously hoping she would then use the one he had given her in 1962. He had not been seen going to the farm, he had not been seen leaving. Despite police investigations at the time, he fortunately escaped the net of their inquiries.

Still dissatisfied, still brooding, he waited eighteen

months. Again unseen he had crept on to the Crewe farm – presumably he had first followed Harvey to Pukekohe to ensure that Crewe was visiting his wife that night. He had set light to the Crewe farm and again unseen had returned to his own farm nine miles away. Again police inquiries did not touch him. Sitting in his Mercer farm with his young wife Vivien he had hatched yet more venom. Again returning to the Crewe property, again unseen, he had set light to a haybarn in June 1969. Again he got away without being seen.

Still dissatisfied, still consumed with the passion he felt for Jeannette, he had again returned to the Crewe farm, this time on the night of 17 June. He had murdered not only Harvey but the object of his passion, Jeannette. He had then somehow removed the bodies from the farm. Neither his coming nor going were seen. He had taken the bodies and dumped them in the Waikato river. Again this activity was unobserved.

The total of exhibits rapidly mounted as the hearing progressed. Bloodstained material from chairs. Blood-stained pieces of carpet. Saucepans, blankets, wheel-barrow, knitting, ashes from the fireplace, the clothing from the dead couple. The list grew longer and longer. None of these items was connected in any way with the accused. Fingerprints that had been found in the Crewe farm were entered as exhibits. Some belonged to Jeannette, some possibly to her husband, some were unidentified; none belonged to the accused.

The cross-examination of Inspector Gaines by Paul Temm gives a clear illustration of some of the diffi-culties that the men defending Thomas faced. Gaines, it may be remembered, was in overall control of the land, sea and air search for the missing Crewes; he was also in control of the subsequent search of the Waikato for the murder weapon and weights that may have been fastened to Jeannette's body. Paul Temm was very aware that the police had brought up a great many items from the riverbed; he attempted a number of times

143

during this Magistrates' Court hearing to obtain an inventory of these items. One would think it would be something that would have been made readily available to defence counsel.

Temm: Did you make an inventory of the things that were brought up by your searching equipment from the river?

Gaines: Any equipment that we brought up was handed to the members of the CIB.

Temm: That tells me what you did with it, it doesn't answer my question.

Gaines: I made no inventory.

Temm: Who did?'

Gaines: This is an exhibit list made out by the CIB. I cannot tell you who made it.

(Of course what the inspector was referring to was not a complete inventory of items recovered, merely those items that the police had chosen to put into evidence.)

Temm: You know that the police have had every opportunity of preventing the defence getting information obtained as a result of your search?

Gaines: I don't know this at all.

Temm: And are you telling us that you don't know, although you were officer in charge of the search, that you don't know who was responsible for recording what was found in your search?

Gaines: Perhaps an explanation of the method would elucidate this.

Temms: Are you telling us you don't know?

Gaines: I'm not saying this at all. If you let me answer the question. When any object was found the person finding the object was despatched with the object to the CIB office; there his version was obtained by whoever was duty officer. And over this period they were numerous.

Temm: That tells me what was done with what was found. Can we go back to my question. Are you telling us that although you were in charge of the search, you don't know who was responsible for recording what you found?

Gaines: No. I don't, sir.

Temm: Do you not think that is rather an extraordinary answer?

Gaines: As officer in charge of the search, I was required to direct and control. I directed staff to the point of official recording and everything that was found was recorded.

Temm: So your job apparently was to direct the search but not to record what you found as a result of your search?

Gaines: Personally, no.

Temm: I suggest that you are being evasive. You know perfectly well, do you not, that I am not suggesting you should have had a pencil and paper. You know that, don't you?

Gaines: I have a complete diary of what we did. But I have no record of the actual objects that were picked up by my staff. This is on the main file.

Temm: The main file is a very elusive document and it never seems to be with the witness giving the evidence.

Gaines: I have in this Court the diary of the day-to-day activities of our search.

Temm: That tells us, Mr Gaines, what you did. What I am asking for is what you found. Do you know where the main file is now?

Gaines: I presume it is in the hands of the Crown Prosecutor.

Temm: Is there, on that file, an inventory of what you found in your search, particularly of the Waikato river?

Gaines: As far as I know, yes. I have not sighted it myself, though.

Temm: Would you recognize it when you saw it?

Gaines: Yes.

Temm: Would you please now produce it so that His Worship and we can see it?

Gaines: I have to have the file produced. I haven't got the file.

Temm: Well get the file. Who was responsible for making the list? Who was in charge of the section?

Gaines: The CIB personnel were under the command of Detective Inspector Hutton and he delegated that, to whom, I don't know.

Temm: So does it come to this, then, that although you were responsible for making a search, you weren't responsible for recording what was found?

Gaines: No, sir, I was not responsible for recording.

Paul Temm asked Magistrate D. MacLean if the witness could be allowed to leave the box and fetch the elusive main file. MacLean rejected the request. Throughout this entire cross-examination the inventory in question was only a few feet from Paul Temm, on the desk of the Crown Prosecutor, David Morris. The above interchange, apart from giving a graphic description of the inefficiency that marked so much of the police investigation in Pukekawa, demonstrates the disturbing degree of commitment displayed by police and prosecution toward obtaining a conviction. Why was Temm not allowed to have a copy of that inventory at that point? His interest in it was far from academic. He had been told that among the items recovered from the area where Jeannette's body had been found were some that incriminated, not Arthur Thomas, but another resident of Pukekawa. Certainly not a single item was recovered and placed on that mysterious inventory that incriminated Arthur Thomas. In view of the fact that the Crown Prosecutor was fully aware how hard Temm had tried to obtain a copy of that inventory his re-examination of Inspector Gaines left a little to be desired.

Morris: It was put to you in cross-examination that you knew the police have had every opportunity of preventing the defence getting information obtained as part of your search? Have you ever had any request to give this information?

Gaines: Never.

Morris: Have you until today ever been approached?

Gaines: No, sir.

Thus Inspector Gaines left the witness box. Paul Temm was still without a copy of that inventory.

When pathologist Dr Francis Cairns gave evidence on 17 December, he told the Court of the detailed examinations he had carried out on the bodies and of his initial inspection of the bloodstained farmhouse. Apart from his theory that Jeannette was knocked to the floor and then shot, he also discussed an alternative that she had been shot from behind her right shoulder whilst seated. With regard to Harvey's death, he told the Court that he thought Crewe had been sitting in his armchair with the chair not in the position shown in police photographs but around facing the fire, and he considered 'he was shot in the back of the head on the left side, from a shot fired from the direction of the door to the kitchen'. Such a theory would of course fit with the police view of a gun through the open kitchen louvre windows. *It equally fits with the theory of the shot being fired from inside the house.*

Careful study of Dr Cairns's evidence reveals nothing that eliminates the theory of murder/suicide. He could not tell how long the bodies had been left before removal and clearly when faced with reconstructing exactly how and in what manner they had died he was faced with grave problems. The bodies were discovered not in that lounge, but months later in the Waikato. Evidence, for example, of powder burns on the heads, a clear indication of very close-range shots, would have been destroyed long before Dr Cairns had an opportunity to examine the bodies. Faced with a room in disarray, such as the Crewe lounge, the theories, the possibilities, the explanations are limitless; all anyone can do, even an expert, is make a calculated guess. It has already been demonstrated that the initial calculated guess of Dr Cairns concerning tomahawks and axes was totally inaccurate. It is possible indeed probable that his subsequent theory of exactly how Harvey and Jeannette Crewe died is also inaccurate.

When evidence about the recovery of Harvey Crewe's body from the Waikato was given by a number of policemen some interesting aspects emerged. The body had been found in just six feet of water. One of the diving team had noticed the wire leading down into the water, yet in a mere six feet of water had not seen, let alone grasped, the axle that had allegedly been attached to the end of that wire. In view of the fact that Inspector Hutton was to testify that while the axle was still attached he had grasped one end of it, clearly the axle was in a horizontal position. Its length is 4ft 6 ins, yet still the divers could not see it in six feet of water. Neither was any wire found tied to the axle. If the wire had *snapped* rather than unwound, where was the piece that in theory would have been *tied* to the axle. Leaving these and other anomalies aside the police had, with the production of that axle, put into evidence the first apparently tangible link with the accused. Other depositions established that the axle had at one time been on a trailer owned by Arthur's father, Allan Thomas.

Details of the various loans that Thomas had received over the years from the State Advances Corporation would have held no surprises for the bulk of the public in the Otahuhu courtroom. It was packed with farmers from Pukekawa and their wives, come to hear the evidence that had been assembled against one of their number.

Nods of recognition passed between a number of them and Thomas. A divided community, drawn together by this macabre case. From now on this cross-section would only meet in courtrooms. The Thomas clan, as they were dubbed early in the proceedings, sat attempting to comprehend what was going on. They sat and listened as Paul Temm and Brian Webb battled with reluctant witnesses and exchanged barbs with David Morris and David Baragwanath.

The gentleman from State Advances was followed into the witness box by Detective Senior Sergeant Hughes. On 11 July he had remarked to Len Demler: 'We have got you now, you've had it.' Now, on 17 December, he told the Court of the visit he had paid to the Thomas farm nine days before he made that remark to Demler. He had been the first police officer to speak to Thomas about the case. His version of the conversation he allegedly had contained one remark that particularly interested Thomas's defence counsel:

Hughes: I said to him: 'I understand that you had some sort of passion for Jeannette Demler some years ago?' He replied: 'Well, sort of.'

Having discussed Thomas's attempts to court Jeannette, the detective sergeant then recalled:

Hughes: He said that he had visited the Crewe farm while working for an agricultural contractor three or four years before. He said that he had met the person whom he believed to be Jeannette's husband, Harvey Crewe, and said he thought he was a decent sort of bloke. He said that he had morning and afternoon teas in the Crewe house and had never been back since. He was then referring to when he worked for the agricultural contractor. He said he had not seen either Jeannette or Harvey Crewe for at least eight or nine months . . .

This latter statement from Hughes can only come under one of two categories. It is either genuine error or deliberate perjury. Whichever it is, it succeeded in placing Thomas on the Crewe farm after the Crewe marriage; that is, from 1966 onwards. If it is a genuine error it is a very serious one. The picture of Thomas sitting having morning and afternoon teas with Harvey and Jeannette exists only in the mind of Detective

Hughes. Regrettably the defence did not pick up this flagrant inaccuracy. What Temm wanted to know about was the first extract of Hughes's sworn evidence that I have quoted.

Temm: Did you make a report of your meeting with Thomas on 2 July?

Hughes: Yes, I submitted a job sheet on this interview.

Temm: Where is that report?

Hughes: It would be attached to the main police file.

Temm: You would recognize that job sheet, wouldn't you?

Hughes: Yes.

Temm: And could you find that job sheet if given the opportunity? If not, why not?

Hughes: I may not be able to but our clerk would.

Temm: I suggest to you that in that job sheet you made no reference to taxing Thomas with having a passion for the girl Demler? Is that suggestion correct?

Hughes: No, this was the reason for the interview initially.

Temm: Did you use the word 'passion' on your report on the job sheet?

Hughes: From memory I did; I haven't seen it for many months.

Temm: Would you please produce the job sheet so that I may inspect it?

Hughes: I have not got it with me. I also made a full entry in my notebook of the discussion between Thomas and myself at that time.

Temm: The job sheet is what interests me. If given time by the Court, would you go and get it?

Hughes: Yes.

At this point Temm broke off his cross-examination to ask the magistrate if the police officer could leave the box and return with his job sheet. Magistrate MacLean said he would consider the request. Clearly the defence was having as much difficulty with the

150

magistrate as they were with certain witnesses. Why should the job sheet not be produced? Temm had not finished with Hughes. The defence counsel remembered what has been described to me by a number of *Crown* witnesses as 'Mrs Batkin's outburst'. He also recalled the headlines that outburst had made. Headlines that this police officer could easily have read.

Temm: On 2 July, Mr Hughes, you had not in any way spoken to Mrs Batkin, had you?

Hughes: I had spoken to a number of people and I do not recall that name. Can you help me?

Temm: I can help you to the extent that she didn't consult the police until long after 2 July.

Hughes: I am afraid I cannot help you; maybe Mr Hutton can and would.

In fact Mrs Batkin had already been interviewed by the police *prior* to 2 July, though her recollections of the Thomas 'passion' did not spring to her mind until the axle was apparently traced to the Thomas family at the end of October or the beginning of November.

As Hughes left the witness box, Paul Temm turned and spoke to Crown Prosecutor David Morris: 'Has Hughes really got the word "passion" in his job sheet?' The Crown Prosecutor's reply was short and to the point: 'He has now.'

Throughout the entire proceedings Paul Temm had wondered about the remark his client had made to him in late October. Thomas had recalled Bruce Hutton saying to him during that long interview on 25 October: 'One other thing, Arthur. I have one other piece of evidence up my sleeve. I'm not going to tell anyone.'

Until Detective Sergeant Mike Charles gave evidence, no 'other piece of evidence' had been revealed to the defence that they were not previously aware of. Mike Charles rapidly changed that situation. What he had to offer in evidence were a number of exhibits, but none so devastating for Arthur Thomas as Exhibit 350, the cartridge case that he had found in a flowerbed in the Crewes' gardens on 27 October. Under cross-examination from the defence Mike Charles made it clear that subsequent testimony from experts would suggest that the cartridge case had come from the Thomas rifle.

It was a bombshell for the defence. Mike Charles was closely cross-examined on this vital exhibit. It was established that Thomas's rifle had been removed from the farm on 17 August, returned to him on 8 September and removed again on 20 October. Mike Charles testified how prior to the search he and Detective Parkes had carried out on 27 October, the enclosure of the Crewe farm had been subjected to a pattern search, 'a thorough, close search'. He told how dry soil poured out of the case when he had found it below the surface, dry soil out of a case that if it had not been deliberately planted had lain under the earth for four months and ten days.

For over seven years now controversy has raged around that cartridge case. As will be shown later in this book many people consider that it was planted, that this piece of evidence was deliberately fabricated to ensure that Arthur Thomas was convicted. That view first surfaced when Mike Charles gave his evidence. The first person to mention such a possibility was the man who found the cartridge case.

Temm: Did it occur to you that a person knowing Thomas was under suspicion at that time, and seeking to heighten that suspicion against him, could achieve that purpose by putting a cartridge case from his rifle where the police could find it?

Charles: No, it hadn't occurred to me, not when I found the shell.

Temm: Has it occurred to you since?

Charles: Yes.

An honest answer from a police officer whom I believe to be honest.

The evidence on the axle, linking it not with Arthur

Thomas, but with his father, followed Mike Charles. It must have been very anti-climactic, though it served to buttress considerably the case that the Crown was successfully building.

Detective Johnston told of finding the stub axles on the Thomas farm tip, stubs that matched perfectly with the axle pulled out of the Waikato.

A variety of policemen also gave their versions of their conversations with Thomas. These included Johnston's final attempt to obtain a confession on the day that Thomas was charged.

'I said: "Did you ask Jeannette for a loan of some money?" He said: "Definitely not." He said: "Had I asked her, she would have given me a loan." ' An innocuous enough exchange that David Morris would soon be using to deadly effect.

In the latter stage of this Lower Court hearing, one witness made a brief appearance. His name was Derek Booth, a former boyfriend of both Jeannette and Heather Demler. It was a name that Thomas had mentioned to the police as a likely candidate if he had been framed. Booth testified that on 17 June he had been working in Whangarei until between 5.30 and 6.00. This was presumably some attempt by the police to demonstrate that Booth could not possibly have had any connection with the deaths of the Crewes. The Court by now was brimming over with participants and spectators; the pile of exhibits grew ever higher: old number plates, metal rims, wheel assemblies, shed sheets showing Cow 4 calved on 17 June, unfired bullets – the list grew ever longer.

One such unfired bullet, already referred to, was to gain in its own way as much notoriety as the Charles case. This bullet, Exhibit 343, was entered into evidence by the man who found it, Detective Stanley Keith. He also deposed that fragment of conversation that he had heard while searching the Thomas's garage. According to Keith he saw, through the cracks in the wall, the two

Thomases in conversation and heard Arthur saying:

'If they think I am guilty, I am and that's that.'

That piece of evidence produced a fascinating interchange between the police officer and defence counsel:

Temm: Were the words that you heard used by Mr Thomas to his wife these: 'If they think I am guilty, I am and that's that'?

Keith: Yes.

Temm: Did I understand you to say that you couldn't hear the whole conversation?

Keith: That is correct.

Temm: Listen now to this sentence, Mr Keith. Listen carefully. 'From their point of view, if they think I'm guilty I am and that's that.' Is what what you heard?

Keith: Yes, sir.

It was simple and very, very effective. Paul Temm sat down satisfied. David Baragwanath rose quickly to his feet.

Baragwanath: In cross-examination, four words were added to the words you gave in evidence-in-chief: 'From their point of view' and then followed the words you gave?

Detective Keith had been thrown a lifeline by the Crown which he grabbed with alacrity.

Keith: Yes, that was an ambiguous question.

Just as quickly Temm rose to his feet objecting to this line of questioning. He pointed out to the magistrate that he had warned the police officer to listen carefully to his question. Yet again Magistrate D. MacLean found himself unable to accept a defence argument. It had been a constant feature of the hearing in his court. He overruled the defence objection and Baragwanath was allowed to continue.

Baragwanath: I have drawn your attention to this point, witness, what is your comment on it?

Keith: I heard the accused say: 'If they think I am guilty, I am and that's that.' I did not hear any other words.

What that interchange illustrates is the danger of quoting a fragment of a conversation and attempting to give that fragment significance. Clearly the reported remark has no context. Keith did not know what followed it or what had preceded it. Evidence of this quality would be better left in a police officer's notebook.

Evidence from DSIR scientist Rory Shanahan followed. In terms of advancing the prosecution case against Thomas some of it was negative, some positive. For example, fragments of rust near the front door that probably came from the Crewe wheelbarrow, the premise being that the bodies had been moved from the house to the wheelbarrow. But there was no forensic evidence from the DSIR examination of the wheelbarrow or the rusty articles that pointed to Thomas. The ashes in the lounge fireplace were probably the residue of a burnt cushion and the hearth carpet, but who placed these objects on the fire and when? Shanahan talked of the various wire samples that he had received at various dates from the police. Study of his evidence confirms that none was removed from the Thomas farm until late September. If, in Thomas, the police had arrested the right man this surely is very lax police work – a man who Detective Inspector Hutton contends was 'always my No. 2'. Why, when wire was removed from Demler's farm within a day of Jeannette's body being found, was none taken from Thomas's? There can only be one logical answer. At that time Thomas was not on the police list of suspects.

With regard to the Charles cartridge case, Rory Shanahan was in no doubt: it had come from the Thomas rifle. His evidence about the condition of the case, however, contained the following comments:

'Had it been exposed to the elements for an extended period of time, I would have expected more corrosion to be present. However, on the other hand, one of the cartridge cases handed to me by Detective Inspector

Hutton showed an amount of corrosion present. So I cannot really say how long this cartridge case had been exposed to the elements. When I say I would have expected more corrosion had it been exposed for an extended period of time, I am talking in terms of months, but I must add it is difficult to give an exact answer.'

Of course the other cartridge case that Mr Shanahan refers to above had had quite a different history. It had not been in the Crewe garden under some inches of earth, exposed to the elements for four months and ten days. To compare the Charles case with it is therefore completely irrelevant.

Shanahan was followed into the witness box by another member of the DSIR, Harry Todd, who was the Crown's wire expert. I will attempt to unravel his evidence later in this book. It is sufficient to say now that he considered there was similarity between some of the wires taken from the Thomas farm and some of the samples recovered from the bodies.

Mr Alexander Aitken, an engineering manager employed by a subsidiary of I.C.I., explained to the Court the significance of the figure 8 that had been found at the base of the murder bullets and also on one solitary bullet among the dozens removed from the Thomas farm. They were three examples of the 158 million such bullets made by the company between 1949 and 1963. These bullets with a figure 8 on the base and three distinctive cannelures are known as pattern 8. Such bullets abound not only in Pukekawa but over the entire country. Before one can accept that Thomas killed Harvey and Jeannette, one must accept that he took two such bullets, disdaining the box he was currently using, to commit the murders, leaving the third in his garage to be found by Detective Keith. It should be noted that Thomas had some ballistic knowledge from his attendances at young farmers' meetings. He was aware that bullets have identifying marks.

Next to depose evidence was Dr Donald Nelson of the DSIR. As the scientist in charge of the forensic side of the investigation his testimony was of necessity long and detailed. He told of examining skin tissue from Jeannette Crewe in an attempt to form an opinion as to the distance from which she had been shot but 'I found no firing residue such as unburned powder and hence I am unable to estimate the distance. I would expect to see such unburnt powder when the weapon had been fired from short range.' What Dr Nelson didn't add was that the immersion of that body in the Waikato for a number of months might well have destroyed such powder burns. He told the Court how he had received from Detective Keith the pattern 8 bullet and cartridge case that had been found in the Thomas garage, the bullet bearing what was obviously considered a significant No. 8. The shell case he described as 'fired'. He described how he had test-fired sixty-four rifles and, comparing the fired bullets with the fragments recovered by Dr Cairns from Jeannette, 'I was able to exclude all but two rifles'. His evidence confirmed that of his colleague Shanahan concerning the Charles case. In his view it had come from the Thomas rifle. He told the Court of the reconstruction that had been carried out at the Crewe farm when Detective Johnston's theory of firing through the open louvre windows had been successfully put to the test. He considered that the condition of the Charles case was 'consistent with exposure to the weather'.

His cross-examination by the defence drew out the fact that the bullet that killed Jeannette may have been fired by a rifle other than the two he had been unable to exclude – the Thomas and the Eyre rifles. His evidence concluded with the fact that he could not link the Charles case with either of the murder bullets.

The case for the Crown concluded with the evidence of the man who had carried for exactly five months the responsibility for the police investigation, Bruce

Hutton. Much of his deposition has already been the subject of comment in this book. What remains will be examined later.

Paul Temm rose at the end of the Crown's evidence and argued that there was no case to answer. He asked the magistrate to dismiss the charges against his client. Not for the first time during the Lower Court hearing, the magistrate disagreed with him. Arthur Thomas was committed for trial in the Auckland Supreme Court. The suitcase of clothes that his wife had brought every day to Otahuhu would have to wait a little longer before being put to use.

Equally the Christmas party that Mrs Ivy Thomas had planned for her son would have to wait a while for its guest of honour.

On Monday 15 February 1971, Mr Justice Henry entered the No. 1 Court of the Supreme Court at Auckland and the task of empanelling a jury in the case of The Queen v Arthur Allan Thomas commenced. Mr Justice Henry, like Arthur Thomas, had not been obliged to queue for admission. While members of the public pushed and shoved each other to gain admission a jury of eight men and four women was sworn in. Prior to the empanelling, the judge took an unusual step which ensured that quite a few potential jury members would suddenly discover pressing personal business. He stated that the jury would be kept together throughout the entire trial, they would not be allowed to return at the end of each day's hearing to their respective homes but would be held incommunicado in the Station Hotel, Auckland. The defence objected to this directive, feeling that it would place the jury under undue strain and pressure. The Crown prosecution, who heartily approved of the move, had taken the precaution of booking rooms at the hotel for the jury weeks *before* the judge gave his ruling. At the time of Thomas's trial it was very rare to keep a jury isolated. To do so, of course, ensured that they could not be got at, tampered with, have their opinions influenced by outside interests. It also meant – and there is detailed research in a number of countries to prove this – that they could possibly build up feelings of resentment towards the accused, identify with the prosecution and the police, members of the police force being constantly at their side, and that they would be vulnerable to inside influences.

The trial Judge Mr Justice Henry was, in the words of Paul Temm, 'A strong judge in the classical sense of that term.' Previously he had been a brilliant defence counsel; as a judge he became a definitive example of poacher turned gamekeeper.

Amongst members of the Auckland Bar Association he had a reputation for being 'a prosecutor's judge'.

Thus the trial of Arthur Thomas began, with a jury in quarantine, a judge with a reputation for harshness and a Crown prosecution that suppressed evidence that would have been favourable to the accused. Leading that prosecution was David Morris, assisting him David Baragwanath. The former a brilliant lawyer with, in my view, a convicting mentality, the latter a clever young man of whom it has been said: 'He won every prize at university except the one for knitting.'

For Arthur Thomas there was Paul Temm who a few days before the trial began had been appointed Queen's Counsel, one of the youngest men in New Zealand legal history to attain such honour; assisting him, Brian Webb, who should certainly have taken some sort of prize for the sheer hard work he had put in on behalf of Thomas in the weeks and months that preceded the trial. But would these two men, who in that period leading up to the trial 'obtained nothing but obstruction from the police', be able to match the total power of the system arraigned against Thomas?

Any who believe that a trial is an arena where truth is sought, where all join together to find justice, would find such a belief a fallacy, a delusion, after the most elementary examination of how the judicial system works in New Zealand. It is a game. Tactics is the name of this particular game. Evidence is put in and taken out depending on how the game is going. When people mouth on about juries being the best judges, that the twelve good men and true hear all the evidence, see all the witnesses, evaluate all the circumstances, it should be remembered that juries are very rarely given this best of all worlds.

For example, the police were fully aware that there was in Pukekawa a witness whose evidence had a crucial bearing on the time that the Crewes met their deaths. But the time would have been too early for the police. Too early for the Crown. They needed a late killing. One that had taken place after Thomas had gone to bed. The evidence of this witness was duly suppressed.

The police were equally aware that there was in Pukekawa another witness who could testify about signs of activity on the Crewe farm on Friday 19 June. Two days after the deaths. At 7.30 on that Friday evening this witness had seen sparks and spurts of flame coming out of the Crewe farmhouse chimney. Without doubt what that witness saw was the murderer cleaning up. Burning a cushion and the hearth carpet on the lounge fire. The sparks must have been unburned kapok. At that time, Arthur Thomas and his wife were in another town, attending a 21st birthday party. The evidence of that witness was also suppressed. It had been given to the police within the first week of their inquiry in June 1970.

The letters the police had found on the Thomas farm from other women, letters that would have put the one they made so much use of, that he had kept from Jeannette, into perspective; these were suppressed.

These are just three examples of what might well be regarded as deliberate suppression of evidence by the police and the Crown prosecution. I could give many more. The defence counsel, totally ignorant of these suppressions, listened as David Morris opened the case for the Crown.

The case that the Crown prosecution outlined to the jury was based entirely on circumstantial evidence. Such evidence immediately presents for a prosecution a very major advantage and an equally large disadvantage. Confronted with only circumstantial evidence counsel can run rife with theories and speculation. Thus having told the jury about the burglary and the fires of the previous years, Morris suggested that Harvey Crewe would not have allowed any unusual movement or noise around the house to go unchallenged. He continued:

'In other words, what I am saying is that the killer of these two people must have used stealth and surprise in committing this double homicide.'

This interesting theory was obviously going to lead to Thomas clambering up windowsills and pushing a .22 rifle through the open louvre windows and picking off Harvey Crewe as he sat unsuspecting in his chair.

It could of course be argued that such stealth and surprise were unnecessary if the killer was a known and trusted friend or relative who they would readily give entry to. This latter theory is the one that the police believed to be the actual explanation for many months of their investigation.

The equally large disadvantage for the prosecution case of circumstantial evidence was that there was no *direct* evidence. No-one had seen Thomas fire the shots or dispose of the bodies. There was no confession. No fingerprints. No bloodstains on his clothes or his vehicle.

Circumstantial evidence can often be very powerful. It can be overwhelming. The difficulty confronting David Morris was that in this case it was neither.

I have mentioned some of the 'tactics' employed by the police and the Crown Prosecutor in this case. Another tactic was the use of the subpoena. This legal

161

device, forcing a witness to testify for the Crown, was used with gay abandon in the Thomas trial. Peter Thomas, the young cousin, living on the farm at the time of the deaths of Harvey and Jeannette, is a good example of abuse of the power of subpoena. He was a crucial part of a triangle, the other two parts being Arthur and Vivien. All three insisted that Arthur had been at home on the evening of the 17th. All three insisted that he did not leave the farm. If believed, whatever the quality of the remainder of the Crown case, Arthur Thomas was already a free man. The only verdict could be 'not guilty'. But Peter had been subpoenaed by the Crown to appear for the Crown, before even the deposition date had been fixed. This automatically prevented the defence counsel talking to him. The Crown used the same technique on a number of the Thomas family, including Arthur's father Allan and his brother Richard. Bruce Roddick was yet another that Temm and Webb were prevented from interviewing before the trial. When people laud our judicial system, it is techniques like this that they are in their ignorance praising. Shortly before the commencement of the trial, Allan and Richard Thomas were advised that the Crown would not be calling them. Finally they could be questioned by the defence. What Temm and Webb discovered, to their consternation, was that months before both had made statements to the police. After the stub axles had been found on the Thomas dump, they were shown to Mr Thomas Snr and his son Richard. Both men took the view and said so in their statements: 'Well, if the stub axles came back from Rasmussen, it's reasonable to suppose that the axle did.' Exactly what they said Temm was unable to discover. The police refused to give him a copy of their statements, but if the two men were accurate in their recall of what they had said to the police they had potentially placed that axle on the Thomas farm, without further proof that it had subsequently left. Temm had to resort to 'tactics' himself. He decided that he dare not risk calling either man.

At the Lower Court hearing, Paul Temm had been unable to nail the story of the police photographing bloodstains in Demler's car. Now having listened as the second Crown witness carefully itemized and described the sixty photographs he was entering as an exhibit he yet again heard no mention of photographs of the Demler car. The last few questions of his cross-examination of this particular witness, Police Constable Stevens, gave him the answer:

Temm: Did you take any photos of any part of the interior of Mr Demler's house?

Stevens: Yes.

Temm: Did you take any photos of Mr Demler's car?

Stevens: Yes.

Temm: Were there any particular stains in that car you were asked to photograph?

Stevens: Yes, on the left front door and on the left front seat.

Temm: As you looked at those stains did they appear to be bloodstains?

Stevens: They did.

Unlike that interchange, much of the evidence was a re-run of that given at the Lower Court. Crime reporter Evan Swain of the *New Zealand Herald* again gave his evidence about certain items that had appeared in the *Herald* between 1 June and 31 July 1970. A number of the items dealt with loans that were being made available to farmers by the State Advances Corporation to help them combat a serious drought that had previously occurred; two other articles referred to police inquiries in September and October when they were attempting to trace the axle ownership. Mr Swain was later to write a booklet that amounts to a eulogy of the police investigation.

Subsequent evidence yet again established that Arthur and Jeannette had been working in Maramarua

163

in 1960. But earlier evidence contained in this book, from Mrs Hessell, concerning Jeannette's stay at the teachers' hostel and the non-appearance of Thomas and the fact that he never featured in Jeannette's conversation, was not put before the Court. The Crown and the police were of course aware of these aspects. The defence was not.

An indication of how desperately insecure was the Crown's case against Thomas can be gauged from the evidence of Mrs Moira Handcock. Her husband had been manager of the Chennell estate, as it was called from 1961 to 1966. The Handcocks left a few months before Harvey and Jeannette moved in. Her evidence of Thomas assisting with the top-dressing, and the teas and meals he had in the farmhouse, was the first piece of evidence elicited by the Crown that indicated the accused had *ever* been on the farm. Mrs Handcock placed these working visits by Thomas and the top-dressing pilot as between 1962 and 1964. Even taking her later date, it was still over two years later that Harvey and Jeannette appeared on the farm. But, as will be seen, this fact did not deter the prosecution or one particular police officer.

Diane Ambler, the old schoolfriend, again testified on her relationship with Jeannette and her memory of the coldness of the Crewe lounge, but the 'fire burning in the fireplace' of the Lower Court was transformed into 'I think it was a space heater at the time.'

Mrs Beverly Batkin recalled for the jury's benefit the local dances of 1956 and 1957, the dirty, untidy Thomas's passion and pestering of Jeannette. The defence had not been idle in this area since the Lower Court hearing in December, as Temm's last question to this witness indicates:

Temm: If it is established that Thomas didn't attend dances until 1959/1960, what would you say?

Batkin: I would say that is rather strange.

Evidence given by an electrician concerning the

1.

Above. Harvey and Jeannette Crewe. A four-year marriage destroyed by two .22 bullets. *Below*. While Harvey kisses his sister-in-law Heather his mother Marie Crewe enjoys the joke. In 1970 Heather and Mrs Crewe found less to smile about as they fought each other for the custody of Rochelle Crewe.

2.

Arthur Allan Thomas. Crown witness Beverley Batkin said in evidence that when Thomas attended dances he was 'usually untidy in appearance... dirty...tie untidily knotted.' This photograph was taken at a dance during the period when he was attempting to court Jeannette Demler.

Below. The same two .22 bullets destroyed the six-year marriage of Arthur and Vivien Thomas.

3.

4.

5.

Above. The Thomas farm at Mercer. The case for the Crown is that Arthur Thomas drove from this farm in the car below, with the trailer attached, to the Crewe farmhouse, *below*, nine miles away.

6.

7.

8.

Arriving at the Crewe farm, the Crown alleged that Thomas took up this position by the kitchen windows. This is a first trial defence simulation.

Below. This, according to the Crown, is the view that Thomas had through the open louvre windows. Sitting in Harvey's chair is Detective Inspector Bruce Hutton.

9.

10.

11.

Having shot Harvey Crewe through the louvre windows the Crown alleged that Thomas jumped down and entered the house through this back door. He went through the kitchen shown below.

12.

13.

Entering the lounge, Thomas, according to the Crown, dragged Jeannette Crewe from the sofa, smashed her in the face and threw her on the hearth rug. He then, according to the Crown, stood over her body and shot her, subsequently burning the hearth rug and a cushion.

The fanciful theory of the louvre shooting was stretched to breaking point when the first trial defence noticed an unnumbered bloodstain. It can be seen behind the right-hand front castor.

Below. The Crewes' dining table showing the remnants of their last meal, with a third flounder virtually untouched in the middle of the table and the morning mail spread out towards a third seat. Is it lunch or dinner? A finished meal or an interrupted one?

14.

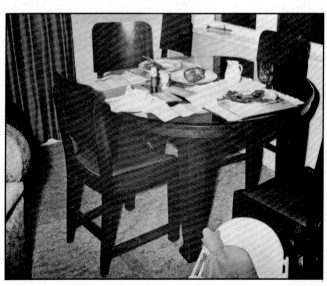

15.

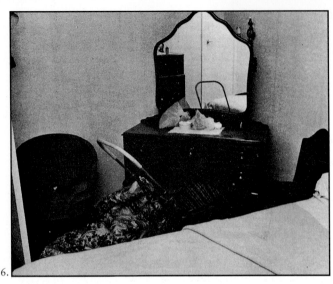

16.

The bedroom of Harvey and Jeannette Crewe as found
by the police. It is devoid of personality. *Above*. A woman's
dressing table with paper bags screwed up.
Below. A dirty change of Jeannette's clothes thrown in a corner.

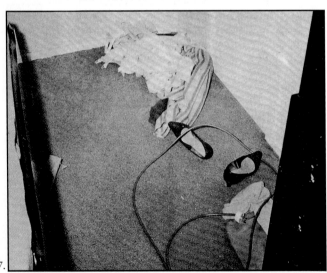

17.

house fire at the Crewe farmhouse was even stranger. He had found nothing upon examination of the house to indicate the fire had been caused electrically. As no subsequent evidence linked this fire, deliberate or accidental, with the accused, I cannot understand why this testimony was allowed. It is totally without relevance, but unexplained fires, like unexplained burglaries, are good 'tactics' when actual evidence is thin.

It is clear from the evidence of stock agent John Gracie and family friend Thirryl Pirrett, visitors to the Crewe farm on the morning of 17 June, that the furniture in the lounge had undergone considerable movement before the police arrived on the scene five days later. This evidence was a prelude to the major argument that would follow concerning exactly how the Crewes had died and where they exactly were at the point of their respective deaths.

Through the evidence of various witnesses the jury were able to glimpse a fragment of Pukekawa life: the ratepayers' meeting, the indoor bowling tournament and the table-tennis competition that had taken place on the night of the murders. These three events ensured that over sixty of the two hundred adults of Pukekawa were on the road that night, yet none saw Thomas. None heard the distinctive whine of his car.

From the Crewes' immediate neighbour, Ron Chitty – 'I never got to know them particularly well' – they may have picked up a hint of the unsociable behaviour of the dead couple.

When Crown witness Peter Thomas took the stand, the first part of the Arthur Thomas triangular alibi was in effect on trial. The eighteen-year-old cousin began nervously to respond to questions from David Morris. The fact that he had been subpoenaed by the Crown and was therefore testifying against his cousin placed him in a curious position. He is by any standard a crucial witness *against* the Crown's case.

He told the Court of how he had been living on the Thomas farm since late 1969; that he worked in nearby Mercer and went home to his parents at weekends; of how he would normally arrive back from work at about 6.15 pm; that he owned a blue Peugeot; that he sometimes assisted on the Thomas farm; that he had on at least one occasion taken material to the Thomas farm dump but had not noticed either the axle or the stub axles; that Arthur Thomas's rifle was normally kept in his, Peter's, bedroom on the farm; of how he had had general discussion about shooting and that Arthur Thomas was not a bad shot; of how Arthur would use the .22 rifle for shooting opossums with the aid of a flashlight; of how he had brought his father's rifle to the farm, kept it there about a week, then taken it back. The examination continued:

Morris: You know we are concerned with events taking place round about 17 June?

P. Thomas: Yes.

Morris: I want you to think back and tell me what you can of your movements during that week, starting with Monday and so on?

P. Thomas: On Monday I went to work. I came home that night and watched TV. I did the same on Tuesday. I was there on Wednesday night but I am not quite sure if I was helping my cousin with the cow that night or what it was. I was there Thursday, and Friday night I went home.

Morris: On those occasions you were home what time would you go to bed?

P. Thomas: 9.30 pm.

Morris: On these four nights who else was in the house?

P. Thomas: Just Arthur, his wife and myself.

Morris: On Monday night did Thomas go out at all?

P. Thomas: No.

Morris: Did he leave the house at all?

P. Thomas: No.

Morris: On the Tuesday did he leave the house at all?

P. Thomas: No.

Morris: The Wednesday?

P. Thomas: No.

Morris: Thursday?

P. Thomas: No.

Morris: On each of these nights was he still up when you went to bed?

P. Thomas: Yes.

Morris: And what about Mrs Thomas?

P. Thomas: Yes.

So there it was safely home, one angle of the triangle. Evidence elicited not by defence counsel but by the Crown Prosecutor, David Morris. As a guide to aspiring Crown prosecutors, it is textbook reading, or should be. Morris knew full well what this series of questions would elicit. Rather than leave the defence counsel to make a full meal, drawing that evidence out of Peter Thomas, with the full impact that such a protracted assertion of Arthur Thomas's innocence would have had on the jury, he had by skilful use of the minimum of words rapidly passed over evidence that was of enormous value for the accused. If, during the course of subsequent cross-examination Paul Temm attempted to enlarge on those answers, David Morris had placed himself in the position of being able rightfully to object on the grounds 'that the question has already been asked and clearly answered'. As an example of how to defuse a bomb that may blow up your own case it had been superb.

He quickly proceeded to what he obviously considered more fruitful ground. He established that when the news of the Crewes' disappearance burst on Pukekawa on Monday 22 June it had been the subject of discussion between the three Thomases. That they discussed the situation the following night. That there had been further subsequent discussions. That the three of them had at some time discussed what they had been doing on the night of 17 June. That Peter had fixed that particular week in his mind by the 21st birthday party they had all attended on the Friday and Vivien had isolated it because it had been the week they had had trouble; and that Arthur, agreeing, had said 'that he had a sick cow in the shed – that it was in calf or something.' It was also established that while Peter was being questioned by the police he had clearly been told by them that his cousin had taken out Jeannette, that he had questioned Arthur about this and Arthur had told him that he had only written to her. In answer to further questions he told Morris that there had never been any discussion about the trailer or any trailer parts. Further aspects of the domestic conversations of the Thomases revealed that Arthur was concerned about drought, cows and farm production and that water problems were causing him some financial worries. One could of course have packed Auckland Town Hall with farmers who had identical problems.

Paul Temm's cross-examination failed to add a great deal, except to clarify what kind of treatment the sick cow had received.

When local delivery man Emmett Shirley testified about the bread, milk, newspapers and mail he had delivered to the Crewe farm during the five-day period a further indication of activity within the house during those days was established. Curtains that had been drawn back on the Thursday morning were closed the following Monday.

The most dramatic evidence of activity during those eerie five days came from Bruce Roddick. In answer to David Baragwanath's questions the mystery of these rustic murders grew deeper. A woman, dressed in slacks, whom Roddick described as 'European', standing near the Crewe farmhouse. Near her, a dark green Hillman which he recognized as being the Crewe car. But who was the woman? Roddick told the Court that at the request of the police he had attended an identification parade in which eight women took part, one of whom had been Vivien Thomas. He had been unable to identify the woman he had seen on the Crewe property.

Paul Temm's cross-examination was brief; many were later to say it was far too brief. He established that Roddick, prior to the sighting, knew Vivien Thomas and that Vivien's hair was black. He also established with the aid of police photographs exactly where Roddick had been working when he had seen the woman. This last aspect was essential if only because Baragwanath had succeeded in confusing his own witness with regard to this aspect by asking him how far he had been from the *Chitty* homestead. Roddick told him 'between 70 and 100 yards'; Baragwanath, a few moments later when repeating the question, promptly doubled the distance. Further questions had produced further variations of distance. None of this could have helped the listening jury determine exactly where Roddick had been, but of one thing there was no doubt, he had seen a woman that Friday morning. Although no charge had been brought against Vivien Thomas, one of the 'tactics' used by the prosecution was to attempt to put into the minds of the jurors that the mystery woman was in fact Vivien Thomas, hence the very careful questions about the identification parade. For Vivien it was trial by innuendo.

If Paul Temm had pressed Roddick's failure to pick Vivien Thomas out on the identification parade, had carefully established that there was no doubt in the young man's mind that whoever the woman was it was not the wife of the accused, much of the power of that innuendo would have been demolished. He chose not to and a fanciful hypothesis from the Crown suddenly took on a dangerous possibility for his client.

Frederick Hoskins, who farmed the land adjoining one side of the Crewe property, contributed further to the mystery. He told how while feeding out on that same Friday morning the cows from the Crewe property came roaring down to the boundary fence bellowing. In his view they could not have been fed on the previous day. No-one asked him if, on the other days before the Crewe farm was discovered to be deserted, he witnessed the same behaviour from the Crewe stock. If they had, they would have been told that he only saw and heard them behave in this manner on the one day. Clearly someone fed those cows in that five-day period.

It is equally obvious that the three dogs on the Crewe property were fed by someone during those five days. As previously noted, Graham Hewson, a man who has bred dogs for over thirty years, saw the dogs within twenty-four hours of the police arrival at the farm. He described their condition as 'fat as seals'. Demonstrably if they had not been fed, three dogs confined in a pen as they were would have been barking so loud and so long that neighbours would have been on the Crewe farm within a day of the deaths.

As the case for the Crown progressed the evidence was producing many questions but precious few answers.

Queenie McConachie told of driving past the Crewe farm on the Saturday shortly after 1.30 p.m. and seeing a child by the front gate a few yards from the road. The child had been wearing long trousers with a bib front. Mrs McConachie thought the colour of the trousers was blue. The description is very similar to the clothes that Rochelle had been wearing on the Wednesday when Mrs Pirrett had morning coffee with the Crewes. Apart from this mystery child Mrs McConachie also noticed a *light*-coloured car parked outside the front of the house. She had looked back as she and her husband had driven by on their way to a football match and taken a second look at the child and watched as it 'sort of toddled back towards the house' . . .'Just at that time

I was going to have a baby myself, and I thought she was a lovely little girl.'

A couple of specific questions from defence counsel would have revealed at this stage an extraordinary situation. The police investigation into the deaths of the Crewes was the most costly police inquiry in New Zealand's history. It was also one of the most crass, banal, amateur investigations ever undertaken in the country's history. In June 1970, after Mrs McConachie had made a statement to the police, she was shown photographs of Rochelle Crewe. She was unable to identify from the photographs the child she had seen by the Crewe front gate. *At no time was she shown the child. At no time was the child dressed in the clothes she had been wearing the previous Wednesday and stood by the front gate for Mrs McConachie to observe.*

By comparison with Inspector Hutton and his men, the Keystone Cops were a model of efficiency. Today, after a police investigation of that calibre a man is serving a life sentence.

I believe the 'lovely little girl' that Mrs McConachie saw was Rochelle Crewe.

Len Demler took the witness stand late on the third day of the trial. The gentle questioning by David Morris drew from the witness some, but by no means all, of the personal and financial details of the Demler family that are recorded earlier in this book. The burglary and the two fires were again trotted out for the jury to consider. Again no evidence was forthcoming that linked any of these events with the deaths of the Crewes or with Thomas. Demler recalled Arthur Thomas calling one day and asking for Jeannette's overseas address, which he had happily given to the young man. He also remembered Thomas calling with the present of the brush and comb set when Jeannette had returned from Europe. There were detailed questions and answers about the normal positions of the furniture in the Crewe lounge. Demler recounted how after five days, during

171

which he had not attempted to contact his daughter and son-in-law, prompted by phone calls from stock agents he had gone to the Crewe farm, discovered it bloodstained and empty of the two adults and found eighteen-month-old Rochelle in her cot, dressed in nappies and pyjama top. Earlier evidence from a stock agent had established that prior to contacting Owen Priest and returning to the Crewe farm, Demler had left Rochelle alone in her cot and returned to his farm, phoned a stock agent to cancel trucks that were due to collect sheep from the Crewe farm. The stock agent had been out but rather than give the simple message 'Cancel the trucks' Demler had left his phone number and waited a quarter of an hour until the stock agent phoned him. His own testimony revealed that even after he and Priest had collected the child and removed her, he did not immediately return to the Crewe farm and resume the search for his relations but spent about half an hour moving sheep from one of his yards. In answer to questions from the Crown Prosecutor he said he had never called at the Thomas property, never borrowed a .22 firearm from Thomas and had not removed any motor vehicle parts from the Thomas farm.

The following morning, Thursday 18 February, he faced the cross-examination of Paul Temm. After discussing with Demler the macabre question of exactly how he had been able to identify the unrecognizable body of Harvey Crewe, Temm turned to the events of 22 June. What follows is the verbatim transcript of the remainder of the cross-examination:

Temm: Let me pass to your discovery that there was nobody in the house but the baby; when you entered the house on 22 June, was the door locked or unlocked?

Demler: It was a Yale lock. I turned the key to get in. The key was in the door.

Temm: The back door?

Demler: Yes.

Temm: You had to turn the key to get in the back door?

Demler: Yes.

Temm: And it was a Yale lock?

Demler: Yes.

Temm: Are you sure?

Demler: The front door has a Yale lock, but the key was in the back door.

Temm: The key was on the outside?

Demler: Yes.

Temm: What is the position?

Demler: I turned the key.

Temm: You unlocked the door before you went in?

Demler: Yes.

Temm: Then I suppose having noticed the disorder in the kitchen the first thing you noticed then was the bloodstains in the lounge?

Demler: Yes, on the way through.

Temm: Did that suggest to you that somebody had been injured in that room?

Demler: I thought there had been an accident.

Temm: Did you notice the bloodstain on the floor referred to as a drag mark?

Demler: As soon as I saw the bloodstain I went to where the baby was.

Temm: You mean you did not notice that when you went in that room the first time?

Demler: Yes, I couldn't help noticing it.

Temm: Then you went to the baby's room?

Demler: Yes.

Temm: The very next thing, from the lounge to the baby's bedroom?

Demler: Yes.

Temm: What did you do after that?

Demler: I had a look at the baby and I decided I would have to find someone to take her so I didn't look any more round the house but went back home.

Temm: You didn't then go straight down to your neighbour Mr Priest?

Demler: No, on the way back.

Temm: You go to the house, through the house, from there back to your house and from there to Priest's house and from there back to the house?

Demler: Yes.

Temm: When you got back to your house did you then ring Mr Wright?

Demler: That is right.

Temm: That was to tell him not to send the sheep or cattle trucks to the farm?

Demler: That is right.

Temm: When did you shift the sheep of which you spoke? While you were there?

Demler: No, after the police were notified and were at the house, I thought I had better do that.

Temm: We understood from Mr Wright you phoned his firm and left a message to ring you back, is that right?

Demler: Yes, he wasn't there at the time.

Temm: Did he telephone you back before you went to Mr Priest?

Demler: That is right.

Temm: It follows that while you were phoning and waiting for his call in reply, Rochelle was alone in the house?

Demler: Yes, that is right.

Temm: Your farm and the Crewes' have a common boundary?

Demler: Yes.

Temm: And you and Mr Crewe would be visible to one another from time to time when out around the farm?

Demler: Very seldom as I was sheltered from the bush. When I was down at the back of the farm was the only time we could see one another.

Temm: Between Wednesday 17 June and Monday 22

June, did you never phone your daughter?

Demler: No, I only phoned her once a week as a rule, if I wanted something.

Temm: How fond of Jeannette were you?

Demler: Very fond of Jeannette.

Temm: How fond of Rochelle were you?

Demler: I was very fond of her too actually.

Temm: But in those five days with which we are concerned you never rang once?

Demler: No, we never communicated by phone. After my wife died I went up every day, then after a while it was every two days, and later it was once a week.

Temm: Did you never drive past the farm during those five days?

Demler: No.

Temm: The outside lights were apparently on throughout the whole period?

Demler: That is right.

Temm: Did you never see those outside lights?

Demler: I can't see those lights, wherever I am. I have the hedge.

Temm: Did you never see those lights during that time?

Demler: No, I did not.

Temm: You told us that you did at one point own a .22 rifle?

Demler: That is right.

Temm: Did the police take possession of a .22 rifle from your farm?

Demler: No, they never took any rifle from my farm.

Temm: Did you give them any particular rifle from any other place?

Demler: No.

Temm: Did you give them any .22 calibre ammunition?

Demler: No, I never had any.

Temm: So you neither owned nor possessed a .22 calibre rifle during the past year?

Demler: That is right.

Temm: When police inquiries were being made into the absence and death of your daughter and her husband, did you make available to them all the information they wanted?

Demler: I did.

Temm: Did the information they wanted include the value of your late wife's estate?

Demler: Some of it.

Temm: What in fact was the value of this estate?

Demler: About $47,000.

Temm: In terms of her will Jeannette was to receive that but you had the use of the farm?

Demler: That is right, till my death.

Temm: Of course there was some cash in that estate apart from the farm, was there not?

Demler: Yes, some cash.

Temm: How much?

Demler: I wouldn't have a clue.

Temm: You know that the defence has asked for this information to be made available?

Demler: Yes.

Temm: And they have sought that information from the estate solicitors, do you know that also?

Demler: No.

Temm: And have you refused permission to give this information?

Demler: I didn't refuse exactly. I didn't see it had anything to do with the case.

Temm: Did you tell the estate solicitors that you would not agree to the information being disclosed?

Demler: Yes, because it has already been disclosed once.

Temm: So you did refuse permission for it to be disclosed?

Demler: That is right.

Temm: What is the value of Jeannette's estate?

Demler: That would be hard to say. Roughly $30,000.

Temm: Is that your answer?

Demler: More than that. It is hard to work out.

Temm: Somewhere near $100,000?

Demler: No, it wouldn't be that.

Temm: The estate solicitors would know the details?

Demler: Yes, they would.

Temm: If I assure you the information is relevant to the case are you now prepared to consider the information being disclosed?

Demler: If you want to know.

Temm: I do want it; do you agree for the defence to know that?

Demler: Yes.

Temm: How much did Jeannette receive when she became of age to do so from the Chennell trust which she and her sister Heather shared equally?

Demler: She got half the farm, but I don't know how much other money she got. There was some other cash.

Temm: At the time she died had she loaned money out on mortgage to other people through the estate solicitors?

Demler: Yes, she had a bit on mortgage.

Temm: How much do you say was out on mortgage?

Demler: I can't say off hand.

Temm: You are the estate's trustee?

Demler: I don't read it up all the time.

Temm: Are you telling the court you don't know how much she had out on mortgage?

Demler: That is right.

Temm: Since her death you have enquired of the solicitors as to her financial affairs?

Demler: It is hardly for me to enquire into that. They would let me know if everything was all right.

Temm: Didn't you have to sign a statement as to her assets and liabilities for the Inland Revenue Department?

Demler: I don't remember signing one of those yet.

Temm: Have you in fact made a return?

177

Demler: It has been put through but it has not been made out properly yet. They are waiting on it now I think.

Temm: Do you say the return hasn't been made out?

Demler: Well, it hasn't been finalized yet anyway.

Temm: I asked if the return had been made?

Demler: Some returns I think.

Temm: Do you tell us that you know nothing about the contents of it as you left it to the estate solicitors?

Demler: Yes.

Temm: Who was the trustee for your daughters in the Chennell estate?

Demler: Alf Hudson and myself. He is dead now.

Temm: Did he die before or after your daughters came into their inheritance?

Demler: He was still alive at the time.

Temm: After the bodies were found to be missing from the house the police had a wide-scale search?

Demler: Yes, that is right.

Temm: Much of the searching was at first inland?

Demler: That is right.

Temm: A great deal of attention was concentrated for a start on caves and the like in the locality?

Demler: That is right.

Temm: Did you assist in searching those limestone caves?

Demler: No, I didn't.

Temm: But you knew your daughter was missing and possibly dead?

Demler: That is right.

Temm: You knew your son-in-law was also missing and possibly dead?

Demler: Yes.

Temm: And we know they were found not in the caves but in the river?

Demler: That is right.

Temm: Were you accused by any police officer of

178

being responsible for the deaths of your daughter and son-in-law?

Demler: I was under suspicion at one time.

Temm: Did anybody directly say to you: 'We have got you now, you've had it' . . .

Before Paul Temm could finish his question Judge Henry stopped him. He ruled that the question was inadmissible. The duel between defence counsel and Len Demler continued:

Temm: What was it that happened that gave you reason to know you were under suspicion?

Demler: A search round my place, that's all.

Temm: Nothing more than that?

Demler: I don't think so.

Temm: Are you telling us that you believed you were under suspicion solely because they searched around your place, is that the whole truth?

Demler: Yes, well, they searched everywhere, I remember them doing it. Then the other point was there was a small bloodstain on the front seat of my car. Jeannette was going to town in my car with the baby and she got a bit of blood on the seat.

Temm: Can we take it that was a bloodstain on the front seat of your car?

Demler: That is right.

Temm: Do we also take it that that bloodstain was from Jeannette's blood?

Demler: I believe that is right.

Temm: Was there also a bloodstain on the door of the car?

Demler: I don't think so.

Temm: If a police photographer says he took photos of what appeared to be bloodstains on the left front door and left front seat, were these bloodstains Jeannette's blood?

Demler: Yes, well, that could be. She carried the baby as she got out of the car.

Temm: Did the police ever question you as to your

movements on Wednesday 17 June?

Demler: Yes, they did.

Temm: How long was spent in that questioning altogether?

Demler: Quite a fair period. A couple of hours.

Temm: On how many occasions were you questioned on that general subject of your movements and association?

Demler: Two or three times.

Temm: Was there an occasion when you were questioned for five or six hours at a stretch?

Demler: For four hours.

Temm: At a stretch?

Demler: Yes.

Temm: When you said a moment ago the time spent in questioning was only a couple of hours, that is not right. How many times altogether were you questioned?

Demler: Two or three times.

Temm: How many times altogether were you questioned in a solemn way about the disappearance of your daughter?

Demler: I said two or three times.

Temm: Did you say to anyone between June last year and October last year that the police were shadowing you?

Demler: I didn't say they were shadowing me. I said they suspected me for a while.

Temm: Did you say to anyone you were being followed by the police and your movements were being observed?

Demler: No, I didn't say that.

Temm: It is not the kind of observation you would forget, is it?

Demler: No, I don't remember saying that to anyone anyway.

Temm: But do you agree that the observation isn't one you would be likely to forget?

Demler: I suppose so.

Temm: Did you have in fact reason to think yourself your movements were being watched?

Demler: No, I didn't think that.

Temm: Did you have a key yourself that would give you access to the Crewe house?

Demler: No, I had no key.

Those who in the past seven years have been so highly critical of Paul Temm's defence of Arthur Thomas would do well to study carefully the cross-examination recorded above. Len Demler was not, of course, on trial although that interchange might well give the impression that he was. All Paul Temm had to do during that trial was convince the jury that reasonable doubt existed. By drawing out of the non-committal Demler the information that he did, Temm was demonstrating, very clearly, there were possibilities other than the one the Crown was urging.

Although the subsequent cross-examination of Len Demler about the financial background that the defence had fought so hard to obtain did not occur until Tuesday, 23 February, I have recorded it here for the sake of continuity. Again it is verbatim from the trial transcript:

Temm: You will remember that I asked you what was the value of your late wife's estate?

Demler: Yes, I didn't know it. I said about £47,000.

Temm: How long have you been farming?

Demler: About forty years.

Temm: Have you prospered in your farming business?

Demler: Yes.

Temm: So in the course of that forty years you had considerable business experience?

Demler: No, I had very little.

Temm: Did you take an interest with your solicitors in your late wife's affairs?

Demler: I went to sign the papers that went through, that's about all.

Temm: I suggest assets in your late wife's estate total $78,000?

Demler: That is correct. The first time it was valued it was about $60,000. After three days it went up to $70,000, something like that.

Temm: You knew then?

Demler: I couldn't think at the time. I gave a rough estimate. I said about $47,000 didn't I?

Temm: Talking about this revaluation you refer to; is the position that at first her share of the farm was taken on Government valuation on 31 March 1966?

Demler: That is right.

Temm: But the duties division said they wanted another valuation as that was out of date?

Demler: That is right.

Temm: When your farm was revalued in 1970 it increased in value by a total of about $30,000?

Demler: Apparently about that figure.

Temm: How much is your farm worth on that valuation today?

Demler: I wouldn't know for sure myself. I forget the figures. About $180 an acre. I wouldn't say that was right or wrong.

Temm: Most farmers know the value of their land per acre?

Demler: It doesn't seem to worry me that much.

Temm: How many acres are there in your farm?

Demler: 465.

Temm: In the Crewe farm next door were there 339?

Demler: Something like that.

Temm: The Crewe farm had been in the Chennell estate?

Demler: Yes, it was.

Temm: That was the estate of your brother-in-law who had died in 1950 in a tractor accident?

Demler: That is right.

Temm: You told us that you were one of the trustees of the estate?

182

Demler: That is right.

Temm: And it was administered by you and your co-trustee for the benefit of your two daughters Jeannette and Heather?

Demler: That is right.

Temm: They were to come into their inheritance on reaching twenty-five years of age?

Demler: That is correct.

Temm: I suggest to you that when Jeannette came to inherit, she received assets totalling just over $20,000?

Demler: Something like that. I am not sure.

Temm: Was it a figure like that?

Demler: I don't remember the figures.

Temm: Do you challenge that figure as being widely inaccurate?

Demler: No, I wouldn't challenge it.

Temm: The defence has now been able to talk to the estate solicitors?

Demler: That is right.

Temm: If I suggest to you that Jeannette came into $54,000, what do you say?

Demler: Somewhere around that figure I would think.

Temm: Did that money include not only her share of Chennell farm but also her share of a number of loans paid by the estate on mortgage?

Demler: A few small loans and a bit of cash in the bank, yes.

Temm: About $5,000 on mortgage?

Demler: Roughly something like that.

Temm: And something close to that figure in cash on deposit at the bank?

Demler: Round about that.

Temm: You were also the executor and trustee under Jeannette's will?

Demler: Yes, I was.

Temm: Preliminary figures for her estate is a figure of nearly $58,000?

Demler: Yes, round about that.

Temm: That is taking the value of the Crewe farm as at 1966?

Demler: Yes, that is right.

Temm: I suggest that when that farm is revalued it will rise in the way corresponding to yours?

Demler: Yes, it will.

Temm: Is there nearly $6,000 out on mortgage?

Demler: Yes, round about that.

Temm: Did she and her husband have a partnership account with the Bank of New Zealand $1,300 in one account in credit?

Demler: I wouldn't be sure of that. They had an account with roughly that figure I suppose.

Temm: Was there also nearly $6,000 in savings bank account?

Demler: I don't know for sure.

Temm: You know they had a savings account with about that figure?

Demler: Yes.

Temm: If I say it is contained as an asset in the combined partnership would you accept that?

Demler: Oh yes, a combined partnership.

Temm: As a result of the provisions of your late wife's will Jeannette's estate will eventually comprise $78,000 in your wife's estate?

Demler: That is correct.

Temm: Plus about another $70,000 in her own estate when the farm is revalued?

Demler: Roughly that.

Temm: That would give a total of over $150,000 altogether?

Demler: Yes.

Temm: When you were asked whether her estate would be somewhere near $100,000 didn't you say no?

Demler: I didn't think it would be that much.

Temm: Are you telling us that for a farmer of your experience you didn't know the size of her estate?

Demler: I didn't add on my wife's estate as she doesn't get it till I die.

Temm: Was there an asset in the Chennell estate which was a firearm, a rifle?

Demler: Not to my knowledge. I have never seen it.

Temm: You know a man named Harry Leech?

Demler: Yes.

Temm: Who is he?

Demler: My brother-in-law.

Temm: Did you ever talk about a firearm in the Chennell estate to him?

Demler: No.

Temm: Did you go with him to talk to another man in Pukekohe concerning that firearm?

Demler: No, I did not.

Temm: At about the time of Jeannette's funeral I suggest to you? Ever seen a man in Pukekohe whom you might have lent a rifle to?

Demler: No, it didn't belong to anyone, it was out of use. It was never used.

Temm: Where is it now?

Demler: I wouldn't know.

Temm: If the records of the Chennell estate show they had a firearm in the assets would you say that is not correct?

Demler: I have not seen a firearm.

Temm: If the records show they had a firearm?

Demler: I don't think that is correct.

Temm: Have you tried to find the firearm of which you have spoken since the deaths?

Demler: No.

Temm: Have you tried to find it?

Demler: No, I have not.

Temm: Is there a rifle in existence?

Demler: A broken-down one, but it wasn't fit for use.

Len Demler was then briefly re-examined by David Morris:

Morris: You were asked about these estates, who

benefits in the long run from Harvey Crewe's estate?

Demler: Rochelle.

Morris: Who takes Mrs Crewe's estate?

Demler: Rochelle again.

Morris: The various interests that Jeannette had in her estate, does that also pass to Rochelle on your death?

Demler: That is right.

Apart from taking the heat out of a gun that initially did not exist at all and subsequently was acknowledged to have existed but now to be missing, the Crown, by establishing the long-term beneficiaries, were clearly hoping to remove all suspicion from the man the police had so long regarded as the No. 1 suspect. Noticeably absent were any questions about short-term beneficiaries.

Thus, despite police obstruction, despite the difficulties put in their way by the Crown office, the defence had finally in the most dramatic manner possible obtained at least some of the information they had sought on the financial background not only of the Crewes but also the Demler family.

Cleverly biding his time, Temm had asked for it in the most public of arenas, the No. 1 Court at Auckland. His questions had clearly indicated to the jury that the defence had been obstructed by Demler. The defence counsel carefully walked Demler into a situation where refusal to allow counsel at least some access to the details of the various estates, when clearly he had given *total* access to the police, would tell heavily against him. Of course the police did not have to ask Demler either publicly or privately for such information; the power of a police search warrant is total. The defence had by no means obtained all the information they had been seeking. The paid cheques of the estate, the wills and other information were denied to them but at least by the time that Paul Temm had finished with the witness who was so full of 'That is right' and 'That is correct' and many other examples of the technique of minimum answer, some information about the financial background had emerged.

The questions and answers about the missing gun had made a reality of a nightmare that Inspector Bruce Hutton had been living with for many months. The in-depth fieldwork of the defence team plus that first look at details of the Chennell estate had been the basis for those defence questions about a missing gun. Hutton had anticipated just such a situation arising in the course of the trial. He said to me:

'The fact that Demler had a rifle that he could not find was always worrying me. I knew that if I eventually got someone else for the murder – God, look at the chagrin the defence counsel would have had. It was bound to get out that Demler had a rifle, which was never bloody found, despite the police searches and all that.'

There was of course also the issue of Demler's own .22 rifle, that was also missing. As the trial progressed, the police redoubled their efforts to find those missing rifles. Meanwhile the puzzles that the jury had to solve grew. The car that Roddick had seen in front of the house on the Friday morning was back in the garage when Owen Priest went to the property with Len Demler. Rochelle's clothing was not dirty; 'It was just sort of used,' he told the Court. Referring to the search that the two men had made outside the house, he referred to the six loaves of bread that he had noticed by the delivery. For good measure there were also a number of bottles of milk and newspapers. Without doubt the farm had been visited a number of times during those five days, yet the daily deliveries had not been moved. This surely would be a fundamental exercise to a killer hiding his or her tracks, unless the risk of being recognized was too great, unless whoever returned did so by means other than the gate by Highway 22.

More and more questions remained unanswered as the trial went on. The Court was told that the clothes-drier was on when the police arrived. They were not told what was in the clothes-drier, or what condition the clothes in the drier were in, or if any attempt had been made by readings of the electric meter to ascertain how long the drier had been on. They learned that the outside light and kitchen lights were on. Again a meter-reading comparison with previous power bills might have indicated just how long these lights had been burning. They were told that only one set of ignition keys had been found, in a cabinet drawer. No-one asked the car dealer who gave evidence if a duplicate set had been supplied with the car.

They were told of the bloodstains that abounded in the house, some of them diluted, of saucepans with traces of blood, clear evidence of someone's attempts to clear up. They were not told if any fingerprints were found on these utensils. Clearly none belonging to the accused were found anywhere, but what prints existed on those saucepans? They were told that the television set was switched to an 'on' position but that a lead running from the set was disconnected from a subsequent lead which was plugged into the mains but switched off. The Crown were to contend that the murders took place after the night's television programmes had finished. Would either of the Crewes get up out of the lounge, go out to the front passageway, disconnect the leads, then go into the master bedroom and switch the wall plug off? Would they really do all that when the alternative was to reach over to the set itself and switch it off? The jury were told of the dirty nappies in the cot, on the refrigerator, on top of the washing machine. They were not told if there were any clean nappies found. From the evidence of Detective Sergeant Murray Jeffries who compiled a complete inventory of all articles that were in the house it is clear that there were no clean nappies. This, like the dirty nappy in the cot, represents very strong evidence that the house was visited during those five days. It is inconceivable that any mother would allow her supply of clean nappies to be totally exhausted.

The dining-table with its curious arrangement of two place settings but the day's mail facing a third chair and a virtually untouched flounder in the middle, indicated to Jeffries a meal for two. Why then does the *morning* mail face a third chair? Would a housewife place a plate with a spare piece of fish directly on the polished wood surface? Surely she would allow it to remain hot and edible in the warming pan on the cooker?

Jeffries told of the tests he had done which would appear to establish that the ashes in the fireplace were the remnants of the burnt hearth mat and a cushion. He told how, when he had burnt identical items in the fireplace there had been very thick smoke before the carpet and cushion burst into flames. I believe that experiment also gives the answer to why the louvre windows were open in the kitchen. They had been opened by whoever cleaned up to allow the smoke to escape rather than choke and distress Rochelle in a nearby room. The fact that they had been left open after the clearing-up operation assumed for the Crown much greater significance. Without open louvre windows, *prior* to the deaths, their theory of how Harvey died is untenable. One gun was found on the property, a Pinea shotgun located in a canvas bag in the washhouse. Surely not the gun that Beverly Batkin has spoken of as 'Harvey's gun, it was quite a good one. Kept in the lounge.' No mention was made of any ammunition being found.

The jury were told of the initial very careful pattern search that was made of the interior and exterior between 23 and 25 June; of the subsequent sieve-search of the gardens on 18 August, specifically looking for a cartridge case.

The cross-examination of Sergeant Jeffries established an interesting variance with testimony given by the first Crown witness, Brian Sly, the surveyor who had drawn the official police plans. According to Sly, Detective Jeffries moved the couch in the lounge from its original position. According to Detective Jeffries, he did not.

The police theory of a louvre window murder depends totally not only on open windows, but on very precise positions for various pieces of the lounge furniture.

The unofficial trial of Vivien Thomas that was proceeding within the official trial of her husband was cleverly conducted by the Crown. During his opening speech to the jury David Morris had told them that 'medical opinion indicated that there was a very distinct possibility that the Crewes' child, Rochelle, had been fed two or three days after her parents were killed. There was evidence to indicate that her nappies were changed at least once between the time of her parents' deaths and the discovery some five days later that the Crewes were missing.'

Suppressing the evidence of Dr Caughey that ran directly contrary to that view Morris proceeded through a variety of witnesses to build up a case against the woman who was not in the dock. Mrs Barbara Willis, Mrs Crawford and Dr Thomas Fox all gave evidence that strongly supported that opening contention from the Crown. The defence asked no questions of any of these witnesses. This I believe to be one of the most serious errors made by Paul Temm. He clearly saw what the prosecution were doing and instead of meeting the issue head on, adopted a profile that was so low as to make him invisible. Better, far better to have made this aspect the central issue of the trial. It is clear that the police had failed to discover who had fed Rochelle. It is clear that someone had. The police failure to discover any evidence that pointed to Vivien Thomas should have been seized upon by the defence to demonstrate just how inadequate the entire police investigation had been. If Thomas was guilty of the murders, then who but Vivien had assisted him? If she had assisted him then why had she not been jointly charged with murder? Who fed Rochelle? Within the answer to that question was the key to who murdered her parents. It was a key that the defence allowed David Morris to place metaphorically at the Thomas door in this trial by innuendo.

With the evidence of pathologist Dr Francis Cairns the Crown case moved through a mixture of fact and theory. The facts of the bloodstains and the incorrect theory of death by blunt instrument were the first such example of this. The fact that Jeannette died as a result of a bullet wound in her head and the theory of how she had received her other injuries followed. Injuries to the temple and abrasions on the throat were caused, in the opinion of Dr Cairns, after death. Injuries to the eye and nose and one of the other injuries to the temple, were in the opinion of the pathologist caused before death. Of the bruise in the left armpit Dr Cairns told the jury he was unable to identify the cause. He considered the injuries to the face *could* have been caused by the butt end of Thomas's rifle.

The fact that sixteen-stone, six-feet-two Harvey Crewe had died of a bullet wound to the head was established. It was followed with the pathologist's theory of how:

'I think that he was sitting in the chair which is indicated as belonging to him, and that he was hit by a bullet which was fired from the direction of the door of the kitchen. I think that this would cause him to slump forward into the right-hand side of the chair and this would explain the bloodstains seen in photo 2. Blood had also seeped down between the arm and the seat. In photo 20 you can see it just appearing above the rear castor on that side.'

191

Morris: Any idea of where direction of shot would come from?

Cairns: I think it came from the direction of the door to kitchen.

Morris: Having seen this house would the wound be consistent with a shot being fired from a .22 rifle from open windows in kitchen?

Cairns: Yes, that was in the same line of fire.

Thus the Crown proposition of exactly how Harvey Crewe was shot had gained the acceptance of Dr Cairns. This theory had clearly not occurred to the doctor when he performed the post-mortem on the body on 16 September 1970. If it had, Detectives Charles and Parkes would have found themselves sieving a flower-bed the following day instead of on 27 October.

The Crown proposition that the injuries to Jeannette's face were caused by the butt of Thomas's rifle took rather a knock during Paul Temm's cross-examination of Dr Cairns.

Temm: And I turn my attention to your description of injury to the right eye and bridge of nose; you were asked whether that could be caused by a rifle blow, and your reply was it could be caused by one blow, do I understand that correctly?

Cairns: That is correct.

Temm: Were you being guarded because there is nobody who could tell now if it was a rifle blow that caused that injury?

Cairns: That is correct.

Temm: Would it be correct to draw the conclusion that the eye and nose were injured similarly by one blow from a blunt instrument?

Cairns: Yes.

Temm: A blunt instrument of course is a term that can cover many things when it is used as a contrast to a sharp instrument. Give us the kind of things you considered. You mentioned a piece of wood?

Cairns: Yes, a hard substance without a sharp surface.

Temm: I suppose if an All Black came out of the forwards with a black eye it could be considered he was struck with a blunt instrument?

Cairns: Yes.

Temm: When it comes to a question of the injuries on the face?

Cairns: There is nothing to indicate the type of weapon used.

The Crown theory concerning the louvre shooting of Harvey Crewe could have been just as effectively demolished but the defence counsel made no attempt to do so. Harvey Crewe could have been shot while standing in a totally different part of the lounge, indeed he could have been shot in a totally different part of the house and his body placed in the armchair shortly after death. That at least is the view several pathologists have given to me.

There can be no doubt that the body of Harvey Crewe was in that armchair for a considerable period of time *after* death but it does not follow that he was in the chair at the moment he was shot. For the theory of the louvre shooting to have any tenability the Crown had to have Harvey sitting in that chair; consequently, the factual pathological evidence of Dr Cairns was extended to a fanciful reconstruction. It should have been demolished by the defence; it wasn't.

Other questions that remained unasked by the defence to Dr Cairns concerned the possibility that one of the Crewes killed the other and the survivor then committed suicide. It was a possibility that Paul Temm laid before the jury in his final speech, but his argument was enormously weakened by his failure to put that possibility to Dr Cairns. I discussed this omission with Temm.

'I came very close to putting a whole series of questions to Cairns with regard to the murder/suicide theory. My worry was that if Cairns said the theory was untenable then I would have been unable to put it to the jury in my final speech. So I decided, and maybe it was a wrong decision, not to ask him those questions, which I had planned to culminate with a demonstration from Dr Cairns of how Jeannette could have killed herself. It's one of those problems counsel have. If you want to say something to the jury, you can sometimes put it forward to them as a comment on the overall evidence which you would be prevented from doing if contradictory evidence had been given.'

When Detective Senior Sergeant John Hughes gave evidence of his conversation with the accused on the Thomas farm on 2 July 1970, it included the following statement:

'Thomas told me that while employed by an agricultural contractor three or four years before, he had worked on the Crewe farm. He said that he had morning and afternoon teas in the Crewe homestead. He said that he had met a man whom he knew to be Harvey Crewe and said that he appeared to him to be a decent type of bloke. He said that he had not seen either Mr or Mrs Crewe for eight to nine months.'

Morris: Did he indicate when the last occasion was that he was at the farm?

Hughes: While working for the agricultural contractor.

There is only one conclusion that the jury could have reached having heard that statement from Hughes, which was not challenged by the defence, and that was that while working for Barr Brothers (the agricultural contractor referred to by Hughes), Arthur Thomas had in either 1966 or 1967 assisted in the top-dressing at the Crewe farm, had had morning and afternoon teas at that time and met Harvey Crewe at that time. *Those conclusions are totally refuted by the facts.*

If Detective Hughes or any police officer had taken the trouble to talk to managing director John Barr of Barr Brothers, as I have and the police have not, they would have discovered a number of interesting facts.

194

Perhaps the most pertinent are that Barr Brothers never worked for Harvey Crewe. The last time they top-dressed the farm was on 15 and 16 April 1966, before Harvey and Jeannette were married and consequently before they moved on to the Crewe farm. In April 1966, both were still living in Wanganui. Even on that occasion in April 1966, Thomas was not part of the top-dressing team; he had finished working for the company during the previous year, on 20 May 1965. In view of the fact that the police did call at Barr Brothers on two occasions shortly after Arthur Thomas was arrested one can only ponder yet again on the entire police investigation. When Detective Johnston called and spoke to the general manager his sole interest was in discussing pubic hairs and Thomas's sex life. In a letter to me Mr Barr observes:

'The questions were aimed to get a view that Arthur was a sex maniac. Johnston wrote down Mr Curley's alleged answer then asked him to sign the statement. After reading it Mr Curley refused because Johnston had written answers in a manner that was not correct and leaned towards the answers they wanted.'

Yet again the unhealthy desire to obtain a conviction is echoed in that statement. Just as it is in the evidence of Hughes, evidence that placed Thomas on the Crewe property at a time when he was not there.

Having been treated to a limited view of the Crewe and Demler finances the jury were given an unlimited picture of Thomas's when his bank manager gave evidence for the Crown. They learned that in June 1970 he was within his overdraft limit of $900, 'with one or two excesses.'

Under cross-examination from Brian Webb the bank manager opined that Thomas 'was making ends meet'.

Details were also given that Thomas had received a suspensory loan from the State Advances during 1970 of $1,000. This was to help him combat the effects of severe droughts in 1969/70. Again the defence were able in cross-examination to put this in its correct perspective.

Temm: Would it be giving a fair picture if I suggest that every farmer in Pukekawa had a suspensory loan?

Witness: Yes.

Unlike those two witnesses the next man to step into the witness box had evidence that was highly relevant to the case against Thomas. The witness was Detective Sergeant Mike Charles.

In his opening address to the jury David Morris had told them that the most important piece of evidence before them would be the .22 Browning rifle, owned by Thomas. Charles, it may be remembered, was the police officer who initially collected and then returned that rifle to the Thomases. More importantly he was the officer who discovered Exhibit 350, a .22 cartridge case, in one of the Crewes' flowerbeds.

Defence questioning revealed the odd haphazard way that sixty-four rifles were collected for test firing. At the Lower Court hearing Detective Charles had described in detail how he and Parkes had searched just one small area of flowerbed on the morning of 27 October. While being questioned by David Morris, an additional piece of evidence emerged which the defence had picked up. Paul Temm questioned the police officer about this:

Temm: You mentioned in your evidence-in-chief that you went and collected a sieve on the way to the house?

Charles: Yes, sir.

Temm: But in searching through the soil you didn't use this sieve, did you?

Charles: Yes, we did, sir.

Temm: Remember giving evidence on this matter once before?

Charles: Yes, sir.

Temm: What did you say about using a sieve on that occasion?

Charles: I can't remember.

Temm: Remember your evidence was recorded?

Charles: Yes, sir.

Temm: Remember it was read back to you and signed as correct?

Charles: Yes.

Temm: Did you sign that record?

Charles: Yes, sir.

Temm: Would you like to look at that record now to see what was there said?

Charles: Yes, sir.

Temm: Would you read it and tell us what you said on that occasion?

Charles: I just mentioned that the soil was raked by Detective Parkes and I searched through the soil to a depth of six inches.

Temm: That answer makes no mention of a sieve?

Charles: No, I didn't mention it.

Temm: You said nothing about a sieve in a lower court?

Charles: No, sir.

This omission in the police officer's initial testimony covering the finding of the most important exhibit in the entire case was clearly something for Paul Temm to exploit. At that point in the cross-examination, however, the fire alarm sounded throughout the Supreme Court. There was a hurried adjournment. It transpired that it was a false alarm; the culprit was not discovered. Paul Temm resumed questioning:

Temm: Since your cross-examination have you been in conversation with the Crown Solicitor?

Charles: Yes.

Temm: You are an experienced officer?

Charles: Yes.

Temm: You know better than that?

Charles: I just happened to speak to Mr Morris.

Temm: Have you spoken to Detective Parkes?

Charles: No, sir.

Temm: He is outside the courtroom?

Charles: He is somewhere in the building I believe.

All very curious, including the last remark by Mike Charles, who was fully aware that Parkes was indeed just outside the courtroom, waiting to be called as next witness.

To any reader wondering why discussions about a sieve, or what Charles did or did not say at the Lower Court, should have particular relevance I would point out – and it cannot be stated too frequently – that the cartridge case found by Mike Charles, which DSIR scientists contended had without doubt been ejected from the Thomas rifle, was the only piece of evidence that *directly* linked that rifle and by implication Thomas with the deaths of Harvey and Jeannette. It is not my intention to nit-pick or quibble with the various changes of evidence that occurred through the many hearings. To compile a list of every such change would fill a fair-sized book. Some of those changes of evidence have been the cause for comment, others will also be, but with regard to this most crucial exhibit in the case against Arthur Thomas any evidence given on it is of the utmost importance when one is attempting to answer the question: Did Arthur Thomas murder Harvey and Jeannette Crewe?

Further cross-examination of Detective Sergeant Charles established that there had indeed been no mention of a sieve at Lower Court. Paul Temm also took exception to the fact that at Lower Court Charles had omitted to say that the soil that poured from the case as he held it in his hands was 'bone dry'. Defence counsel would have been better employed seizing on this honest description of the condition of the soil in the cartridge case. Mike Charles had with his honesty in the witness box handed the defence a remarkable fact. *He had described a scientific impossibility*.

I have conducted many tests during my past twelve months' research into this case. A number of those tests were with .22 cartridge cases. One test in particular was to ascertain if cartridge cases, some placed on top of the soil, others a few inches below the surface but all with soil inside them, would still have *dry* soil inside them four months and ten days later. Dry soil was put in some of my cases, wet soil in others. A number of locations were used: Auckland, Pukekawa and Wellington. The one common factor was the earth was exposed to the elements, to the rain, wind and sunshine of New Zealand. Every single cartridge case was retrieved after precisely the same period of time that in theory the Charles case had lain in the Crewe garden – four months and ten days. *Every single cartridge case contained wet soil. There was not a single instance of bone dry soil. There was not a single instance of soil pouring or falling or running out.*

I do not expect the police or the DSIR to accept my word for this. I invite them to conduct the same experiment, with independent observers, preferably in that flowerbed, which is still there, on what was the Crewe farm.

Paul Temm's subsequent questioning of Mike Charles established exactly the condition of the soil in the flowerbed:

Temm: When you found this cartridge case did you pick it up?

Charles: It was already in my fingers when I saw it. The first time I noticed it was when I had soil in my hands. I was fingering the soil, the soil broke away and there it was.

Temm: But you didn't find it while shaking the sieve?

Charles: No, sir, I was using my fingers at the time.

Temm: You were not using the sieve at the time?

Charles: No, I found the soil being damp as it was, it was not breaking up sufficiently for the sieve to be of correct use.

When he re-examined his witness, David Morris confined himself to just one question:

Morris: Why was it you went to that particular bed?

Charles: It was because Detective Sergeant Jeffries

had told Inspector Hutton that that particular bed had not been sieved and Inspector Hutton instructed Parkes and myself to go and search it.

He little realized it at the time but that simple question and answer, designed merely to take the heat out of the defence attack, would cause David Morris a headache that was destined to last for years.

Detective Sergeant Parkes duly followed his colleague into the witness box. One time bomb that was destined to explode in the faces of the police and the Crown prosecution had just been unwittingly set ticking by the simple question and answer recorded above. Now the time bomb in the shape of the brush and comb set that Thomas had given Jeannette in December 1962 was about to ignite in the face of the accused. Parkes had been the officer who had found the brush and comb inside a cupboard in a spare bedroom of the Crewe farm and the small card attached to it that 'Arthur' had signed. He told the jury that on 12 August 1970 he had shown the card to Thomas, that the accused had admitted he had given Jeannette a brush and comb set, when he had 'wanted to court her'. The Court also heard of the other gifts and letters Thomas had sent to the accused; of how he had called on her once or twice when she was at the teachers' hostel at Maramarua.

The long verbal third-degree session that Parkes and Detective Sergeant Seaman had had with Thomas on 7 September was also covered by David Morris, though the manner of its telling to the Crown prosecutor left something to be desired. The way that Parkes told it in the witness box created the impression that it had been a friendly chat over a cup of tea.

A slightly different picture emerged when Paul Temm cross-examined the police officer. Parkes admitted that he had attempted to bluff Thomas into confessing; that he had lied to him about it being his rifle that killed the Crewes; that it had been a deliberate act by the police officer to give Thomas the impression that there was no room for doubt. It was also established that not only had Thomas vehemently protested his innocence but he had also volunteered to do anything he could to prove that he was not responsible.

Several witnesses established a trail of ownership of a particular trailer that led ultimately to Arthur's father, Allan Thomas. Part of the original assembly of that trailer had been the axle that the police had recovered from the bed of the Waikato river. The engineer Rasmussen testified that he had replaced that axle with a new one 'round about 1964/5' and that the old one and the original stub axles were not left with him as he would have liked, but were collected when the renovated trailer was picked up. Building on this the Crown then called the officer who had been given the responsibility of tracing the axle. Having taken the story as far as Rasmussen, Detective Johnston continued:

'On 13 October 1970, I went to Mercer Ferry Road, Pukekawa, and there saw the accused, Thomas. I showed the accused the axle in question, Exhibit 293, and asked him whether he had seen this axle before. He said he hadn't. He said, "The only axle on the farm is down on the tip and this has two wheels attached to it." I later saw this axle in the position he indicated. I then produced a photograph of a 1929 Nash motor car and trailer. It was the same one that appeared in the *NZ Herald* on 10 October. I asked whether he had ever seen this photo in the *Herald* and he said he had. I asked him whether he recognized the trailer in the photo. The accused said it was similar to the trailer his father had on the farm one time and it could have been painted blue. I then asked the accused for all the .22 ammunition he had in his possession, and with that he produced a box of .22 ammunition from somewhere in the kitchen. I produce that box of ammunition as Exhibit 318. I asked the accused about the ammunition and he said he used it in a rifle he had to shoot rabbits on the farm. He said he also had a shotgun which he used during duckshooting seasons. I asked the accused whether he knew if Jeannette had used the brush and comb set that he had given her. He said he didn't know, it could still be wrapped up for all he knew.'

Mr Justice Henry, who had been listening attentively to the evidence, made careful note of that last remark. It would feature heavily in his summing-up to the jury.

Detective Johnston, continuing his evidence, related how Thomas had recommended that the police talk to his father about the trailer. Thomas gave the police officer his father's address, phone number and instructions on how to get to Thomas Senior's farm at Matakana.

Having interviewed Thomas Senior, Johnston had returned on 15 October and he and Arthur Thomas searched for the stub axles and other scraps of the original trailer. If Thomas had murdered the Crewes this was surely inexplicable behaviour. A police officer comes enquiring about a trailer, Thomas tells him the photo he is shown is similar to a trailer belonging to his father and gives every possible detail to enable the police to contact his father. His father in turn suggests various places where the scrap items might be and Arthur Thomas then assists the police in looking for them. They are unsuccessful and return five days later and after digging around on the dump find the stub axles. Arthur had six days during which he knew the police were specifically looking for those stub axles. Six days in which he could have located them on the dump and removed them.

By leaving them untouched Thomas had enabled the police to discover a powerful piece of evidence indicating that not only the axle stubs but the axle itself had until recently been on his farm.

As had the Lower Court before so now the Supreme Court began to resemble a scrap-metal merchant's yard with the amount of rubbish that was entered as exhibits.

When Derek Booth, whose alibi until 6 p.m. on the night of the murders apparently satisfied everyone, gave evidence, his involvement with the two Demler sisters was taken a little further under cross-examination. At the Lower Court he had only referred to going out with Heather, now he admitted he had also taken out Jeannette. Asked by Paul Temm to put a date on the period when he was taking her out he said he thought it was 'the end of 1963, late in the year'. He said he was aware that Jeannette had been overseas before that and that at the time he was taking her out he thought she was teaching 'over Mangatangi way, but I actually took her out from her home at Pukekawa'.

It is clear that Mr Booth's memory had deserted him in the witness box. At the end of 1963 Jeannette was living and working several hundred miles south of Pukekawa, at Wanganui. If Booth took her out when she was teaching 'over Mangatangi way' then his relationship with Jeannette was either between February 1960 and January 1961, or if it was after her European trip it was between February and April 1963. Jeannette had talked to her friends at Mangatangi of a man who called on her, whom she saw at dances. Booth, on his own sworn evidence, was seeing her during this period.

Detective Keith took the witness stand and recalled the fragmented remark he had heard Thomas make during one of the police searches: 'If they think I am guilty I am, and that's that.' For the benefit of Paul Temm he also recalled how in the Lower Court that phrase had been preceded with the words: 'From their point of view'. Subsequently, for the benefit of David Morris and despite strenuous objections from Paul Temm, he was allowed to look at his notebook then revert back to his original recollection of this meaningless phrase.

Keith also offered into evidence as an exhibit the

solitary round of .22 ammunition he had found in the Thomas garage, which when dissected had the number 8 on the base of the bullet.

When DSIR scientist Rory Shanahan gave evidence the defence launched a major attack on the Charles cartridge case. Paul Temm was primarily concerned about two aspects: the overall external condition and the marks on the base of the cartridge case. He held the view that a cartridge case exposed to the elements for as long as this one allegedly had been would show a far greater degree of corrosion. It was also the defence counsel's belief that the firing marks on the base differed markedly from the marks left on cartridge cases that had been indisputably fired from the Thomas gun. Both lines of attack would have been immeasurably stronger if the defence had called experts in these areas. Certainly experts existed who could have testified about the marks on the base of the case, but with regard to corrosion Paul Temm was to be the first of many people to discover that the study of corrosion on metals is a veritable minefield. Before the trial commenced Temm arranged for Professor Tichener, head of the engineering faculty at Auckland University, to examine the Charles case. The following is an extract from his report:

'The case appeared rather less corroded, both inside and outside, than I would have expected in view of the length of exposure it had presumably suffered in the soil; but not to the extent that I felt it possible to say with any conviction that it could not have been exposed for this length of time. In this connection it must be realized that corrosive attack is notoriously variable, and that nominally identical articles exposed for the same period to similar environments frequently show markedly different degrees of attack.'

Certainly the Charles case was subjected to markedly different descriptions from a variety of witnesses. It became a ballistic Jacob's coat of many colours.

Rory Shanahan: 'Somewhat duller than the other cartridge cases.'

Dr Donald Nelson: 'It was darker than other freshly fired ones.'

Inspector Hutton: 'Heavy ink type of stain running from the bullet end of the cartridge case at its widest end and tapering down towards the rim.'

Detective Charles: 'I would say darkish brown . . . Yes, in a way chocolate brown would be a better description.'

Without the comforting knowledge that he would be calling his own experts to justify certain defence contentions, Paul Temm attempted by comparison photographs to establish fundamental differences between the marks on the bottom of the Charles case and one fired from the Thomas rifle. But whereas Shanahan had used photographs merely to demonstrate to the jury conclusions reached from microscopic examination, Temm relied solely on photographs to justify defence conclusions. It was a line of attack that was extremely vulnerable. As defence counsel took him through photograph after photograph, Rory Shanahan readily agreed that there were indeed marked and significant differences but as he had previously observed: 'A photo can never ever fully reproduce what one can see through a comparison microscope. You cannot pick up shade, depths and highlights. They merely attempt to illustrate previous findings.'

Later Shanahan explained that such differences that existed in his photographs and the enlargements of them made by the defence could be caused by lighting. He also referred to minute marks that could only be observed through a microscope. Clearly the answer would have been to set up either in the DSIR laboratory or the courtroom itself a comparison microscope for the jury to look through. Such a demonstration was first performed in an English court in 1928; evidently the idea had yet to reach New Zealand.

Shanahan was followed into the witness box by another DSIR scientist, Harry Todd. His testimony was largely concerned with comparison of the wires found around both bodies and around a bedspread that was recovered close to Harvey Crewe's body. He had been given thirty segments of wire to compare with what were rather gruesomely called 'the body wires'.

During the course of my research I discussed with a considerable number of scientists the need for a scientific ombudsman, someone who could give the jury an independent assessment of forensic evidence. A number of the men and women I spoke to welcomed the idea, others objected or felt counsel representing an accused person would object. I believe there is a desperate need for such a person to be incorporated into our legal system, not only when there is a direct conflict of scientific evidence, but also to explain in lay terms exactly what the hell a particular witness is talking about. The Thomas jury was made up of twelve ordinary people: housewives, shopkeepers, etc. Does any reader honestly believe that they made sense of the following extract from Mr Todd? Remember, unlike the reader, the jury only heard it, and only heard it once:

Baragwanath: Were you asked by Mr Shanahan to make comparison between on the one hand certain wires which were labelled as having come from the bodies, and on the other hand certain wires said to have come from neighbouring farms?

Todd: That is correct.

Baragwanath: Did you initially separate the samples in the bag visually to copper and non-copper?

Todd: I used two techniques, the visual and the magnet.

Baragwanath: Which picked out the ferrous samples?

Todd: That is right.

Baragwanath: So we have a term to use for ferrous samples, a common term used to describe these?

Todd: It could be called galvanized iron.

Baragwanath: Did the sample received include the following: sample X 6626 (1)?

Todd: Yes. Snip from Ex 288 (1) or wire no. 1.

Baragwanath: Did you also receive sample X 6626 (2)?

Todd: Yes. Snip from Ex 288 (2) or wire 2.

Already it will be noted that every sample has three different identifying sets of numbers. This was just for openers. After going through a whole series of samples that Todd had received, each bearing a triple designation, it was established that the three samples of galvanized wire taken from Harvey's body *differed from each other* and also differed from the samples collected from a number of Pukekawa farms. It was also established that the copper wires removed from both bodies were apparently identical.

When Todd talked about the second batch of wires he had received on 22 October, the Crown dealt initially with the copper samples:

Baragwanath: Did all these differ appreciably from the copper samples you had from Harvey's body and one from Jeannette's body?

Todd: Yes, they differed appreciably.

Baragwanath: How many pieces of galvanized iron wire did you receive in this second batch?

Todd: There were again 11 samples.

Baragwanath: How did the gauge of these 11 samples compare with the gauge of steel of the galvanized iron wires 1, 2 and 4?

Todd: They were nominally the same.

Baragwanath: Did you conduct tests to see how wires 1, 2, and 4 labelled as being 1 and 2 from Harvey and 4 from bedspread, compared with these other 11 galvanized iron samples?

Todd: I did.

Baragwanath: Deal with these wires in turn; firstly wire 1, lab No. 6626 (1)?

Todd: Comparing sample 1 and the 2nd batch, there is excellent agreement in composition between sample 1 and 4 of the batch. 320a, 323, 325 and 334.

Baragwanath: Were you able by the tests conducted to differentiate between wire 1 and the four galvanized iron samples to which you just referred?

Todd: No, I wasn't. Within my experience they were indistinguishable.

Baragwanath: Did you also test a sample 328d against wire 1?

Todd: That is correct. That is also in good agreement.

Baragwanath: Referring to wire 2, how did this compare with other wires?

Todd: There was some good agreement between wire 2 and sample 324a.

Baragwanath: You refer to wires 1 and 2; did you also check to see whether wire 4, bedspread wire, compared with the 11 other wires?

Todd: Yes, I thought at first there was a possible agreement but the subsequent work convinced me that there wasn't a full similarity between sample 4 and any of these wires.

Baragwanath: You referred to wire 1 as being indistinguishable within the limits of your tests, are you able to say categorically whether on the basis of your tests two pieces of wire are necessarily from the very same coil?

Todd: No, I could hardly say that. I could say that they were different, but the samples if of a similar composition they could be from the same coil, but they needn't be of course.

What the lay jury made of that I do not know. But in his last answer Mr Todd had totally demolished any probative value his evidence might have for the Crown. He honestly admitted that he was not in a position to say if one particular piece of wire had come from the same coil as another particular piece; all he could do was talk of similarities to a lesser or greater degree.

With regard to comprehension of this scientist's evidence, it is not without significance that the newspapers of this country either carried no reports of it at all, or passed rapidly over it.

Equally I have yet to read, in any of the books, articles or statements of the Thomas case, covering a period of nearly eight years, an accurate assessment of Mr Todd's evidence. Many writers have mistakenly asserted that the scientist was only able to find one sample taken by the police from the Thomas farm that was in agreement with the body wires.

In fact in the scientist's opinion four of the samples taken from the Thomas farm were in 'excellent agreement' and two were in 'good agreement' with the body wires. If Thomas is indeed the double murderer this poses an extraordinary situation. He used copper wire from a source as yet untraced and a mixture of galvanized wire some of which was similar to the body wires. It conjures up a picture of Thomas walking around his farm picking up odd bits of wire and then, ignoring his own copper wire rolls in his shed, acquiring from an unknown source, copper wire. Of course every odd piece that he used would increase the risk of detection. If one were aware that wire could be traced why not use just one roll of wire and throw the remainder in the Waikato. Why would a farmer use sixteen gauge wire, more suitable for wrapping small cartons when there was an abundance of eight gauge wire on his farm. The sixteen gauge wire would be extremely unlikely to support an axle weighing over 35lb.

Although previous witnesses had identified the bewildering array of wire sample numbers, the Crown made no attempt while questioning Mr Todd to identify the source of the various wires.

Into this veritable foggy maze came another man from the DSIR, Dr Donald Nelson.

He enlarged on his Lower Court evidence concerning

his examination of the skin tissue that had been removed from Jeannette Crewe's head. The absence of soot or powder burns might, he told the Court, be accounted for because the skin tissue had originally been covered by hair and had also been in water for a long time. He was therefore unable to form an opinion as to the range that Jeannette had been shot from.

If he had subjected the skin tissue to a neutron emission test it is possible that he might have found traces of barium carbonate or nitrate, antimony and lead styphnate, which would have proved the range to be very short. Such tests have been performed in the United States and England on skin tissue subjected to water for longer periods than two months with significant success. The question of range of shot is crucial when considering the possibility of murder/suicide in this case. And as Dr Donald Nelson said to me when referring specifically to the deaths of Harvey and Jeannette:

'We cannot rule out the possibility of murder/suicide.'

Asked why he had been unable to exclude two of the sixty-four rifles tested Dr Nelson replied:

'On two of these rifles the width of the land markings was identical with the bullet 234, and in addition in the land markings of these rifles there was very little characteristic detail which would leave a further exclusion.'

The characteristic detail; that is, the secondary markings or striations which are produced by each individual weapon and no other, are what pinpoint a specific weapon. Clearly none existed on the bullet fragments retrieved from the two dead people. This does not need the legal doctrine of reasonable doubt applied to it, merely common sense. In terms of determining which rifle was used to kill Harvey and Jeannette Crewe, the Crown and the DSIR are no nearer a specific positive conclusion today than they were seven years ago.

Dr Nelson told how he had taken part in the reconstruction of the louvre theory shooting, but he stressed to the Court that he had nothing to do with the placement of Harvey's chair. That responsibility had been left to Inspector Hutton. Dr Nelson's conclusions about the theory were: 'It was quite possible, in fact relatively easy, to shoot accurately at a target in the armchair using the room lighting in the sitting-room from the position where I was.'

Under cross-examination it turned out that the reconstruction he had just recalled so vividly had been less fresh in his mind two months earlier. In the Lower Court version he had his left foot on the brick wall and the right foot on the windowsill. At the Supreme Court the feet positions were reversed. The sharp eyes of a member of the defence team had spotted the switch. After some reflection Dr Nelson elected to stand by his current version. His memory also did not recall whether the lounge floor was carpeted during the reconstruction, an absolutely vital factor. He was equally ignorant about potential movement in the louvre windows themselves. Now these are crucial aspects if the police theory was to be demonstrated as tenable. The louvre windows, for example, do not open beyond a horizontal position. This would be the maximum rifle access a marksman could obtain, yet the DSIR man made no test on the windows, did not check if the carpet was in its correct position, did not check if there was a carpet laid at all. He waited until everything was to Inspector Hutton's satisfaction then climbed up and aimed a rifle through an already horizontally opened louvre window and fired.

Later in his cross-examination, Paul Temm turned to the bullet fragments recovered from the two bodies:

Temm: And these bullets might or might not have been fired from that Browning belonging to the accused?

Nelson: Yes, sir.

Temm: And might have been fired by that Remington?

Nelson: Yes, sir.

Temm: And might have been fired by another weapon altogether that you have not tested?

Nelson: Yes, sir.

Temm: Turning to the cartridge case found by Mr Charles, are you able to say that the bullet that killed Jeannette Crewe came from that cartridge case?

Nelson: No, sir.

Temm: From your examination of the two objects you can't say that the one came from the other?

Nelson: No, sir. I might add . . .

Temm: From your examination of the cartridge case and the bullet that killed Harvey Crewe can you say the bullet came from that cartridge case?

Nelson: No, sir.

The final point that Temm established from Nelson was that the DSIR had only compared the Charles cartridge case with cases fired from the Thomas rifle. It had apparently not been considered necessary to call back in the initial sixty-four rifles collected, let alone bring in new ones.

Late on the afternoon of 24 February, the main prosecution witness, Inspector Bruce Hutton, commenced giving evidence. Efficiently, step by step, he told the story of the police investigation that he had controlled. It was not the story outlined earlier in this book of wild accusations being levelled at a variety of Pukekawa residents. The Apaches who had run wild through the farms were replaced by careful, calm, cavalry officers. Step by inexorable step the hunt was led towards Arthur Thomas. The axle, the wires, the brush and comb set, the louvre reconstruction, the reasons why that particular flowerbed had not been searched before, the finding of the Charles case, it was an impeccable performance. The following morning when he continued his evidence Hutton even threw in a surprise. He had, it seemed, gone back to the Crewe farm after the Court had risen the day before, this time with a photographer. While he posed in an armchair, the photographer shot him through the louvre windows, with his camera.

All the statements made by Thomas prior to the accused being cautioned and charged were introduced. Details of conversations about sick Cow 4, whether he was jealous of Harvey, how the drought had hit him, the alibi, the ejection tests that had been carried out with the Thomas rifle to determine how far a case could possibly go. Tests carried out after the Charles case was found. The final flourish which initially was meaningless to jurors, was when Inspector Hutton produced two new exhibits. The first was Thomas's watch. The second was a copy of the *Franklin News* (a local newspaper) in which was a photograph of Arthur and Vivien.

I have spoken to a number of police officers who served in the force with Bruce Hutton. One comment in particular I recall from a man, now a detective sergeant, who trained under Hutton:

'He was remarkable the way he organized his mind when giving evidence. I remember one occasion a number of us, including Hutton, were giving evidence. While the rest of us fretted and rehearsed our lines outside the Court, Bruce Hutton just sat there very calmly waiting. We went in and made rather a hash of it. Hutton came in last. It was an incredible performance. He knew, God knows how he knew, but he knew every mistake the rest of us had made. As he went through his own testimony, he patched a hole here, covered a shaky piece there that the rest of us had created. It was a masterful performance. The accused was found guilty of course.'

Paul Temm rose to cross-examine. He got the inspector on the run immediately:

Temm: Did I understand you to tell the accused in the last interview on Armistice Day last year that you

213

asked him for an explanation of the fact that the axle had been traced to his farm?

Hutton: I did, sir.

Temm: I understand from the evidence thus far that the last time the axle was seen before it was found on Harvey Crewe's body was by Mr Rasmussen in Meremere in 1965?

Hutton: I understand it as the axle which was found near the body of Harvey Crewe was the one I was referring to when speaking to the accused.

Temm: The point is that the last time it was seen by anyone was by Mr Rasmussen in Meremere in July 1965?

Hutton: Yes, I would agree.

Temm: Did you also ask him for an explanation as to how wire on Harvey's body had been traced to his farm?

Hutton: I did, sir.

Temm: That is not correct either?

Hutton: I did ask him.

Temm: It was not correct that wires were traced to his farm?

Hutton: I think the total evidence indicates that.

Temm: Did you also say to him that it was his rifle that fired the fatal bullets?

Hutton: I did, sir.

Temm: That was I gather then a matter of your deduction on your part?

Hutton: This is what I believe, sir.

As the former inspector explained to me, he had a number of techniques for dealing with defence counsel. They ranged from pausing before answering, asking counsel to repeat the question through to answering a question that had not been asked. His initial response to Temm's questions about the axle is an example of the latter technique, answering a question that has not been asked. It failed to deflect Temm but at the Lower Court hearing the same technique had, on at least one occasion, been totally successful as this interchange illustrates:

Temm: What was the first occasion on which you personally interviewed Thomas?

Hutton: The first occasion was when I called and spoke to him and obtained the authority off him.

Temm: That tells me what you did. I asked you when you did it?

Hutton: May I refresh my memory (*REFERS TO HIS NOTEBOOK*). I would say 22 October.

Temm: When you questioned Thomas about his movements in June, did he have any way of refreshing his memory in your presence?

Hutton: I didn't question him in June.

Temm: About his movements in June?

Hutton: Are you referring to when my officers interviewed him?

Totally deflected from the very valid point he had been attempting to make Temm proceeded to question Hutton about how long the interview of 22 October had been. Hutton's techniques were clever, very clever; of course they had nothing to do with justice.

As the cross-examination in the Supreme Court continued, Inspector Hutton told of other deductions he had made. That Jeannette had been sitting in the sofa near the fire. That television had finished for the evening. That Harvey was shot as he sat in his chair. That there had been a fire burning, because the night was wet and windy. It was all very neat and on initial examination logical. The logic begins to evaporate out of open louvre windows; open, on a night that was wet and windy? Open when the wind was squalling at speeds of up to 35 mph? Open and therefore exposing the lounge to such wind? A lounge that according to Diane Ambler, close friend of the Crewes, was, on an August afternoon, 'so cold that even with the fire going we had to keep our overcoats on'. The fact that the television was disconnected led Hutton to deduce that they had been watching it that evening and watched it until closedown at 11 p.m. As Detective Dedman, the officer in charge of fingerprinting the Crewe home, had delicately observed, 'Mrs Crewe did not appear to be an extremely successful housekeeper.' An entire change of her clothing piled in one corner of the main bedroom for at least forty-eight hours and a change of Harvey's clothing slung over a door amply justify that tactful observation. The television set could have been disconnected and switched off at the mains, days before the deaths. In their desperate need to have the Crewe deaths occurring after television had finished, the police totally discarded logic. The reason for the need was simply to weaken the alibi of Arthur Thomas. Thomas creeping out of his bed and quietly leaving a sleeping wife, carefully dressing, leaving the house without disturbing his sleeping cousin, driving off and hours later returning without disturbing either of the other occupants; this was the picture that both police and prosecution were determined to fix in the minds of the jury, even though such a picture strains credibility to breaking point. But Thomas, up, awake, alert, eating his meal and watching television with a conscious wife and cousin keeping him company, at the time the Crewes died is a totally different proposition. By stating the murder occurred late Hutton was astutely weakening an apparently impregnable alibi. It was of course only deduction, it had nothing to do with justice.

The cross-examination of the detective inspector continued with a discussion of the financial affairs of the Crewes. The defence had gleaned a considerable amount of information about this aspect from the police inventory. The fact that by utilizing that inventory Paul Temm was now able to get certain facts before the jury was particularly galling to Hutton. In Paul Temm's words: 'Hutton was furious when he heard we had obtained a copy of the police inventory of the Crewe household. It was illuminating because it told us something about their financial affairs that we had not previously known.'

Temm: A joint account of $1667?

Hutton: Yes, sir.

Temm: And Mrs Crewe had three savings bank accounts, first credit, $1636?

Hutton: Yes, sir.

Temm: Another with credit of $1500?

Hutton: Yes.

Temm: And a third with credit of $1500?

Hutton: Yes.

Temm: That is a total of $4,640?

Hutton: I will accept that, sir.

Temm: Mr Crewe had only two savings accounts?

Hutton: That is true.

Temm: The amount he had in his accounts both together came to $34?

Hutton: Yes.

Temm: From the investigation of the financial affairs did you find Mr Crewe had taken out a very heavy mortgage on the farm with SAC?

Hutton: Yes, there was a mortgage.

Temm: Was it $36,000?

Hutton: I couldn't say.

Thus the defence counsel demonstrated to the jury the curious imbalance in the respective bank accounts of the Crewes.

Subsequent questioning covered the police theory of exactly how Harvey was sitting in his chair. Paul Temm asked Hutton whether he agreed with Dr Cairns' theory that Harvey's weight would have been to the front of the chair at the moment he was shot. The reply from Inspector Hutton is for me, in the light of events connected with the Thomas case over the past seven to eight years, the most ironic comment of all:

Hutton: It would be pure guesswork. He could have been in any position. One would be a brave man to say the way he would be. So many theories have been proved wrong.

The finding of the axle was a subject of considerable discussion between the two men with Hutton observing: 'I had always dreamed and believed the body would be weighted.'

Another of Hutton's many techniques for dealing with clever defence counsel is to make them lose their temper. But when Temm took the photos of Hutton's reconstruction of the previous evening and suggested that on the evidence of those photographs a marksman aiming through the louvre windows would hit, not the head of Harvey Crewe, but the cocktail cabinet, it was the inspector who lost his renowned cool. 'This is ridiculous,' he shouted. 'One knows with photos you can completely alter angles and position of door handles.'

Mr Justice Henry, now Sir Trevor, recalling Hutton's performance in the box, said to me: 'He was a good witness, but what worried me about Hutton was his hardness. I thought it quite likely that he might alienate the jury. That they might dislike him.'

Aware that such alienation might well be occurring at this point in the inspector's evidence, the judge came to his aid. He told Paul Temm that 'photographs are two dimensional and unless angles and lines are confirmed by expert evidence they are not to be used in this way'.

In view of the fact that he had previously allowed Inspector Hutton to enter these same photographs as exhibits to prove the police contention of a louvre window killing that ruling is hard to follow. Hutton had not qualified as an expert in photography. Why allow the prosecution to prove a theory with certain evidence and not allow the defence to disprove that theory with the same evidence?

The defence had no alternative but to change tack. Temm suggested to Inspector Hutton that the wire trailing from Harvey's body had been attached not to the axle but to the bedspread that was also found nearby, jammed in the branches of a partly sunken tree. It was a suggestion that Hutton vigorously rejected. He was sure that the object he had felt under the water and near to the floating body had been one end of the axle, that it had slipped from his grasp when one of the divers putting some strain on the body had unwittingly snapped the wire attaching the axle to the body.

The defence counsel went on to ask a great many questions about an incident that had been reported to the police. On the day after the Crewes died a man had been seen near the Tuakau landing at 10.30 a.m. He had a blue car that was backed up to water's edge and was washing it out. Despite close questioning in which the judge joined in, Inspector Hutton could not enlighten the Court about this curious event. He said he would look up the report. If he did it never reached the Court.

Yet again the cross-examination returned to the crucial question of the louvre reconstruction. Brian Webb, while studying the mass of police photographs had noticed a curious omission. The police marked every blood stain or group of stains with a number, but one stain remained unmarked. The sharp-eyed Webb had picked it up, a stain on the carpet, on the right-hand side of Harvey's chair. Why was this clearly discernible stain left unmarked? It is immediately in the area, where if one accepts the police theory, Harvey Crewe died. Paul Temm was sure he had the answer. By placing the right-hand rear of the chair over that stain so that stains 2 and 3 and the unmarked stain were in uniformity with each other, he contended that a louvre shooting was an impossibility. He was reassured by the inspector that the police had considered this and although it 'certainly wasn't easy, it was possible'. No-one else gave evidence on this 'possibility'. Before the

219

trial had commenced the jury had been taken out to the Crewe house and various other relevant places in the Pukekawa area. Why not a return visit? Why not re-lay the carpet? This particular bloodstain was still visible during the trial. Why not place the chair on it and demonstrate to the jury the 'possibility'? A man was on trial for a double murder here. This was no academic bar-room debate. It had taken nearly five million dollars of public money to get this far. For a few dollars more justice would have been immeasurably better served. As it was, theory and counter theory were allowed to run rife in this case where 'so many theories have been proved wrong'.

When Inspector Hutton completed his evidence, it was generally considered that David Morris would rise and tell the Court: 'That is the case for the Crown.' Instead he called another witness. At the eleventh hour William Eggleton, jeweller of Pukekohe, entered the box. His evidence could be heard by all, but few knew the curious background leading to his appearance in the No. 1 Court. My research produced some interesting and disturbing facts.

It has been said by several people writing on the Thomas case that the defence were 'caught by surprise' with regard to the evidence of Eggleton. They were not. It has been said that the defence objected against his evidence being heard and were overruled. Again this is untrue.

The story that Eggleton was to tell in the witness box was a fascinating one. A week after it was known that the Crewes were missing he had been discussing the affair with 'a friend' in his jeweller's shop. During the course of their discussion a man entered the shop. The man was 'fairly large, a bit bigger than I am, an outdoor type. He was wearing a black singlet, an open-necked shirt white in colour.' The man wanted Eggleton to repair a watch, the glass was broken. Eggleton took the watch and told the man to call back later. Upon further examining the watch the jeweller noticed that it was stained with blood and mucus. The watch was rolled gold, with a leather strap. Having replaced the glass Eggleton could not remember if he had served the mystery man when he returned or one of his staff had. In November he saw a photograph of Arthur Thomas in a local paper and 'knew it was the person who had brought the watch in to me'. On 23 February while the Crown were presenting their case against Thomas, William Eggleton finally contacted the police.

Detective Sergeant Murray Jeffries, at Hutton's instructions, went immediately to Pukekohe and took a statement from Eggleton. Later that day, copies of the statement were given to David Morris and he detailed his junior, Baragwanath, to deal with the matter. A copy of the statement was given to the defence. When I interviewed Sir Trevor Henry he vividly recalled the sequence of events that followed:

'Baragwanath and Temm came to see me on the Tuesday evening and said: "We've got this." I said to Temm: "Well, what about it? Did you have any objections to this evidence?" I also offered him an adjournment to give him time to consider if he would be prejudiced in any way by its admission. Paul Temm said he would think about it and see me again before the Crown finished presenting its evidence. They came back to see me on the Thursday morning (25 February). They told me, Temm and Webb, that they had no objection to the evidence going in. I just about fell through the floor. I had expected them to object strenuously to Eggleton's evidence being heard. If they had objected I would have upheld that objection. There is no question about it. The lateness of the statement. I also considered Eggleton's evidence unimportant. The probative force was so small, the prejudicial effect so great. That piece of evidence was ready to go out as far

221

as I was concerned. It was admissible evidence. One cannot tell the Crown that they must not offer it. If there is no objection from the defence then it goes in. If I had been Morris I would not have countenanced offering such evidence. Baragwanath is a very meticulous sort of fellow. Everything he's got must go in. He often failed to see the wood for the trees.

'It was the shock of my life when no objection was raised. I thought about it and came to the conclusion that the defence must have an ace. It's a common and very effective technique for defence lawyers to use. Demolish one aspect of the Crown's case and it acts as a demonstration of just how brittle their entire case is. It's like money for jam. So we heard Eggleton's evidence, and I sat back and waited.'

Eggleton's evidence-in-chief was much as I have already outlined. He was shown the newspaper photograph and the watch, the items Inspector Hutton had produced as exhibits at the end of his examination by David Morris. Of the photograph he said it was the one that he had just referred to. Of the watch he said it was totally different from the one that the man had brought in. At no time was he asked to directly identify the man who was sitting a few yards away from him in the dock. The brief cross-examination by Paul Temm established that Eggleton had broken his silence of four months because 'It was worrying me.' Asked if he was also nagged by the thought that he could be mistaken he replied: 'No.'

And that was the case for the Crown.

Mr Justice Henry offered the defence a brief adjournment, which they gratefully accepted. The judge, a former defence lawyer of great ability, realized intuitively that the defence might want a little time to reconsider what is often the biggest of problems for defence counsel. Should they call the accused? Most criminal defence lawyers whom I know believe it is a mistake to call the accused in a murder trial. They argue that a man charged with murder is invariably the worst possible witness to put in the box. Not because of guilt, because of pressure. Juries are apt to be influenced heavily by the performance of the accused in the witness box. They regard the accused, often wrongly, as the most important witness. A man facing a life sentence rarely gives of his best if called.

During the adjournment Paul Temm and Brian Webb agonized over the decision. From the outset, the plan had been to call Thomas; now at lift-off time there were tiny spasms of doubt. Eventually Temm decided to follow their initial plan: they would call Arthur Thomas. Paul Temm smiled at me when he discussed this aspect and said: 'And thank God I did, in the light of subsequent events, otherwise I would have been cut to pieces by the retrial syndrome.'

Certainly there are people who feel that Thomas in the box was his own worst witness. It is not a view shared by the judge:

'Under the circumstances, standing accused of a double murder, Thomas was an excellent witness.'

When I interviewed Arthur Thomas in New Zealand's maximum security prison, Paremoremo, I did not ask him for a self-evaluation of his performance in the box. But we did discuss how he felt.

'As the first trial approached I had very high hopes that I would be acquitted. I had nothing to hide. I was going to get into the witness box and tell the jury where I was on the night of the crime and what I was doing. As far as telling the jury what happened on the Crewe farm I had no more idea of what had happened than anyone else. I lived miles away. Even going to town would not take me past their place. I've always told Vivien and Peter, tell the truth. I don't care if I get a third trial, fourth trial, fifth trial. Tell the truth. We have nothing to hide.'

Facing the gentle friendly questions of his own counsel Paul Temm was one thing. David Morris, sitting waiting, would be quite another game, played with a different set of rules.

Before calling his first witness Paul Temm spoke to the jury. He told them he did not intend to address them at length. He continued:

'I submit that the Crown has not proved its case. The evidence you have heard is circumstance piled up on guesswork. Arthur Thomas denies he had anything to do with the deaths of Harvey and Jeannette Crewe. You will hear him testify that he was at home on the night in question. He will tell you of the events of that particular week and his wife will confirm his evidence.

'If, indeed, you accept the submission that Thomas had not been proved guilty and you accept his evidence that he was at home that night, you may ask yourselves: "Then who was it that did it?"

'It is not part of the defence case to do the job of the police. In many ways it would be dangerous for an accused person to try to solve a crime. The defence do not propose to try to tell you how the Crewes died. I call Arthur Allan Thomas.'

Arthur Thomas, guided by his counsel, began to fill in some of his background for the benefit of the eight men and four women who would determine his fate. .

He told them that last time he had spoken to Jeannette had been about six months before her death when they met in the nearby town of Tuakau, when they had chatted for ten or fifteen minutes. The examination very rapidly and inevitably came to Cow No. 4. Thomas explained how two or three weeks before her calving he had called the local veterinary surgeon Henry Collett out to examine the animal; of the special diet the cow was put on; special equipment that was bought to lift the beast up with.

Temm: Do you know somebody named David Leyman?

Thomas: Yes, I know him well.

Temm: Did he ever help you with the cow?

Thomas: Yes, he did at times.

Temm: What did he help you with? Remember?

Thomas: No, not in particular.

That interchange illustrates some of the difficulties that the defence were labouring under. Even thrown a prompt line Thomas was not astute enough to give the answer Paul Temm was seeking which was that Leyman had stayed at the farm until 1 June 1970 and had helped him with the sick cow 4. Thomas was later to come under ferocious attack from the Crown because he had not, when the police first visited him, immediately given them a detailed, blow-by-blow account of his movements throughout 17 June from dawn to bedtime. Yet here he was on trial for a double murder and despite the promptings of Paul Temm, still not giving the full detailed picture. Nothing to do with guilt. Leyman would later go into the witness box and give the testimony himself. No, not guilt. Simplicity, unawareness, naivety. As Margaret Smith, his Pukekawa friend and neighbour observed in her private diary of Thomas in the box: 'Arthur was just Arthur.'

Slowly, almost painfully Paul Temm extracted the information. The sick cow had calved in the late afternoon or early evening of 17 June. Vivien had helped him with the calving. They had had dinner around 8 p.m.; Thomas, his wife and Peter. None of them went out that night. It was established that Vivien looked after the herd records, that his wife assisted with running the business side of the farm.

Temm: Let's go back a little in time, before this fatal night, go back to the time we heard Mrs Batkin speak of, you heard her evidence?

Thomas: Yes.

Temm: I ask you, did you go dancing in 1956/1957?

Thomas: I definitely did not go to one dance.

Temm: When did you first go dancing?

Thomas: In 1959.

Thomas then continued to explain how he had a

friend just up the road, 'a very shy quiet person; he and I were going together as cobbers and we decided to learn to dance in 1959.' His dancing lesson card for April 1959 was duly entered as an exhibit.

Subsequently Thomas talked of his early working life, details of which are recorded earlier in this book. He talked of the variety of policemen who had called during the investigations at his farm, during the course of which he elevated Detective Senior Sergeant Hughes to an inspector. He recalled the session he had been subjected to with Detectives Seaman and Parkes. His account of it was even more gentle than that given by Parkes.

With regard to the axle, he had not seen it before Detective Johnston walked on to his farm with it. Shown the photograph that had appeared in the *Herald* of the trailer, he had told the police: 'It would pay you to go and see my father, I vaguely remember him having a trailer like that.' Of Eggleton and his evidence, Arthur Thomas swore that he had never owned a gold watch, did not know Eggleton, had never been to his shop and that he was not the man Eggleton was talking about.

The examination-in-chief concluded with:

Temm: What assistance have you given to the police during their inquiries?

Thomas: I have given them every assistance that I can give them.

Temm: Did you have anything to do with the things that happened in the Crewe house on 17th June?

Thomas: I certainly did not.

David Morris, like a patrolling barracuda, had been quietly waiting. Personally, having met both men I would not have put Thomas in against Morris, even if the former was armed with a machine-gun.

If a couple of experts in spectrographic analysis had been needed on the jury for Mr Todd's evidence on the wire a few farmers among those twelve good men and true would have helped during the evidence of both Arthur and Vivien Thomas.

The opening cross-examination had about it a pastoral quality full of questions about the problems of cows, calving, artificial insemination, due calving dates, actual calving dates. In view of the fact that David Morris was primarily concerned with the calving records and he had just heard Thomas say that these were kept by his wife, one would have expected him to curb his understandable impatience until Vivien Thomas took the stand, but presumably a Crown solicitor has to begin somewhere. Having had it repeated to him that Vivien kept these records, Morris withdrew from that particular farming cul de sac and went down another avenue.

He wanted to know when Thomas, his wife and his cousin had first discussed what they were doing on the night of Wednesday, 17 June. Bruce Hutton had previously testified that Thomas had told him that they first discussed this aspect about a week later. David Morris was under the impression, mistakenly, that they had discussed what they had been doing about a week after the fact was known that the Crewes had vanished. Again, the naive Thomas dug a bear trap for himself..

Morris: The discovery was 22nd, would that discussion be around the 28th or 29th?

Thomas: About the 23rd I think we had our discussion, when we first saw it on TV.

Morris: I am asking you at this stage not when you first discussed the disappearance, but when you and your wife and cousin sat down to discuss what you had been doing on Wednesday 17th June?

Thomas: I think it was the 23rd.

Morris: The night after the disappearance was first on TV?

Thomas: Yes.

Morris: You tell us you and your wife were discussing what you were doing on the night of 17th June?

227

Thomas: When we saw headline news on TV it was natural for us just to go back to that week in normal conversation and say: 'We're all right, we were home,' just a normal conversation.

Morris: Why did you pick out 17th June as the specific night?

Thomas: I think it was on TV, that it was about 17th June. I am not sure but it is a possibility.

Morris: If it wasn't on TV that night why was it you decided on 17th June?

Thomas: The first I heard it was 17th June or thereabouts was on the news.

Morris: Do you think that was news on Monday night the 22nd?

Thomas: Yes, I think it was.

Morris: Was that radio news on Monday night?

Thomas: The 23rd, Tuesday night.

Morris: The radio news that night?

Thomas: Or TV.

It was yet another example of the simplicity of Arthur Thomas. This was a man who if one accepts the Crown case was clever enough to commit two acts of arson and burglary over a three-year period, without leaving a trace or being seen. Was clever enough to murder the Crewes, leaving not a fingerprint or any atom of forensic evidence in the farm. Remove the bodies and dump them in the Waikato river without being seen. Yet here he was within the first hour of cross-examination leaving himself in the most terribly vulnerable position. Why should he and the two other residents of the Thomas farm discuss what they were doing on the 17th, when news of the disappearance first hit the nation? Why the 17th? Why not the 18th or the 19th? The premise is at once simple and damning. If the Crown could prove that no mention of the likely date of disappearance had been made public by the evening of the 23rd, they were home and dry in the most potent manner. While David Morris continued to cross-examine he quickly scribbled a note for a member of his staff to check on what information had been given out on the radio and television media on the evening of 22 June. Paul Temm, listening to this interchange, was equally alert. As his hair grew greyer with every moment that Thomas was being cross-examined, he too started doing a little research.

As the cross-examination continued David Morris used a technique that is all too familiar in courtrooms where the concept of British justice is played out. A technique that I have personally seen applied to men who ended up dangling from a rope. I call it the 'So he is lying too' gambit. The object of the exercise is to get the accused to disagree with as many prosecution witnesses as possible. One then begins to tally it up.

Fortunately for Arthur Thomas the rope, or capital punishment as we are pleased to call it, has been abolished in this country, at least temporarily; though liberal-thinking people would do well to know that the gallows is still in Mount Eden prison, waiting.

David Morris initially applied the technique to the evidence of Detective Sergeant Hughes. Thomas had a different version of their conversation. That segment of cross-examination had a predictable conclusion:

Morris: So if he did not ask you that question, then he is lying, that is what you say?

Thomas: I suppose so.

The Crown Prosecutor then attempted to add to the number by cross-examining Thomas about the evidence of Parkes and by inference Seaman, though the latter has always remained an unseen witness through the entire Thomas saga. He refrained from uttering this well-worn and deadly legal cliché but forced Thomas to remark:

'I am not saying the police are lying, all I am saying is it was 17th June.'

This was connected with the wretched animal that stalked the entire proceedings, Cow No. 4 and when it calved.

Of his dialogue with Detective Johnston about the equally wretched brush and comb set Morris shortly before the adjournment on the afternoon of 25th February, drew the following from the accused:

Morris: Did you say to him you didn't know whether she ever used it and that it could still be wrapped up for all you know?

Thomas: Yes, I possibly could.

Morris: Did you say that it could still be wrapped up for all you knew?

Thomas: I could have said that.

Morris: Was that just a choice of words on your part or because you had seen it there on the night of 17th June, wrapped?

Thomas: Just a choice of words.

It was powerful, very powerful. The technique of asking the same question several times is another common and very effective legal ploy when a lawyer has elicited an answer he considers favourable to his point of view. Previously David Morris had reminded the jury through his questions and answers that the blanket wrapped around Harvey's dead body came from the same spare bedroom where the brush and comb set were found by the police. The 'So he is lying too' gambit was played with vigour by Morris the following morning:

Morris: Do you recall Detective Keith giving evidence?

Thomas: Yes.

Morris: You heard him say he made a note of a conversation between yourself and Mrs Thomas?

Thomas: Yes.

Morris: He noted the conversation as you saying to your wife: 'If they think I am guilty I am and that's that'?

230

Thomas: Yes, I remember him saying that.

Morris: And he referred to his notebook when he said that?

Thomas: Yes.

Morris: Do you say no such conversation took place?

Thomas: Yes, I do say that.

Morris: So that detective is mistaken, is that what you say?

Thomas: He only heard part of the sentence if he heard that sentence.

Morris: So he got it wrong?

Thomas: That is if I said it.

Morris: Did you say anything like that?

Thomas: Nothing like that at all.

Morris: Then he has got it entirely wrong then?

Thomas: Yes.

Morris: Mr Eggleton the jeweller who gave evidence, you heard him identify you as the person with the watch?

Thomas: That is right.

Morris: You tell us he is entirely mistaken in his identification?

Thomas: He is definitely mistaken.

So the number of people that Arthur Thomas disagreed with slowly but surely mounted. Morris showed him his own watch, quite different from the one that Eggleton had testified about. Thomas told him it was two or three years old, that he seldom wore it when working on the farm and that he had bought it from a man named Jim Connelly.

Morris: Is he a jeweller or something?

Thomas: Yes, I bought it from him.

Morris: Do you possess another watch?

Thomas: Yes, I have a broken-down watch at home.

Morris: Do you ever wear that about the farm?

Thomas: No, I never wore it about the farm.

Morris: Have you worn that in the last three years?

Thomas: No, I have never worn it on the farm.

Morris: Do you normally wear a black singlet when you go to town?

Thomas: Not when I go to town.

Morris: When you are dressed to go out do you wear a black singlet?

Thomas: No, never.

Morris: With an open-necked shirt when you go to Tuakau would you wear a black singlet?

Thomas: No, never.

The Crown Prosecutor showed him the newspaper photograph that Eggleton identified Thomas by. It shows Arthur and Vivien at the pyjama dance they had attended in October 1970; clearly visible under his pyjamas is a black singlet. Presumably the Crown felt there was a link between wearing a black singlet at a pyjama dance and going into Tuakau for a day's shopping. In fact Thomas frequently could be seen in Tuakau dressed in a white shirt, open at the neck and with a black singlet underneath. My research clearly established this fact and when I questioned Thomas about this aspect he readily admitted it. Why then the denial? It had cost him dearly in Pukekawa. That one denial of something that many of his neighbours knew to be a fact convinced them of his guilt.

David Morris moved on to the evidence of Mrs Batkin, finishing that aspect with the by-now inevitable:

Morris: As far as you are concerned she is wrong?

Thomas: Yes.

A discussion followed about the fact that Thomas had only learned to dance at the age of twenty-one. Morris found it odd that Thomas had not taken dancing lessons earlier in his life. The accused's schoolboy crush for Jeannette was touched upon. Of how subsequently he had seen her twice at Maramarua. Of how he had written to her when she was in England and the final attempt to court her during December 1962. Nothing of any significance was elicited. There was no evidence to show that Thomas had persisted in his attempts to court her after 1962. He had previously volunteered the information that he had on one occasion chatted to Jeannette outside a store in Tuakau; this had been late 1969 and the conversation had been for about ten or fifteen minutes. The police and the prosecution were ignorant of this meeting until advised by Arthur Thomas, during the course of the trial; hardly the action of a guilty man.

Detailed analysis of the entire cross-examination clearly demonstrates the weakness of the case against Thomas. Of motive, there was none. Try as they might, the Crown simply could not produce anything approaching motive. Of course it is not an essential ingredient in a homicide, but as Inspector Hutton would say: 'If you haven't got a motive, then boy you are in trouble.'

What the Crown did have was circumstantial evidence of varying degrees of quality. Morris attempted to build something out of the fact that Thomas kept his rifle in a variety of places around the farm whereas Peter Thomas had testified that the rifle was usually in his bedroom. A guilty man would surely have leapt at the evidence of his cousin and readily agreed that yes, it was *always* in Peter's bedroom. By moving it around the farm Thomas was in fact giving an accurate picture not only of his own carelessness with firearms but also how the bulk of Pukekawa residents treated them, if the thirty farms I have visited in the area are anything to go by. I find an odd kind of innocence in the answers that Thomas gave in the witness box. For a man standing in grievous peril, his responses are not those of a guilty man. Rather a simple man who felt sure that 'she'll be right'.

Morris: One bullet that was found on your farm had a No. 8 on it?

Thomas: Yes.

Morris: Ever use that kind of bullet?

Thomas: I wouldn't have a clue.

Morris: That one was apparently on its own.

Thomas: Yes, on its own.

Morris: When you saw the trailer photo in the newspaper you knew it was connected with the inquiry into Jeannette?

Thomas: That is right.

Morris: You told us you were anxious to give every assistance to the police?

Thomas: Yes, that's right.

Morris: You followed the case with some interest?

Thomas: Yes, I did.

Morris: When you saw that trailer was it something like the one your dad had?

Thomas: That is right, but you couldn't see much of the trailer.

Morris: Did you go to the police about that and help them?

Thomas: No, I wasn't sure enough.

Morris: Did you think about going?

Thomas: I thought about it when I saw the photo in the paper and I said to Vivien my old man would be sure to see it and he knew more than me.

A copy of that photo in this book indicates just how little of the trailer can be seen.

A considerable discussion followed about who had first suggested that Thomas had been 'framed'. Was it the police or Thomas? Does it matter?

Other fragments of his conversations with the police were re-introduced to buttress the Crown's case:

Morris: You will remember Mr Hutton saying that you told him 'I know I am sitting on rocks, I have got to stick to what I have already told you otherwise I am a goner.' Did you say that to him?

Thomas: Yes.

Morris: What did you mean by the words 'I am a goner'?

Thomas: The fact I can remember my times, I can

remember my cousin and my rifle being at home, and that is all I have to go on.

Morris: Why use the words 'I am a goner'?

Thomas: If I can't remember anything and all this has come off the farm, this is what I am referring to.

When Thomas had used the words 'and all this' he had pointed towards the pile of exhibits.

David Morris then finished his cross-examination with a further fourteen questions about Thomas's watch and the man called Connelly who had sold it to him. Clearly, despite the vast intellectual gulf between the two men, despite the ingenuous answers, the Crown Prosecutor had not furthered his case against the accused. The one potential exception to that position was quickly covered by Paul Temm when he re-examined Thomas. After establishing yet again that the accused had never owned a gold watch he turned to the dinner conversations that had taken place on the Thomas farm after the disappearance of the Crewes was made public knowledge.

Temm: You were questioned about how you and your wife talked about your whereabouts on the night of 17th June?

Thomas: Yes.

Temm: What newspapers do you receive at your house?

Thomas: The *New Zealand Herald* and the *Franklin Times*.

Temm: At the time of the disappearance of the Crewes becoming public did you receive a *Herald* then?

Thomas: Yes.

Temm: Remember reading about this in the paper?

Thomas: Yes, I read most of it.

Temm: I show you a *Herald* for Tuesday 23rd June and ask have you seen a copy of this newspaper before?

Thomas: Yes, this is familiar.

Temm: Did you read this article?

Thomas: It is possible I did.

The article was then read aloud and entered as an exhibit. Within the *Herald* article was the crucial phrase, 'The baby, 18-month-old Rochelle Crewe, is believed to have been alone in the house since Wednesday night.' Further on there were several other references indicating that whatever had happened to the Crewes had happened on 17th June. Thus the puzzle of why the Thomas family were discussing their movements for the 17th on the evening of the 23rd was solved.

Paul Temm's research had paid off which, in view of the fact that he had seen that morning at the Auckland Supreme Court a well-known television news reader talking to David Morris, was fortunate for Thomas.

Brian Webb's examination-in-chief of Vivien Thomas once again brought back into the courtroom the reminder that this was a rustic murder case. The city girl who at the time of her arrival at Pukekawa knew nothing about farming other than how to milk a cow went into detailed information about dairy farming that clearly indicated she had learned a great deal in the intervening four years.

During the Lower Court hearings, the whole procedure had taken on for Vivien Thomas almost a dreamlike quality. It all seemed totally unreal. At times, she told me, 'It did not even seem serious, but when they found there was a case to answer it became serious. During the Supreme Court hearing it was difficult to comprehend what was going on but towards the end it became increasingly obvious that there was something terribly wrong.'

The rising fear was well masked during Brian Webb's questions. Page after page of questions dealing with dairyfarming were designed to establish that Cow 4 had calved late on the afternoon of 17th June. It was an aspect that obsessed the Crown. In view of the fact that the Crown's case was that Thomas had committed the murders after television closedown at 11 p.m., I find such concern with what the man was doing at 5 p.m.

236

inexplicable. Nevertheless with the aid of her dairy records Vivien Thomas was able to support her contention that Cow 4 had calved on 17th June and had been subsequently shot on 23rd June.

I equally find it odd that such stress was placed by the Crown on the fact that the Thomas family discussed where they were and what they were doing on the evening of 17 June 1970. I know exactly where I was and what I was doing when I heard the news of President Kennedy's assassination. Over the years literally hundreds of people have been able to tell me exactly what they were doing when they heard of the death of JFK. For tiny Pukekawa, the news of the bloodstained farm and the disappearance of the Crewes was an equally shocking event. Curious how normal natural behaviour can be made to seem abnormal and unnatural when a clever lawyer is let loose.

What was more pertinent was Vivien Thomas's assertion that on the night of 17th June Arthur Thomas did not leave the marital bed once they had retired to it at about 9.15 p.m., and that he had not left the house earlier that evening.

David Morris nominated his junior Baragwanath to cross-examine Vivien Thomas. He told me that this was a deliberate ploy to reduce the apparent importance of the witness.

Baragwanath was clearly preoccupied with the fact that Arthur, Vivien and Peter Thomas had had those dinnertime discussions. His first twenty-three questions were concerned with this aspect. At one point when he had quite obviously irritated the judge, Mr Justice Henry remarked: 'We all agree it was a topic and people talk about it.' Undeterred, Baragwanath pressed on. A sample of what had annoyed Mr Justice Henry follows:

Baragwanath: I am concerned about the first discussion of your husband's movements on that Wednesday night, when was the topic of your husband's movements on Wednesday night, 17th June, first discussed between you?

Vivien Thomas had already answered this same question three times and told counsel that it was a 'week perhaps, after the news was broadcast. I can't say any closer than that. I am sorry I just don't remember.' She again virtually repeated that reply. The Crown Junior continued:

Baragwanath: My next question, on the occasion when his movements were discussed between you, what brought it up?

Vivien: General discussion from the paper and the news.

Baragwanath: Can you enlarge on this a little, what was the relevance of his movements on that night?

Vivien: No relevance.

Baragwanath: I put it to you that the ordinary person who has no reason to suspect they are under suspicion would have no reason to discuss his movements on that night, do you agree?

Vivien: Yes, I would agree with that.

Baragwanath: Yet you say this subject was discussed between yourself and your husband?

Vivien: And Peter Thomas.

Baragwanath: Can you help me and take your mind back to what brought up this unusual topic?

Vivien: It wasn't unusual, it was all in the paper and on TV.

It was at this point that Mr Justice Henry intervened with the observation recorded above. Eventually the prosecution turned to a discussion about shed sheets and calving dates. Here the error, slip, or mistake that Vivien Thomas had made during that long interrogation on 25th October at Otahuhu police station was exploited to the full by Baragwanath. At the time of that interrogation she had told Detective Johnston that the sick Cow 4 had been shot two days after it had calved. When she had returned home and checked her records she discovered this to be incorrect and subsequently advised the police that it had been six days after the birth that the cow was shot. For approximately forty-five minutes Baragwanath asked question after question on this aspect. It is evident, even from a reading of the trial transcripts that Vivien Thomas, self-composed when questioned by her own counsel, gave way under Baragwanath's questions, becoming a hesitant, bewildered woman. Despite the hesitancy, the brittle element which is an aspect of Vivien Thomas still shows through. It is an aspect that cannot have helped her husband's position during the trial. Juries are very often emotional, irrational and illogical. They will take a dislike to a particular witness and bring in a verdict based on that dislike. The judge in this trial clearly recognized that factor when he talked to me of his fear that the jury might take a dislike to Bruce Hutton. He did not express the same fear about Vivien Thomas but he felt that 'she fell apart on cross-examination'. A view that I would agree with. Many who knew the Thomases as a married couple have stated to me that Vivien was the strong one of the marriage. It is a view held by people as diverse as Bruce Hutton and Kevin Ryan. Yet under the pressure of cross-examination the farmer from Pukekawa was strong while the typist from Farnham was weak. Indicative of guilt? Many would say and have said to me definitely 'yes'. If that be so was Arthur Thomas's strength under cross-examination indicative of innocence? Why the clever typist became foolish and the simple farmer became clever has, I believe, little to do with guilt or innocence. David Morris may well diminish the role his colleague played but Baragwanath, the man who took every prize except the one for knitting, is nobody's fool. The questions he asked were cleverly convoluted. Vivien Thomas remembers him as a man who 'belonged to the fifteenth century when they were burning witches'. He certainly made things hot for Mrs Thomas on the morning of Friday, 26th February 1971.

Baragwanath: How long was it after the birth of the calf that Cow No. 4 died?

Vivien: She didn't die, my husband shot her.

Baragwanath: When was she shot?

Vivien: 23rd June.

Baragwanath: How long in dates or terms of period between date of birth and the date the cow was shot?

Vivien: She calved on the 17th. Six days.

Baragwanath: How do you remember that?

Vivien: You count from 17 to 23.

Baragwanath: That of course presupposes that you have the two dates firmly fixed in some way or another?

Vivien: Yes, I have it recorded in the shed sheet when she calved and in the other book as to when she was shot.

Baragwanath: It's those entries I put to you that give you the basis of your recollection at this point of time? Is it on the basis of looking now at the documents you have in front of you that you establish the two dates, 17th to 23rd from which you do your subtraction to get the six?

Vivien: Yes.

Baragwanath: Was your memory do you think clearer on this particular topic at a time nearer to the date when the cow was killed?

Vivien: Possibly yes.

Baragwanath: That is the normal state of affairs, isn't it, the nearer it would be the better the memory of it?

Vivien: Usually, yes.

Baragwanath: On 25th October, Detective Johnston asked you to make a statement?

Vivien: Well, I made one so I suppose he must have asked me.

Baragwanath: You made only one statement, did you, to Johnston, it is a written statement I refer to?

Vivien: Yes, I think there was only one, yes.

Baragwanath: As at 25th October you were well aware I suggest that the movements of your husband on the night of 17th June had long been the subject of inquiry?

Vivien: What do you mean by long?

Baragwanath: As at the date of Johnston's interview of you, you were aware that the police had, prior to that date, been inquiring into your husband's movements on the night of Wednesday 17th June?

Vivien: Yes.

Baragwanath: I put it to you that it would be important if possible for an alibi to be established in respect of his movements that evening, would that be right?

Vivien: That would be right.

Baragwanath: If possible there should be made known some truthful explanation as to your husband's movements which would show that he could not have committed the crime?

Vivien: That is correct.

Baragwanath: And you would be aware before the interview started that it would be your husband's movements that would probably be asked about on that night?

Vivien: Not really, he said he wanted to know everything.

Baragwanath: Did you on that occasion tell Detective Johnston that the cow was destroyed two days and not six days after calving?

Vivien: Well, unless I read my statement to see, I can't exactly remember.

So, of course the statement was duly shown to her, it established that she had indeed said that to Johnston. The rather too confident way in which she had earlier demonstrated to the Rhodes scholar how to add seventeen and six was thrown back at her.

Baragwanath: Again I suggest it is a matter of simple arithmetic, if your book exhibit 348 is right in saying that the cow was killed on 23rd June, if your statement to the detective is correct, the calf was not born until two days before 23rd June, namely Sunday 21st, is that not a matter of arithmetic too?

Vivien: Would you repeat that too? Could I say when I made the statement to Detective Johnston that is what I genuinely believed, that the cow had been shot two days later, until I looked this book up and I saw it was the 23rd.

On reflection I believe Baragwanath should have been given the knitting prize as well. By accepting the erroneous date of the killing as a sacrosanct fact, the prosecution had moved the calving date from the 17th to the 21st and if believed by the jury had demolished the bulk of the Thomas alibi for the hours between 4 p.m. and 7.30 p.m. on the day the Crewes died. Again it must be pointed out that the Crown contended that the murders took place after 11 p.m. so in terms of demolishing an alibi it was a wasted exercise. What the cross-examination did was equally important. It threw into doubt Vivien Thomas's credibility. One error, one mistake. Well then, perhaps there are other errors? Other mistakes? After further questioning about the calving habits of cows, Baragwanath turned the questioning to cover the trial that was going on within the trial of Arthur Thomas. The unofficial trial of Vivien..

Baragwanath: When you are on and about the farm do you regularly wear slacks?

Vivien: Yes, I do.

Baragwanath: Do you also drive a 1965 Hillman car painted *light* green?

Vivien: Yes.

Baragwanath: How would you describe the colour of your hair?

Vivien: Dark brown.

Baragwanath: What is it like in the sunlight?

Vivien: The same colour, dark brown.

Baragwanath: Whereabouts were you on the morning of Friday, 19th June, at 9.30 a.m?

Vivien: Probably doing my housework.

Baragwanath: Can you not remember?

Vivien: The 19th, that would be normal at that time of day. If my husband had gone to feed out hay I would be with him, if not I would be in the house.

Baragwanath: Whereabouts was he at that time of day?

Vivien: How can I remember that now?

Baragwanath: Have you not been asked before as to where you were at that time on that date?

Vivien: I think we were asked for our movements of all the days of that week. That date is not particular from any other date asked about.

Baragwanath: This was the day on which a woman wearing slacks with light brown hair was seen on the farm of the Crewes, I have told you that now, do you say this is the first time you were informed of this?

Vivien: No, it is not the first time.

Baragwanath: When was the first time?

Vivien: I am not sure whether I heard it in general conversation, whether I read it or I was told by a police officer.

Baragwanath: I ask you a similar question in respect of the following day, Saturday 20th June. In the morning you had been to a cat show in Auckland?

Vivien: Yes.

Baragwanath: What time did you return home?

Vivien: About the middle of the morning.

Baragwanath: What sort of vehicle were you driving?

Vivien: Hillman Minx.

Baragwanath: *Light* green in colour?

Vivien: Yes.

Baragwanath: What were the movements of your husband at 1.40 that afternoon?

Vivien: I don't know.

Baragwanath: This is the date on which a car of *light* colour, like the one Jeannette Crewe used to own, was seen at the Crewe farm; understand the reason for my question?

Vivien: Yes.

Baragwanath: Tell us about your movements at the time this car was seen at 1.40.

Vivien: Well, we would have been at home.

Baragwanath: Your husband was not at the football that afternoon?

Vivien: No, he was not at the football that afternoon.

And so it continued. The fact that the Thomases, knowing they had to milk and could not attend both football match and subsequent dinner and dance, had elected for the latter so that they could milk during the afternoon assumed a significance at least in the eyes of the Crown. Of course it did no such thing. What the Crown was intent on establishing was the guilt of both Arthur and Vivien. The fact that only one was officially on trial was an irrelevance. This is what lawyers call 'tactics'.

In re-examination Paul Temm, attempting to put the error that Vivien Thomas had made at Otahuhu on 25 October into perspective, established that Vivien had not had access to her calving records or notebooks on the day of the interrogation. He was in the process of establishing with regard to the crucial date of 17 June that her statement to Johnston and all subsequent statements including her present testimony were entirely consistent with each other when the judge took exception to the question. Subsequently he obtained from Vivien Thomas a categoric statement that she had not been on the Crewe farm on Friday 19 June.

Vivien was replaced in the witness box by an aunt of Arthur's, Rosemary Thomas. On the night of 17 June, Mrs Rosemary Thomas testified, she had phoned Arthur and Vivien asking them to accompany her to the ratepayers' meeting. They had declined because they had yet to have their dinner and they were running late because of trouble with a sick cow. As a pertinent comment on the quality of the police investigation Brian Webb also obtained from Mrs Rosemary Thomas the information that her husband owned a rifle that was identical to Arthur's and that the police had not requested it for testing. So yet another person who had been within three miles of the Crewe farm, with access to a rifle *identical* in terms of rifling marks had not been investigated.

There followed into the witness box a number of farmers and neighbours of the accused whose evidence reads almost like a plea of mitigation after a verdict of guilty. They all told the jury that Arthur was well liked, highly regarded, a good farmer and all the rest of it. I fail to see the relevance of such testimony before verdict. I have met some thirty men and women who have murdered. The majority of them were very charming people. It is not my intention to disparage these good honest people who stood up and in essence declared their belief in the innocence of Arthur Thomas. I admire that, but as *evidence* it is not relevant. The pity is that stuck among these men was one whose evidence was not allowed. Evidence I would have thought relevant. Stock agent Roger Burrell had called on Arthur Thomas the morning of 18 June; which, if one accepts the Crown's case, was the morning after Thomas had shot the Crewes. Burrell was in the process of telling the jury that Thomas on that morning had been perfectly normal when Mr Justice Henry intervened to rule that such evidence was inadmissible. Curious that evidence of Thomas pestering at dances some fourteen years before the deaths was allowed, and evidence of his behaviour less than twelve hours after the deaths was not allowed. Sir Trevor Henry justified that ruling to me with the remark: 'If we allow that sort of evidence to be given we will have suspects manufacturing evidence after they have perpetrated crimes.'

I think that a very valid point. It would, however, be equally logical to rule as inadmissible alleged statements made by the accused before he is officially cautioned. Statements like those made by Thomas and his wife from early July 1970 through to early November 1970, to so many policemen, statements that were allowed to feature so heavily in this trial.

Several witnesses gave evidence about the quantity of .22 shells that proliferated all over the Thomas farm, the premise being that anyone could have walked on to the Thomas farm, picked up a used .22 cartridge case and then dropped it in the Crewe flowerbed.

David Leyman confirmed that he had been staying on the Thomas farm between 23 May and 1 June and had helped his host look after a sick cow that if he remembered correctly was in calf. Veterinary surgeon Henry Collett testified that he had been called to the Thomas farm in June to attend a sick cow that was in calf. Dentist Garth Brown recalled that both of the Thomases had attended his surgery between 12 and 12.30 on 17 June. Further questions from the defence would have elicited the information that he had invited them to have a coffee and look around his new house and they had declined because they wanted to get back to look after a sick cow that was about to calve. Those further questions were not asked. Neither was Garth Brown asked if the police had made inquiries either to him or his staff about the dental appointments of Arthur and Vivien. Throughout all this coming and going to the witness box the Crown adopted an astute silence. Until Merv Cathcart gave evidence, that is. He was the 'quiet shy cobber' who had taken dancing lessons with Arthur in 1959. His evidence directly contradicted that of Beverly Batkin's about Arthur attending dances in 1956/57. Like many others Mr Cathcart had not attended the ratepayers' meeting of 17 June. If asked, and nobody had until I did, he would have told the jury that he too phoned Arthur Thomas that evening and had spoken to the accused. One aspect of Mervyn Cathcart's evidence might appear whimsical to a townie but would be significant to anyone living in the country. To get to the Crewe farm, Thomas would have to go past the Cathcart farm. At that time Mercer Ferry Road was a cul de sac ending at the Waikato river. The Thomas car had a very distinctive whine in the differential – as Mr Cathcart said to me: 'You knew every time that car of his went by. I was in that night. I went to bed about 9.30 p.m. We slept right on the front of the house, about fifty feet from the road. You could hear the noise of his car over half a mile away. It was such a well-known noise. I never heard it that night.'

When David Morris rose to examine Cathcart he attempted to diminish the power of the noisy differential with comments about how windy it was that night. But more significantly, he established that this close friend of Arthur's had not known of the existence of the dump on the farm. It would become a powerful piece of ammunition for Morris in his final speech.

The louvre shooting theory was brought back to prominence with the evidence of several defence witnesses. Temm had taken to heart the judge's strictures that evidence deriving from photographs could only be given by experts. Hutton during the course of his evidence had taken a trip out to the Crewe farm to attempt to prove for the benefit of the Crown how Harvey had been killed. During the course of the defence evidence a photographer had been sent out to Pukekawa to disprove with his own photographs that same theory. With the photographer had gone a marksman and a man with over thirty years' experience of firearms. They had taken a number of Court exhibits and had effected their own reconstruction. *Their combined evidence demonstrated, effectively, the sheer lunacy of the police theory of louvre shooting, when the armchair is placed with the right-hand rear castor over the bloodstain the police neglected to mark.*

It was a very strong finish to the case for the defence, only marred by the fact that the judge refused to allow a psychiatrist and a bank manager to testify. From the former, Paul Temm had intended to elicit the fact that

Thomas did not have an obsessive nature; from the latter he had hoped finally to get access to the cheques that had been drawn and the deposits made by the Crewes shortly before their deaths. In both instances he was balked by Mr Justice Henry. The judge considered that the evidence from the two men was 'inadmissible'.

Prior to the intervention of the judge, the defence had established from the bank manager that the police had indeed had access to the information that Paul Temm wanted. Why then had they suppressed that information? Why not make it available to the defence? There can be no doubt that Mr Justice Henry would have very quickly thrown such evidence out unless he considered it relevant. Such information would reveal, for example, if the Crewes had withdrawn from their accounts a large sum of cash shortly before their deaths, money that was not found in the farm by the police. Such information might open up a powerful motive for the deaths.

The crowds who had queued, pushed and shoved their ways to seats in the public gallery throughout the trial once again rushed for seats before David Morris began his final speech to the jury.

It was inevitable in a case that relied on circumstantial evidence that conjecture would run rife through his speech. 'The Crown contends that Thomas shot Jeannette and Harvey Crewe on the night of Wednesday 17 June. That he shot Harvey Crewe by firing through the open louvre kitchen window while Harvey was sitting in his chair. That subsequently Thomas burst into the house, knocked Jeannette down and shot her. At some stage he wrapped their bodies in bedspreads and then weighted the bodies before depositing them in the Waikato river.'

David Morris told the jury that he would pose three questions to them:

1. Were the Crewes killed on 17 June?

2. How and when on that night did they meet their deaths?
3. Who did the evidence indicate was the person who committed the two killings?

The first was quickly dealt with on the basis that the couple had last been seen alive at a stock sale on the afternoon of Wednesday, 17 June. Telephone calls went unanswered on the Thursday and newspapers were uncollected.

The Crown Prosecutor then immediately moved into speculation when he observed: 'Evidence establishes they had eaten their evening meal. It must have taken place after that.' The meal of course could have been lunch eaten before the stock sales. Did they really wait until 7 p.m. to read mail delivered at 9.30 a.m? The fact that the table was not cleared is entirely consistent with the clothes slung willynilly in the bedroom. From the fact that Rochelle was found in her cot, dressed in night clothes, Morris deduced she had been put there by the parents. He cited the evidence of Len Demler that the child was normally put to bed around 6 p.m. He told the jury that it was clearly established that they had been killed later in the evening 'certainly after television had finished'. The lead on the television was disconnected but the television was still on. In fact apart from the disconnected lead in the hall the set was also switched off at the mains in the master bedroom.

The ingenious David Morris continued:

'At the time Harvey was shot he was sitting in his chair and Jeannette was sitting on the sofa knitting. She had jumped up, dropped stitches and taken the other needle to defend herself and dropped it bent.

'There was no doubt Harvey was shot in his chair from the evidence of Dr Cairns and the bloodstains and drag marks on the carpet,' asserted the Crown Prosecutor. He continued:

'A defence witness had said it was perfectly possible to carry out the sort of shot that killed Harvey. It was certainly not a difficult task for someone accustomed to shooting opossums and there was light present.'

In fact, the defence witness, Percy Brant had said:

'I found that position for one my size was quite uncomfortable and I would not guarantee a steady sight in that position. The eave was close to my head, my knees were bent, and I found it quite difficult. I suppose a shot could be fired. There was a certain amount of restriction with both top and bottom louvres, there was a very limited angle at which to get an offhand shot.'

Building on the conjectural story, Morris dropped in a contradictory fact: 'The weather that night was windy and unpleasant.' How that equates with wide-open louvre windows, Mr Morris did not enlighten the jury.

Supported by the evidence of Dr Cairns he elaborated on the Crown theory of exactly how Harvey and Jeannette had been murdered. In view of the initial theory of Dr Cairns of tomahawks, axes and pieces of wood, Morris was seeking justification from a proven fallible witness. When he turned to the third question he had posed to the jury he observed:

'The Crown case is that whoever fired the shots and did the killing also tied the axle to Harvey Crewe's body, and the shell case found by the police was ejected as the killer reloaded, having fired the first shot, before bursting into the house.'

With regard to the axle, his task would have been infinitely easier if the axle had been recovered attached to the body. The Crown case would in those circumstances have been immeasurably stronger. Their case would have been stronger still if from the vast collection of rubbish recovered from the Waikato a weight had been produced linking the Thomas farm with the disposal of Jeannette Crewe.

With regard to the axle the Crown's case was that it must have been attached to the body of Harvey Crewe and fell away as the police pulled the body into the cradle.

Tracing the previous history of the axle, the Crown came to a full stop at engineer Rasmussen's yard. In view of the fact that the other redundant components had been found by the police on the Thomas farm dump Morris considered the axle had gone back to the farm as well. 'I suggest it, too, was left on the farm until the night of Harvey's death, when it was used to weigh him down in the Waikato river.'

The trailer conversion had taken place a year before Arthur Thomas took over his father's farm. *Prior to its discovery on the riverbed on 16 September 1970, no evidence had been brought of the axle's history over the previous five years.*

Of the Charles cartridge case David Morris said:

'There can be no doubt whatsoever, after hearing the evidence that the cartridge case was ejected from the accused's rifle.'

Certainly powerful evidence from DSIR scientists had been adduced in support of the statement but a few moments later the Crown Prosecutor made a statement that was in direct contradiction to those same scientists' opinions:

'This case was from the bullet which killed Harvey Crewe. This rifle on the desk in front of me fired it.' .

Why Paul Temm did not leap screaming to his feet at this point I do not know. Why the judge did not stop Morris and insist that he withdraw that remark and instruct the jury to ignore it I do not know. Not only was there no evidence to support that statement, there was very significant evidence to contradict it.

Temm: So it comes to this does it, that the two rifles left were the accused's Browning rifle and another I suggest a Remington rifle?

Nelson: That is correct.

Temm: And these bullets might or might not have been, might have been fired from that Browning of the accused?

Nelson: Yes, sir.

251

Temm: Might have been fired by that Remington?

Nelson: Yes, sir.

Temm: And might have been fired by another weapon altogether that you have not tested?

Nelson: Yes, sir.

Temm: Turning to the cartridge case found by Mr Charles, are you able to say that the bullet that killed Jeannette Crewe came from that cartridge case?

Nelson: No, sir.

Temm: From your examination of the two objects you can't say that, that the one came from the other?

Nelson: No, sir. I could add . . .

Temm: From your examination of the cartridge case and the bullet that killed Harvey can you say the bullet came from that cartridge case?

Nelson: No, sir.

What Dr Nelson might have said, if not interrupted by the next question was: 'I could add that I would not normally expect to be able to link a particular bullet to a particular case.' And quite clearly with regard to the Charles case he had not. When people talk of Thomas having had two fair trials they should consider situations like this. In a closing speech for counsel to assert as a fact something that has not been established as such is a serious breach of his duty to the Court.

The quality of much of the remainder of the Crown Prosecutor's speech was in keeping with the extracts already quoted. The motive for Thomas in Morris's view 'was probably jealousy stemming from a childhood passion'.

I have contended throughout my study of this trial that there were two trials taking place simultaneously. Officially Arthur Thomas. Unofficially Vivien Thomas. The cross-examination of Vivien Thomas by Baragwanath clearly proves that contention.

In his final speech David Morris told the jury that Thomas's story had, of course, been supported by his wife.

'This is not a trial of Mrs Thomas. The Crown does not suggest she knew anything about the murder. She may have visited the Crewe farm on the Friday to feed the child, to minimize the tragedy, this would explain the apparent inconsistency of the careful and meticulous planning by the murderer and the seemingly foolhardy behaviour in feeding the baby and attempting to clean up.

'Mr Roddick has described seeing a woman with light hair and wearing slacks at the farm.

'You may well think she is a determined, resourceful and loyal wife.'

In those words a Crown Prosecutor calmly stated: 'Vivien Thomas is an accessory after the fact of murder.' The cynicism of first blandly stating she was not involved in the murder and then accusing her of being an accessory after the murder is a revealing insight into the mind of David Morris. Nearly eight years later that 'determined, resourceful and loyal wife' has yet to have any charge brought against her.

The Crown Prosecutor reminded the jury of how Vivien Thomas had faltered under cross-examination. She had not corroborated her husband 'on the vital evidence of the watch'.

Indeed she had been asked no questions at all on 'the vital evidence of the watch'. Mr Justice Henry had listened as Arthur Thomas had talked of buying his own watch from a man called Connelly 'a few years ago'. Thomas had been hazy about where the sale had taken place; it 'was either at his flat or on the farm'. And hazy about how much he had paid for it. He had said that Vivien would be able to answer those questions. The judge had waited for the ace to be sprung. At the end of Mrs Thomas's evidence he was still waiting.

Referring to Thomas's alleged remark that the brush and comb set might 'still be wrapped up for all I know' Morris asked the jury:

'Was it purely coincidental that he described the set exactly as it was although he had not seen it for eight years?' He concluded his address to the jury with the following words:

'In the Crown's submission, the whole of the evidence taken together leads inevitably to the conclusion that on the night of 17th June 1970, the eve of the Crewes' wedding anniversary, the accused, Arthur Allan Thomas, shot them to death.'

Rising to his feet, Paul Temm began with a long detailed explanation of circumstantial evidence and direct evidence. He pointed out to the listening jury that the Crown's case depended totally on the former and told them how in his view they should consider such evidence. He continued:

'In our submission, this man is innocent and comes here because the inquiries that were made were less than adequate.'

Eggleton the jeweller he called 'a patently honest man, but I submit his identification of the accused was a case of mistaken identity'. He read to the jury a letter written on 24 February 1961. It was from Jeannette Demler, thanking Arthur Thomas for the present of a writing compendium and pen. It was a chatty, friendly letter. Paul Temm asked the jury to compare the words written by the dead woman with the evidence given by Mrs Batkin, in considering the relationship at that time between the accused and Jeannette Demler. He could have equally read out to them another letter from Jeannette that Arthur had kept, written ten months later, in December 1961. A Christmas card from Britain that read:

'To Arthur, Christmas cheer and best wishes for the New Year from Jeannette.' Inside was written:

'Dear Arthur, What a surprise to find a present of beads and stockings at the OVC. Thank you very much. The beads were lovely and you were a good guess with the size of the stockings. You certainly seem to be seeing lots of different parts of the North Island with working at Barr Brothers. Life is still just as hectic as ever over here. I am stopping work to go for a skiing holiday in Austria early next year. Yours sincerely Jeannette.'

Hardly a note from a young woman who had been pestered by Thomas, whose life had been made a misery by this man. As for the brush and comb set that he gave her at Christmas 1962 – does anyone seriously think that this woman would still have it, albeit wrapped up, eight years later, if she had the slightest reason for disliking Arthur Thomas? This woman who 'was pestered at dances', 'lived in fear of her life because of fires and a burglary'?

Temm hammered away at the unmarked bloodstain in the Crewe lounge. He called it 'the key to the whole case'. He elaborated:

'Consider the fact that you were told nothing whatever about it till Mr Hutton was cross-examined – a significant feature if ever there was one. If the defence had not noticed it, you would probably have been told nothing about it.

'I invite you, in weighing up the circumstances of this case to weigh up the conclusions with great care, in case you take a piece of one and a piece of another and put them together when they do not make a whole.'

He returned to that unmarked bloodstain:

'If the chair is put over that bloodstain it is pretty clear conclusion that a person sitting in the position of Harvey Crewe was just not within range of a bullet fired from the louvre windows.'

Referring to the reconstruction that Inspector Hutton had so dramatically carried out during the trial he made two telling points. The inspector had said that the chair used was identical to the bloodstained armchair, known as 'Harvey's chair'. Temm had clearly established during his cross-examination of Hutton that it was not. He rammed the point home:

255

'I put it to you that it is abundantly clear they were not the same.'

The defence counsel also asked how during that particular reconstruction the chair had been over the unmarked bloodstain, when there was no carpet laid.

'The police cannot point to the surveyor's plan as the bloodstain is not marked on it.'

The defence counsel pointed out that the last known sighting of the axle was in 1965. He queried whether it had actually been attached to the body; that nobody knew that it had been tied to the body. 'Would you expect the body to be floating with that axle tied to it? I put it to you it was never on the body at all. It's a classical example of thinking up a theory and putting evidence to it. I submit the axle was there by pure chance and when found by the diver it was treated by the police as being connected to the body and everything started from there.

'Can you say this axle was on that body as a weight? It's almost certain that the body was held by the bedspread which was jammed up against the tree and held to it by wire.'

This was, of course, possible but it would seem to me that Paul Temm was walking at that point on ground as unstable as the Waikato river. It had been established during the trial that Thomas had on at least two occasions dumped rubbish on the Tuakau tip, which was immediately next to the river about two miles from where Harvey's body was found. The premise was that the axle might have been dumped with other rubbish.

More effective, in my view, was his review of the accused's relationship with the dead woman. He talked of the early attempts to court her, of the letters and presents.

'Is there anything to be seen in that of a sinister quality? Is there anything in that which would provoke a cold-blooded murder ten years later? Thomas has said he had never got in touch with her again after Christmas 1962. There was no evidence that he ever called again or telephoned her again or wrote to her again. There was not a single witness to suggest anything to the contrary.

'Mrs Thomas had said her marriage was a happy one and that it took place in 1964. Jeannette Demler had married two years later in 1966. Was he still supposed to be carrying some passion for this woman? It's the point that this whole thing is founded on. There's no proof at all for any reason why this man should do the monstrous thing he is accused of.'

Easily the most controversial aspect of Paul Temm's final address to the jury concerned the possibility the Crewes' death had been caused by murder/suicide. Many dismiss it as a desperate plea from a desperate defence counsel, I do not. What I would criticize Paul Temm for is not establishing firm evidence during the course of testimony that justified such a possible solution. Those who have subsequently criticized the QC for introducing this possibility into the trial would do well to remember that the first person to find that bloodstained farm was Len Demler. His first reaction, repeated a number of times in front of Owen Priest, was that Harvey had murdered his daughter. Now if the father of the dead woman, a man as close to the dead Crewes as anyone was, could come to that conclusion, if the police during the early days of their inquiry could come to that conclusion, it certainly merits close examination. On the basis of this possible solution, the police had told the farmers assisting them in the land search to 'Look up in the trees as you walk. One of them might have hung themselves.' Certainly talking to me over seven years after their deaths it is a solution that Dr Nelson of the DSIR did not rule out. He said: 'We cannot rule out the possibility of murder/suicide.'

Certainly none of the evidence of pathologist Dr Cairns rules out the possibility.

Again from Dr Donald Nelson:

'There is a 60 to 70 per cent chance that the murderer will be the spouse, the ex-spouse or the de facto spouse.'

With those kinds of odds who would dare rule out such a possibility? To return to Paul Temm's final speech:

'It is not open to us to prove who committed this crime. You may finally come to the conclusion on the facts before us it is perfectly reasonable, the police might through all these months be searching for a murderer who no longer exists. There is a distinct possibility that this was a case of murder and suicide.

'It's hard to know sometimes what goes on inside a marriage. Very little is known of this couple. Any disagreements would not be heard because of the loneliness of the house. We know their financial positions were very different. From her savings account she had a substantial amount, but Harvey Crewe had an account of only 34 dollars. This was a wealthy young woman. Isn't it strange that there were no curtains in the living room, baby's room or main bedroom?'

He drew their attention to other singular aspects of the Crewe home then continued:

'You see in all this perhaps financial problems arising between a wealthy wife and a not so wealthy husband.

'Perhaps there was some discussion and sharp words. The injury to Jeannette's face might have come from her husband's fist.'

He theorized that, after an initial argument Jeannette may have left the house, that Harvey had turned on the outside light to look for her and failing to find her returned to the lounge. Reminding the jury of the missing firearm that still remained missing, he wondered if there might not also have been some old ammunition on the farm.

'Perhaps the last act of the drama had been for Mrs Crewe to put the rifle to her husband's head and then shoot herself. Did someone with the interests of the family at heart, to conceal what had taken place, and in the hope it would remain unknown put the bodies into the Waikato? Perhaps so that Rochelle would not know what had happened? Can you say that's impossible?

'You might think from the evidence emerging in this Court, there is something more to be seen than you have been told.'

Referring particularly to the drawn cheques and deposits in the Crewe accounts, details of which he had sought for in vain throughout the period between arrest and trial, Paul Temm, remarked:

'Was it not a great pity that the police had not made a thorough search of the financial records of the Crewes? It could be that the root of the double murder, if it be double murder, lay somewhere in that area.'

Many of the details recorded earlier in this book would have strengthened the theory of murder/suicide. But Paul Temm had only had two months from the Lower Court hearing to dig for information. The interests of justice, it would seem, are often best served by a rush to judgment.

The defence counsel did not know of the recorded instances that demonstrated Harvey had a violent temper; did not know that he did indeed feel disturbed about the imbalance of wealth in the marriage; that Jeannette had expressed regret about this aspect. Paul Temm did not know of the gun that Mrs Batkin had seen in the Crewe house, one that was considered valuable, surely not the gun the police found in the washhouse? Neither did he know what her father's first reaction was. Why was that his immediate reaction?

Clearly for such a theory to be tenable required the involvement of a third party. Clearly a third party was involved. The sighting on Friday and Saturday confirm that third party as a fact.

Of the wire that had been recovered with the bodies Temm reminded the jury that Mr Todd had not been able to say that two pieces of wire came from the same coil, only that they had the same chemical content. He asked:

'How many pieces of gauge 16 wire would there be in a farming community? One ton of metal produces thirty-eight miles of wire. It is a fair inference to draw that large supplies of wire would be delivered to the same store from the same source and would have the same chemical characteristics. How many other farms would have been found to have a similar piece of wire if the police testing had been done thoroughly and methodically?'

It was a very valid point. Including the Thomas farm, wire samples were taken from only eight farms in the Pukekawa area. A strange counterpoint to the sixty-four rifles.

He reminded the jury that it had not been established that the Thomas rifle had fired the fatal bullets:

'That's not the position. Nobody has been able to, or dared to, say that the bullets in the bodies came from this rifle and no other. They could have come from a Remington rifle that was also tested or another untested rifle.'

The one person, of course, who had dared to say that it was the Thomas rifle and none other that had fired those bullets had been David Morris in his final speech.

Temm queries the time of deaths, reminding the jury that Hutton had said more than once that the shootings had happened after television had finished for the evening. Referring to the photographs showing the positions of the chairs and couch he argued against this theory, contending that there was nothing to suggest that the television set had even been switched on that evening. In the defence counsel's view:

'It could have been any time that night they came to their deaths. I suggest it was some time soon after tea and therefore before the ratepayers' meeting.'

Again and again he rightly, in my view, attacked the quality of the police investigation:

'Police investigations were not adequate. They did not have a category for all the rifles of people who were abroad that night in the area to be tested. It is not right for the police to say that because someone was at the ratepayers' meeting they were not guilty.'

He was working on the assumption that the Crewes died before the meeting. The Crown worked on the assumption that they died after the meeting. No evidence has ever been revealed that gives any clear indication of the time they died. I have discovered such evidence. It was known to the police and, like so much else, suppressed.

Turning to the Charles case, the 'most crucial piece of Crown evidence', Paul Temm trod a delicate line. In his own mind he was quite convinced that it had been planted, that it was a fabricated piece of evidence. To say so would have been to run a grave risk. It is well known that when allegations of that kind are made in a courtroom, no matter how justified, the risk of alienating the jury is very great. Jurors, who will accept that there is corruption in all professions, in all walks of life, very frequently give to the police officers they listen to an infallibility which is unreal. It only requires the slightest suggestion and the Crown will protest about 'wicked unfounded allegations'.

Moving into this dangerous area, Temm first reminded the jury of the photographic enlargements that indicated significant differences in firing-pin marks. An expert in the witness box indicating from his own microscopic examination of those cartridge cases the different features would have strengthened this argument. He was on stronger ground when he asked:

'How did it get where it was found? Three thorough searches of the area. Would you expect it to be buried under the surface? If it fell from the rifle of a marksman and was ejected and flung out as suggested, it would be there to be seen by the police.' He cited the evidence of DSIR scientist Rory Shanahan that he would have expected more corrosion on a case that had been outside for four months.

'Police evidence against the accused on 26 October involved the axle, the wire, the possibility of a rifle, and some vague connections between Jeannette and the accused. The finding of the cartridge case had been a critical piece of evidence for the police. The case had been found on 27 October, the search for the murder rifle was stopped at 3 o'clock on 28 October and Mr Shanahan looked at three cases on the 28th, and fired 14 more bullets on the 29th. His testing was not completed till the 29th and yet the search for the rifle was stopped on the 28th.'

This was as near as Paul Temm was prepared to go in front of that jury to indicate that the case was, in his view, planted.

Of the accused, his counsel observed: 'He is a man of almost guileless simplicity. A less honest man would have hedged with the police. Instead he has been completely truthful in his dealings with the police.'

Of the attack that had been made on Vivien Thomas, Paul Temm said to the jury:

'There is a wholesome quality about Mrs Thomas that almost radiates from her. Theirs is a happy marriage and they sleep in the same bed. In all probability the man who did this thing must have taken several hours. Mrs Thomas has said that she is a light to moderate sleeper. Wouldn't she have known if her husband was out? Do you think that woman, if she had known her husband had been out, do you think that woman, if she had known her husband had done that, would go back and lie alongside that man? If she had compassion for the baby and had gone back to feed it as the Crown stated, do you think she would have gone back to this man if he had killed these two?

'This man is innocent, and if he is convicted he will

be done wrong, in my submission, which can never, never be put right.'

All that remained on that afternoon of 2 March 1971, was Mr Justice Henry's summing up to the jury.

For sixteen days the jury had listened to 96 witnesses; they had seen 163 exhibits. Nightly they had returned to the Station Hotel. There had been the police-supervised bus trips to Maraetai, to the hot pools of Parakai, boat trips to the One Ton Cup races and to Motuihe Island, excursions to the Mercury Theatre, trips to the movies, and always the entire twelve, always with at least two police officers. Totally cut off from their families, they had to varying degrees closely followed the ebb and flow of the trial. Soon they would have to sing for their many suppers by returning a just verdict. First there were to be the final words from Mr Justice Henry.

The judge's final speech will be found verbatim at the end of this book. When I interviewed Sir Trevor Henry I asked him for his personal evaluation of a number of the central participants in the trial. Of Crown Prosecutor David Morris, he said:

'Morris is a good counsel. A fine keen mind. His trouble was that he was too gentle. He lacked the killer instinct.'

Those who are familiar with the performances of David Morris in the courtroom may gasp at that evaluation. I have watched this man in action and he is ruthless. I find the former judge's evaluation illuminating, not of David Morris, but of Sir Trevor Henry. In his final speech he gave not only Morris but the entire court a definitive example of 'killer instinct'. As a closing speech from the prosecution, I feel it could not be bettered; as a speech designed to ensure that only one possible verdict could be reached by the listening jury it was superb. The trouble is that it was coming not from David Morris, but from the trial judge. In terms of a summing-up favourable to the Crown's point of view, I have only ever once seen an example to top it: Lord Chief Justice Goddard's speech in the trial of Craig and Bentley. That too ended in a verdict that is now widely regarded as a miscarriage of justice. During the course of my discussion with Sir Trevor he observed: 'I expressed no opinion at any stage on any part of the evidence. A judge of course is entitled to express an opinion but it would be wrong to do so and then qualify it with: "Of course it is a matter for you".'

If the reader cares to he may count up the seventy times that Sir Trevor used the expression: 'Of course it is a matter for you' or a similar qualifying term.

In fairness to the judge, it should be recorded that he dismissed what the Crown had put forward as a motive for the murders, as he remarked to me:

'I do not believe that any real motive for the murders was established by the Crown. I referred to the interest that Thomas had shown in Jeannette Crewe some years before his marriage as "early background". That's all it was, no more. Certainly not a motive.'

He also dismissed the evidence of Eggleton, the jeweller. He had waited for the defence ace on that aspect and it had not come; nevertheless he considered that evidence as 'dubious and suspect' and made no reference at all in his closing address.

Clearly Mr Justice Henry believed that Rochelle had been fed. In view of the fact that all the evidence on that aspect that had been presented pointed to that conclusion, he could have reached no other. The judge's summing-up (in Appendix 5) contains the clearest indication that the person responsible was Vivien Thomas. The trial within a trial had succeeded beyond the wildest expectations of the Crown. Yet talking to me Sir Trevor said:

'I do not believe that Vivien Thomas fed the baby. If Thomas killed them and that baby was fed, then Thomas fed the baby. But that assumes he did it. I think whoever killed them acted alone.'

During his final speech the judge made powerful use of the alleged remark by Thomas about the brush and comb set being still wrapped up for all he knew. Sometimes Mr Justice Henry referred to it as 'an unwrapped gift', sometimes it was 'still wrapped up' which must have added to the jury's confusion, but the judge's point came over with crystal clarity:

'Now when Harvey's body was recovered there was a blanket near it, and according to Mrs Crewe senior, the bedspread, call it what you may, was usually in the spare bedroom, and I draw your attention back again to what I have already mentioned, that that was in a place in a room where the unwrapped gift was found. Is it possible that the accused has in some unguarded moment given himself away? By itself, of course, this would carry little weight, but you ought to bear it in mind.'

It was powerful, very powerful. I pointed out to Sir Trevor that subsequent to those remarks it had been established that Arthur Thomas had been told by Detective Parkes on 12 August that the brush and comb set were still wrapped up. And that he allegedly reiterated this remark to Detective Johnston on 13 October. The former judge was aware of this development.

'Yes, the alleged remark was significant at the first trial but in view of the evidence of Detective Parkes at the second trial the remark becomes irrelevant.'

The second trial lay well in the future as again and again Mr Justice Henry returned to the brush and comb set remark. After rightly criticizing, in my view, the defence attempt to challenge the expert testimony that the Charles case had come from the Thomas rifle with the aid of photographs instead of experts the judge stated:

'Please do not think I am suggesting it, but you may well think that any suggestion of the planting of a shell has little merit or validity.'

In late 1977, during our discussion Sir Trevor said:

'The cartridge case that was found in the Crewe garden may well have been planted. I do not think it was, but one cannot rule out that possibility.'

Early in his speech to the jury Mr Justice Henry said to them:

'You must, of course, always bear Mr Demler in mind, and he must be excluded before you can convict the accused and, as I have told you, so must every other reasonable possibility.'

Clearly the reasonable possibility of planting was excluded from the judge's mind during his summing-up. Clearly also was Mr Demler, for very late in his speech he devoted as will be seen considerable comment to the fact that Arthur Thomas had taken no part in the searches for the Crewes. Completely absent is any comment about Demler's own non-appearances in the searches for his daughter and son-in-law.

Mr Justice Henry was most certainly a strong judge in the classical sense of that term. I have discussed with many who sat through that speech their views on it. Many were so libellous they cannot be recorded. Here is just one opinion. That of a man called Ted Smith, a Pukekawa farmer and neighbour of the Thomas family:

'I sat there and listened to Mr Justice Henry summing up. I could not believe my ears the way he was distorting evidence, slanting it towards only one possible verdict. I wished at that moment that I had had on me the medals they pinned on me during the Second World War. I wanted nothing more than to go up to that judge and slap those medals on his desk and tell him that if this was democracy, if this was what I had fought for then you can stick it, and you can stick these medals with it. I have always believed in the justice system. Always believed in the integrity of the law, the honesty of the police. I sat there during the trial and listened and watched, and as I did, one by one, those beliefs were stripped away from me.

'If God had stood up and objected, Judge Henry would have fined him for contempt of court and put him in jail for thirty days.'

Ted Smith would be the first to admit that he is not an intellectual. This is no Rhodes scholar or a man who can drop the neat clever Latin phrase. To me he is much more. He is the very bread of the life of this country. His name, like the man, is so average as to be a cliché. Such men represent to me all that is good in New Zealand. The justice system, as Ted calls it, is for men like him. When judges speak to convicted people about society having to be protected from them, it is the Ted Smiths of this country that the judges have in mind when they say 'society'. His reaction has a wide and deep significance. In terms of the Thomas case it also had a highly pertinent one. Many felt exactly the same as this man and their feelings were to produce a powerful catalyst. One so powerful, that it has shaken the Establishment of New Zealand to its roots.

The jury retired to consider its verdict. To many that verdict was a foregone conclusion. Vivien Thomas watched as crates of drinks were wheeled into the Crown Prosecutor's office.

'I didn't object to them having a drink, but to flaunt it in front of everybody standing around waiting for the jury to return. To hear them saying "Let's celebrate". It wasn't very nice.'

The celebration was barely premature. In a little under two hours, the jury were back. The verdict was guilty on both counts. There was not a great deal of reaction from the packed court, a couple of whispered 'Oh no's' from two women. The judge asked Arthur Thomas if he had anything to say and Paul Temm rose to say that in view of the injunction on the judge there was nothing the defence could usefully add. He was referring to the statutory life sentence, which was then passed by Mr Justice Henry.

As they left the Supreme Court, some of the

267

bitterness that was within some of those residents of Pukekawa welled up. Two of the police team walked by. Angry comments were shouted at them. One Pukekawa farmer invited Bruce Hutton to 'come outside'. The farmer obviously thought a fight might settle the matter. Hutton ignored the offer. Neither he nor the farmer realized that the fight, far from ending, was only just beginning.

I think the final word on that first trial should be from the man who dominated it, Mr Justice Henry. During my interview with him he said:

'It was to my mind a local murder. No stranger could have gone on to that farm, committed a double murder and carried out the various acts that were unquestionably carried out. How all that was achieved by the murderer I will never know. No-one saw or heard anything. It defies belief.

'It was truly extraordinary that there was no forensic evidence to link Thomas to the murders. No prints, no hair, no blood. They usually leave some trace somewhere. But in this case not a single thing anywhere. No clothing of Thomas destroyed, and whoever did it must have been covered in their blood at some stage. It defies belief.'

6

The Hunt Ball

The clothes that Vivien Thomas had brought every day to the Auckland Supreme Court for her husband to change into were once again put away in a cupboard on the farm.

The day after the verdict Vivien went to see Arthur, this time not at the remand prison of Mount Eden, but his new home, Paremoremo maximum security prison. During the course of the visit the man whom twelve of his 'peers' had decided was responsible for murdering Harvey and Jeannette Crewe broke down. Crying, he told her that all his life was gone. That he had only lived for Vivien, his parents and the farm.

While the market gardeners of Pukekawa pondered over their sweetcorn and their gherkins, while the farmers milked or fed their stock and wondered, the rest of the nation began to consider the trial of Arthur Thomas. Even in those first few days after the verdict many people far removed from Pukekawa had doubts. Telephone calls began to come into local radio stations until eventually callers were asked to stop ringing on 'The Thomas Case'. Other elements of the media saw a very newsworthy story. It was quite clearly considered by certain sections of the press and television that there was a ball to be had with this story. Very quick off the mark was the newspaper *8 o'clock*. Its edition following the jury verdict was headlined:

PUKEKAWA BACKS MRS THOMAS:
MY MAN'S INNOCENT.

It was the opening shot in what was to become yet another bizarre episode in an already uniquely bizarre murder case.

While the then Chief Justice of this country, Sir Richard Wild, was telling the Auckland Chamber of Commerce on 19 March 1971: 'The world is changing, and the law must change with it,' many of his fellow countrymen and women were forming the opinion that with regard to the trial of Arthur Thomas, the law was in need of a few immediate changes. Ironically at almost exactly the same time as Sir Richard was speaking, Auckland barrister Peter Williams was reviewing his profession in rather more critical terms. Talking to a Rotary club at Te Awamutu this man who Bruce Hutton described to me as 'very, very clever, good thinking, radical but clever' fairly lashed into some aspects of the law. One of the facets that particularly distressed Peter Williams was:

'The prosecution might have some information of value to the defence, which it does not bring forward because it's not in the prosecution's interests. The names and addresses of witnesses who are not called by the police should be made available as early as possible to the defendants, who may utilize these witnesses if they wish.'

What made these statements by the Chief Justice and the barrister doubly ironic was that in the years that followed them, both men would be drawn deeply into the Thomas case.

Public disquiet at the verdict was showing in a number of ways. Pamphlets attacking the verdict were distributed in the streets by late March. Inspector Hutton and his officers promptly seized them. What concerned him was that the appeal had still to be heard. He clearly considered that the leaflets might influence the appeal and also that they were in contempt. Under our legal system you are only allowed to criticize a legal decision after appeal. This ensures that you cannot

270

object to the horse bolting until he is in the freezing works.

The appeal was heard in the first week of May. There were three grounds on which Paul Temm appealed on behalf of his absent client, incarcerated in Paremoremo. The first was that Mr Justice Henry had failed to put the defence case adequately. The second was that the judge had failed to direct the jury correctly on the standard of proof to be applied on circumstantial evidence. The third ground was that the trial judge had been wrong in ruling that the evidence of psychiatrist Kenneth Newton was inadmissible.

With regard to the first ground, failure of the judge to put the defence adequately, Paul Temm pointed out to the Appeal Court in Wellington that: 'His Honour summed up the defence case in only five lines, which was rather inadequate considering the attention given to the prosecution's case.' Temm also argued that the absence of motive in the Crown's case should have been strongly put by Mr Justice Henry to the jury. That the Thomas alibi had been given short shrift in the summing-up. That the judge had 'brushed it aside'. That the reasonable possibility that the accused's rifle could have been used by someone else, without Thomas's knowledge, was ignored.

David Morris and David Baragwanath appeared for the Crown to support the conviction. Quoting his opening address at the trial, Morris submitted that the Crown were not greatly concerned with establishing a motive. One can only wonder, if that was so, why people like Mrs Batkin were called. Why statements about fires and burglary were made. Why policeman after policeman gave evidence about the friendship of Arthur and Jeannette. The aspect of the brush and comb set and the 'It could still be wrapped up for all I know' remark were discussed. Temm complained to the Appeal Court that the judge had unfairly weighted that aspect against Thomas. When David Morris submitted that Mr Justice

Henry had qualified his remarks with 'that is a matter for you to decide', he drew from one of the appeal judges, Mr Justice Turner, the observation:

'A trial judge cannot take refuge after making an unfair remark by saying "but that is for you to decide." In this instance the trial judge has only put forward the one interpretation on the remark and this was unfavourable to the accused.'

Smartly retreating, Morris agreed that it was perhaps an unfortunate omission by Mr Justice Henry but he submitted that it did not invalidate the whole summing-up.

If one removes from that final speech every statement by the judge that is preceded or followed by 'of course it is a matter for you', there would be no case for the Crown left.

It is very rare in my experience for this first ground of appeal to succeed. The regularity with which it is pleaded is only matched by the regularity with which appeal courts reject it. There are of course exceptions, most of which can be found in case law as precedent.

The reader will find in my book *To Encourage The Others* a verbatim report of Lord Goddard's summing-up in the trial of Craig and Bentley. After publication of that book there was a debate in the House of Lords, initiated by Lord Goodman. Quoting extracts from Lord Goddard's summing-up, he stated that the speech was a disaster and the result of a mental aberration. Yet in 1953 Derek Bentley's appeal judges found the speech 'a model of perfection'. Bentley was hanged a few weeks later. I can see echoes of those British appeal judges in the remarks of the president of the Court of Appeal to whom Temm put his points. The president was Mr Justice North.

Paul Temm cited the evidence of Detective Keith concerning the remark he allegedly overheard: 'If they think I am guilty, I am and that's that.' He pointed out the different version the police officer had given to the defence at the Lower Court, a version that was confirmed at the Supreme Court. No mention was made by Mr Justice Henry of the differing versions. Temm submitted that His Honour had ignored the doubt cast on this evidence. Mr Justice North rejected this submission and stated that the present case involved a brutal murder, many months of searching to find the bodies and the judge should be very careful in considering the evidence. 'He should not let anyone off lightly.' The first ground of appeal failed:

'Having studied the summing-up carefully we are of the opinion that there is really no substance in this complaint.'

The appeal also considered that the trial judge had dealt fairly with the 'somewhat slender evidence as to the existence of a possible motive for the crimes'.

The third ground, the judge's refusal to allow the evidence of psychiatrist Dr Newton, was also tossed out. His evidence would have been that the accused did not have an obsession for Mrs Crewe. This 'obsession' had been the keystone of the Crown's theory about 'motive' during Morris's opening address. The appeal judges considered that, if the jury felt the accused's attitude toward Jeannette during her lifetime was at any stage relevant, then he himself was best able to depose that very fact and to rebut Crown evidence. Thus an accused can only answer allegations made by lay people such as Mrs Batkin with his own lay opinion; he may not call an expert.

Temm had complained to the Appeal Court that Mr Justice Henry had not dealt adequately with his contention in his final speech about the possibility of murder/suicide. The appeal judges expressed surprise that he raised such a theory and felt it would have been immediately rejected by the jury. It might well have been, particularly as Mr Justice Henry had inverted what Paul Temm had said. Temm had argued about the possibility of Jeannette killing Harvey and then herself.

273

As will be seen in the judge's final speech he reversed this and had Harvey killing Jeannette and then himself.

Mr Justice Henry freely admitted to me that he had been unable to hear Paul Temm talking on this aspect and only realized after the verdict that he had inverted the defence counsel's contention.

The second ground for appeal – 'That the trial judge had failed to direct the jury correctly on the standard of proof to be applied to circumstantial evidence' – was also rejected and in doing so, the appeal judges made a decision with far-reaching consequences. Their ruling is now in the law books. It is now precedent on how circumstantial evidence should be evaluated. Arthur Thomas has now found himself a place in law.

'In a case depending on circumstantial evidence the jury is not bound to proceed by a series of separate steps, weighing each item of evidence separately, and requiring each item to be proved beyond reasonable doubt before relying on it in arriving at their verdict: it is "the essential factual components of the crime" that must be proved beyond reasonable doubt, and "it is the totality of the narrative to which the formula 'beyond reasonable doubt' applies (*R. v. Thomas* 1972, N.Z.L.R. 34, 38)." While each juror must be convinced on "every essential element of the crime charged" including in some cases particular facts without which the Crown case must fail, it is not necessary that they should agree collectively on the circumstantial facts on which they individually rely (per Turner J., p. 41). (See also *Essays in Criminal Law in New Zealand*, 1971: Sweet and Maxwell, pp 72–4.)'

In my view this is a highly dangerous ruling. Put simply and relating it to the Thomas case it means this. And it should be remembered that 'the essential factual components of the crime' were not defined by Mr Justice Henry. When that jury retired to consider their verdict a situation like this may have occurred:

1st Juror: You know they've not proved it was his gun that fired the fatal bullets.

2nd Juror: Well, if it wasn't his, whose was it? I'm sure it was his gun. Mark you, I think that cartridge case they found in the flowerbed is bloody suspicious. I think that might have been planted.

1st Juror: Planted? Who planted it then?

2nd Juror: I dunno. Could have been the police. Could have been someone trying to frame him.

1st Juror: No, I can't accept that. Police don't go around planting evidence. I'm not sure about those fatal bullets though, you heard what they said. Could have come from some other gun.

2nd Juror: They came from his gun all right, I'm sure of it. What was it Morris said? 'The bullet that killed Harvey came from this gun.'

1st Juror: He also said that cartridge case did.

And so it continues, until an odd kind of agreement is reached. Neither juror can agree on *both* pieces of evidence. Eventually a 'Well, I think they proved the bullets and you think they proved the cartridge case so in a way they've proved both things' situation arises. A third juror might have rejected both of those pieces of evidence but have been heavily swayed by Eggleton's evidence regarding a bloodstained mucus-covered watch. Indeed a man claiming to have been a member of the jury phoned lawyer Kevin Ryan and said precisely that.

Paul Temm lost the appeal on all grounds. He wanted to press on, to take the case to the Privy Council in Great Britain. The question of the importance of each individual item of circumstantial evidence was one that affected the entire Commonwealth. He felt totally sure that he could persuade the Privy Council to throw out that Appeal Court judgment. He never got the chance. The case was taken from him by the Thomas family.

'I suppose they lost confidence in a two-time loser,'

he ruefully observed to me. The man was hurt by the treatment he received. The hurt still shows.

Paul Temm's final involvement with the case was dramatic. It was the stuff that fiction-writers dream of:

'I had been in Wellington. This was after the trial. After the appeal had been dismissed. My secretary phoned to say a man who refused to leave his name was telephoning continuously. She thought it had something to do with the Thomas case. No reason, just a feeling. I rang the man. His name was Graham Hewson. I just wished to God that I had had that man in the witness box during the trial. I went to see Hewson and eventually obtained from him a sworn affidavit. I believe Hewson. I'm sure he was telling the truth. He had sieve-searched in the Crewe garden in August. He'd helped the police. One of the flowerbeds that they sieve-searched then was the one they found the Charles case in during October.'

Having taken Hewson's affidavit Paul Temm then handed it to the man the Thomas family had chosen to replace him, Kevin Ryan.

By now the Hunt Ball was in full swing. The tabloid press of New Zealand, sensing a growing undercurrent of unease at the verdict amongst the public, came to the party with a vengeance. *Truth* newspaper 29.6.71:

VIV'S FIGHTING FOR HER MAN

'HE'S INNOCENT'

'I EVEN MADE TEA FOR THE POLICE'

The *Sunday Times* 20.6.71:

BLOOD-SOAKED FARMHOUSE:

CYCLE OF A DOUBLE SLAYING.

ARTHUR WAS 'GOOD BLOKE'

CARTRIDGE CASE A KEY

The *Sunday News* 25.7.71:

'LAY OFF OR BE KILLED'

This one referred to death threats that had been made to a private detective firm who were considering making further investigations into what the *Sunday*

News called 'the slaying' of the Pukekawa farm couple Harvey and Jeannette Crewe.

The fight that that unknown farmer from Pukekawa had offered Bruce Hutton in the foyer of the Supreme Court was now reaching national proportions. *Truth* newspaper showed in particular a total commitment to the argument that there should be a retrial. It told its readers on 17 August 1971: '*Truth* will continue to inquire into the Thomas affair until it feels that justice has been served.' Various aspects of evidence that appeared unresolved were seized on by *Truth* and other newspapers. Headlines screamed: 'THOMAS: GOLD WATCH RIDDLE' and 'GUNS NEGLECTED' and 'POLICE IGNORING THOMAS MURDER MUDDLE'.

A retrial committee was formed, headed by Vivien Thomas's uncle, Pat Vesey. He had made a brief appearance during the first trial, testifying on behalf of Arthur Thomas that there was a profusion of used .22 cartridge shells lying around the farm, the premise being that anyone could have picked one up and dropped it into a Crewe flowerbed. He little realized when he formed that retrial committee in July 1971, the years of frustration that lay ahead for him and the other committee members.

Members of the public began sending cash donations to the retrial committee. Quite suddenly the name of Arthur Thomas was on everyone's lips. While he remained locked in a maximum security prison the debate raged in clubs, pubs, offices, from Whangarei and Auckland in the north to Christchurch and Dunedin in the south. Nowhere was there greater debate and argument than in the small settlement where it had all begun, Pukekawa.

Pukekawa's division burst out into the open. Those who supported the verdict, including some who had been witnesses for the Crown like the jeweller Eggleton and the poultry farmer Priest complained of

277

intimidation and harassment. Eggleton, it was alleged, had actually been subjected to bodily threats unless he changed his testimony. Owen Priest talked to the press of cars that drove slowly past his farm, stopped, then accelerated away. To combat the retrial committee, another emerged. It included farmers Ian Spratt and Priest. They were convinced the verdict was just and asked the press to approach the issue objectively. Both groups denied there was a vendetta. Both groups denied they were harassing the other. Shots were fired up Ian Spratt's driveway. Other shots were fired at the home of Ted Smith. Julie Priest complained that she was being followed when shopping in nearby Pukekohe.

Inspector Hutton and some of his men moved back into the area. Hutton defended the case that the police had assembled against Thomas. He also said he intended to give the Crown witnesses full protection. Regarding protection for people like Ted Smith and his wife and children he made no statement. He said that the identities of a number of the culprits were known, yet strangely there were no arrests. While a French medium offered his services, an Auckland medium instructed the supporters of Thomas to look in the bush on Len Demler's property for a rifle.

The very frightening aspect for the citizens of Pukekawa, who significantly locked their doors at night, took on elements of farce when the *Sunday Times* on 8 August published a photograph of a smartly dressed gentleman crouched and peering through fieldglasses over open countryside. The caption underneath read: 'One of the persons observed by the police on the Demler property and suspected of harassing Crown witnesses from the murder trial.' As the circulation battle hotted up *Truth* gleefully reproduced the photograph the following week plus the confirmation they had obtained from Bruce Hutton that the man in the photograph was in fact a policeman.

Old-age pensioners, young children and wealthier

people sent their cents and dollars to the retrial committee; and Detective Inspector Hutton told the press that the file on who fed baby Rochelle was not closed. He added:

'The child was obviously fed during the time between the killings and when she was found.'

The New Zealand *Weekly News* published a double-page spread entitled: VIVIEN THOMAS: 'MY HUSBAND IS INNOCENT'.

Petitions headed 'LET RIGHT BE DONE' came out of Waiheke.

Other papers cited the Mareo case as justification that a convicted murderer could obtain a second trial.

Television crews, radio teams, newspaper reporters and most of all sightseers roamed through the lanes of Pukekawa.

More official petitions were distributed by members of the retrial committee.

While all this furore and much more was exploding, life, normal, sometimes dreary, everyday life had to be lived. The cows on the Thomas farm, singularly unimpressed that the woman who tended them, had become overnight a personality, demanded to be milked. With the aid of sister-in-law Lyrice and brothers-in-law Lloyd and Desmond Vivien Thomas, in between posing at the farm gate for a magazine, or on a tractor for a newspaper, got on with the essential job of running the farm. There was also the routine of the weekly visits to Paremoremo prison. While some members of Pukekawa attempted to establish the innocence or guilt of Thomas with the aid of fortune-tellers, clairvoyants, spinning glasses and ouija boards, the two people who knew the truth met in what Governor Hobson described to me as 'the end of the road, for any prisoner'.

When the retrial committee tested rifles, but would not tell the press why, when they dug up the Thomas farm tip and declined to say what they were digging for, one man at least knew – Inspector Bruce Hutton. He had an excellent intelligence service operating in Pukekawa. As fast as the retrial committee came up with an idea, Hutton moved to combat it. In case any reader wonders how I know this, the ex-inspector told me.

Clearly it was open invitation to this particular Hunt Ball. A great many people were running around in ever decreasing circles in the hunt for 'the real murderer' or 'the mystery woman'. Yet, in truth no *real* hunt for either person was ever undertaken. The retrial committee was totally concerned with destroying the case that had been built against Thomas. If the same amount of energy, time and effort had gone into establishing exactly who had killed the Crewes I believe Thomas would have been released from prison years ago, with a full pardon.

When the *Sunday News* attempted to interview members of the jury they were promptly threatened with legal action by Solicitor-General R. C. Savage, QC. He effectively gagged them.

The press gag by the Solicitor-General is a clear indication that the pressure was beginning to bite. The newspapers that had taken up the issue had many readers. People who read newspapers also vote.

Attacking its rival in the Thomas stakes, *Truth* called the action of the *Sunday News* irresponsible and backed the Solicitor-General. Clearly the very important issue of press censorship did not occur to the then editor of *Truth*.

Internal newspaper politics aside, the popular press kept up an unremitting campaign on behalf of Thomas. It was by late 1971 the most controversial murder case in the history of New Zealand.

In August 1971, Vivien Thomas had finally told her parents in Farnham, Surrey, that their son-in-law had been convicted of a brutal double murder. In the same month yet another television team came to Pukekawa.

The group interviewed were either members of the retrial committee or people who believed in the innocence of Arthur Thomas. Amongst them was Margaret Smith. She talked on television of the effect the whole case was having on the children in the district, how it was discussed in the schools. This drew upon her the ire of at least one local headmaster who insisted that none of his schoolchildren discussed the affair. Palpable nonsense. It was not only discussed – it became part of the school curriculum. One end-of-term exam at Onewhero secondary school had as the subject of its comprehension test: 'Arthur's dump'. In the same English paper the pupils were asked to write an essay; among the subjects they could choose from were 'Prison: Punishment or Reform?' 'The Power Of The Press' and 'Capital Punishment'.

In September 1971, the flowering ex-typist from Farnham spoke at a lunchtime forum to the students of Auckland University; also speaking were Pat Vesey and the man who so long ago had insisted that Thomas get a lawyer, farmer Brian Murray.

The pressure was mounting, the screw tightening. Trajectory tests that illustrated the improbability of a cartridge case flying backwards nearly sixteen feet tightened it just a little bit more. Friction between members of the retrial committee on the best way to proceed loosened it again.

There was further friction on the Thomas farm between Vivien and the members of the Thomas family who were helping her, though this was not made public. There was further friction in the home of many in Pukekawa. The strain was beginning to tell. Margaret Smith's relations, for example, were critical of the fact that she appeared to be spending more time collecting signatures on petition forms than she did looking after her children. What primarily mattered to both of these women, Margaret and Vivien, was 'the cause'. They and many others were determined that there should be a retrial, that justice should finally be seen to be done. By October over 20,000 signatures had been collected on the petition forms.

While *Truth* attacked the *Sunday Times* for being first critical and then capitalizing on the Thomas case, and a former member of the retrial committee attempted to bring a private prosecution against three Crown witnesses, alleging perjury, the people of New Zealand kept on signing petition forms.

As *Sunday News* columnist Odette Leather rightly observed in an article published on 12 September: 'The trial of Arthur Thomas has ended but in its stead a strange new trial has begun. The defendant in this instance is "the system".'

Even more pertinently she observed: 'Allegations quite serious in their implications have been made but the defendant remains silent.'

In mid-November a petition asking for a retrial for Arthur Thomas was presented to the then Governor-General Sir Arthur Porritt. With the petition went 22,000 signatures, all collected by a handful of people within the space of a few months. Also with the petition went the reasons why a second trial was being asked for. They took the form of a number of sworn affidavits. There were a considerable number, but clearly the most important was that from Graham Hewson.

While the Executive Council pondered, articles and stories on the case continued to stream from the presses. One that should take a Pulitzer Prize for the most ridiculous heading read: THE GUILTLESS-NESS OF ARTHUR THOMAS. AN OBJECTIVE APPRAISAL by Stephen Chan. The article was as 'objective' as the heading.

On 19 December Acting Minister of Justice David Thomson announced that the case would be reviewed by former Supreme Court Judge, Sir George McGregor. It was an unusual step to take. Section 406 of the Crimes Act 1961 – and it was under the provisions of this Act that a retrial was being asked for – gives the Governor-General several alternatives, but with an application like that of Thomas these were reduced to one: refer the matter to the Appeal Court. Sir George, as a retired Judge, was not a member of any court. It should have given the retrial committee and Thomas's supporters a whiff of what was to come. It didn't.

Sir George gathered around him the trial transcripts and the Appeal Court records and withdrew to his Wellington home.

Over a year had passed since that moment when Detective Mike Charles had remarked to Vivien Thomas: 'I admire your loyalty.' It had been a twelve months that few can imagine for the quiet, rather prim girl from England. She had become the focal point of the entire campaign mounted on behalf of her husband. She had been subjected to publicity on a scale that is very difficult to comprehend. From the quiet obscurity of a small farm, she had had press and television cameras thrust in her face, her every thought and word recorded. She had watched powerless as her marriage was broken irretrievably. She had been accused in the most clear terms by the Crown Prosecutor of being an accomplice to murder. There had been letters of support but there had been the other kind, always anonymous, of course, saying: 'You should be serving life too, you bitch.' And: 'Get out of our country, you Pommy bastard.' The vivacity shown to the Auckland students masked the reality of the mud and cowshit of her everyday life. She had coped with the strictures from her husband on visiting days about how she should be running the farm; had coped as best she could with the icy silences that so often greeted her in the Pukekawa store. She had a thousand friends but no-one to hold in bed through the long nights. By December 1971 she was taking at her doctor's instructions sleeping pills and tranquillizers. By January 1972, she took a lover.

'I was not looking consciously for anybody or any-thing. It was just a situation that evolved. I think in that three-month period before I went to England that I contemplated marrying . . . in a silly sort of way. Probably because I knew when I left that farm in May 1972, that it was the end of my marriage.'

The brief affair was the beginning of many years of moral blackmail for Vivien Thomas. She wanted to state publicly that her marriage was over, that she desired to seek a new life. Always there were people to say: 'Remember Arthur. Think of the Cause. It will damage our work. You know how people think, they'll assume he must be guilty.' Vivien Thomas was beginning to find by early 1972 that there is more than one form of prison. Strange the way so many of us equate im-morality with criminality.

On 17 February Sir George McGregor's conclusions were known. Not to Arthur Thomas or his wife Vivien. Not to Pat Vesey or Mr Thomas senior, in whose names the petition had been presented. Not even to the legal representatives of the committee. The first people to be told were the news media. Vivien Thomas's first information about the report was obtained from the radio.

The report itself was as inept as the manner in which it had been made public. It was a disaster and was considered to be so by people on both sides of the Thomas case. One quote should suffice here to illustrate that Sir George, the retired judge, should have stayed retired:

'The expert evidence in effect decides that the shoot-ing was done with the accused's rifle.'

I am aware that Sir George McGregor is now dead. Like Voltaire I believe we owe the dead nothing but the truth. His report was riddled with inaccuracies like the one just quoted. We once had a man in Great Britain who produced on behalf of the then government a very similar report on a murder case. In this man's mind, justice had most certainly not miscarried in the case he had been asked to study. The man's name was Scott-Henderson. The case he was studying was that of Timothy Evans. A number of years after that report Evans was granted a posthumous pardon.

When Sir George's findings were made public and his conclusion that with regard to the Thomas case 'there had been no miscarriage of justice', it was considered a shattering blow to the retrial committee. It was nothing of the sort. It was the most perfect ammunition on which to mount a major campaign.

The then Attorney-General and Minister of Justice, the late Sir Roy Jack, expressed his delight with the report. 'Justice had been done,' he told the nation. 'We have been fortunate in having the benefit of a very careful and thorough examination of all the papers made by the Hon. Sir George McGregor, a recently retired Supreme Court Judge.' Sir Roy felt that McGregor had been the 'ideal person' for such a task. His homily concluded with:

'The decision of the Governor-General in council has been taken after consideration of Sir George's report, and I hope that the public will share my confidence that justice has been done in this case and are now prepared to accept the verdict and the decision of the Court of Appeal.'

It was a vain hope. He knew the legal system itself was on trial.

The retrial committee, newspapers like *Truth* and *Sunday News*, all made it quite plain that they did not believe that justice had been done.

Aspects of the report were torn apart. It was, for example, pointed out that Sir George had, when considering the information laid before him that clearly established the fact that Arthur Thomas did not own and never had owned a gold watch, accepted that evidence and dismissed Eggleton from the proceedings with: 'I am not impressed with the evidence of Eggleton

285

. . . It would seem to me that Eggleton was mistaken. I think this doubtful evidence would not have influenced the jury in its decision.' Sir George had justified his ability to read the minds of the twelve jurors by pointing out that neither judge nor counsel had referred to Eggleton's evidence in their final speeches. As has already been shown, both counsel referred specifically to Eggleton's evidence.

While impassioned pleas that their son was innocent were being made by his parents, people totally unconnected with the family or the retrial syndrome were also expressing private doubts. Among them was the Labour party's spokesman on justice, Dr Martyn Finlay. Then in opposition, he was widely tipped as the Minister of Justice if Labour came to power at the next general election. When I interviewed him he recalled that period for me in the Thomas saga:

'Immediately the first trial was over I was uneasy about it. I obtained the notes of evidence and the judge's summing-up from Paul Temm and read them through with some care. The theory of the louvre shooting worried me. From this very unsteady and strained position he had to shoot with the absolute requirement that the shot be fatal. That seemed to me to be stretching a possibility to breaking point. That was the first flaw I saw in the Crown's case. Logic pointed to the murders having been committed inside the house.'

Of the report by Sir George, Dr Finlay said to me:

'I read his decision with the most profound surprise. It really seemed a totally inadequate job. Just a superficial review. He had not really touched on the essential points at all.'

It was by no means all one-way traffic in early 1972. The retired Supreme Court Judge's report had its supporters, apart from Sir Roy Jack. The *New Zealand Herald* considered Sir George McGregor had 'one of the finest judicial minds in the country'. It editorialized that the handling of 'the Arthur Allan Thomas case in toto is a gratifying exposure of British justice at its best', or rather it considered the detached observer could be excused for thinking that.

In Pukekawa things were getting hotter. Owen Priest's workshop was broken into by people searching for the missing Chennell rifle. Bruce Roddick's home was broken into, presumably by a passing transvestite as the only item stolen was a home perm belonging to Mrs Roddick.

Vivien Thomas, at this stage acting out the role of dutiful wife, continued her weekly visits to prison. Other inmates recognizing her as she left on one occasion shouted out: 'Good on you, Viv' and: 'Get your husband out of here, Viv, he doesn't belong in this place.'

The strain on the woman was beginning to show. At least one doctor advised her that unless she underwent a period of complete rest she would be in Kingseat institution within six months. The treble life of national personality, loyal farmer's wife and lover was taking their cumulative toll.

'I remember around that time coming back from a prison visit, the cattle were wandering around the road. Next week when I went to see Arthur someone had told him and he gave me a rocket. During the first year after his conviction we had a good season. I only lost one cow. The farm went into profit. The cow that died was the first to calve, it died of milk fever. Arthur's comment was: "Well, that's a good way to start the season. If you're going to carry on like that you won't do very well." We didn't lose any more. We had 113 calves. You see, David, what everyone, including Arthur, forgot was that I am a human being. The pressure of the farm work. The prison visits. The press and television interviews. The feeling that I had become public property. You had no life of your own. You had to forget that you were a human being. I had to eat, sleep and breathe "The Arthur Thomas Case". That was the expectation of the Thomas family, the lawyers, the retrial committee and the general public. The hypocrisy disturbed me and screwed me up. It still does. If I had been able to do what I wanted to do in the very beginning and everybody had left me alone I think I would have been all right. It had nothing to do with Arthur's guilt or innocence. I *know* he's innocent and he *knows* he is innocent. We are the only two who *know*. You are the only person that has ever been allowed to interview him. You've interviewed me. What do you think?'

I told Vivien Thomas that my answer to that question would be found in this book.

By May 1972, it was clear to Vivien Thomas that she needed total rest. News from England that her father was ill resolved the problem. She flew back to England. An example of the police enthusiasm about the entire case occurred at Auckland airport. When friends and well-wishers came to see Vivien off, there in the background watching were Bruce Hutton and police officer Abbott.

The police thought they had seen the last of Vivien Thomas just as they hoped they had heard the last of the Thomas case. They were to be doubly disappointed.

With the screw being tightened again by constant press attacks on the McGregor Report and promises at a public meeting by Dr Finlay that if a Labour government was elected later that year and a new trial had not been granted in the interim period he would take steps to facilitate a further application for a retrial to be put before the Court of Appeal, the game was afoot with a vengeance.

Further petitions were made to the Governor-General. With them went the same sworn affidavits that had been previously referred to Sir George McGregor, plus a few new ones. The only new element was that certain members of the retrial committee had carried out corrosion tests by burying cartridge cases for virtually the same period of time that had elapsed from the deaths of the Crewes to the discovery of the Charles case. The petitioners argued with the aid of colour photographs that the cases they had buried then dug up from soil 'adjacent to the Crewe farm' showed very distinct corrosion, unlike the Charles case. At this stage those particular affidavits were not supported by any from a forensic scientist. Clearly the main thrust of the petitioners' arguments was exactly the same: that the affidavit of Graham Hewson indicated the Charles case had been deliberately planted; that Eggleton the jeweller was wrong; that Bruce Roddick's affidavit clearly indicated the person he had seen on the Crewe farm was not Vivien Thomas.

What was rejected in February was accepted in August. The arguments were considered strong enough to justify referring the matter back to the Court of Appeal.

The former Prime Minister of Great Britain, Harold Wilson once remarked that 'a week in politics is a very long time'. Clearly six months in New Zealand politics is an eternity. The Thomas case had become a political hot potato. The decision to refer the issue back to the Court of Appeal was less than three months before the general election of 1972.

If the National party, then in power, hoped to salvage the votes they had undoubtedly lost because of their previous attitude over the case, they were doomed to suffer disappointment. With the issue safely in the limbo land of awaiting a Court of Appeal hearing they were voted out of office in November 1972.

Dr Martyn Finlay duly became the Minister of Justice and Attorney-General in the new Labour government. He had no need to fulfil the pre-election promise he had made, his predecessors had done that for him.

The man who had master-minded that successful application to the Governor-General was Auckland lawyer Kevin Ryan, head of the retrial's legal advisers. In late July while still awaiting the Governor-General's decision, Ryan had arranged for a number of the exhibits from the trial to be sent to Great Britain for examination by Home Office forensic experts. These exhibits included the Thomas rifle, the fragments of bullets recovered from the two bodies, the Charles cartridge case and a DSIR bullet that had been test-fired from the Thomas rifle, two days after Jeannette's body had been recovered from the Waikato river. There was one unfortunate omission from the parcel that was flown to Great Britain: the Remington rifle, commonly known as the Eyre rifle. It did not occur to Kevin Ryan, the DSIR or anyone else that to have given the Home Office experts *both* rifles might have meant an expert conclusion that one was more likely than the other to be the murder weapon.

The Home Office experts were unable to establish that the Thomas rifle was the murder weapon. Of the Charles case the British experts were in no doubt; they were satisfied that it had come from the Thomas rifle. The most significant detail in the report from the British Home Office was that they held 246 .22 firearms with the same rifling characteristics as the Thomas rifle and 15 with the same groove and land width features that they had found on the exhibit bullets. If those 15 guns had been in private hands in Great Britain at the time of the deaths of Harvey and Jeannette Crewe then clearly on the quality of evidence on that specific in the Thomas case the Crown prosecution could have proceeded against any of those fifteen people.

At the same time as the Home Office men in England were considering these items, the public of New Zealand had the opportunity to consider a retrial-committee-backed book on the case written by Terry Bell. It argued the case for a retrial with considerable power. Although presenting in some instances totally illogical arguments – for example: 'One essential

290

ingredient of every murder is motive' which is nonsense – Terry Bell did a fair destruct job on the McGregor Report and an unfair destruct job on Paul Temm. For example, Bell took the QC to task for not calling Arthur's father and brother to give evidence on the axle. Apart from the small matter of the Crown's subpoenas which kept both men tied up until shortly before the trial, if Bell had spent five minutes with Paul Temm he would have very quickly learned why in the final event the QC did not call them. Their statements made to the police in October would have been powerful weapons in the hands of David Morris as he sought to establish a connection between Arthur Thomas and the axle.

At this time, too, elements of the gutter press in this country decided that the real reason Vivien Thomas had gone to England was to have an abortion. Having read many private letters that Vivien Thomas wrote during that period and listened to tape-recordings she sent to friends here and, perhaps more pertinently, probed this aspect in England, it is clear to me that there is not a vestige of truth in the story. Apart from earning a living as a temporary secretary while she was in England, her most exciting moments appear to be when she was babysitting for friends. The fact that according to the Crown Prosecutor of this country a murderer's accomplice was looking after their young ones does not appear to have worried the parents.

One of the letters referred to above contains a particularly poignant passage. It is Vivien's response to the news that she was 'pregnant', courtesy of a fevered reporter's imagination:

'I'll be blessed if I'm going to a doctor for a non-pregnancy certificate etc. I've been examined internally several times when it was necessary and I don't see why I should do this unless the committee wants one.' Then later in the same letter:

'Back to this pregnancy jazz, if the committee wants a doctor to examine me and make a statement, better let me know and I'll get one.'

That was written less than two weeks after she had arrived in England. To me the poignancy is how clearly those remarks illustrate the public property Vivien Thomas had become. Her internal physical examinations determined by gutter press and retrial committees. For the record, the brief love affair that Vivien Thomas had was over before she flew away from this three-ring circus.

To the surprise of the police and the cynics who had asserted that she would never come back, Vivien Thomas returned to New Zealand in October after a five-month stay with her parents. There was no returning to the Pukekawa farm, by then being run by other members of the Thomas family, but what of her marriage? Although in retrospect when we talked in late 1977, Vivien asserted that it was over when she had left the farm in May 1972, she clearly did not feel that when she returned in the October of that year. She had come back to fight – for her husband's freedom and for that marriage. Moving into an Auckland flat the weekly visits to Paremoremo began again as they waited for the referral to be heard by the Court of Appeal. In August 1972, Sir Roy Jack had said that 'no time will be lost in referring 'The Thomas Case' to the Court of Appeal'. It was February 1973 before it was heard. On the fifth day of that month Kevin Ryan got to his feet and called his first and most important witness, Graham Hewson. This man who remarked to me: 'If Arthur Thomas did it I wouldn't want him in prison. I would want him hanged,' was not prepared to see Thomas convicted on what in one crucial area was incorrect evidence. The flowerbed that Detectives Charles and Parkes had sieve-searched on 27 October 1971, solely because that particular bed had not been previously sieve-searched was, on the sworn testimony of Graham

Hewson, sieve-searched in August, two or three days after Jeannette's body had been found.

Graham Hewson said to me: 'I was not prepared to stand by and allow what I knew to be fabricated evidence put against the man.'

His deposition explained why he had not come forward earlier:

'That I did not come forward during the trial because I had given a great deal of information to the police and believed that if I was required to give evidence, the police would contact me. I considered also that if any evidence that I had to give was helpful to the defence this information would have been given by the police to counsel for the defence. I did not know until after the hearing of the appeal that the defence knew nothing of my participation in the search and had not heard of my existence.'

The affidavit went on to explain that ironically it had not been until the Evan Swain booklet had been published that Hewson had seen a photograph of the actual flowerbed that the Charles case had come from. Ironic that the booklet which is little more than a paean for the police should unwittingly result in some of those police officers having to come back into a courtroom and explain the inexplicable.

Opposing Kevin Ryan in that Wellington Appeal Court were the two men who had successfully argued the Crown's case through a lower Court hearing, a trial and an appeal: Morris and Baragwanath.

David Morris got to work on Hewson. He showed him a plan of the area immediately around the Crewe house and asked Hewson to familiarize himself with it. Then pointing to a chalked enlargement of the plan on a blackboard Morris requested: 'Please mark on the plan in blue all the beds within the enclosure.' Hewson duly did. He was then asked to mark the beds that he had sieve-searched; again he obliged. Morris then demonstrated that he had omitted one bed and had not marked as sieve-searched another bed that was. Neither bed was the relevant one where the Charles case had been found but the object of the exercise for the Crown was to demonstrate fallibility, not relevance.

Hewson pointed out that it was now nearly three years since the events in question. Morris chose to ignore that observation. Hewson could have also pointed out that he had first given this information to the defence nearly two years before this cross-examination. Doubtless the Crown Prosecutor would have ignored that too. Morris asked him for the name of the police officer he had helped. Hewson groped for a moment then remarked that it could have been 'Higgins, or something like that'.

Intent on a destruct job Morris asked question after question pertaining to the time lapse between the sieve-search and Hewson coming forward. The Crown Prosecutor clearly felt that newspaper articles would have advised Hewson of exactly where the cartridge case had been found much earlier. It might have helped the Crown's argument if he had produced an article written before the verdict that did this. He did not. The reason was simple; there was none that would have buttressed his argument. Hewson explained that at the time of the trial he was back living in Woodville and reliant on local coverage of the trial.

The police had not been idle since Hewson had first come forward. They had dug into his personal life. They had questioned his wife, his friends, anyone that could give them something 'useful'. Morris then mounted what I consider an unwarranted personal attack on Hewson. The three appeal judges had, before this hearing began, placed a total press ban on the reporting of these proceedings. As they rightly pointed out when announcing the ban any information published might prejudice 'any new trial that may or may not follow from the Court's determination'. This then was a closed court, a secret court. Few then, will have had an opportunity to read any of the testimony. There was only one reason for Graham Hewson's presence in that courtroom and that was to establish if the police had in fact sieve-searched a particular flowerbed on a particular day.

Morris: Did you have a lot of personal worries of your own about this time?

Hewson: Oh, yes.

Morris: These worries extended about this time and when you had been helping at the Crewe farm?

Hewson: Yes.

Morris: Did they include your financial position?

Hewson: Yes.

Morris: Your matrimonial position?

Hewson: No.

Morris: What caused you to worry about your financial position over this period?

Hewson: Everyone has financial troubles.

Morris: Had you not been issued with warrants for debts? Distress warrants?

Hewson: Yes.

Morris: Wasn't one issued against you for $2,000?

Hewson: No.

Morris: What was the largest one?

Hewson: Might have combined to that sum but not one particular one.

Morris: This concerned you?

Hewson: Yes.

Morris: Did you not have to borrow money from Mrs Crewe?

Hewson: No.

Morris: Did she not in fact pay $500 for you, Mrs Crewe senior that is, to a man called Pat Nelson?

Hewson: A lady called Pat Nelson.

Morris: Did she or did she not?

Hewson: Yes, I knew nothing about this for three months.

Morris: Have you repaid?

Hewson: No.

Morris: Did she ask you for it?

Hewson: No.

Morris: Also obtain money from Mrs Knox?

Hewson: No.

Morris: A friend of Mrs Crewe's?

Hewson: No. Mrs Crewe paid up Pat Nelson without me knowing for months.

David Morris then asked a series of questions about the various dogs that Hewson and Harvey Crewe had exchanged or Hewson had sold to his friend. The clear drift was that after the Crewes had died, Hewson had removed dogs from the farm that belonged to Harvey. Morris then returned to more personal aspects of Graham Hewson's life.

Morris: Between the time of this search between 1970 and 1972 have you had domestic trouble?

Hewson: Yes.

Morris: Has that also upset you?

Hewson: Yes.

Morris: I am putting to you over the period of this search and up to now, in fairness to you, you have had money worries and domestic troubles on your mind?

Hewson: That's right.

The 'in fairness to you' may be regarded as somewhat cynical. Some would say the last thing the Crown Prosecutor was doing was being 'fair'.

The domestic troubles that Morris kept alluding to were based on the information that police officers had discovered. Graham Hewson and his wife were separated at the time of this referral, not at the time of the police sieve-search in August 1970; they separated some six months later. The reader may well ask what any of this had to do with the central issue of whether or not a particular flowerbed was sieve-searched on a particular day. It has nothing to do with that central issue. The premise was clear. This man had personal problems, financial and matrimonial.

296

Consider his state of mind. How could a man under that pressure remember sieving a flowerbed? If that kind of legal yardstick was applied daily in our courts we would all be declared unfit and untrustworthy witnesses.

The entire episode is a revealing example of the desperate position both police and Crown Prosecutor found themselves in. I am saddened that the then Chief Justice, Sir Richard Wild, and Mr Justice Richmond and Mr Justice McCarthy sat listening to such blatant attempts by a Crown prosecutor straining to maintain and justify a conviction, and yet made little or no adverse comment.

It was clear that the Crown fully accepted that Hewson had indeed been present and had helped the police in their search of the Crewe gardens. Demonstrably they could not accept his sworn evidence about that particular flowerbed. To have done so would have been virtual admission that the Charles case had been planted; that the piece of evidence that the Crown prosecution had considered the most important of all in their case against Thomas was a fabrication. Thus the man who had assisted the police by giving them detailed information about Harvey and Jeannette Crewe, assisted the police by giving them daily accounts of his conversation with Len Demler, assisted the police in their searches, had to be destroyed. During my interview with Graham Hewson I questioned him about the allegation that he was a dog thief.

'I went to the police. To Len. To Mrs Crewe. I asked all of them what should be done about the dogs. The police were not interested and Len and Mrs Crewe told me to take the dogs back south. Mrs Crewe even came with me when I put them on the train.'

I questioned him very closely about the sieve-searching and asked him if he was absolutely certain in his mind, now, that he sieve-searched that particular flowerbed.

'Yes, I am absolutely certain. There is no doubt in my mind now. There never has been. Along with those police officers, I sieve-searched that bed in August. We did the lot. Those photos showing the shrubs still in place must have been taken before the sieve-search. All the garden plants were removed. We went right round the house. It took several days. We were looking specifically for a cartridge case. Jeannette had been found. It was known that she had been shot with a .22 bullet. It was a .22 cartridge case we were looking for. I went over and borrowed the mower from the Chittys. I was in the car when we collected the sieve from Tuakau. I may have been confused about where we picked that sieve up from. I thought it was a council yard. It turned out to be a company yard. But there is no confusion in my mind about being in that police car with them or with being on the Crewe farm with them. They say we hadn't sieve-searched that particular area but I know bloody well we had. One of the police deliberately planted an entire bullet and case for me to find, for a joke. I was very excited when I found it, then we all had a laugh. I was there all right and they know I was there. Why they said I wasn't, I'll never know. When I gave evidence at Wellington I thought: "Well, there's no dispute about my evidence. It'll be straight-forward." Then Morris got into me about all manner of personal things. I felt awful. It was a terrible experience. He began to make me feel as if I'd committed some crime, that I was on trial. The police seemed to be a good crowd of lads when I was up there helping them. Good blokes. All of a sudden they changed after I came forward to give evidence. Now why should they change? Bruce Hutton came up and spoke to me, as did the others when there was no-one around. This was at the Wellington Court. They were friendly then, told me not to take it personally: "The Crown does this to everyone," they said. They passed it off as a joke.

'According to the evidence of the various police officers, they sieve-search the beds near the house, they then carefully examine the lawn, they then miss a small bed, go out into the paddock, cut the grass and subject the paddock to a very careful search. It's bloody ridiculous to think they would leave those few yards. It's unbelievable.'

Clearly Mr Justice McCarthy and Mr Justice Richmond also found it unbelievable.

Graham Hewson's references to collecting a sieve from Tuakau were subjected to a strong attack during the Court of Appeal hearing. He had contended in his affidavit that he had accompanied three officers in a car when the sieve was collected. He was under the impression it was a council yard, in fact it was the yard of a local company. It did not alter the fact that he had been present at that time but it enabled Morris to make a further assault on Hewson.

George and Ella McGuire of Tuakau had a curious tale to tell the three listening judges. It concerned the jeweller Eggleton, who was a friend of many years' standing. The McGuires had been in Eggleton's shop on 15 December 1970. A local newspaper containing a photograph of Eggleton's two daughters became the subject of some discussion. In the same local paper was a photograph of Arthur and Vivien Thomas. The McGuires asked Eggleton if he knew the couple. He studied the photograph and told them that he did not know them and had never seen them.

Subsequently, when Eggleton had come forward and sworn that Arthur Thomas had brought a bloodstained mucus-covered watch into his shop about a week after the Crewes had died, the McGuires were shocked. They drove to Auckland and in the foyer of the Supreme Court had a conversation with Hutton. According to Mrs McGuire's sworn testimony, Hutton had told her that he 'was not interested'. According to Mr McGuire Inspector Hutton then asked him if he knew where the watch was. When McGuire said he didn't, Hutton had replied that he did and left.

On 6 February Dr Thomas James Sprott took the stand. He had been retained by the defence to give expert opinion on the corrosion or lack of it on the Charles cartridge case. Sprott is an industrial and consulting chemist and analyst from Auckland. A large part of this judicial hearing was taken up with conversations about metal corrosion. The 'experts' had threatened to take over the trial and were now bidding fair to do the same with the appeal hearing. For Dr James Sprott this involvement with the case began as no more than a relatively small task. Over seven years later the case now totally consumes him.

A number of cartridge cases that had been buried by members of the retrial committee and then dug up again had been compared by Jim Sprott with the Charles case. In view of the fact that Sprott's first sight of the Charles case was some two years after its discovery, the corrosion comparison would seem to me to be of little scientific value. As Dr Sprott observed in his affidavit: 'It is regrettable that a detailed report is not available describing accurately the condition of Exhibit 350 when found, and the condition of the earth in which it was found.'

Metal corrosion is not a consistent phenomenon, but Dr Sprott's evidence gave the three judges further food for thought as they considered the now much maligned Charles case.

The evidence of DSIR scientist Rory Shanahan that followed clearly indicates just how well Inspector Hutton's intelligence network of pro-police citizens had functioned in Pukekawa. He had been tipped off about the tests that were being carried out by the retrial committee. 'At the request of the Crown Solicitor' Shanahan had carried out some of his own. His results differed from those of Dr Sprott. The trial by experts had arrived.

On the evidence of the four police officers who had searched the Crewe gardens and paddock on 18 and 19 August, Graham Hewson was an invisible man. He had not been in the police car that picked up the sieve from Tuakau. He had not helped in the sieve searches. Constable Higgins recalled Hewson being 'about the house on the 18th'. Detective Jeffries recalled Hewson searching the roof and that was about it. As far as the four men were concerned he had appeared by some unknown means on the property while they were searching and had subsequently vanished in the same manner.

Eggleton the jeweller brought back to the courtroom more basic issues. Asked whether the evidence of the McGuires was correct he said it was. Asked for an explanation he declared: 'I didn't want her to know what I was doing or how I was going to become involved. I was hesitant about becoming involved at that time.'

Cross-examined by Kevin Ryan, Eggleton stated that he had lied to Mrs McGuire, then lied to Mr McGuire. Further cross-examination revealed that an uncle of Arthur Thomas's who bore a physical resemblance to Arthur had been in and out of Eggleton's shop around the period that Eggleton had been allegedly dealing with the bloodstained mucus-covered watch. The uncle had been chasing a watch repair. It was a hornet's nest.

Those who consider that Arthur Thomas had a fair trial should ponder on this testimony that helped put him inside prison.

When Inspector Hutton, final witness for the Crown's rebuttal, gave evidence he was equally adamant that the evidence of the McGuires was wrong. He recalled a conversation with them outside the Supreme Court but 'she did not refer to the evidence of Eggleton'. He also swore on oath that his conversation with the McGuires had taken place actually while Eggleton was giving evidence, not on a subsequent day. 'The evidence of Mr and Mrs McGuire is mostly untrue.'

The three Court of Appeal judges were obviously intrigued by the evidence of Bruce Roddick and they recalled him for further examination.

On 26 February the Court of Appeal announced its decision. It was a decision without legal parallel in New Zealand's history. 'The order of this Court is that there will be a new trial of the indictment.'

Retrials, as in the case of Mareo, had occurred before, but that had been a retrial of basically the same evidence. A new trial had also been ordered prior to the Thomas case, but the alleged crime was not murder.

The judgment made it clear that the Court were not saying that a miscarriage of justice had occurred. What they were saying was that if the evidence that had been put before them on behalf of Arthur Thomas had been put before the first trial jury that jury might well have come to a different decision.

For the retrial committee, for the press who had campaigned, for Kevin Ryan, for every person who had written or spoken on the case expressing doubts, it was a stunning victory. For the Crown, the police witnesses, the DSIR experts it was a crushing defeat. Joy and anger respectively ran through the ranks of the two camps. That joy would soon be crushed in its turn. That anger would ensure the most appalling travesty of justice ever seen in this country. The verdict was quashed. Arthur Thomas, no longer a convicted double murderer was moved from maximum security Pare-moremo to the remand wing of Mount Eden prison. He was overjoyed, literally speechless. It had been almost two years to the day that he had been convicted and sentenced to life imprisonment. Now after what many considered would be only a formality of a trial he would be a free man. Free to try to repair his marriage. Free to return to his Pukekawa farm. As had been indicated not all shared his delight. Apart from those who had

dedicated themselves to ensuring his successful conviction in the first place there were men in the corridors
of legal power who disagreed and disagreed strongly
with the quashing of the verdict and the order for a
new trial. One such man was the then Chief Justice of
New Zealand, Sir Richard Wild. He had been outvoted
by his two brother judges at the Court of Appeal.
Another who objected in the world of wigs and gowns
was the judge who had been president of the Appeal
Court in front of whom Paul Temm had vainly argued,
Sir Alfred North. Both judges were to take more than
a passing interest in the future events connected with
the Thomas case.

These men and others considered the granting of a
new trial to be an indictment of the judicial system.
Public affirmation by the Court of Appeal that something had perhaps gone seriously wrong in the Thomas
case was viewed by some members of the Establishment
both political and judicial as dangerous precedent.

For two years, judges, barristers, police officers, the
entire system had been subjected to attack and criticism
that was without parallel. Such pressure has its dangers;
it can produce a devastating reaction. It can produce in
men an overwhelming desire to vindicate themselves,
to prove that they were right because by this time
objectivity on both sides had long since been lost. Paul
Temm, now an onlooker in the continuing fight discussed with me some of these aspects:

'You must remember that by the time the second trial
came on the situation was entirely different. By then,
Thomas had faded into the background as far as the
police and the Crown were concerned. The judge had
been vilified, so had Morris, so had Baragwanath, so
had the police. Everybody involved in the case was
under an extraordinary attack. It was by this time a very
personal contest, I think between Morris and Ryan. The
desire for conviction is not common but in that second
trial at least, the desire was there, it was very deep, it

was very personal. By now bigger issues had come up. The whole system of trial by jury was on display and under investigation. That second jury had been, as we all had, subjected to a barrage of newspaper publicity over a very lengthy time. I felt certain that Thomas would be acquitted, that the Crown would have no show of getting anything but possibly a disagreement among the jury. That would be the best they could hope for. I think the defence thought it would be a bus ride and that nobody foresaw the strength and the venom of the Crown case. It was a reaping of the whirlwind.'

Dr Martyn Finlay, then Minister of Justice and Attorney-General, shared Paul Temm's view about the outcome as the second trial approached:

'I was certain that the outcome would be an acquittal, simply on the grounds of doubt. There was so much doubt. For some reason unknown to me the defence did not rely on what was the most salient point, doubt. They tried to introduce other theories which confused the issue. I would have thought it was sufficient to rely on the conflict, on the inherent improbability of some of the material used by the Crown.'

Neither man knew then, or knows now, just how far that 'desire for conviction' would go. It went far. It went in many directions. The Roddick family were one group it touched.

The Crown yet again used the power of the subpoena to keep Kevin Ryan and his colleagues away from key witnesses. One of the many people subpoenaed was Bruce Roddick. He had been an invaluable witness for the Crown during the first trial with his evidence of the mystery woman. His testimony had been the keystone on which the Crown built its unofficial trial of Vivien Thomas.

At the Wellington referral, to the chagrin of the police and the Crown, his evidence had clearly influenced the decision to grant a new trial, but they still

304

kept a tight grip on the young man as the second trial approached.

Detective Johnston appeared in Pukekawa. He wanted Bruce to come up to the Chitty farm with him and show him exactly where he had been standing when he saw the mystery woman at the Crewe farm. Roddick, by now more than a little wary of police techniques, declined to go immediately and arranged to see the police officer the following day. When the police officer returned he found that Roddick was no longer alone. His mother and a family friend were also there. Mrs Roddick explained the reason why to me:

'Bruce phoned us. We were staying up in Auckland, which of course the police knew. They had wanted to get him back on the Chitty farm on his own. He thought they were going to try and pull a fast one, so did we. I drove down to Pukekawa and we were all there waiting when Johnston returned.

'We all went up to the Chitty farm and climbed over the fence. Johnston started walking up to the house, seeking the exact spot where Bruce had been working. He called Johnston back saying: "I wasn't up there. I was here. Near the road. That's where I was." During the second trial they told Bruce they had measured the distance. If they did, they did it after we left.'

Three days before the second trial began David Morris advised Kevin Ryan that he would not be calling Bruce Roddick and consequently he was available for the defence. Lawyers call that 'tactics'.

Prior to the commencement of that trial Allan Thomas remarked to Ted Smith:

'I hope when Arthur is acquitted at this trial that there will be no stigma on the police. I realize that there is no love for them now, particularly among the young people but I hope they do not pursue it any further just because of Arthur. I just want my son out, I don't want the system upset.'

At about the same time, the 'system' was

305

demonstrating just how upset it already was.

Three weeks before the second trial, the names and addresses of the jury panel were made available to the police from the Justice Department of the Auckland Supreme Court. The list had already been scrutinized by Supreme Court staff and anyone with 'certain characteristics' had been removed. Certain people because of their professions or because they have a criminal record are automatically disbarred from jury service. That is common knowledge and such scrutiny is, as the law stands, perfectly proper. What subsequently happened to the list of potential jurors for the second Thomas trial was not proper. What happened to that list is in itself another extraordinary episode in a most extraordinary case.

The task of checking the jury list was given to the Criminal Intelligence Squad. Its normal function would be to check for any convicted person on the list. This work is normally carried out by any member of the squad. Arthur Thomas was accorded VIP treatment; the checking was done by the officer in charge of that section. Extensive inquiries followed throughout the Auckland area. Any person of certain political leanings was taken off the list; any person who might possibly be, no matter how slightly, anti-police, was removed from the list; any person with a family background which could affect their feelings towards the police was removed.

Unless this was an attempt to ensure that the jury would be entirely pro-police one would expect that anyone who might conceivably have been favourably disposed to them would also have been removed. It would in this instance be an expectation that was not realized.

Talking to me about jury lists, Sir Trevor Henry observed.

'The jury list should be available to defence and prosecution at the same time.'

For this second trial, the defence received the jury list one working day before the trial began; three weeks after it was in the hands of the police.

Over ninety names appear on that list. Ryan had to decide in a matter of hours which six jurors he would object to. Unlike the Crown who, by standing down, can object to an unlimited number, defence is only allowed a maximum of six challenges.

As in the first trial, the second trial judge, Mr Justice Perry, (now Sir Clifford Perry) decided that the jury would be kept in isolation throughout the trial. As Paul Temm had objected before him so now did Kevin Ryan. He too was overruled. As in the first trial so now in the second, accommodation for the jury had been booked at the Station Hotel, weeks before this judicial decision.

Before the jury were sworn in, the judge advised the group of over ninety of his decision and invited any of them who felt they might be severely inconvenienced to make application to be excused. Among those who made application to be excused was Bob Rock. The jury list showed his occupation as 'advertising manager'. He was in fact a taxi-driver. Anxious to build up his business, he applied to the judge to be excused. His application was denied. Twenty-two of the ninety-three people on the jury list made such applications. Nine of them were excused. Seven others listed as potential jurors were not present when their names were called. This clearly put them in contempt of court. No action was taken against these seven. The Crown asked that a further seven who were present should stand down. The defence used up its maximum of six objections and a jury of twelve were sworn in. It is said that a jury selects its foreman. In this particular case only two men expressed the desire to be foreman. One of those two was elected; it was the reluctant juror, Bob Rock. Prior to two policemen being sworn in to 'take care of the jury during the period of the trial' Kevin Ryan raised strenuous objections to the incarceration of the jury.

He told the judge that he had not applied for this measure and that as far as he knew the Crown had not either. Mr Justice Perry told him that he had made the ruling 'in the interests of a fair trial'.

On the following day, 27 March 1973, David Morris made his long opening address on behalf of the Crown. On at least three occasions he referred specifically by name to Detective Sergeant Hughes and told the jury what evidence they would hear from that particular officer. Bob Rock, the reluctant juror, now foreman, recalled that day for me:

'When I heard David Morris making references to Johnny Hughes and the evidence he would give I thought: "Right, that's it, now I'll get off this jury." I was in the Navy with Hughes, had known him for years. I advised the judge through the Court Registrar of my association with Hughes. The reply was: "It doesn't matter, he's not related to you." '

Kevin Ryan knew nothing of this. He had no knowledge of the association of the two men and remained ignorant of that fact until the trial was finished, when he was informed by the Court Registrar.

During the first week of the trial Kevin Ryan noticed a familiar face among the onlookers. He was then a chief inspector. His name was Graham Perry.

'I also discovered after the trial that he had been in the Navy with Detective Sergeant Hughes and with the foreman of the jury, Rock.'

I have discussed these aspects with a number of people who have been deeply involved with the Thomas saga. It will be clear from my earlier remarks that I do not regard the first trial judge Sir Trevor Henry as a weak man but a man who if he leaned in any direction would favour the prosecution. Perhaps his view of what I have just recorded might carry more weight with this country's government than, say, the view of Kevin Ryan.

Sir Trevor said to me: 'That jury should have been

308

dismissed once it was established that the foreman had been in the Navy with Hughes. I would have dismissed them and ordered a retrial.'

I would suggest to the government that Sir Trevor Henry would be an excellent choice as chairman of a public inquiry into the background of the entire second jury. The odds of Bob Rock being on that jury list by accident are about on par with the odds against Prime Minister Muldoon telling the nation to vote Labour at the next General Election.

The fact that the foreman's profession was incorrectly shown on the jury list might also be food for thought for the team who publicly inquire into that second jury. Rock told me he had been a taxi-driver for only three weeks before that second trial and before that had indeed worked as an advertising manager.

Kevin Ryan: 'I rang *Truth*, the *Star*, the *Herald* and a number of other sources connected with advertising. I could not find one person who knew him.'

Kevin Ryan also subsequently discovered that the foreman of that second jury is related to the McGuires, the married couple who gave evidence on behalf of Arthur Thomas and against Eggleton the jeweller. It might be thought that as they had been defence witnesses at that referral this might in some odd way balance the fact that Bob Rock had known a key prosecution witness for many years. That might be thought until one discovers that the McGuires and Bob Rock were not on speaking terms at the time of the second trial.

The more I researched, the more apparent it became that the second trial of Arthur Thomas was a travesty of justice. All that work by the press, the retrial committee, the Ted Smiths of this country, the defence lawyers was in vain, a total and complete waste of time. Thomas has yet to have a fair trial, if by 'fair trial' we mean a hearing when all the evidence is heard by an impartial jury. Leaving aside the possibility that either jury was biased or set up, one clear fact emerges: *neither jury heard all the evidence available.*

Before the second trial Kevin Ryan had considered handing over the task of defending Thomas to another barrister. He felt that he might have become too emotionally involved in the case during the long fight to get the second trial; that he might be lacking in total objectivity. He discussed with barristers Peter Williams and Michael Bungay the possibility of one of them either leading for the defence or alternatively assisting him.

'I gave it a great deal of thought and finally concluded: "Well, you've got this far, Ryan. You've got to see it through. If a barrister is lucky he gets at least one really big one during the course of his career. I'd had big ones before and since but this was *the* one. I wanted to win that case because apart from believing that Thomas was innocent I realized just how important it was. There were very big issues at stake. With that trial there was an opportunity, given the right verdict, to go on and effect a number of changes in our legal system that needed to be made. They still need to be made."'

Consequently Kevin Ryan, assisted by his brother Gerald, defended the farmer from Pukekawa in a trial in which the odds were heavily weighted against the defence before the first witness had been called. With a jury that had been chosen from a list that had been subjected to three weeks' intensive screening by the police. With a jury that had as its foreman a man who clearly recognized that he should not have been on it, a jury that was kept locked away in the Station Hotel, a favourite haunt of Auckland police officers.

All of that was just for openers. There were many other factors that ensured the verdict would be a foregone conclusion. One such factor was a police caravan parked near the Supreme Court. It was thought at the time that the purpose of the caravan was simply to provide a restroom for police officers waiting to give evidence. It was nothing of the sort. I had already uncovered that caravan's real purpose before interviewing Bruce Hutton.

'There was criticism, why there was criticism I don't know but there was, of my set-up at the Supreme Court. I knew I was dealing with a case of great magnitude. I knew that certain tactics would be used. I operated something that has never been done before or since. I operated a very big nerve-centre there; instant checking of any developing trend during the trial. Defence counsel's questions to various witnesses clearly indicate possible lines of defence. Everything that was said, every name that was mentioned was checked, checked, checked. A team of officers was out in the field immediately to go into any detail or new aspect or any attempt to change our evidence. To change our evidence into something which wasn't as we saw it. It's never been done since. I've been criticized for doing my job really. Kevin Ryan will tell you that the set-up was very effective in breaking down some of the loosely presented evidence for the defence. I personally believe the police should approach all trials with that standard of efficiency. Because, as I say, unfortunately we are now living in a day when a number of counsel are bending the rules, in their attempts to obtain a "Not Guilty" verdict.'

I suggested to Bruce Hutton that possibly Crown prosecutors might also be bending the rules the other way to obtain a 'Guilty' verdict. He said, 'That could happen, certainly. Must do.'

What the former inspector was describing was a monitoring centre. Day by day, hour by hour as the case progressed, the evidence was being studied and analysed. With the many police officers that Hutton had at his disposal he effectively destroyed piece after piece of Kevin Ryan's defence by acquiring further evidence that was promptly fed into the courtroom for the Crown to use.

Inspector Hutton and the men serving under him were clearly angered at the allegations that had been made by so many between 1971 and 1973. The allegation that the Charles case had been deliberately planted had resulted in a secret internal police inquiry, conducted by Deputy-Commissioner Robert Walton who held the view 'that if planting had taken place it was far better that the police established the fact and reveal it than have it exposed by other persons or judicial processes'.

Walton came to the conclusion, after interviewing Inspector Hutton, Detectives Charles and Parkes and a number of other officers, that he could find no flaw in the circumstances surrounding the Charles cartridge case.

There were most serious allegations. Bruce Hutton told me that before being interviewed himself he had made his own inquiries into the possibility of planting and that he advised the deputy-commissioner of his own findings, that the allegations were unjustified. Talking of the deputy-commissioner's inquiry he said:

'I'm quite sure if the public knew how a police inquiry of this nature is conducted they would feel very comforted indeed. I've done a number myself. I have been responsible for putting a number of men out of a job. I can say that when such an inquiry is conducted in this country it is done with total efficiency. The attitude of the men in the police force, right down through the ranks is: "If there is a bloody rogue there then let's get rid of him." They'll turn on their own mates as soon as they are convinced that this particular police officer has broken the rules. They'll turn and hunt him like a bloody dog.'

It is clear that Inspector Hutton and the men who had served under him during the investigation into the deaths of the Crewes were anxious at the start of the second trial for public vindication. The presence of that police caravan by the Supreme Court and its

312

purpose are examples of just how deeply that anxiety went. It was indeed the reaping of the whirlwind.

'The Thomas-Crown Affair', as one newspaper billed the second trial, attracted huge crowds to the Auckland Supreme Court. Queues of many hundreds of people were a daily feature. Circuses have always been popular and this one was no exception. Within the No. 1 court itself there was throughout the trial a strange atmosphere. This culmination of two years' pressure produced in that room much more than understandable excitement. Anger, bitterness, resentment, venom, all of these emotions were in constant attendance.

In view of the fact that I consider it was a mistrial before it had even begun it would be futile to analyse the evidence in any great depth. To do so would be to merely compound the pointless exercise that passed for a fair trial. Some aspects, however, are worth noting: the changes of evidence; the legal tactics of the Crown and defence. Within the first week the jury of twelve was reduced to eleven through the illness of one of its members. The eleven that remained must have had moments when they too wished they had been excused.

Changed evidence, perjury, genuine error, call it what you will, occurred with regularity throughout the trial. It began on the first day evidence was heard. It began with the second witness called by the Crown, Police Constable Stevens. Cross-examination from Kevin Ryan established that Stevens had taken photographs of the bloodstains on the passenger seat of Len Demler's car and also photographs of what appeared to be bloodstains on the nearside door. Ryan asked him about other photographs:

Ryan: Take any photographs of the interior of Mr Demler's house?

Stevens: No, sir.

Ryan: Sure of that?

Stevens: Yes, sir.

From the first trial cross-examination of the same witness:

Temm: Did you take any photos of any part of Mr Demler's house?

Stevens: Yes.

Difficult to justify that change of evidence on the grounds of genuine mistake.

Diane Ambler had told the first trial jury that she had been to school with Jeannette Crewe. The second trial jury heard her say that she had not. When the defence questioned her on this aspect she said that she had been mistaken at the first trial.

A more significant change in her evidence, however, escaped unchallenged. At the Lower Court she had testified about a visit to the Crewe farm in August 1966. With regard to the Crewe lounge she had said that even with the fire burning the temperature inside the room was very cold and they had been obliged to keep their coats on throughout most of the afternoon. At the first trial the burning fire had become a space heater; now at the second it became a heater that was not operating. This evidence has a direct bearing on the likelihood of the Crewes sitting on a cold wet stormy winter's night with open louvre windows.

Beverly Batkin's evidence now contained the additional information that Arthur Thomas wearing a black singlet in the streets of Tuakau was a usual sight, that in fact it would be unusual if she had seen him not wearing a black singlet. Her cross-examination by Ryan produced explosions both from the witness and the counsel. This sole witness of Thomas pestering Jeannette Crewe at dances which by her own testimony were attended by between 100 and 250, said to me:

'I was a nervous wreck after Kevin Ryan had finished with me.'

Ryan: You only learned his name was Arthur following the homicides?

Batkin: Well, my memory was refreshed after the homicides.

Ryan: Who refreshed it?

Batkin: I would say the newspapers, mostly.

Ryan: How much more of your evidence is obtained from the newspapers?

Batkin: My evidence is fact.

Ryan: If evidence is given, called in this Court, that this Arthur Thomas did not learn to dance until 1959 and did not go to dances in those two halls you described until that year would you say that your evidence is wrong?

Batkin: I would say that I am very glad to hear he learned to dance, because prior when he was making a large pest of himself he was a very poor dancer.

Ryan: Who was he dancing with when you saw him at these dances?

Batkin: Jeannette.

Ryan: You actually saw him dancing with Jeannette?

Batkin: Yes.

Ryan: If evidence is given he didn't go to any dances at Pukekawa until 1959 do you say that evidence is mistaken?

Batkin: I would say that I am not prepared to commit perjury.

The acrimony between the two grew as the cross-examination progressed until:

Ryan: What clothing did Thomas wear at these dances?

Batkin: It was not so much the clothing he wore but the way he wore it. He would wear grey trousers, white shirt, tie and black dirty shoes. The tie was usually rather untidily knotted.

Ryan: Many people at the hall looking like that?

Batkin: No, not many, very few in fact. It was not fashionable to be untidy and dirty in the late 1950s.

Ryan: You actually hate Arthur Thomas, don't you?

Batkin: No I don't.

Ryan: Don't you?

Batkin: No I don't.

Ryan: Sure?

Batkin: I feel rather sorry for him.

Ryan: How sorry for yourself?

Batkin: I don't feel sorry for myself.

Ryan: You have told lies in Court.

Batkin: That is very unkind to say to anyone. I have told not one lie in this Court. I could not live with my conscience if I told a lie.

Ryan: If you had a conscience.

Kevin Ryan was rightly rebuked by Mr Justice Perry for the last remark and told to confine himself to asking questions. He promptly sat down.

It may be recalled that David Morris had told the Court of Appeal after the first trial that the Crown 'were not greatly concerned with establishing motive'. Demonstrably they had been very concerned to establish motive, they had strained visibly to do so with the evidence of people like Mrs Batkin. Again in this second trial they strained, this time even harder. In his opening address Morris had spoken at length about Thomas 'the persistent suitor who had deep feelings for Mrs Crewe, but these were not returned'. He had told the jury of Mrs Batkin's view that it was 'more passion than a schoolboy crush and his attentions distressed Jeannette'. Just how hard the Crown were straining to establish a motive can be evinced from the testimony of the woman who followed Mrs Batkin into the box, Beverley Willis. Mrs Willis, unlike Diane Ambler, was an old schoolfriend of the late Jeannette Crewe. She had made a statement to the police within a week of the Crewes' disappearance. The police had quietly sat on her statement. Now as a measure of the Crown's desperation to establish motive it had, after three years, been dusted over and was put up for the jury's consideration.

In the first trial Paul Temm had objected to the

introduction of evidence about the fires and the burglary; consequently that aspect had been played down by the Crown. With no objection coming from Kevin Ryan, the Crown were free to run riot with evidence that should not have been allowed. Mrs Willis was only one of a number of witnesses who testified about these earlier incidents. Nothing she or anyone else said linked them with Thomas but her testimony also contained references to conversation with her late friend, in which Jeannette had talked of Thomas pestering her at dances. It was hearsay evidence and as such inadmissible, yet it was admitted.

In the first trial Sir Trevor Henry had refused to allow a stock agent to testify about the demeanour of the accused on the morning after he was supposed to have murdered two people:

'If we allow that sort of evidence to be given we will have suspects manufacturing evidence after they have perpetrated crimes.'

Surely those same suspects should be protected from hearsay evidence of alleged conversations that occurred eleven years before the crimes of which they stand accused? How could Thomas rebut the evidence of Mrs Willis? Clearly he could not. He had not been present during these alleged conversations.

In his opening speech David Morris had told the jury that the Crown's case was that Thomas did the killings himself but later received assistance from some person or persons. The tactic of a trial within a trial was used again. Knowing that Bruce Roddick would this time be asked directly if the woman he had seen was Vivien Thomas the Crown had prevented him from being made available to the defence until shortly before the commencement of this second trial. Roddick, who had been such a vital witness for the Crown during the first trial, was then released from his subpoena. The object of the exercise as far as the Crown were concerned was to hold on to the fact that Roddick had seen a woman

317

but to throw as much doubt as possible on his assertion that the woman was not Vivien Thomas.

Ron Chitty, the farmer who had employed Roddick and had been driving the tractor when Roddick had seen the mystery woman, was called by the Crown. Careful questioning of Mr Chitty was designed to demonstrate to the jury that Roddick might well have been busy at the moment he saw the woman, hence how could he be sure that it was not Mrs Thomas. The Crown had not, of course, asked Ron Chitty these questions during the first trial.

Len Demler's marital status had altered between trials; he had remarried. His evidence changed a little too. He told the Court that Jeannette had gone to Wanganui to get well away from Arthur Thomas. He also told for the first time of how stock agent Joseph Moore had telephoned him on Wednesday, 17 June at about 7 p.m. and of how Moore had advised him that he had been trying to contact Harvey Crewe by phone but could get no answer. Demler went on to say that he took no notice of this and did nothing until the following Monday when he was phoned by transport manager Ron Wright who advised him that he had been trying to contact Harvey since the previous Thursday. without success.

Why was Joseph Moore not called by the Crown at the Lower Court? Why did the Crown avoid asking questions of Moore at both trials that would have revealed he had phoned Len Demler on Wednesday, 17 June at about 7 p.m? Where was Harvey Crewe at 7 p.m? Where was Jeannette? Clearly neither was answering the telephone. Why did the Crown avoid asking questions of Demler during the first trial that would have revealed this information? What price Arthur Thomas murdering two people at 11 p.m. who are not answering their telephone at 7 p.m? Why did Len Demler do nothing for five days?

As at the Lower Court, Demler yet again got his days

mixed up and put himself on the Crewe farm on the night they died:

Morris: On the Tuesday night you had dinner with your daughter and son-in-law, which day was this?

Demler: The day was Wednesday.

Morris: The Wednesday following the dinner . . .

Demler: Not the Wednesday following, it was the next Wednesday, not the one following.

Morris: The day you had a ring about the stock?

Demler: Yeah.

When Kevin Ryan began his cross-examination he initially asked about the additional information that Demler was now giving for the first time about the reason his daughter went to Wanganui:

Ryan: You have given information on oath on two prior occasions, have you not?

Demler: I have.

Ryan: And you knew it was in relation to a charge against this accused for murder, didn't you?

Demler: Yes.

Ryan: Did you make any mention on either of those prior occasions that your daughter had gone to Wanganui to get away from Thomas?

Demler: No, I didn't mention it at the time. I didn't think it was . . . I didn't have to.

Ryan: Did you tell it to a police officer?

Demler: No, I didn't worry about telling anyone about that.

On the basis of the information given to me by the woman who taught with Jeannette at Maramarua, on the basis of the information given to me by the woman she lived with for three years in Wanganui, Len Demler's version of why Jeannette went to teach in Wanganui is a total contradiction. Somebody has to be wrong.

During the course of that same cross-examination the missing shotgun from the Chennell estate suddenly appeared. The gun that had worried Bruce Hutton so much. The gun that had remained lost for nearly three years had been found by Len Demler a few days before he gave evidence. 'It was lying in a shed in the corner. I thought I gave it away to someone and it was chucked outside the manure shed and it was right down in the corner. I found it when I was shifting the other day and I gave it to Mr Hutton.'

Still missing was Harvey's gun. The gun that Mrs Batkin had previously seen in the lounge. It is still missing. Still unaccounted for was the .22 rifle that Len Demler had once owned. It is still unaccounted for.

Yet again Len Demler displayed his apparently phlegmatic attitude to the death of those nearest and dearest to him:

Ryan: While your wife was in hospital did you visit her at all?

Demler: Yes, we went down quite a lot.

Ryan: How many times would you visit her in the home in Epsom?

Demler: I always went, sometimes I took Jeannette, it was nearly twice a week anyway; towards the finish there it might have been only once if I was busy.

Ryan: On the day your wife died were you playing bowls?

Demler: No, I was back home. I knew she was dying, you couldn't do anything for her.

There were clearly a number of points that worried Kevin Ryan.

Ryan: You are aware that there were bloodstains in your car?

Demler: Yes.

Ryan: You are aware they are the same blood type as Jeanette's?

Demler: Yeh, Jeannette put them there; she hurt her finger one day when we were going to see her mother.

Ryan: It must have been in January when they were put there?

Demler: Yes, in January.

Ryan: No-one washed them off?

Demler: There wasn't much to wipe off; I never touched them.

Ryan: Did anybody else sit in the passenger seat after Jeannette?

Demler: That's hard to say.

Towards the end of his cross-examination Kevin Ryan confronted Demler with the essence of what was troubling him:

Ryan: Did you take the bodies of Jeannette and Harvey Crewe to the Waikato river after 17 June 1970?

Demler: I didn't do anything of the sort.

Ryan: Why didn't you help the police when they were searching for your daughter and Harvey?

Demler: I did search for them two or three times.

Ryan: Did you ever mention to anybody, 'They won't find them on the land, they will be in the river?'

Demler: No, I never mentioned that to anybody.

Ryan: On your birthday on 6 July you had a party at the Paerata Hotel, before the bodies were found?

Demler: That's right, we just did that to release the tensions; if you had lost your son-in-law and daughter you would be worried too, wouldn't you?

Ryan: Wouldn't you look for them?

Demler: I was worried about it but there were plenty of others doing all the looking and search.

Demler's reference to having searched for the missing couple two or three times, like his reference as to why his daughter went to teach at Wanganui, is in conflict with all the other evidence. In the case of the searches, the alternative evidence that he took no part in them comes from the police.

The defence battled on and battle it was. They were not only fighting to get the truth from a variety of witnesses whose testimony varied from previous sworn testimony; they were not only fighting in the courtroom David Morris and Baragwanath, and out of the courtroom Inspector Bruce Hutton and his caravan;

there was also the battle with the judge Mr Justice Perry. Again and again he overruled Ryan's objections.

When Ryan attempted to cross-examine police witnesses about what they had said during the referral hearing at Wellington that had resulted in the order quashing the verdict and granting a new trial, the judge upbraided him in front of the jury. Ryan was severely criticized for asking perfectly proper questions. In chambers the judge telephoned Chief Justice Sir Richard Wild and advised him that 'Mr Ryan was experiencing some difficulty and needed help. Would it be in order for him to ask such questions?' Chief Justice Wild declared that it would be perfectly in order. The press ban placed on the referral hearing clearly lapsed when the second jury had been sworn in. In truth it was Mr Justice Perry who was 'experiencing some difficulty', not Ryan. The defence counsel's 'difficulty' was Mr Justice Perry. Though he had been admonished in front of the jury, no public retraction was forthcoming from the judge, no acknowledgement for the jury that such a line of questioning was perfectly proper.

Graham Hewson, who in the eyes of four police officers had been invisible during the Wellington hearing, remained in much the same condition during this second trial. Detective Sergeant Murray Jeffries, the man in charge of the sieve-search that Hewson insisted he had helped with, was pressed hard about the invisible man by Ryan.

Jeffries had no knowledge of a police bullet being excitedly found by Hewson, no knowledge of Hewson borrowing a mower from the Chitty farm for the police to mow the paddock, no knowledge of going with Hewson to a Pukekohe hotel to meet Mrs Crewe senior on the evening of 18 August. The last piece of 'no knowledge' had an interesting sequel when Mrs Crewe senior gave evidence:

Ryan: Are you outside the court in a green Valiant car?

322

Mrs Crewe: Yes.

Ryan: Did Mr Jeffries, a police officer, sit in the car and talk to you?

Mrs Crewe: Yes, Mr Jeffries told me he was going home to paint his house.

Ryan: He got inside the car?

Mrs Crewe: He got in the front of the car.

Ryan: You were both talking and speaking for some time?

Mrs Crewe: Yes, and we were talking about him going home and about his wife and children.

Ryan: Was any mention made of him seeing you at the Pukekohe Hotel in August?

Mrs Crewe: Yes.

As the cross-examination progressed Kevin Ryan established that Mrs Crewe had been driven up to Pukekawa by Hewson after Jeannette's body had been found in mid-August, that Hewson had indeed stayed at the hotel, that he had brought the police officers back, that he had gone off and assisted in the search in the Crewe gardens. Mr Justice Perry at the end of the cross-examination asked a question about the curious episode of a police officer who had just given evidence risking contempt by talking to a Crown witness who was about to go into the witness box.

Perry J: You tell me the conversation in the car was Mr Jeffries saying he was going home to paint his house?

Mrs Crewe: That's right sir. *He did just mention something about coming to the hotel.*

Cross-examination of Detective Constable Higgins, another of the police equivalent of the three wise monkeys – 'See no Hewson. Talk no Hewson' and 'No work with Hewson' – established that a complete bullet had been dropped onto the ground during the August search. He was certain that Hewson was not present during this demonstration. The question that remains begging is: 'How did Hewson, the sheepfarmer and dog-breeder from the Wairarapa, know about this complete bullet?' Such demonstrations are standard practice for the police in a search of this kind. The only conclusion is that not only was he there, assisting in the sieving and searching, but he did in fact find the demonstration bullet. If the police case against Thomas was so strong, so overpowering, why the need to discredit Hewson? Why the special screening of the jury list? Why the police caravan? Why the need for Detective Jeffries to discuss with Mrs Crewe a particular meeting which involved Hewson?

Ryan had been fighting from the commencement of the trial to obtain a photograph of the bloodstains in Demler's car. On the perhaps not inappropriate date of 1 April he finally obtained a photo of the stains on the passenger seat. Stevens, one of the police photographers, was recalled and submitted a copy of the photograph as an official exhibit.

During my very long interview with DSIR scientists, Dr Donald Nelson and Rory Shanahan, the subject of those bloodstains was raised. Both men insisted that they were minute marks. Indeed Dr Nelson demonstrated with a drop of his own blood just how small the marks in the car had been. In the minds of both men the bloodstains were no bigger than a few dots the size of a pin-head. The photograph in this book may help the reader to judge their evaluation. I pointed out to both men that the police photograph showed considerably more. Dr Nelson observed: 'That photograph is misleading.' He would presumably say the same of the verbal evidence given by the police photographer: 'The bloodstain is approximately two and a half inches in length.'

As previously recorded, one Crown tactic during the first trial was the assertion that the child had been fed, and fed by Vivien Thomas. Two years later with Vivien Thomas still uncharged it was apparent to the police and the Crown a change of tactics was called for. Dr

Fox was called and again testified that in his opinion Rochelle had been fed during that five-day period. He was followed into the witness box by the late Dr Donald Caughey, a consultant child physician with considerable experience. His evidence had been suppressed by the Crown at the first trial. Now to bolster their 'well, perhaps the child was not fed' tactic it was used. Dr Fox had initially examined Rochelle on 23 June 1970, within 24 hours of her discovery in the cot. His second examination had been three days later. Dr Caughey did not see Rochelle until 1 July 1970; *nine days after she had been found in the cot and eight days after Dr Fox's initial examination*. Dr Caughey's opinion, which flies in the face of not only Dr Fox and Professor Elliot, but the many people who saw the child in the *hours* after her discovery, was: 'Her clinical state was, I believe, consistent with her not having been fed.' It transpired that he had not conferred with Dr Fox and he was basing his conclusion on the unproven theory that she would have had an evening meal with her parents on 17 June.

Eggleton the jeweller was yet another Crown witness who had different evidence to offer since his last appearance. He told this second jury of his initial reaction of disgust when the watch had been handed to him. He also advised that he had first talked to the police about it in December, 'just after the depositions'. This was totally contrary to the evidence he gave during the first trial. The reason he had lied to Mrs McGuire was because 'she is a very vicious woman'.

Detective Senior Sergeant John Hughes was another to be added to the ever-growing list of Crown witnesses with altered testimony. His additions, unlike the jeweller's, were deadly for Arthur Thomas.

It is my contention that Hughes by particular phrasing during the first trial gave the impression that Thomas had worked on the Crewe farm *after* Jeannette and Harvey took it over. Other observers disagree.

There can be no disagreement about the testimony he gave to the second trial jury. Hughes told them of his conversation with Thomas that had taken place on 2 July 1970:

'He went on to tell me that, while employed by an agricultural contractor some three or four years before, he had actually worked on the Crewe farm; he said he would have morning and afternoon teas in the house and he met Harvey Crewe there; he described Harvey as being "a decent type of bloke". He said he had not been back to the Crewe farm since that time, meaning three or four years before; he said the last time he had seen either Jeannette or Harvey was some eight or nine months before.'

If one accepts this evidence Arthur Thomas, anxious to be charged and found guilty of a double murder and to be sentenced to life imprisonment, told Hughes that while top-dressing for Barr Brothers, he had met the dead couple on their farm and had morning and afternoon tea with them.

Arthur Thomas terminated his employment with Barr Brothers on 20 May 1965. Harvey and Jeannette did not move on to the farm until June 1966. As previously recorded in this book, Barr Brothers never top-dressed the farm during the entire period that the Crewes were in residence. The one abortive attempt to do so occurred during early March 1967, nearly two years after Thomas had ceased working for them.

This deadly addition from Hughes passed unnoticed by Kevin Ryan. But not by David Morris.

The name of Eyre began to feature significantly in the case as the Crown evidence continued. Paul Temm during the first trial had capitalized on the fact that a rifle removed from the Eyre property by the police had not been excluded by the DSIR as a potential murder weapon, but he had studiously avoided direct questions about the Eyre family in general and Mickey Eyre in particular. Kevin Ryan considered this a significant omission from the first trial defence, one that he would not have made. He most certainly made up for that omission during the second trial. Questioning Detective Mike Charles about the sixty-four-rifle collection, he elicited the information that the officer had been told by Mrs Eyre when the rifle her son used was uplifted that they did not have any ammunition at that time. It was Ryan's first shot across the bows in the direction of Mickey Eyre. More were to follow which makes Ryan's omission of a request that the Eyre rifle be sent to the British Home Office forensic experts all the more inconsistent. He was clearly running Mickey Eyre as another possible fox to the jury.

The ephemeral Graham Hewson gained a slightly longer life span in terms of the August police searches when the then manager of the Crewe farm John Handcock gave evidence. Handcock remembered him being there at the time in question and thought he recalled Hewson with something in his hand: 'It could have been a fork or something like that; he might have been loosening the soil. He appeared to be working with the police party or close by.'

In view of the obvious attack that the defence had mounted on Len Demler, they allowed one piece of information from Mr Handcock to pass unexploited. It transpired that on the day that Charles found the now much maligned cartridge case, both Handcock and Demler had been on the Crewe farm.

When Detective Senior Sergeant Parkes was cross-examined by the defence an explanation of why Thomas had possibly remarked to Detective Johnston on 13 October of the brush and comb set: 'I don't know, it could still be wrapped up for all I know' became apparent.

Ryan: On 12 August 1970 you took a card that you had located with this brush and comb set to the accused's farm?

Parkes: Yes.

Ryan: And you showed him the card?

Parkes: Yes.

Ryan: And asked him was it his handwriting?

Parkes: Yes.

Ryan: Did he ask you where you had found it?

Parkes: I am not sure whether he asked me or I told him.

Ryan: I put it to you he asked you where you found it and you told him you found it in a brush and comb set still wrapped up?

Parkes: No, I certainly wouldn't use the words 'still wrapped up' because I didn't consider it was still wrapped up.

Ryan: Did you say it was wrapped up?

Parkes: I have a recollection of saying that.

It became clear as the cross-examination progressed that the police officer's objection was to the word 'still'. All right, let us take that word out. Two years after the first trial judge Mr Justice Henry had hammered Thomas into the ground with his constant comments during his final speech to the jury on the significance of that remark, Kevin Ryan in the space of a few moments' cross-examination had established that the remark had about as much potency as a bag of cold chips.

Another man made his first appearance in the Thomas saga, a man whose evidence clearly demonstrates the lengths that the Crown, who David Morris had said were not very concerned with establishing a motive, went to in their attempts to establish one. To be fair to the Crown Prosecutor, he had made that remark about the Crown's case in the first trial. Perhaps this was another change of tactics. The new witness, Charles Liddell, had been chief engineer for Barr Brothers at the time Arthur Thomas had been employed. He had a tale to tell of a visit to a fortune-teller that he had made in the company of two married ladies and Arthur Thomas. Liddell's evidence may have given the jury and the packed public gallery with their packed lunches some light relief, but what it had to do with the guilt or innocence of Arthur Thomas is difficult to see.

The visit to the fortune-teller 'would be early 1963, it may be even a little before that'. Before the visit Arthur had spoken very highly of Jeannette 'as if he probably would have been in love with her. I could not give his exact words but they would be . . . I feel he had ideas of marrying her.' Then later after regaling the Court with how he had paid five shillings to have his fortune told he said: 'My impressions were he thought a lot of her. I would even say he was probably very much in love with her.' The last question from the Crown was obviously designed to set the seal on this nebulous love affair. He was asked: 'Did he ever mention any other girls?' Clearly Liddell was expected to respond with something to the effect that Thomas's entire conversation was about Jeannette Demler. His response was: 'Oh, yes.'

Pathologist Dr Cairns came and went unquestioned by Kevin Ryan who clearly wanted no part of murder/ suicide theories or of Dr Cairns's initial theory of murder by axe or tomahawk.

An echo of the curious between-trials incident between Detective Johnston and the Roddick family was brought into the courtroom when the police officer testified. Johnston produced photographs taken on the Chitty farm giving a view of the Crewe farmhouse, taken from a distance of 357 feet. He told David Morris that it was difficult to distinguish the facial features of any person at that distance. The Crown were clearly hotting things up for Bruce Roddick. Just how hot they intended to make it can be gauged from this interchange between the Crown Prosecutor and the detective:

Morris: At the time these photographs were taken, to your knowledge had the police received certain information from a man called Roddick?

Johnston: Yes.

Morris: Who *claimed* to have been working on this farm property in the immediate foreground of photo three on that afternoon?

Johnston: And he later showed me the position from where he *alleges* he saw this woman. (The italics are mine.)

Morris: In relation to that photograph and the position from where the photograph was taken, how does that compare to the position he was in?

Johnston: Approximately the same position within two or three feet.

There was already considerable confusion as to exactly where Roddick had been standing, partly through his own conflicting evidence and partly through a series of conflicting and confusing questions he had been asked by Baragwanath at the first trial. The object of the above interchange was to increase that distance.

Detective Johnston then produced the certificate of registration covering the missing Chennell gun, a double-barrelled, breach-loading .360 rifle. This was the gun that Len Demler had said he had given to the police 'a few days ago', that is, March 1973. According to Johnston he had received the gun a few weeks after the first trial had finished in 1970. It was all very odd. It got odder during Ryan's cross-examination. He established that Johnston had gone to the Thomas farm with the axle on 13 October and had shown it to Thomas; that the accused had given the name and address of his father and stated that the photo of the trailer looked similar to one that his father owned. On 15 October Johnston had returned and together with Thomas searched for the other axle components without success. On 20 October Johnston and Parkes had returned and found the matching axle stubs on the farm tip. Thomas had had seven days to remove the stubs, seven days during which he knew the police were looking for them. Would a man who had so cleverly murdered two people that he had left not a trace of his

330

presence behind leave incriminating axle stubs on his property? Would the same man when the police returned on 21 October looking for more components come down to the tip and help them and suggest various ways in which they could carry out the search productively? Murderers certainly do make mistakes but I have yet to meet one who behaved with the same degree of blind innocence and naivety as Thomas did.

The name of Eyre which had been bouncing about during this second trial took on physical shape in the presence of Mrs Eyre in the witness box. But why not Mickey Eyre? I am aware that he has a speech and hearing impediment. I am equally aware that he can communicate and communicate very precisely. As it was the Court and the jury had to make do with his mother.

Mrs Eyre, a widow at the time of the second trial, told the Court that the Eyre rifle that the DSIR had been unable to exclude as a possible murder weapon was in fact owned by a family friend Mr Jack Brewster but at the time of the Crewe murders had been in the Eyre household, loaned to her other son Colin. The Mr Brewster in question subsequently married Mrs Eyre in late 1973. During her examination-in-chief Mrs Eyre told the jury that because of his disabilities Mickey did not go out at night-time unless accompanied. In view of the information Kevin Ryan had acquired it was an assertion that he took issue with when he rose to cross-examine:

Ryan: Do you swear that John Michael (Mickey's full name) does not go out at night by himself?

Mrs Eyre: I do.

Ryan: Has he ever been out at night with a rifle?

Mrs Eyre: No.

Ryan: Has he assaulted someone in the last two or three weeks?

Mrs Eyre: No.

Ryan: Was he blamed for an assault in the last two or three weeks?

Mrs Eyre: I have no idea.

Ryan: Did your son use to go on to the Crewe property?

Mrs Eyre: At haymaking time, when he was working for them.

Ryan: Did he get ordered off the Crewe property by Harvey Crewe on one or two occasions?

Mrs Eyre: No.

Ryan: Is there a drum on the Crewe property with your face painted on it?

Mrs Eyre: I have no idea, I have not seen it.

Ryan: Ever hear about a drum with your face painted on it?

Mrs Eyre: No, I have not.

Ryan: Is John Michael a good shot?

Mrs Eyre: I should say so. He is a duckshooter.

Ryan: The farmer next door to the Crewes, is he a vintage car enthusiast? On the Brewster property?

Mrs Eyre: No, not in Pukekawa.

Ryan: The other road goes right down to the Waikato river?

Mrs Eyre: The road past my property? One way it goes straight to Tuakau Highway 22, the other way it goes out to Glen Murray still Highway 22.

Ryan: You are on a corner?

Mrs Eyre: Yes.

Ryan: Does the other road go right down to the Waikato river?

Mrs Eyre: It would go to Rangiriri or to Orton.

Ryan: Orton is next to the Waikato river?

Mrs Eyre: Yes, towards Rangiriri.

Ryan: There are good places for boats or launching pads?

Mrs Eyre: Not that I am aware of.

Ryan: What was the weather on the evening of 17 June 1970?

Mrs Eyre: As far as I can remember it did rain towards morning.

Ryan: Did John Michael destroy sheep by breaking their backs with his hands?

Mrs Eyre: My son John Michael is an extremely kind person, he is an excellent shearer and he is very kind to animals.

Ryan: Has he ever broken the back of animals with his hands?

Mrs Eyre: No.

Ryan: How big is he?

Mrs Eyre: Approximately 5′ 9″.

Ryan: His weight?

Mrs Eyre: Approximately 11½ stone.

Orton is in fact the exact place where I believe the bodies of Harvey and Jeannette were put into the Waikato river.

Apart from the fact that Ryan was in possession of evidence that indicated Mickey Eyre wandered abroad at night, with a rifle, the defence counsel had also discovered that the young man did in fact have a violent temper, had allegedly attacked not only a variety of animals but also a member of the Pukekawa community, shortly before the commencement of the trial, had been ordered off the Crewe farm by Harvey at least twice, on one occasion for cutting the wrong paddock, and indulged in the bizarre pastime of using a drum with his mother's face painted on it for target practice.

DSIR scientist Rory Shanahan was another of the many experts who gave evidence. Sir Trevor Henry when justifying to me his decision not to allow the defence to call a psychiatrist in the first trial had said: 'What we have to avoid is trial by experts,' a sentiment that I fully endorse. The second trial fairly bulged with experts. Experts on child care, death, corrosion, wire, bullets, small arms manufacturing. Some of their evidence was highly relevant, some of their evidence had no relevance at all. For example, Shanahan

333

occupied a great deal of his time in the witness box with evidence about the variety of corrosion tests he had carried out between trials. He had buried cartridge cases at twenty-one different locations in the Auckland area. All the jury were concerned with were any corrosion tests carried out in the flowerbed where Charles had found a cartridge case. Soil conditions, like corrosion itself, vary enormously. Corrosion on a case buried in Remuera has nothing to do with Pukekawa, some thirty miles away.

Answering the Crown's questions Shanahan said that thirty-seven of the cases returned to him had been buried for the same period of time that had elapsed between the night the Crewes died and Charles finding a cartridge case. He was primarily interested in what corrosion had occurred but in passing he observed that thirteen had no soil inside them, sixteen had dry soil and eight had wet soil. I have already commented on my own tests with dry soil in a cartridge case.

One fact stands out clearly from Rory Shanahan's cross-examination: he had not taken factors relating to the condition of the soil into account when conducting these tests and, as he himself honestly admitted: 'I am not an expert in this field.' He had earlier remarked, 'I am not a soil scientist.'

Alexander Aitken, an engineering manager with a subsidiary of I.C.I., testified about .22 bullets manufactured by his company that bore the figure 8 on the base of the bullet. It will be recalled that the bullets that killed the Crewes had a figure 8 on their base and that Detective Keith had found a round in a box of nuts and bolts at the Thomas farm which when broken open revealed a figure 8. The Crown's premise on this aspect is totally clear. Arthur Thomas used .22 bullets with the figure 8 on the base of the bullet. Two such bullets killed the Crewes; therefore two and two must make four. In this particular instance they made 158 million, that being the total of bullets with a figure

8 on their base that were made by the company between 1949 and 1963 and sold in New Zealand.

What was not revealed at any judicial hearing of the Thomas case was that the police had broken open a number of the bullets taken from the box of ammunition he was *currently* using. None of them had the figure 8 on them. If Thomas murdered Harvey and Jeannette Crewe here then is yet another extraordinary act. He disdains the box of ammunition in his kitchen that he was currently using. No bullets bearing figure 8 were found in the carcass of the sick Cow 4 or the carcass of an old blind dog also shot during this same period.

DSIR wire expert Harry Todd appeared, to baffle yet another jury.

The DSIR were by now bidding fair to take over the entire proceedings. Rory Shanahan had indicated that while he knew nothing about soil, a later witness knew all about it; the later witness also from the DSIR followed Mr Todd into the witness box. His name was Allan Metson, and he had some thirty to forty years' experience as a soil chemist. Vast as his experience undoubtedly was, impressive as his qualifications assuredly were, his evidence was, in my view, totally useless to that jury. He knew of no published work on short-term corrosion. He and the Crown talked of tests done in the United States over a period of six years, but the soil in America was not similar or comparable to the soil in the Crewe garden at Pukekawa. He had never examined a cartridge case that had been in the ground for four months. He could not pass an opinion as to what degree of corrosion one would find on such a cartridge case. He was not asked by either counsel for an opinion about the likelihood of dry soil pouring out of a cartridge case that had been found at least three inches beneath the surface in wet soil, which to my mind is the one area that Mr Metson might have helped the jury with.

335

Metson was followed by another man from the same government department, Wilfred Braithwaite. His speciality was corrosion and his advice had been sought by the United Nations. In essence, he said he agreed with the conclusions of Rory Shanahan. He was 'sunk without trace' by Kevin Ryan in a few brief questions that established he had never conducted such corrosion tests himself. He had no knowledge of what type of soil the Charles case had been found in. He had never examined the Charles cartridge case. Next in to bat was Dr Donald Nelson.

For the second time in front of a jury Dr Nelson recounted how 'relatively easy' it had been to shoot a person sitting in Harvey's armchair. Asked if he agreed with the Home Office report on the recovered bullet fragments Dr Nelson observed: 'One might almost say, sir, that report agrees with me.' Referring to the role of a DSIR member giving evidence Dr Nelson observed to me:

'It is important for us when giving evidence to pitch it at the right level so that we do not give it more probative value on behalf of the prosecution.'

I found it a valid, responsible point of view. How it equates with Dr Nelson's evidence when cross-examined by Kevin Ryan is a moot point. Ryan attempted to establish from this highly qualified man a number of simple facts. Reading the trial transcript gives a clear indication of just what kind of uphill battle he had with Dr Nelson. For example: it had already been established that at least 158 million rounds of bullets bearing the pattern 8 had been manufactured and sold in New Zealand between 1949 and 1963. This is the beginning of Ryan's cross-examination of Dr Nelson:

Ryan: On the base of the two bullets examined by you taken from the heads of the two deceased you found stamped figure 8?

Nelson: Yes, sir.

Ryan: Would you agree that this type of bullet would be in common supply throughout the North Island at least during the period in question (June 1970), easily available to persons?

Nelson: Well, you are asking me a question now you should be asking someone else, but what I understand is you could not purchase it at this time.

Ryan: If evidence is called that at least eight people have this type of bullet now wouldn't that be so?

Nelson: No, you could easily round up people with old ammunition of this number, in fact I could have answered your advertisement myself; I have some number 8 myself. I have number 8 and no doubt any cartridge collector in the country will have too, plus other people who hold old ammunition.

Ryan: How long have you had your number 8 cartridges in your possession?

Nelson: Probably from the 1950s, I couldn't give you the exact date.

Ryan: You are aware of the quantity of number 8 ammunition produced?

Nelson: Yes, I have heard other people give evidence, the figure is large.

Ryan: Is this type of ammunition drawn in the Colonial Ammunition factory at Mount Eden?

Nelson: You are asking me a hearsay question.

Ryan: Know where it is stored?

Nelson: Not of my own knowledge, sir, but once again I could hazard a guess of hearsay.

It is not common to see an expert witness, to whom the hearsay rule does not apply, hiding behind such a rule. Seven years after they had ceased to make pattern 8 bullets, there were literally thousands of them in the country. There still are. Dr Nelson was aware of this. Why not say so?

To me, a certain pomposity came through during his cross-examination:

Ryan: You know Dr Sprott, do you not?

337

Nelson: I know he is in court.

Ryan: Do you know the man personally?

Nelson: I know to whom you are referring.

Ryan: Do you agree that he is an eminent scientist?

Nelson: That is a loaded question. My speciality differs from his. I am giving evidence now as a forensic expert. I don't think he has done very much work in this area on which I am at the moment giving evidence.

In fact Dr Nelson had not only known Dr Sprott professionally for many years; they had actually both given evidence for the defence in a previous trial. Despite interruptions from the judge and from David Baragwanath that Ryan could not develop this aspect, Kevin Ryan at least succeeded in getting a fragment of it brought out in front of the jury, obviously to the chagrin of Donald Nelson who remarked of that previous trial: 'Your behaviour then, as now, is very offensive.'

The last question in re-examination speaks for itself:

Baragwanath: Is it consistent with your evidence that the Harvey and Jeannette bullet has in fact come from Exhibit 350 (the Charles case)?

Nelson: Oh, entirely consistent, sir.

There is no way that the Charles case could be matched to either bullet. Nelson had already said as much in earlier evidence. Why the absence of qualification on this, the last question he was asked?

Harry Todd, the Crown's wire expert, was recalled so that what the defence's wire expert would say could be put to him for his reaction and opinion. If the earlier questions and answers of this witness were a trifle obscure then what followed would have meant nothing at all to the listening jury. In essence it transpired that the defence had experts who would disagree with Mr Todd's conclusions and, with regard to the body wires that he had found similar to wire taken from the Thomas farm, would say they were totally dissimilar.

The final witness for the Crown was the man David

Morris considers the 'best witness I have ever led' –
Inspector Bruce Hutton.

His evidence varied considerably from earlier testimony. In the light of subsequent events one aspect of his examination-in-chief is of particular interest:

Morris: Is it normal practice for police after an appeal has been dismissed to retain exhibits indefinitely?

Hutton: No, for a very good reason. Space is the problem and for this reason always within a short time of the result of the appeal all exhibits are destroyed.

Morris; Some time after the appeal did you receive from the officer in charge of exhibits an instruction to destroy all exhibits involved in the Arthur Allan Thomas case?

Hutton: Yes, I received that on at least two different months following possession by myself.

Morris: Who was that officer?

Hutton: Chief Superintendent Ross; I did not comply with that instruction.

Morris: Why was that?

Hutton: Well, I felt some of the exhibits were of historical value so far as the police were concerned in this particular case. I felt they should be mounted and exhibited in the police museum in Wellington; for this reason the axle stubs and rifle were to be mounted on a more extensive basis than they are now for presentation and in addition to this I intended mounting the various shells and some of the wire also under the same exhibit groups.

Morris: What would your purpose be in forwarding these exhibits to the police museum?

Hutton: The purpose is very clear to my way of thinking. That it demonstrated to trainee detectives at the training college what can be acquired through tenacity and following up leads however remote they may be, and in addition to that necessity to be so vigilant when searching the scene of homicides.

At this point Kevin Ryan, feeling he had heard quite

enough of this police commercial, objected. Apart from anything else, these statements of Hutton's were begging the very issues that were in question in this second trial. The fact that the verdict had been quashed and Thomas sat in that courtroom an innocent man makes the statements of the former inspector all the more astonishing. They were to rebound with a vengeance at a later date. The reason that Morris had drawn them from Hutton during the course of the second trial is abundantly clear; apart from their highly prejudicial value for the Crown they helped to explain why the Charles case had undergone such a dramatic transformation, a transformation that is based on the recollection of Hutton and other Crown witnesses as to its original appearance.

Step by step Hutton went through the investigation that he had controlled. It all sounded so logical, so calm, so correct. It sounded none of these things to the accused Arthur Thomas. When Inspector Hutton started to recount his version of the conversation he had had with the accused on the day he had arrested him, Thomas could take no more. He groaned out 'No' and collapsed. After being examined by a doctor the trial was adjourned until the following morning, Tuesday, 10 April 1973.

Continuing the next day Hutton, in answers to questions from Morris, declared that he had verified from two other people Len Demler's version of how the blood from Jeannette got on to his car seat. Who these two people are he did not say.

One of the additional pieces of information that this jury were privileged to obtain from Bruce Hutton concerned the subject of wrist watches.

It had become obvious to the police and the Crown that the Eggleton rolled-gold wrist watch did not belong to Arthur Thomas. Too many people had sworn on oath that he had never owned such a watch for that proposition to be pursued at the second trial. Consequently

340

in another change of tactics the police and the Crown also changed wrists, they attempted to put the blood-stained mucus-covered watch on the arm of the dead Harvey Crewe, hence:

Morris: Anything missing from the body?

Hutton: Yes, in particular I was interested to look at this body to see if there was a watch on it.

Morris: Was there a watch on it?

Hutton: No, sir.

And later during the same examination:

Morris: You mentioned in your evidence there was no watch on the man's body, Harvey's body, when found in the water, was any watch at all found in the Crewe farm?

Hutton: No, there was no gents' wristlet watch found; there was a farm pocket watch found in the house which appears on page eight in the inventory and also some ladies' wristlet watches found inside the house.

Evidence, like certain feastdays is movable. This attempt to make Harvey the owner of the mysterious watch that Eggleton had repaired, *a watch that has never been produced*, would have been immeasurably strengthened if evidence had been laid before the jury that Harvey did in fact own such a watch. If for example his mother Mrs Crewe, his father-in-law Len Demler, his neighbours the Chittys, the Spratts, or the Priests had got into the witness box and sworn that he had owned a rolled-gold wrist watch, it would have strengthened this attempt to put such a watch on the dead man's wrist. There was only one reason why none of these people gave that testimony. To have done so would have been to commit perjury. *Harvey Crewe never owned such a watch*. His wrist watch, apparently missing when the police carried out their inventory, was one with a stainless steel exterior. My source of information on this aspect includes not only friends of Harvey but his near neighbour Mrs Spratt. It is inconceivable that Inspector Hutton or members of his

341

large investigating team had not ascertained this fact before the second trial; yet here was the Crown trying to establish something as a fact that elementary research would have instantly disproved.

At twenty minutes past ten Kevin Ryan rose to cross-examine. It was by any standards a crucial moment for both defence and prosecution. These two men, fighting on opposite sides, had been on each other's backs from the moment that the move to obtain a retrial had begun in the middle of 1971. Now nearly two years later the man who had triumphed in that fight to obtain a retrial was about to question the man who had so vigorously resisted. It was not the first time they had faced each other across a courtroom. For Ryan there had been other clients who had been placed in the dock as a result of Hutton's investigations. Each held very clear opinions of the other. Hutton on Ryan:

'The truth is that Kevin is a great orator, that's where his secret lies. Not a worker. I know from experience that if you upset Kevin Ryan you've won and in that second trial I did it purposefully. These are tactics. I baited him and he went berserk in the first minute of cross-examination. Kevin's a dangerous man when he gets on his feet. I used to train my detectives. I would drill it into them: "Now remember this, Kevin Ryan has not prepared his case, he derives his next question out of your previous answer. Keep the answer to the minimum." I had a couple of Englishmen who went up against him (police officers) they were beauties: "Yes, sir. Yes, sir. Yes, sir." Another thing about Kevin is that he cannot remember his questions. He hasn't got it written down. He will ask it, you take a little time answering, then say: "Would you mind asking that again?" More likely than not he will ask you a totally different question. Of course all the time the trained mind is thinking what answer to give to that first very pertinent question. We beat Kevin and his brother up, just like that.' At which point Bruce Hutton snapped his fingers.

Ryan on Hutton:

'Thomas has always maintained that prior to his arrest Hutton said: "I've got something up my sleeve which I won't tell you about now but you'll find out about it." Now I believe Hutton did say that to him but having over the years seen Bruce Hutton's performance in the witness box, his capacity as a prosecution witness, it was pointless to challenge him on this point. Here you are dealing with a very clever, sophisticated police officer.'

So these two men faced each other in a packed courtroom. A courtroom with such a curious atmosphere. Odette Leather, at that time writing a weekly newspaper column, talked to me of that atmosphere:

'I have been closely involved with the law and legal proceedings for over twenty years. Never before or since have I experienced an atmosphere like that one that existed throughout that entire second trial not only in the courtroom but in the entire building. The antagonism of the court officials, the registrar, even the judge. There were two camps in that courtroom, you were either anti-police or pro-police. The court officials refused to reserve seats for the Thomas family. Even his parents, and his mother was an elderly woman who was very ill, had to queue. I spoke to one court official about this. It seemed so degrading that Mr and Mrs Thomas were merely being taken to the front of the queue and obliged to endure the pushing and shoving, the comments and the stares. I said to this official: "Surely you could reserve seats for Mr and Mrs Thomas?" His reply was: "Piss off." Kevin Ryan had a particular problem during the course of the trial. I know you are aware what it was. He discussed it with me during one lunch recess. After lunch Detective Abbott engaged me, not very subtly, in conversation.

He wanted to know about my friendship with Kevin Ryan, who I was, my views on the case, my views of the innocence of Thomas. If he'd bothered to read the newspaper I was writing for at the time he could probably have worked out the answers to most of his questions.'

What Kevin Ryan's 'particular problem' was will become clear shortly.

In this atmosphere the defence counsel began to cross-examine the prosecution's chief witness:

Ryan: You have mentioned a brush and comb set. Did that inventory say that brush and comb set was found on the floor of the wardrobe?

Hutton: It does not but it points out what was found on the top of the wardrobe and I clearly remember where it was.

Ryan: One or two witnesses remember it was in the top of the cupboard.

Hutton: On the top shelf?

Ryan: Yes.

Hutton: It wasn't there. There were a lot of picture frames there.

Ryan: One of your witnesses said that was where it was found.

Hutton: He was mistaken, the inventory tells us exactly where it is.

Ryan: The other matter you mentioned, about how fair you were supplying a list of cars to the defence. When did you supply it?

Hutton: I supplied it as soon as I received a direction from the Crown Solicitor and it took me two and a half days of going through a police file which is some six feet thick.

Ryan: Were there some problems before this was received?

Hutton: Yes I understand there were problems; I received a direction from the Crown Solicitor and as a result of you frequently breaking arrangements with me concerning appointments I referred the matter to the Crown Solicitor.

Ryan: I put it to you that you are a liar.

Hutton: I am not lying.

Hutton had succeeded in some ten questions in provoking Kevin Ryan into the public outburst that the inspector sought. The background of frustration and obstruction at every turn by the police that Paul Temm had suffered had been Kevin Ryan's pre-trial lot as well. The car list referred to was a schedule of vehicles seen near the Crewe farm between 16 and 22 June 1970. Ryan had battled for weeks before the trial to obtain a copy. He had also battled to get samples of the body wires for his own experts; that took a Court order issued only a few days before the trial began. The frustration that had been welling up within Kevin Ryan was calmly exploited by Inspector Hutton. All great fun and games in this trial where a man faced a life sentence if found guilty. All part of the rich fabric of the legal system admired and praised by so many of us.

The obvious animosity between the two men grew as the examination proceeded. They argued about Hutton's refusal to allow Dr Sprott to inspect wire samples, they argued about whether Sprott had inspected the Charles case prior to the referral in Wellington. In fact he had but Ryan had to dynamite that admission out of Hutton. During his examination-in-chief Bruce Hutton had for the first time described the appearance of the Charles case on the day it had been found as inky blue. They argued about why he had not previously used that description. This bore on the all-important matter of just how corroded the case had been at the time it had been discovered.

They argued about what Detective Charles had said at the referral and what Hutton himself had said. There was indeed great validity in the questions that Ryan was asking. Charles had been specifically asked at the referral if the cartridge case he had found had a bluish or an inky blue colouring. He had no recollection that it had. Hutton had made no mention of this during his evidence; now during the second trial and for the first time he testified about an inky blue colouring. Here is just part of the interchange between Ryan and Hutton covering that aspect:

Ryan: You didn't give evidence that the cartridge case was inky blue?

Hutton: I wasn't asked by Mr Morris or by you, sir.

Ryan: Why didn't you say so?

Hutton: I wasn't asked by you.

Ryan: You didn't say anything about the cartridge case being inky blue at Wellington?

Hutton: I wasn't asked to give that evidence.

Ryan: You only give evidence as to what you are asked?

Hutton: I give material evidence relating to my transactions, not someone else's.

Ryan: This cartridge case was of some importance in Wellington was it not?

Hutton: Perhaps to you, sir, it was.

As for giving material evidence relating only to his own transactions his evidence-in-chief at all hearings concerning this case is full of detail and information involving other officers. The slugging match ranged over many subjects. Hutton informed Ryan and the listening jury that after making certain inquiries following the first trial about Bruce Roddick he and the Crown Solicitor David Morris had felt Roddick's evidence was unreliable and that he should not be called for the second trial. Why then keep him under Crown subpoena until a few days before the commencement of that second trial? Did it really take three years to make 'certain inquiries'? If indeed Bruce Roddick was an unreliable witness and played such an important part in obtaining the conviction at the first trial would that not indicate that the first trial was a miscarriage of justice?

346

I talked at great length to Bruce Hutton about Bruce Roddick and his sighting of the mystery woman on that Friday morning. He took the view that what Roddick saw was Jeannette Crewe on a day prior to her death, that Roddick's personal background and his 'mental capacity' made him unreliable. Bruce Hutton talked of his conversation with Roddick's employer of that day, Ron Chitty, and of Mr Chitty's view that Roddick was inclined to be vague and unobservant. The former chief inspector said to me: 'I was convinced prior to the first trial that Roddick had made a mistake. But I felt that the jury are the people to make the decision and that's why I made the decision to call him in the first trial. The option was not open at the second trial because he was a defence witness.'

A defence witness who until a few days before the trial was under subpoena to appear for the prosecution.

The next person to get the treatment from Bruce Hutton during his cross-examination was Mrs McGuire. He told Ryan that he would not be surprised to hear that Eggleton the jeweller had described her as a nasty woman. He continued:

'I know she has threatened him; I have had police officers engaged in watching this woman; she had threatened this man in no uncertain terms; this woman has gone out of her way to put this man out of business, she has also subjected his child to the same kind of treatment.'

The next one to get the treatment was Graham Hewson. In front of the three appeal judges at Wellington Hutton had agreed with the defence suggestion that Hewson 'was a reasonable sort of chap oh yes, typical farmer, liked to talk'. Now during the second trial:

Hutton: At first he was helpful but when he stole Mr Crewe's dogs that was the end of it as far as I was concerned.

Ryan: When did you find out he stole the Crewes' dogs?

Hutton: After he left.

There was more on Hewson in similar vein. Hewson ceased being temporary manager of the Crewe farm at the end of July. When he returned on 16 August Bruce Hutton had readily accepted Hewson's offer to help with the sieve-search of the Crewe gardens.

Questioned about the letters that Thomas had kept, letters written by girlfriends at the time he was according to the Crown passionately courting Jeannette; letters taken by the police and suppressed until after the first trial had finished, Inspector Hutton, the man in charge of the investigation, could not recall any such letters.

Questioned about police investigations of Thomas's previous employers Hutton answered:

'Yes, in particular Barr Brothers, everyone was interviewed there.' As earlier parts of this book establish, everyone was most certainly not interviewed at Barr Brothers and the police never asked for any information regarding the dates that Thomas was employed by the company. Crucial information by any standards if they were to find support for the remarks that Detective Hughes alleged Thomas had made to him.

Questioned by Ryan if the police had checked on the dental appointment that Arthur and Vivien had in Pukekohe on the day of the killings, Hutton replied:

'We checked and they were there. Arthur and Vivien were at Pukekohe that particular day and so were Harvey and Jeannette; they went to a stock sale but returned to Pukekohe that afternoon.'

Clever to put all four principals in the same town at the same time. I do not know Inspector Hutton's source of information regarding the Crewes. I do know that neither he nor any police officer checked with dentist Garth Brown or any of his staff about the Thomases.

The former chief inspector may well feel that he broke the Ryan brothers with a snap of his fingers. The trial transcript tells a different story. Yes, he certainly caused Kevin Ryan to lose his temper. But Ryan with his questions established a clear picture of the methods of the man in charge of the Crewe murders.

So the 'finest witness that David Morris ever led' left the witness box and the case for the Crown was concluded.

Kevin Ryan, like Paul Temm before him had agonized about whether or not to put Arthur Thomas into the witness box. Both lawyers shared a view that is very widespread among defence counsel, that your client is often his own worst witness. In Ryan's case there was a special reason for his anxiety. Towards the end of the first week of the trial Kevin Ryan made a phone call from his private residence. This phone call and what subsequently happened are the clearest indication I have ever known in my life of telephone tapping. The man Ryan phoned was Keith Christie, the pilot with whom Thomas had usually worked when they were both employed by Barr Brothers on top-dressing. The reason for contacting Christie was to ask him if he would be prepared to give evidence on behalf of Thomas. Christie readily agreed. He then dropped a couple of bombs on Kevin Ryan. 'Did you know about the business of the pubic hairs? If they cross-examine me surely it's bound to come out?' He explained to Ryan what he was talking about; it shook the lawyer rigid. Information about a pubic hair collection of long ago from a man named Christie seemed to Kevin Ryan to be straight from the Rillington Place murders. When Christie went on to say that he was sure he had seen the axle on the farm after Thomas had taken the farm over in 1966, Ryan freaked. He told Christie that he did not want to hear any more and he would contact him again if he intended to call him. Unknown to both men Kevin Ryan's phone was bugged. Their phone conversation had taken place shortly after 10 p.m. on Friday, 30 March 1973.

Twenty minutes after that conversation, Keith

Christie had another phone call at his home on the outskirts of Hamilton. This call was from the local police station. Christie was told: 'Inspector Hutton has just telephoned us from Auckland and asked us to contact you. He would like you to give evidence for the Crown in the case against Arthur Thomas.' Christie advised his local police that he had been approached by the defence and that he was standing by to be called on behalf of Arthur Thomas.

If one uses that common sense that judges are always telling juries to use, it would be stretching common sense not to suspect that Ryan's telephone had been tapped.

I heard many allegations concerning phone tapping during my research, some were undoubtedly based on fear, persecution complex or paranoia. Others like the example of the Christie/Ryan phone call are not. Indeed Kevin Ryan was ignorant of the fact that Christie had been contacted by the police within minutes of their phone call until I told him.

In the event Ryan did not call Christie as a witness and by then a Crown subpoena would have served no purpose. The information was however tucked away. A few months before I interviewed Keith Christie in late 1977, at his Hamilton home, a police superintendent appeared at his door. Under his arm was a large file on the Thomas case. In the superintendent's car was the axle. There had at that time been a number of public statements from retrial committee members and others that they had solved the puzzle of the axle. The superintendent was clearly looking for a different solution and took a statement from Christie. This is an aspect I shall return to.

This example of telephone tapping is not unique in the Thomas case. In a country which has just passed highly controversial legislation authorizing its secret service to tap telephones, what has now been made legal has been par for the course, certainly with regard to the telephones owned by supporters of Arthur

Thomas. Kevin Ryan's was undoubtedly tapped throughout the second trial. Pat Vesey, chairman of the retrial committee, was another whose telephone was tapped during the same period. On one occasion when attempting to telephone a number in Tuakau he was put through to a South Auckland police station. On another occasion he passed confidential information to Kevin Ryan concerning the number of no. 8 bullets that had been collected. A police witness subsequently quoted precisely the same figure during the second trial when asked how many he would expect to receive if he had advertised as the retrial committee had.

Thomas's father, Allan Thomas, was staying at a private residence during the period of the second trial. The telephone was subjected to constant interference. Finally when the subscriber complained she was advised: 'It will not be necessary to send a serviceman as today is the last day of defence evidence. You will not have any trouble tomorrow.' She didn't. I could cite many other examples. It would seem that the recent legislation authorizing such practices is superfluous.

From the time of the phone conversation with Christie Ryan had worried and fretted. Having interviewed his client he knew that the story of the pubic hairs was true. With regard to Christie's comments about an axle, Thomas insisted that if Christie had seen an axle on his farm it was not the one that the police had pulled out of the Waikato river.

As the trial progressed Ryan worried more and more about those pubic hairs. While he could reason that this was some youthful quirk of Thomas's, which in view of the fact that he had thrown them away long before he had met Vivien, had demonstrably passed, he was fully aware of the damage that Morris would inflict if he could get such a piece of information out in front of the jury. It had nothing at all to do with the trial, nothing to do with the alleged murders, it could be objected to on many grounds, prejudicial and irrelevant were just two. But such information would ensure that a trial that had in many respects moved away from an examination of the relevant evidence would become a trial of sexual standards, an inquiry into morals or sexual aberrations.

After a short opening address to the jury Kevin Ryan called his first witness at 2.45 p.m. on the afternoon of 10 April 1973. It was the accused, Arthur Thomas.

Kevin Ryan took him through his early life, his schooling, his work, his interest in Jeannette and in other girls. He took him through the day and evening of 17 June 1970 until:

Ryan: Did you leave the house that night?

Thomas: Neither Vivien or myself left the house that night.

Ryan: You know the Crown case is you murdered Jeannette and Harvey Crewe on the night of 17 June?

Thomas: I did not sir, as God is my witness I did not murder either of the Crewes.

Thomas told later how he was shown by Parkes the small greeting card and was told that it came from a wrapped-up brush and comb set. He told of the subsequent interrogation by Parkes and Seaman and that he thought they had again mentioned the wrapped-up present. He denied taking a rolled-gold watch into Eggleton. Asked if his memory was very good on some matters he replied: 'I haven't got a very good memory, sir; I wasn't very brilliant at school.' His examination-in-chief concluded with:

Ryan: Did you wrap the wire around the body of Harvey Crewe?

Thomas: I did not.

Ryan: Did you assist in any way the putting of the bodies of Harvey and Jeannette Crewe into the Waikato river?

Thomas: I did not, sir.

Ryan: You know how a cartridge case which must have been fired by your rifle came to be in the Crewe garden?

Thomas: I don't know, sir.

Ryan: Did you have anything to do with the homicide of the Crewes?

Thomas: I did not, sir, as God is my witness, I did not have any involvement with the Crewe murders in any way.

The cross-examination of Arthur Thomas by David Morris stretched over two days. Because of its length a verbatim record of it within this book is not possible. Fragments of it may give an indication of its quality. It made many who heard it wince, including members of the legal profession. David Morris, who had told three appeal judges in the middle of 1971 that the Crown were 'not greatly concerned with establishing motive' spent several hours during his cross-examination in the second trial attempting to do just that – establish a motive. Right at the start of his cross-examination after asking Thomas how old he was, it began:

Morris: Were you ever in love with Jeannette Demler?

Thomas: I was fond of her, yes, at one time.

Morris: Were you ever in love with her?

Thomas: No, I wouldn't say that.

Questions of love, passion, schoolboy crushes, depth of feelings, feelings as he grew to be a man, poured from Morris in a torrent. He threw at Thomas the hearsay evidence of Mesdames Batkin, Willis and MacGee. He re-activated the 'so he is lying too' gambit; beginning amazingly enough with the dead woman, Jeannette Crewe.

This illustrates exactly the point I have already made about the inadmissibility of Mrs Willis's evidence, as also with that of Mrs MacGee. At least Mrs Batkin alleged that she was *present* when Thomas allegedly pestered Jeannette at dances. How Thomas was expected to refute what a dead woman had allegedly said about him when she complained of his pestering to Mrs Willis when he was not present I do not know.

I defy any member of the legal profession in this country to tell me. Morris invoked the alleged words of the dead woman on a number of occasions during his cross-examination. The fact that when she returned from her European trip she worked in the Maramarua area for only a few months before going to Wanganui was laid at Thomas's doorstep. Strengthened of course by the additional evidence offered by Len Demler.

Morris: What were you doing to her to make her complain to her father and travel to Wanganui to get away from you?

Thomas: I don't believe she did, sir.

Morris: You know she went to Wanganui?

Thomas: Yes.

Morris: It is apparent from the dates she stayed at the hostel that she had left early in the year. She had not completed her course there, something had made her go to Wanganui; what were you doing to make her travel to Wanganui to get away from you?

Thomas: I am telling you the honest truth, sir, that in 1962 when I gave her the brush and comb set, this was when she told me she had another boyfriend and from that time on I had not seen her or asked her out or done anything.

Morris: What were you doing to her?

Thomas: I hadn't written to her or anything after 1962.

At this point because New Zealand's legal system is based on the British system everything stopped for tea for fifteen minutes. On the resumption:

Morris: Remember I was asking you what you had been doing to Jeannette to make her want to complain to her father, to make her travel as far away from her home as Wanganui and you told the jury you had been doing nothing to her. So really if what you say is correct . . .

Thomas: It is true and correct.

354

Morris: Jeannette has been making up all these things she has been telling about you?

Thomas: Her friends.

Morris: You suggest friends of hers in different parts of the country have made up stories about you?

Thomas: I am telling you that from 1962 onwards I had not pestered her, that's what I'm telling you; if you can say asking her out three times is pestering.

The Crown Prosecutor when opening to the first trial jury had said among other things that 'Thomas to his credit had not attempted to court Jeannette after 1962'. Not a shred of evidence at that trial or the second took the accused's abortive attempt to court the girl beyond that date, yet here was the Crown Prosecutor attacking, and attacking in a most virulent manner, the accused for driving her to Wanganui in April 1963, A man stood that day charged with the most serious crime a person can commit in this country. He had already been in prison since his arrest in November 1970. He faced an automatic life sentence if found guilty.

The Crown Prosecutor saw fit to attack Thomas because of the accused's relative poverty, relative to the wealth of the Crewes that is. He attacked him for taking over his father's farm. He inferred it was so that Thomas could be near Jeannette. He attacked him because he had hardly seen the Crewes since their marriage. He attacked him because when he had seen Jeannette in the street he had had the temerity to speak to her. He attacked him about the fires and burglary that had taken place on the Crewe property. He asked Thomas to speculate on who was jealous enough of the Crewes to have done these things. He then asked the most extraordinary question I have ever heard come from the lips of a prosecution counsel:

Morris: Do you know anybody with more reason than you to be jealous of Harvey?

Kevin Ryan assures me that he leapt to his feet objecting. I do not know. I was not there and the court verbatim transcript does not record an objection. The question is on a par with: 'Have you stopped beating your wife, answer yes or no.' Thomas stared at Morris in bemusement, then replied with the naivety that totally sums up the man:

Thomas: I do not, sir.

Why not ask the wretched man if he knew of anybody with *less* reason than himself to be jealous of Harvey?

In the first trial Morris had slipped in a similar kind of question when he had asked Thomas if he knew of anybody who hated him enough to frame him. He attacked Thomas when the accused had the temerity to say that the evidence of Detective Sergeant Hughes was wrong. Thomas had little alternative other than to say that Hughes was wrong. Hughes was wrong.

Curious, the length of time that David Morris dwelt on the evidence of Hughes. Far longer than in the first trial.

The following day after an hour or so of questions that virtually amounted to a final speech to the jury, David Morris concluded with:

Morris: For these various acts of murder, as done, aren't they the type of acts you would expect of a person taking every precaution to avoid having himself connected with the murders?

Thomas: I would say that, sir, as I see it.

Morris: All these things; throwing the bodies in the water, weighing them down, are consistent with a man covering his tracks?

Thomas: I would say so.

Morris: Is that not the reason why after killing the bodies you wrapped them up, weighed them and threw them in the Waikato river?

Thomas: Not me, sir.

Despite everything that Morris had thrown at him, including showing him the grotesque photographs of Harvey Crewe's dead body, Thomas had not broken. With regard to that ploy of showing the photographs

356

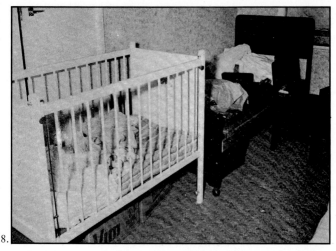

18.

Rochelle Crewe's bedroom as discovered by the police. Did Rochelle survive for five days in this cot without any food or drink?

Below. Rochelle Crewe. This photograph was taken only days after the child had been found in the blood-spattered home. Could anyone seriously argue that this child has just suffered five days of total starvation?

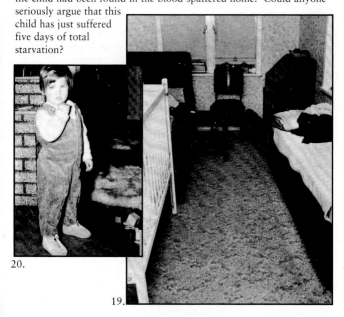

20.

19.

Len Demler. 'He was my number one,' Detective Inspector Bruce Hutton said to me.

Below. One of the reasons why the man in charge of police investigations placed Len Demler at the top of the list of suspects. Jeannette's bloodstains found on the passenger seat of Demler's car. Stains nearly three inches long that DSIR expert Dr Donald Nelson assured me were 'no bigger than a pin head.'

21.

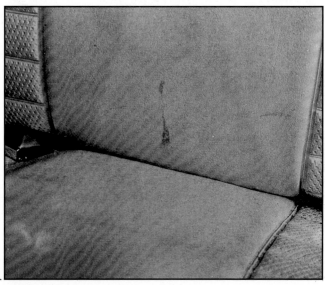

22.

After Jeannette Crewe's body had been found with a fatal bullet wound in the head, the police yet again took the Crewe gardens apart. Photo shows the earlier pattern search made in June 1970. The strings indicating a pattern search can be clearly seen. *Below.* Taken at the scene of another police investigation this shows just how thorough a pattern search is. Yet despite searches like this at the Crewe farm in June and again in August 1970 no cartridge case was found.

While the most extensive and most expensive search in New Zealand's history continued for his daughter and son-in-law, Len Demler rode his farm and threw a birthday party to 'take his mind off it.'

Below. September 16, 1970. The Waikato River. Inspector Hutton holds an axle recovered from the riverbed. To his immediate right is Inspector Gaines who had led the search for the bodies; in front of Hutton the wrapped-up remains of Harvey Crewe.

25.

26.

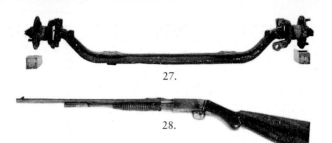

27.

28.

29.

A close-up of the axle with the stub axles that the police allege they found on the Thomas farm-dump.

The .22 rifle of Arthur Thomas that the Crown wrongly asserted was the murder weapon.

Wire found around the body of Harvey Crewe. None was found around the axle.

Below. Some of the men from the DSIR seen here examining the Crewes' car. Dr Nelson is on the right and Rory Shanahan on the left.

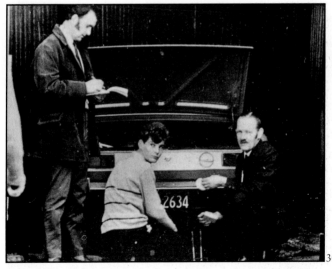

30.

31.

Arthur Thomas told his counsel Paul Temm that Hutton had asserted during the interrogation on 25 October: 'I've got another piece of evidence up my sleeve.' All the evidence against Thomas had been shown to him during that interrogation. Two days later a cartridge case allegedly fired by the Thomas rifle was found in the gardens of the Crewe farm. Photo shows Detective Charles, who found the cartridge case, pointing to the marker that indicates the exact spot, nearly sixteen feet from the louvre windows.

Below. The Charles cartridge case, the most discredited Court exhibit in the history of New Zealand.

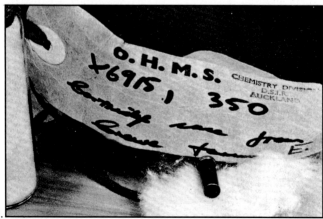

32.

33.

34.

Top Left. October 24, 1970. Arthur and Vivien Thomas at a
'pyjama stir.' Hours after the party had finished they found
themselves facing an all-day interrogation from the police. From this
photo the jeweller Eggleton claimed to recognise Thomas as the man
who had brought a bloodstained mucus-covered watch into his shop
for repair a week after the Crewes were known to be missing.
Top Right. John Fisher. In January 1971 he took this watch,
bloodstained and mucus-covered, into Eggleton's shop. This evidence
was suppressed for over five years. *Below.* Moment of arrest. Arthur
Thomas walking into Otahuhu police station with Detective Keith.
On Thomas's arm is the wrist watch that would become the centre of
one of the first trial controversies.

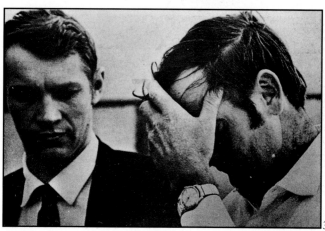

35.

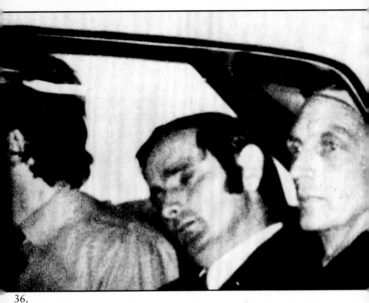

36.

Above. Arthur Thomas returns to Paremoremo prison.

Below. Arthur Thomas's family. Left to right: Vivien, Lloyd Thomas (brother), Rita Tyrrell (sister), Richard (brother), Mr Allan Thomas, Robyn Thomas (sister-in-law), Desmond (brother), Mrs Ivy Thomas, Ray (brother), Margaret Stuckey (sister), Mrs Ethel Hill (aunt), Lynette Hooton (sister).

37.

of the dead man, Morris had turned to the press bench at the end of the previous day's hearing and remarked of Thomas: 'He might look sick. But he doesn't look half as sick as Harvey and Jeannette Crewe.' To which I would add, or the face of justice. Recalling the ordeal that his client went through during that cross-examination Kevin Ryan told me he was delighted with Arthur and the manner he had answered the questions. 'He didn't lose me any marks.'

Vivien Thomas, who followed her husband into the box, was engaged by Baragwanath in another of those interminable conversations about the mating habits of cows. She was followed by the family dentist Garth Brown, the gentleman who according to Inspector Hutton had received a visit from the police, checking on that aspect of the alibi, but who has yet to receive that visit from the police. Apart from confirming that both Thomases had attended his surgery that day he added the significant piece of information that when invited to join him at home for coffee they declined because they had to rush back to attend to a sick cow.

Arthur's aunt testified that the Thomases had declined to join her at the ratepayers' meeting because of trouble they were having with a cow. Her telephone call to the Thomas farm had been made at approximately 7.30 p.m. on the night of the 17th.

Arthur's father, Allan Thomas, took the stand and told the court that it had been his idea for his son to take over the Pukekawa farm in 1966, which should have put the Crown's allegations about Arthur returning to the area to be near Jeannette into perspective. He was questioned by Kevin Ryan about the work that Rasmussen had carried out on his trailer. He had no recollection about what had happened to the original axle after the engineer had replaced it and could not remember seeing the stripped-down axle back on his property. His subsequent evidence told of young men taking the odd piece of machinery and vintage car parts

357

from the farm and of some of them tinkering about with an old car they had dumped on his property in mid-1965. He told Ryan of Detective Johnston's visit to his farm before his son had been arrested, of how he had answered their questions and given them access to his business files, of how he had signed a statement prepared by Detective Parkes in which as far as he could recall the expression that 'if other parts of the old axle assembly had been found on his farm in Pukekawa it would be reasonable to assume that the axle had come back from Rasmussen to the farm'. At that time Mr Thomas senior had been trying for three years to get a copy of that statement from the police; they had refused to give him a copy. Over seven years later they still refuse to give him a copy of the statement drafted by Parkes and signed by Thomas senior. He had been and still is trying to get certain records covering the business transaction with Rasmussen back from the police.

Subsequent witnesses called for the defence confirmed that access to the Waikato river on the Mercer Ferry road leading from the Thomas farm was impossible on 17 June, that Thomas had first had dancing lessons two years after Beverly Batkin allegedly saw him dancing with Jeannette, that his car with the distinctive differential whine had not been heard on the road that night, and that Pukekawa was an area alive with scavengers collecting old car parts, scrap metal and cast iron.

Several young men testified to moving various metal objects from the Thomas farm in 1965. One actually referred to 'the axle' but he was unsure what sort of axle it was they had moved. Other vintage car enthusiasts testified to searching over the Thomas farm at the end of February or the beginning of March 1970 and declared that if they had seen an axle like the one the police brought up from the bottom of the Waikato they would have grabbed it.

The name of Mickey Eyre shot back into prominence

with the testimony of Frederick Brooks. He had been working in the Pukekawa area in 1969 and 1970. In view of Mrs Eyre's testimony that her son Mickey was not allowed out alone at night because of his physical handicaps, the evidence of Mr Brooks was particularly interesting. He swore on oath that at about ten o'clock on an October night in 1969 he had seen Mickey on the road, alone, with a rifle.

His final evidence should have been of particular interest to Dr Nelson, the expert who had opined that pattern 8 .22 bullets would by 1970 be a collector's item. Mr Brooks had *bought* two packets of .22 bullets from a store in Te Kuiti in either May or June 1970. By the time the number 8 had any significance he had used one packet; he had broken open all of his remaining bullets, purchased in mid-1970, and they all had the figure 8 on them. Significantly the Crown did not cross-examine Mr Brooks about either Mickey Eyre, pattern 8 bullets, or anything.

Quite evidently Mrs Eyre did not keep a very good check on her son. The next two witnesses, Mr and Mrs Hooker, testified about finding him on their porch one evening with a rifle in his hand. That had been about 1959. Ten years later Mr Brooks sighted Eyre, rifle in his hand, out alone at night.

The jury had heard so many policemen talk about the non-appearance and non-existence of Graham Hewson that at this stage of the proceedings they might well have been coming to the conclusion that Hewson was a figment of the defence's imagination. Before he took his place in the witness box the Court heard evidence from Patrick Vesey. Related by marriage to Vivien Thomas, Vesey had provided a home for the young woman when she had arrived in New Zealand and had subsequently introduced her to Arthur. For nearly two years he had battled and worked for this second trial. Reminiscent of a latter-day Sancho Panza in stature, his role in the campaign for Thomas had been that of Don Quixote, tilting at legal and political windmills of very real substance. He had organized petitions, written articles, held press conferences, dug up tips, taken part in burying cartridge cases on the Crewe property for corrosion comparison tests. He had also done his best to give the marriage of Arthur and Vivien Thomas some continuing semblance of reality. Certain Court officials had throughout the trial been winding the jury up, telling them that they were being heavily protected by the police in case the retrial committee attempted to get at them; there was even talk that attempts might be made on the jurors' lives. One jury member had been stopped in the toilet of the Supreme Court and told: 'Don't forget Arthur Thomas is innocent.' He complained to the registrar and was told: 'Don't worry, that's the retrial committee.' I know exactly who the man was; he was nothing to do with the retrial committee but it serves no purpose telling that second jury that now. At the time of the incident it would have seemed clear evidence to those eleven jurors that attempts were indeed being made to get at them. In fact no attempt by any member of the retrial committee was ever contemplated, let alone made.

When Pat Vesey strode to the witness box, the word went around the jury: 'That's one of the Thomas clan.' It was like something out of a Western movie.

Pat Vesey testified about the proliferation of fired cartridge cases around the Thomas property, many of them fired by his sons. The premise being that fired cases from the Thomas rifle were easily available to anyone wanting to drop one into a Crewe flowerbed. He also told the Court of his part in burying test cases. Perhaps the last part of his testimony was the most pertinent. It certainly should have been to Dr Nelson who had refused to accept Ryan's suggestion that there might still be quite a few pattern 8 bullets around the country. The retrial committee, in an attempt to demonstrate just how many there were, had placed several small advertisements in newspapers. In a very short while they had been sent over 5,000. Pat Vesey was followed into the witness box by Graham Hewson.

In examination-in-chief he gave details of his friendship with Harvey and Jeannette Crewe and of how on hearing of their disappearance he had driven from Woodville to Pukekawa to render what help he could. He told the Court of how he was subsequently appointed temporary manager until a more permanent manager could be found. Upon the discovery of Jeannette's body, having previously returned to Woodville to look after his own business affairs, he had once again driven to Pukekawa, this time with Harvey's mother. Details of how he had been with the police when they collected the sieve from Tuakau and his participation in the subsequent sieve-search followed, including his finding of a full round of ammunition. As to being a stealer of Harvey's dogs, he told the Court of his conversations with Mrs Crewe, who urged him to take them; and of his conversations with the estate solicitors and Demler and Hutton who were all quite happy for the dogs to be shipped down to Woodville.

Under cross-examination Morris taxed him about the errors he had made at the referral at Wellington. There was much discussion about the quality of Hewson's memory, of exactly what beds had been sieved in the Crewe gardens in mid-August. Hewson remained adamant. The bed that Charles found a cartridge case in had been sieve-searched by Hewson and the police officers in August. Morris finished with a series of questions that implied Hewson's evidence was based on what Kevin Ryan had told him to say. On re-examination Ryan demolished that particular innuendo by establishing that since Hewson had arrived in Auckland to give evidence he had spent less than five minutes with defence counsel.

George McGuire told the jury of his conversation

with the jeweller Eggleton in December 1970 and of Eggleton declaring he had never seen either Arthur or Vivien Thomas. Strangely there was no cross-examination from the Crown. There is a droll quality about the last few questions Ryan asked this particular witness.

Ryan: What is the size of your wife?

McGuire: She is about five foot three or four I suppose. She is not the vicious type if that's what you are talking about.

Ryan: Mr Eggleton said she was.

McGuire: I read about that in the paper.

Ryan: You are married to her, is she a vicious woman?

McGuire: Never found her that way.

Bruce Roddick took the stand. It was predictable from the treatment he had received at Wellington and earlier evidence in the trial that the Crown would attack him as they had attacked Graham Hewson.

In answer to questions from Kevin Ryan he told the Court of the mystery woman he had seen on the Friday morning. For the first time in front of a jury he was asked about Vivien Thomas. He said he knew her and that she had not been the woman. The last piece of information that Ryan elicited from the young farmer concerned Mickey Eyre:

Roddick: Yes, when I was working for Mr Allen out at Glen Murray on his sheep farm Mickey was employed to crutch the lambs, and one lamb wouldn't sit still for him so he just grabbed it around the throat and throttled it.

He was cross-examined by Baragwanath who initially attempted to conjure up a picture of Roddick and his employer racing around the paddock at breakneck speed to get the job of feeding-out completed. Such an image would of course reduce the amount of attention that Roddick would have paid to the woman he had seen. Such questions, of course, were not put by the

Crown during the first trial, when Roddick was their witness.

The curious pre-trial episode of Detective Johnston and the Roddick family on the Chitty farm was also a feature of this cross-examination. Johnston's calculations of the distance between Roddick and the woman were given by Baragwanath. Roddick observed, very pertinently: 'I wasn't there when he measured it.' The Crown then asked one of its former key witnesses:

Baragwanath: Have you on occasion had difficulty in remembering matters over a relatively short time?

Roddick: No.

Baragwanath: Have you found it necessary for Mr Chitty to repeat instructions he has given you about your work?

Roddick: No.

Baragwanath: Do you think it likely or not you were confused about the day on which it was you saw that woman?

Roddick: No.

Further questions followed pointing out an earlier estimation of the distance between himself and the woman that Roddick had given. The cross-examination finished with:

Baragwanath: In fact did you not initially think the lady you had seen had been Mrs Crewe?

Roddick: Yes.

Baragwanath: After the showing of the photograph in book A, the photograph right at the back?

Roddick: Yes.

Kevin Ryan rose to re-examine:

Ryan: Had you seen Mrs Crewe prior to 19 June 1970?

Roddick: No.

Ryan: Is that why you thought the person you saw there was in fact Mrs Crewe?

Roddick: Yes.

Ryan: Regarding your knowledge of the accused's

wife had you been to any social function where she was present?

Roddick: Yes.

Ryan: Seen her there?

Roddick: Yes.

Ryan: Been to other occasions at which she was present?

Roddick: Yes, there were parties, dances and there was a football match.

Ryan: Although she wasn't known to you well she was known to you by sight?

Roddick: Yes.

Ryan: On the statement you gave to the police in June 1970 . . .

At this point there were strenuous objections from Baragwanath. Apparently although he considered it was perfectly in order for the Crown to attack Roddick about the deposition he had given to the Lower Court concerning distance, he objected to Ryan asking about the *initial* statement that Roddick had given to the police. Mr Justice Perry ruled that the question could be asked.

Ryan: Can you recall what distance it was you said in your statement to the police you were away from the person when you saw her?

Roddick: Between 75 to 100 yards.

In fact as has been previously recorded in this book Roddick's original statement states: 'I was about 75 yards.' At the Lower Court he had said approximately a good 200 yards and Detective Johnston's calculations put the distance at about 120 yards. I have not measured the distance but I have stood in exactly the area where Roddick was working that day with Ron Chitty. Two women appeared from the direction of the kitchen entrance of the Crewe farm. This had not been arranged – it was pure chance. One of them I instantly recognized as the wife of a Pukekawa farmer. The other I had never seen before. Perhaps if either jury during their respective guided tours of the Crewe and Thomas farms and areas by the Waikato had been taken across the road to that paddock they would have been in a far better position to assess Roddick's evidence. There is no doubt in my mind that if he had known the woman he would have recognized her from that distance. Clearly he did not.

To combat the array of Crown experts the defence produced a few of its own. It had become what Sir Trevor Henry so rightly objects to: 'A trial by experts'.

The first defence expert called was the highly qualified Ian Devereux. His contribution to the Thomas trial concerned the wire. He took exception to the conclusions of the Crown's wire expert Harry Todd. Using a different method of analysis he had concluded that the body wires and the wire removed from the Thomas farm had significant differences.

David Baragwanath when cross-examining Dr Devereux spent about half an hour stating in essence: 'Our expert is more expert than your expert.' Eventually Mr Justice Perry decided to intervene. The judge insisted that the content of trace impurities in the wires be expressed in percentages, rather than parts per million, and he failed to appreciate the significance of differences between the Todd tests and the Devereux tests. The conversation between the judge and the expert contained this interchange as it approached its conclusion.

Devereux: I can't see you can apply Mr Todd's results to my figures.

Judge: I am not proposing to do that; the greatest variation you found in copper was .014.

Devereux: Yes and on the basis of those figures that is a significant difference.

Judge: He has been willing to allow for a possible error variation of .01 so the difference would be .004 after allowing for your .014.

Devereux: I don't follow that.

Judge: You say the biggest gap in all those six samples of copper was .014. Mr Todd said he was willing to allow or agree there could be . . . you see his .01, if he had put there .014 you would have been in agreement?

Devereux: No, all that means is that two things agree within a large area of say, a five-foot man and a six-foot man, within a foot. This is a very important scientific fact, I have quoted the maximum error I have to be applied to my figures and on the basis of that the chances of those two wires being the same would be something like approaching 1 million.

Shortly after that the judge withdrew from the discussion.

In the first trial, evidence from the final witness for the Crown, the jeweller Eggleton, had come as an apparent bombshell to the defence. This book makes it clear that though Paul Temm's knowledge of that evidence was not acquired until two days before the testimony he nevertheless was at that stage aware of what Eggleton would say.

In the second trial, the boot was on the other foot with a vengeance. Sensational evidence for the defence was to come from the man that Kevin Ryan called on the final day of the case for the defence, Dr James Sprott. The events surrounding that evidence are as strange and bizarre as anything in this strange and bizarre case.

As had been indicated by the evidence of Pat Vesey, newspaper advertisements were placed requesting .22 bullets bearing the pattern 8. The object was for the defence to demonstrate just how widespread such bullets were throughout New Zealand. They got more than they bargained for. A lot more. Packets, envelopes, boxes of .22 bullets began to arrive at Dr Sprott's laboratory in Parnell. Among those sending samples was a man who is largely unknown in the Thomas case. A man who to my mind is the unsung hero in a story noticeably short on heroes. His name is Jack Ritchie, a former police detective.

At the time of the Thomas trials Ritchie had left the police force and was in business in Dannevirke. The nature of his business was a gun shop. The police must certainly rue the day they allowed Evan Swain to write his booklet, 'The Crewe Murders. Featuring Photographs Previously Unpublished'. One such photograph in that booklet had alerted Graham Hewson. Another alerted Jack Ritchie. The photograph of the base of the Charles cartridge case. Reading the booklet the former detective learned of the pattern 8 bullet fragments that had been recovered from the bodies of Harvey and Jeannette. One of those apparently useless pieces of information that we all have dancing round inside our heads started Jack Ritchie looking through his large stock of .22 bullets to check that piece of information. Examination of his own stock confirmed what he already knew. Carefully placing some cartridge cases and bullets inside three envelopes he mailed them to Sprott's laboratory with certain suggestions. Sadly they lay for several weeks among the boxes and packets of bullets that members of the public had sent. In the final week of the trial, Pat Vesey, idly sorting through the many samples that had been sent in, picked up the small box that had come from Dannevirke. When he opened it and digested the contents he went running in search of James Sprott. What Jack Ritchie, the ex-policeman, had sent to the defence was not just a few bullets and cartridge cases but a bomb that caused an explosion of such magnitude it is still reverberating in this country. Tragically when the experts got loose on the information Ritchie had made available it moved the Thomas case into the rarefied atmosphere of experts and beyond the comprehension of the ordinary man.

Put simply, what Jack Ritchie had discovered was that the markings on the base of the cartridge cases differed. All of them had I.C.I. stamped on them but his sharp eyes had noticed significant differences in the shape and the size of the letter C. In terms of cartridge bases, therefore, there were different categories. One particular category in Jack Ritchie's experience never carried a bullet with the pattern 8, the murder bullets. That category appeared to be the same as the base of the Charles cartridge.

It was explosive. It established beyond any doubt whatsoever that the Charles case, which experts were agreed upon had come from the Thomas rifle, had no connection with the deaths of the Crewes and had been deliberately planted for Mike Charles to find.

Sprott began to check through .22 samples. His excitement grew with each check. He found what he considered four clear categories of case. Three of the categories always contained a pattern 8 bullet, the fourth always had a bullet with a blank base. Ironically he was surrounded by thousands of bullets that the public had sent in. What he now needed was complete unfired bullets so that each cartridge case could be compared against the actual bullet it held. He remembered that there in the Supreme Court was another bullet with its cartridge case: the Keith bullet, the one example of pattern 8 that the police had found on the Thomas farm. It had been dissected by the police but the cartridge case with it was in a small perspex phial, under the safe keeping of Deputy Court Registrar Ian Miller. Sprott phoned Ryan at the lawyer's private residence and told him he wanted to examine the Keith exhibit. He told him why. To do so of course on a tapped telephone was tantamount to announcing the discovery on the front pages of the national press, but then neither man was aware of the fact that the phone was tapped.

The following morning a curious scene was enacted in No. 1 Court. At 8.30 a.m. Miller, having unlocked the precious exhibit from the court safe, was standing watching Dr Sprott and his assistant subject the Keith cartridge to microscopic examination. Both Sprott and his assistant Douglas Gifford had examined and had advised Kevin Ryan, who was also present in the otherwise deserted courtroom, that it was in accordance with the categories that Sprott had established. At that point Inspector Hutton, who told me he 'happened to be walking by', burst in. Douglas Gifford described Hutton's demeanour.

'He began shouting and screaming: "You are interfering with a police exhibit. You have no right. This is a very important exhibit on which I am going to bring further evidence."'

Inspector Hutton's recall of the incident was not dissimilar:

'I had the tightest security ever known around those exhibits, particularly the Charles and the Keith exhibits. I had a firm undertaking from the court registrar that those particular exhibits were not to be brought out of the court safe unless the exhibits officer was present. Now in spite of those instructions, as you well know, I came into that court about 8.30 a.m. and he had conned the young deputy registrar into taking it out of the safe so that they could examine it in the empty court, in the absence of the police. Now this is a police exhibit. That should have cost Sprott his practice. My God, I'd say I got upset. What would you do? I crashed in. I happened to be walking past and thought: "What's that light doing on in there?" I told Bob Walton: "If anything has been done to that exhibit that's when it was done." He had no authority to examine that exhibit. After further application was made, yes. But at that time no authority. I think he made an error right there and then in his measurement.'

James Sprott had previously examined the Charles cartridge on a different morning and was satisfied that it fitted into category four, the sole category that did not carry pattern 8 murder bullets.

Dr Sprott had in fact asked Kevin Ryan for access

to the exhibit. Kevin Ryan assures me that he had obtained official permission. I can well understand Bruce Hutton going berserk, it was indeed a very important exhibit. If, however, the defence had stood up in open court and asked the judge for permission to examine it they would have been obliged to state why they wanted to see it. Nothing unreasonable about that in the normal course of events but here was a background of obstruction that the entire defence had experienced for months, a background of a police communications nerve centre parked near the Supreme Court, of a jury that if not fitted was screened to a degree to warm the cockles of a CIA agent's heart. If Ryan did not go through the proper channels it is to be deplored. If he chose to use the tactics that were being used against him it is to be understood. In the middle, though, was a man named Arthur Thomas.

On Friday, 13 April Dr Sprott gave evidence. It largely consisted of further discussion about corrosion, wire elements, soil and who was better qualified than whom; but it also contained this vital new element concerning the Charles cartridge. To all intents and purposes it was a bombshell, Kevin Ryan's express roaring right through the middle of the prosecution's case. Copies of a hastily drawn diagram from the witness were handed to members of the jury for their consideration. In his cross-examination, which was of some length, David Morris wisely kept his questions on this particular subject to a minimum. The only points of significance that he established were that Sprott in the short time available had only been able to acquire .22 bullets complete with cases from six different sources and that he had not checked his findings with I.C.I. Australia in the twenty-four hours since he had come to his conclusions.

The final witness for the defence who gave evidence that he had seen Mickey Eyre beating and kicking a dog until it foamed at the mouth came almost as an anti-climax.

In view of the evidence of Dr Sprott the Crown sought an adjournment. There was a conference in the judge's chambers. Kevin Ryan recalls:

'David Morris and I saw Mr Justice Perry in chambers. The judge remarked that Sprott's evidence on the cartridge categories was obviously important and that he had noticed the foreman of the jury studying Sprott's hand-drawn diagram very carefully. Morris asked if Dr Nelson could examine the cartridge cases. I had no objection to that. I pointed out to both of them that I had not been able to put Sprott's evidence to Nelson because it had only been in the last couple of days that Sprott had been able to establish the categories. I told them both that I was sure that Dr Nelson would come to the same conclusions. At that stage the judge merely granted the Crown the right to examine the cases within the Supreme Court.'

The adjournment, in fact, stretched over four to five hours. Rebuttal evidence on behalf of the Crown was then heard. The first witness David Morris called was John Shea, a general manager employed by a subsidiary of I.C.I.; for many years he had been concerned with the company's manufacture of .22 bullets. He conceded that there had over the years been variations in the I.C.I. pattern stamped on the cartridge cases but felt that Sprott's categories three and four were in essence one and the same category with a difference in the height of the letter C considerably less than Sprott had detected; that they were in his view of the same basic nominal size. In cross-examination Ryan drew from him the admission that although the two categories were related they were not identical. His cross-examination of this witness was not easy, and the chief difficulty centred on a phone call that the prosecution had made to I.C.I. in Australia during the adjournment. In essence I.C.I. Australia had said that Sprott's various categories did not exist. Faced with an adjournment of many days while the Crown flew the I.C.I. man over from Australia, Ryan took the dubious alternative of accepting the evidence although he had not of course been able to cross-examine the man in Australia.

Rory Shanahan was recalled to dispute Dr Sprott's evidence on corrosion, but at this stage such evidence was surely academic when contrasted with what had now become the all-important issue of categories of cartridge cases. The final witness called by the Crown in rebuttal was Dr Donald Nelson. He told the Court that after the adjournment he had examined the Charles and Keith cartridge cases at the court. He had been unable to find any difference between the letter C stamped on the bottom of both cases. The cases had then been taken to the DSIR laboratory in Auckland and subjected to microscopic examination. Again he could find no difference at all.

Kevin Ryan's express had apparently gone off the rails.

The following morning before final speeches Dr Jim Sprott, microscope in hand, appeared early at the Supreme Court and pleaded with Kevin Ryan to be allowed to re-examine the Keith and Charles cartridge case. To Ryan's great credit, because he felt sicker in his heart at this apparent let-down than ever before in his life, he attempted to get Sprott an opportunity to look at the cases. He spoke to Baragwanath, who refused: 'We have had a gutsful of Sprott. He doesn't get to see anything.'

This attempt by Dr Sprott and the refusal by the Crown took place on Saturday morning, 14 April. If ever an overwhelming argument has been established for a forensic ombudsman to assist a jury it had been established in this trial. A trial that had experts by the dozen on apparently every subject under the sun except one, common sense. Sprott's evidence on the categories of cartridge cases was vital. The rebuttal evidence from

Shea, Nelson, and I.C.I. Australia on this subject was vital. Someone was clearly wrong, very wrong. Was it the defence or the prosecution evidence that was in error? How were the jury to determine the issue? They were to determine it on a rough drawing from Sprott plus his verbal evidence. They were to determine it on the verbal evidence of Shea. They were to determine it on a rough drawing from Nelson, plus his equally rough drawing on a blackboard in the courtroom, plus his verbal evidence. They were to determine it on the gist of a phone call made to I.C.I. Australia. A man was on trial in this courtroom charged with a double murder facing a life sentence if found guilty and the quality of evidence presented by both sides resembled the trial in *Alice in Wonderland*.

At no stage while presenting evidence did Sprott, Shea or Nelson pick up the Charles and the Keith cartridges and show the jury what they were talking about by demonstrating with the actual exhibits. Shea in fact had never examined them. At no stage was it decided that a comparison microscope set up in the courtroom, or for that matter in the nearby laboratories of Sprott or Nelson for the jury to examine the exhibits, would serve the interests of justice. At no stage did anyone even take microscopic photographs of the bases of the two cartridge cases. It is said that justice is blind. It certainly was during the Thomas trial. We *cannot, must* not, allow the fate of an accused person to be determined in such an amateur haphazard manner. Two people had died. A third stood accused of murdering them. All three deserved something better than this.

All that remained then in this circus that passed for a judicial hearing was the final speeches from counsel and the judge's summing-up.

The final speech for the Crown from David Morris will be found verbatim in the appendices.

As a short story it is brilliant. It grips. It is atmospheric. On initial reading or hearing, powerfully convincing. In terms of obtaining a conviction it is in my view only bettered by the judge's summing-up in the first trial and Lord Goddard's speech in the trial of Craig and Bentley. In terms of fact, the reader can at his leisure compare it with the evidence contained within this book. I will merely cite here one or two examples for the reader to consider how faithfully the facts were put to jury in the second trial:

'Jeannette hears the shot and hurries to her feet as the murderer enters the lounge through the kitchen and attacks her. We fortunately do not know how long elapsed between the time Jeannette realized her husband was dying and her own death or just what happened in between.

'We do know that at some stage she received a violent blow consistent with being from the butt of a rifle to her face; and that when she was finally shot, she was lying on the floor. We also know that a long hearth mat and cushion were at some stage burned by the murderer, and also that the room was heavily blood-stained. Whether the burning of these items was like the use of two saucepans with a view to concealing the blood, or whether it was done to conceal other marks traceable to the killer or his treatment of Jeannette we do not know.

'The murderer was impelled by some overwhelming motive, and that motive may have been more than merely to destroy Harvey, perhaps out of jealousy, and to silence the only other witness. The evidence is equally consistent with a desire to get to Jeannette, even if this entailed first killing her husband and later Jeannette herself. Whether the murderer was impelled by a combination of these motives only he can say, but there is nothing to suggest any alternative.'

Sir Trevor Henry comments:

'With regard to Morris's final speech in the second trial and his reference to a sexual attack, I do not think that should have been said by Morris. There was absolutely no evidence of a sexual attack. I would not agree to a Crown prosecutor saying such things.'

And Kevin Ryan:

'With regard to the remark he made about a sexual assault by the murderer on Jeannette I was so staggered and amazed by it I simply did not know what to do. It was improper, it was prejudicial, it was without any foundation whatsoever. If I had commented on it I felt I would merely be drawing more attention to an outrageously improper statement. I thought of going to the judge but in view of his performance throughout the trial that would obviously have been a complete waste of time. It was a shameful thing for Morris to do. If he had questioned Thomas on this aspect, given him a chance to deny it, if he had led that aspect correctly about a mad sexual attack it might, if he had been allowed to lead on such a subject, have been referred to in his final speech. To do it the way he did was disgusting.'

David Morris says:

'Yes, it was without foundation.'

Bob Rock:

'The jury considered David Morris's final speech to be entirely factual. As foreman of that jury I believed the reference to a sexual assault to be fact. Why was the carpet burned if not to get rid of seminal fluid?'

During his cross-examination of Arthur Thomas, David Morris had asked:

Morris: Do you know anybody with more reason than you to be jealous of Harvey?

Thomas: I do not, sir.

I could quote many members of the legal profession who were scathing in their criticism of Morris for asking that question. Perhaps just one of them will suffice: Paul Temm, QC, a highly respected member of the Auckland bar and the man who defended Thomas at the first trial. During my very long interview with Temm, one

375

particular aspect animated him and angered him more than any other. It was that question asked by Morris.

'The question about jealousy that Morris asked was an objectionable question. It should have been objected to. It was most improper. He should not have been allowed to ask such a question. It is inadmissible.'

I would ask the reader to consider the question and answer for a moment, then consider this comment from the final speech of David Morris:

'On his own admission his was not a normal attitude of a married man seeing an old girl friend interested in someone else; in cross-examination he agreed that "no one in Pukekawa had more reason than me to be jealous of Harvey Crewe". That you may think was a very significant piece of evidence. No doubt Harvey Crewe appeared prosperous and had a well-liked wife, and no doubt Thomas was having his troubles financially along with other farmers in the area who had been hit by the drought. But to think of Harvey Crewe in terms of such jealousy, particularly in his very cautious answers in cross-examination is the plainest evidence that Thomas viewed Harvey differently from the apparently prosperous farmers in the neighbour-hood.'

As the reader will see from a reading of the full speech that was not the end of it. Any further extracts, like any further comment would be superfluous.

David Morris spoke for two and a half hours. It was then Kevin Ryan's final opportunity to speak on behalf of Arthur Thomas.

I have already recorded Paul Temm's view of the defence at the second trial that he considered they took it easy, that it was going to be 'a bus ride'. Curiously it is a view that Ryan holds of the defence performance at the first trial: 'I think Temm took it easy. I think he thought it was one he was going to win.'

Perhaps both men are right in their view of the other's performance. Both men certainly made serious mistakes which they freely acknowledged to me but I believe that both men gave of their best. Certainly it drained the very lifeblood from both counsel and at the end of the day both were exhausted. Kevin Ryan observed:

'Towards the end I was very tired. I make no excuses but it did affect my performance. I should never have given that final address that Saturday. It was a mistake.'

But give it he did. He spoke for about an hour. While copies of the *Auckland Star* were on the streets with the headlines;

CROWN: JEALOUSY IS A MOTIVE FOR
'WELL EXECUTED KILLINGS'

and a summary of a large extract of the Crown's final speech that the jury would be able to read before considering their verdict; Kevin Ryan had yet to begin his final speech. When he did he told the jury that the defence was one of alibi. 'It was a positive assertion. Thomas could only call his wife and cousin to support that alibi. How many people in Pukekawa area could do better than that for that night?'

He pointed out that the Crown had set great store by the fact that Peter Thomas knew nothing of cow 4 calving on that day. That the Crown believed the cousin on that aspect.

'If that be so the Crown should also believe the same witness when he swears that Arthur Thomas could not have left the house that night. If you believe Peter Thomas that is the end of the whole trial.

'I am aware that you have been kept together for three weeks and have been confronted with evidence which must have taxed the credibility and credulity of some of you. If there is any reasonable doubt then Thomas must be given the benefit of it. "Reasonable doubt" are not glib words from a defence counsel. If you laugh away those words, injustice will creep in. Never forget those principles.'

He attacked the introduction by the Crown of

evidence relating to the fires and the burglary. 'They ask you to infer he did these things. There is no evidence at all that he did but because it suits the Crown it is put before you.'

He talked of the allegedly petrified, frightened Jeannette that the Crown had painted and contrasted that with the facts that no blinds were pulled, no barking dogs kept near the house, and the back door was unlocked. He talked of the Crown case having 'too many coincidences. If Thomas is guilty he would know that he had left a cartridge case behind. Yet he made no attempt to dispose of his rifle or alter it either before or after the bodies were found. When the police came looking for trailer parts he had days in which to dispose of the other parts, yet did not.'

Of the expert testimony that had so heavily featured he observed:

'It is important that you realize that scientific evidence can be the worst kind of evidence. Scientists said that thalidomide was a good drug, but you have seen the results.'

He contrasted the considerable length of time the murderer had spent in wrapping bodies, moving them in the wheelbarrow, if one accepted the Crown's contention about that, washing the wheelbarrow out, burning mat and cushion and cleaning up, with the 'panic of light left on after this desperate search for a lost cartridge'. He reminded the jury that the DSIR expert had spent two months examining the wires and the defence had only been given samples the Thursday before the trial commenced. He also drew their attention to the contrasting expert testimony on the cartridge case, and the wires.

'On every single ingredient that the Crown has placed before you there are large areas of doubt. And Thomas is entitled to the benefit of that doubt.'

He was critical of the corrosion tests carried out by Rory Shanahan: 'What good, for example, are such tests if cartridges are placed in different soils and different environments to that on the Crewe farm?'

He reminded them of the evidence of Graham Hewson who 'had no reason to lie for Thomas'. Of Eggleton he said: 'Since he accused a lady who can't defend herself, I say Mr Eggleton is a liar and a coward and you can't believe what he says. His evidence should be ignored.'

He told the jury that he had made mistakes during the trial and that he took the blame for them: 'Do not blame Thomas.'

He continued: 'Juries too can make mistakes. You can't ignore what happened at the last trial. We have not got hanging in this country and so sometimes a man is given another chance. Why? Because he is innocent. All Thomas is asking is, give him a fair go, give him a fair trial.'

Referring directly to comments that Morris had made in his final speech about resources being available to the accused under our legal aid legislation, Ryan observed:

'When I referred in my opening speech to the fact that it was difficult for the individual to fight against the state I was not talking of counsel and specialist fees. When you are in this court you can't chase around looking for witnesses. You can't have a caravan placed by the court and plugged in like the police have.'

Referring to the Charles case this man who knows police methods in New Zealand as well as any other defence lawyer said to the jury:

'I did not ask police officers directly if they had planted the cartridge case found in the Crewe property. This is not a Perry Mason television trial. What is the use of asking police officers: "Did you plant the cartridge case?" The police officers themselves from their own assertions had raised that question.'

He concluded with:

'All I can implore you is don't let Arthur Thomas's

ghost come knocking on your door in the future.

'The Crown evidence is made up like rope of many strands but the alibi of Thomas cuts it straight through and there is no rope to link Thomas with the crimes.'

I do not have a verbatim copy of Kevin Ryan's final speech. No copy exists. I hope the extracts quoted, based on interviews with many people, including, of course, Kevin Ryan, plus quoted extracts that appeared in the press, fairly represent the sum total of the speech. In terms of oratory it would seem to me to have the power and the eloquence I would expect from the man. In terms of a final speech for Thomas it would seem to be clearly inadequate. What was needed was a point by point rebuttal of the speech made by David Morris. Leaving aside the innuendo, unsupported allegations, assumptions and speculative comment from the Crown prosecutor he had clearly made a number of points that needed answering. As indicated earlier, Kevin Ryan was extremely honest when we discussed this aspect. He was clearly exhausted but there was more to it than that:

'I felt I had been let down at the last moment. What was to be my bombshell became my damp squib. It meant that in my final address I had to go very easy on this whole business of categories in cartridge cases. The domino theory was working with a vengeance that day. Apparently one vital piece of forensic defence evidence had been discredited. That could and probably did in the eyes of that jury destroy a great deal more of the expert defence testimony. Always in the back of my mind as I stood there talking to the jury was this business of Sprott and the measurements and I thought, "He's done me." '

Mr Justice Perry adjourned the proceedings after Ryan's final speech and advised the jury that he would sum up the following Monday, thus putting nearly forty-eight hours between his own well-chosen words and the final defence speech.

On the Monday, when Kevin Ryan arrived at the Supreme Court he saw entering at the same time, Inspector Hutton.

'For the first time throughout the entire trial he was smiling, very relaxed. He had attacked my brother Gerald at the end of the previous week when Gerry rang Australia trying to find out what I.C.I. had told the Crown. Hutton came up to him and raved: "I've got a tape recording of you impersonating a police officer. Trying to get information out of I.C.I." It was bloody nonsense and Gerald had said to him: "Listen, if you've got a tape recording there's no problem, is there. It'll prove I didn't try to impersonate one of your lot." Hutton had mouthed on threatening to arrest him. When I saw him on the Monday I tackled him about it, said to him: "They tell me you threatened my brother. I don't like that." He smiled at me and said: "Oh forget it. Not important now." I said to him: "Do you know something I don't know?" He just grinned. I discovered later that on the previous Friday, after Mr Rock's efforts to control his ship, only three of the jury were considering acquitting. That was confirmed to me by Hutton. Now how would he know that?'

How indeed?

Mr Justice Perry, who had not read the first trial transcript, had most certainly read the final speech by Mr Justice Henry. Although the constant 'of course it is a matter for you' is missing, it represents a very powerful final speech on behalf of the prosecution. The most ironic line in the speech for me is the remark: 'Each side has been free to call every relevant witness.' That might well apply to the Crown, it most certainly did not apply to the defence. Suppression of certain witnesses by the police had ensured that.

An indication of how heavily the speech weighed against Arthur Thomas can be gauged from the manner in which the judge embraced the Crown contention that the murders happened late at night. The uncomfortable fact that Demler had received a telephone call from a stock agent as early as 7 p.m. on Wednesday the 17th advising him the Crewes were not answering their phone is completely ignored. The fact that Demler normally ate with the Crewes 'around 7 p.m.' is ignored. The contradictory evidence of Mrs Crewe senior that they ate 'terribly late about 8.30 p.m.' is highlighted. Roddick's evidence is demolished with 'whether it was Mrs Crewe whom he saw, whether she was alive at the date he saw her, or alternatively whether he may have been mistaken as to the day on which he made this observation . . .' The possibility that Roddick had seen a woman other than Mrs Crewe on that Friday morning was not even put to the jury.

At five minutes past three on the afternoon of Monday, 16 April 1973, the jury retired to consider its verdict. While the Thomas family and their friends waited, some chain-smoking, some pacing the corridors of the building. While Mr Justice Perry sat in chambers drinking tea and checking on the phone number of his brother judge, Mr Justice Henry (one of his first actions after the verdict was to advise Mr Justice Henry of the result.) While Kevin Ryan talked to his brother Gerald and wondered what else he could have done. While David Morris and David Baragwanath relaxed in the Crown robing room near Court No. 1. While all of this was going on the jury were, in theory, considering their verdict.

I say in theory because the eleven were at one very quickly. For a short while three of that eleven did indeed hold for a verdict of 'not guilty'. But as foreman Bob Rock explained to me: 'They were quickly persuaded to change their mind.'

The jury ordered more tea. They were aware that the first jury had been out a little under two hours. This jury felt obliged to stay out longer, though they had made their minds up within a few brief minutes. One of their number suggested a debate on whether

382

the cartridge case was planted. Now this in reality had nothing to do with the verdict; that had already been determined, but it would help pass the time.

At 5.30 p.m., having satisfied themselves that they had stayed out longer than the first jury, they returned to the courtroom. One of the three women on the jury, unhappy at the verdict they were about to give, had already broken down in the juryroom. Now as they sat she was yet again on the verge of tears. The crowd rushed to the court at the news that the jury were back. Some female members of the Thomas family were knocked over. Others were locked out, like Arthur's brother, Richard. Also pushed back and locked out were close family friends and neighbours from Pukekawa. Arthur Thomas was brought up from his cell. He waited anxiously to hear the verdict that would free him of his guards.

'Members of the jury, have you unanimously agreed upon a verdict?' asked the court registrar.

Bob Rock stood up:

'Yes.'

'On the first count, do you find the accused guilty or not guilty?'

'Guilty.'

The second verdict of guilty was lost in the uproar. There was a total eruption in the courtroom. That one word had triggered an extraordinary response. Sir Alfred North, who subsequently heard a tape-recording of this reaction, likened it to the mob at the French Revolution. One of that 'mob' was Margaret Smith, Pukekawa neighbour and close friend of Viven's.

'The wail that went up when the verdict was announced was an unearthly sound. It was like a hurt animal. I suddenly realized that I was making that noise too. It was a sound that came from deep within. No rise. No fall. Just a constant tone. It was weird, yet it was coming from all of us. I have never before or since heard such a sound.'

Like many hurt animals this one became angry. People collapsed. Others began chanting: 'He's not guilty. He's not guilty.' The chant was heard by those outside in the foyer.

In the courtroom as the uproar continued unabated Arthur Thomas, visibly shocked, was trying to talk, his lips were moving but none could hear his words. He looked towards the jurors. None met his gaze. His head was shaking· in disbelief. Calls from court officials brought a temporary silence. The verdict on the second count, that of murdering Jeannette Crewe, was also guilty. Asked the ritualistic question as to whether he had anything to say Arthur Thomas looked the judge directly in the eyes and declared:

'I want to say that I had nothing whatever to do with that crime and I was home on the night of the 17th of June.

'I had nothing to do with that crime. I am completely innocent of that crime.'

In a low voice Mr Justice Perry, also visibly shaken, spoke quickly. Just one line: 'I sentence you to life imprisonment.'

As Thomas was bundled below pandemonium broke out. Vivien Thomas rushed towards the jury and screamed:

'What sort of people are you? He's innocent. You're murdering him.'

Police appeared from everywhere. Inspector Hutton, ever a methodical man, had expected this. The judge and jury sat like stone. Eventually the court was cleared but the uproar continued in the foyer. With a classic touch of insensitivity the police asked not David Morris or Baragwanath to reassure the frightened jury but Kevin and Gerald Ryan. With the same courtesy and charm that I found deeply impressive the defence lawyers agreed to do what they could. Gerald went to the jury room and reassured them with calm words. Gerald who with his brother had battled so long and so hard for their client comforted the eleven people who had said to them: 'You lose'.

Arthur Thomas, after a brief goodbye to Vivien, was driven yet again to that maximum security prison on the North Shore, Paremoremo. Kevin Ryan, again at the request of the police, calmed the angry crowds outside the Supreme Court. He told them:

'You are not doing anyone any good by this. Please go home.'

Subsequently Kevin Ryan picked up his books, his papers, his carton of notes and decided he needed a drink. He went to the nearby Station Hotel; the building that had been home to the jury throughout the trial. The people he saw in the bar were hardly those whose company he was seeking. David Morris, David Baragwanath and Bruce Hutton. He joined them for a drink. He recalled to me part of the subsequent conversation:

'Hutton said to me: "We had the jury list three weeks before the trial." I said to him: "How the hell did you get it three weeks before the trial?" Hutton said: "It doesn't matter. We just had it, three weeks before and of the jury that were put on eight of them were category A. Eight were A.1. We had them down as A.1." '

I recounted this to Bruce Hutton. He laughed and said he remembered the conversation with Kevin Ryan.

7

After the Ball Was Over

So to the anger of some and the astonishment of many the Crown's case against Arthur Allan Thomas had triumphed again. Morris, Baragwanath, Hutton, Nelson, the police force, the DSIR had all been vindicated. Apparently against all the odds they had won. Apparently with all the odds in their favour Thomas, Ryan, the retrial committee, the press that had campaigned, had lost. In fact, as the previous chapter demonstrated, the odds were reversed. If the defence had won it would have been against all the odds. If the Crown had lost after the precautions it had taken it would have been like the favourite coming second in a one-horse race.

In July 1973, the Court of Appeal heard the defence appeal against the conviction of Arthur Thomas. There were a considerable number of grounds on which the defence argued; they were all dismissed. The three judges listening to that appeal were the same three who had decided that there should be a new trial: Chief Justice the late Sir Richard Wild, Mr Justice McCarthy and Mr Justice Richmond. The president of the court that rejected this appeal against the second conviction was the man who had strongly opposed the granting of the second trial, Chief Justice Richard Wild.

The second trial had left many unanswered questions. While Vivien Thomas told the press that she had adopted an expression from the Bible to help her through the times that lay ahead: 'Let us not be weary of well-doing, for in due season we shall reap' (Galatians chapter 6, verse 9), one man in particular thought it was time to start digging. His name was Pat Booth, deputy editor of the *Auckland Star*. Booth's interest in the Thomas case was initially no more than that of a journalist protecting his newspaper's investment. The *Star* had contracted to buy the Thomas life story in the event of an acquittal. As events turned out they were to get a much more sensational story than the 'I was born at an early age' kind of thing they would have had.

Pat Booth dropped into the second trial hearing from time to time. He was there the afternoon that David Morris cross-examined Thomas. He didn't like what he heard; in fact the venom of that cross-examination disturbed him deeply. He was there on the evening the verdict was announced. Photographs of the post-verdict scenes in the foyer show a wide-eyed disbelieving Booth in the background.

In the months that followed as Sir Richard Wild extolled the jury system and publicly thanked the second trial jury, as lawyer Peter Williams attacked the jury system and declared that it was 'loaded against the accused', Pat Booth began to probe. As he investigated, the Thomas case continued to reverberate.

Terry Bell, writing an article for *Rolling Stone*, attacked not only the police investigation but also the performance of the jury, not for the verdict that they brought in but for the high capers he alleged they were cutting in the Station Hotel. He wrote of 'musical beds and of parties where the drink had flowed freely'. He quoted one employee of the Station Hotel who had talked to him of the final party on the eve of the verdict: 'The whole lot of them were in it. They were paralytic.' Acting without a court order the police seized copies of the issue from Wellington to Auckland. The seizure was not followed up with a prosecution.

The *Sunday News* ran a poll among its readers. The

results showed that just under 80 per cent of the people who responded believed Thomas was innocent.

The *Sunday Herald* linked the names of Watergate conspirator John Dean and Arthur Thomas. At that time Dean was giving sensational testimony against President Nixon to a United States Senate hearing and he had offered to undergo a lie-detector test. Thomas had asked for the same after the second verdict. Indeed he had asked to be given a lie-detector test before he had been arrested.

In June 1973, several weeks before the second appeal had been heard Commissioner of Police (later Sir Angus) Sharp announced that Detective Inspector Bruce Hutton was to receive a certificate of merit, the police department's highest internal award. Sharp said the award was for Hutton's 'devotion to duty over many years and particularly for diligence and zeal shown during the Crewe murder inquiry.

'His meticulous care in preparing the file for prosecution, and the outstanding assistance he gave the Crown prosecutor during the trials, combined to bring a successful conclusion to an extremely difficult and arduous inquiry and was in accord with the highest traditions of the New Zealand police.'

A considerable number of people took exception to those 'high traditions'. They demanded that the award be withdrawn. Among those who bitterly complained about the award were, predictably, the retrial committee. To their amazement they received a letter from Commissioner Sharp which stated that among others who had recommended the award had been defence counsel Kevin Ryan.

In fact after the appeal hearing Kevin Ryan had complained to the commissioner about the announcement being made before the second appeal was heard. He rightly felt that the timing not only prejudged an impending appeal but that it might seriously prejudice the hearing. Ryan was not alone in this view; at least two members of the Cabinet complained to Sharp. David Morris who was present during this conversation was most enthusiastic in his praise of Hutton and stated that he had earned the award. Sharp asked Ryan for his views and Kevin Ryan, so reminiscent of a character from a John O'Hara novel, replied with lines worthy of O'Hara:

'I must agree no-one has worked harder for the conviction of Arthur Allan Thomas than Mr Hutton. I have no doubt that except for his hard work the rebuttal evidence would not have been given as only he and I knew of Mr Shea's existence. He beat me to the telephone by a quarter of an hour.'

While the attack on the judicial process that convicted Arthur Thomas continued unabated Sir Richard Wild was joined on the barricades by brother judge Sir Thaddeus McCarthy. Speaking at a dinner in Wellington he acknowledged the legal system was under attack but he had a quirky view of who was doing the attacking: 'Our institutions from top to bottom are under attack by restless youth and a dissatisfied intelligentsia'. If Sir Thaddeus had cared to do a little research before making that speech he would have discovered that the vast proportion of people attacking the legal system, with regard to the Thomas case, fell in neither of his two categories but consisted of the Ted Smiths of New Zealand.

Pat Booth meanwhile was making some interesting discoveries about New Zealand's most famous *cause célèbre*. A full account of his research can be found in his book *Trial By Ambush*, or the series of articles that appeared in the *Auckland Star* in August 1973. Perhaps the most potent piece of evidence he published concerned the sensational last-minute testimony of Dr James Sprott. Booth found that the .22 cartridge cases did indeed fall into various categories, when one compared the I.C.I. stamped on the base. There were clear differences, not so much in the size but in the shape of the middle letter C. But as he recounted to me:

'By that time the second appeal had been and gone and Kevin Ryan had not made an issue at that appeal of this aspect.'

The material that Booth gathered was for the book referred to above. The *Auckland Star*, recognizing the significance of Pat Booth's research, decided to run a series of articles on the case entitled 'You be the Jury'. The articles, like the book that followed them, by no means tell the whole story. My main criticism of both would concern the people that Booth chose for interviews. Anti-Thomas people are noticeably absent when one lists the people Booth did speak to, but it was crusading journalism, not an attempt at objectivity. During the course of that year Booth joined forces with Dr Sprott. They make an oddly assorted couple and both recognize that fact. As Pat Booth remarked to Jim Sprott on one occasion:

'We make an odd team, I'm a left-wing trendy and you're a right-wing reactionary.'

The press articles and the public meetings such as the one at Auckland Town Hall on 27 August 1973 could not pass unnoticed. At that meeting packed with over 2000 people, with hundreds more battering at the doors to get in, the retrial committee plus some distinguished guests argued the case for Arthur Thomas. Among those guest speakers was the lawyer that Bruce Hutton described to me as 'radical but clever' Peter Williams.

In late October 1970, Arthur and Vivien Thomas had sat in a solicitor's office in Pukekohe and discussed which barrister should be briefed to defend Arthur if he were arrested. Three names had featured largely in that discussion: Paul Temm, Peter Williams and Kevin Ryan. Williams had been ruled out on the grounds of price. Two of those men, Temm and Ryan, had battled in the courts on behalf of Thomas. Now in mid-1973, the Thomas family were pinning their hopes on Peter

Williams. Perhaps the radical element in the man can be questioned, but there is no doubting his intelligence and gifts as a barrister.

Addressing the packed gathering he concentrated not on the specifics of the Thomas case but on the flaws in the system that the case highlighted.

Similar meetings were held throughout New Zealand. The Thomas case would not lie down and die. In Nelson, Christchurch, Hawke's Bay, people in their thousands expressed concern. It was a concern that was to turn to anger and contempt in the light of subsequent events.

The results of the joint Booth/Sprott investigations were submitted to Minister of Justice, Martyn Finlay. In the light of those submissions Dr Finlay offered an independent assessment of the evidence that had been given on the cartridge cases at the second trial. It was an offer that was widely approved by the press and the public. It was an offer that in the event would never become a reality.

The offer from the Minister of Justice was made public in the first week of September 1973. The following week Dr Finlay stated that he was 'desolated and deeply troubled'. What had caused that desolation and deep concern for the Minister was the revelation that the police, or to be more specific Bruce Hutton, had dumped the cartridge cases on the Whitford rubbish tip in Auckland.

After the second appeal had failed and at the suggestion of Crown Solicitor David Morris, the Charles and the Keith cartridge cases along with another 135 exhibits had been unceremoniously thrown away.

Bruce Hutton had spoken at length during the second trial of why he had cleaned, polished and brushed the Charles cartridge case. The reader will find his exact words earlier in this book. He had considered that the Charles case and a number of other exhibits had 'historical value so far as the police were concerned, in this particular case. I felt they should be mounted and exhibited in the police museum in Wellington.' They were, Hutton went on to say, to serve as an example to trainee detectives as to what could be achieved by tenacity and vigilance. Their disposal after the second trial when clearly their historical value had doubled, when the example they would give to those trainee detectives would have been multiplied many times, should serve as an example to those same trainee detectives of perhaps the most maladroit piece of bungling in the history of the New Zealand police force. Why dump cartridge cases no bigger than a thumbnail and keep an axle weighing 35 pounds? Why dump the Charles case and keep the rifle that it allegedly came from? If the police considered that the rifle was the property of Arthur Thomas and therefore could not be dumped, clearly they considered the Charles case was the property of Thomas. Their contention that it was his was the key piece of evidence in both trials. If Sprott and subsequently Booth were wrong, what better proof than to subject the cartridge cases to independent assessment? If the police were right then it would inevitably mean the demolition of the central argument which both men were expounding.

The items had been allegedly dumped on the Whitford tip on 27 July. Normal police procedure was to contact the site foreman and advise him they wanted to dump items. The site foreman has no record of the police appearing at the tip on 27 July.

On being advised what had happened Dr Finlay ordered an immediate search of the tip. He was advised by the police that the area that the exhibits had been dumped in could not be narrowed down to less than three acres and the possibility of finding the exhibits was hopeless.

On 20 September, a week after the revelation of the dumping had been made public, a front page *Auckland Star* article revealed exactly what the Booth/Sprott submissions to Dr Finlay had contained. The essential conclusion they had reached after a joint trip to Melbourne and access to I.C.I. records was backed with photographic evidence and supported by information obtained from I.C.I. It was startling. The Charles case, they contended, did not and could never have contained a pattern 8 bullet. Quite simply, if their opinion was correct, the fatal bullets had no connection with what had been the Crown's most vital piece of evidence in the case against Arthur Thomas.

The information that the I.C.I. company had given to the Crown during that dramatic adjournment on the last day evidence had been heard, had been given in good faith, but it had now been established that it was incorrect information. Company records had indeed shown no official change in the design of the lettering on the base of the cartridge cases, but further company investigation prompted by Booth and Sprott had revealed that at certain dates engravers had indeed changed the I.C.I. stamp on the base. Further investigation showed that the use of pattern 8 bullets had ceased before the first shipment of cartridge cases from Australia bearing the design on the Charles case.

The dumping of some of the trial exhibits was not an illegal act. Disposal of court exhibits once an appeal has been turned down is normal practice in this country. But at the time of the dumping in late July it was known in police circles that a series of articles on the Thomas case were imminent. Clearly in a case as unique and important as this one had become, authority for the dumping should have come from much higher up the line than from a man who was deeply involved in the case. David Morris told me that he had told Hutton to get rid of the exhibits. That decision merely added massive fuel to the fire of controversy that far from dying down after that second appeal had raged unabated.

While many newspapers called for the instant release

of Thomas and declared that he should be pardoned, Prime Minister Norman Kirk made public his own unhappiness about the exhibit dumping. The isssue had reached white heat within the country as can be clearly seen from the hundreds of letters written to newspapers. Not all by any means were pro-Thomas; a significant percentage resented bitterly the attack that had been made on the police and on the legal system. They considered that Thomas should be left to rot, and a number lamented the passing of capital punishment.

The Establishment in the shape of Dr Nelson of the DSIR and Inspector Hutton were not idle. They too flew to Australia to do their own research.

In November 1973, Minister of Justice Dr Finlay announced that he had recommended that the Court of Appeal should review new evidence that was available in the Thomas case. The announcement came after months of delay. Delay not from the Minister but the police and the DSIR as they researched and prepared their rebuttal to the arguments of Pat Booth and Jim Sprott.

The bitterness between the two camps grew. The gulf between the two positions widened to unbridgeable dimensions as counter-accusations followed accusations. In the middle was the Minister of Justice doing his level best to be fair, urging both parties to adopt a reasonable attitude but reasonable attitudes have been in very short supply in the Thomas case. Egos were wildly tripping, they still are. Reputations and the protection of them became paramount. Over two years passed before Dr Finlay's recommendation that the Court of Appeal should review the new evidence became a reality. This was not just the familiar story of the law moving slowly. Peter Williams, Kevin Ryan, Pat Booth and Jim Sprott were engaged in a battle with a machine, a machine that demonstrably procrastinated and blocked every effort. The police had been given the Booth/Sprott submission in September

1973. When Assistant Commissioner Walton forwarded the police response to the Minister of Justice, a recommendation that the response should not be given to the men fighting on behalf of Thomas went with the police report. To his great credit Martyn Finlay ignored that recommendation and made the information available. Over a five-year period tenuous police and DSIR theory hardened into fact. The possibilities that the DSIR could be in error, that the police could be in error, that the Crown solicitor could be in error: none of these possibilities appears to have been seriously considered by the individuals concerned. To err is human but in this case to admit error was unthinkable. While lawyers manoeuvred and experts flew back and forth across the Tasman seeking information that gradually became more and more complex, Arthur Thomas waited in Paremoremo prison and his wife waited in her Auckland flat. There was about their marriage a strange pendulum quality. Arthur never veered for one moment from his love for Vivien. The indecision, the doubts were the exclusive property of his wife. In late 1974 she began an affair that was to last eighteen months.

'There was no thought of marriage or living with this man. I was very fond of him but I had enough sense to know he was not the man for me on a permanent basis. Yes, you're right there was this on/off quality about my marriage at that time. It was in part caused by my own confusion. It was also in part caused by the lawyers. They told me to keep Arthur happy, not to upset him, that there were fresh developments about to happen in the case. There were always fresh developments happening. They did indeed happen but none of them got Arthur out. In the meantime I had a life to lead. I was living in a limbo world. We both were.'

Mrs Thomas alone with her thoughts in Pukekawa and then Auckland. Mr Thomas alone with his in Mount Eden and then Paremoremo.

Vivien was still continuing her regular visits to Paremoremo and still vigorously campaigning on behalf of her husband but the lifeblood of their relationship was being inexorably drained from her. The frustration of waiting for this court hearing that never seemed to come allied to the deception were biting very deeply into the woman. She wanted to tell her husband the truth but again and again those around her prevailed upon her to play out the role of a faithful wife. She was still public property and was as effectively living in a cell as Arthur Thomas.

As a result of yet another petition to the governor-general two questions were referred to the Court of Appeal in December 1975, for the court's opinion. Those questions were:

1. Has it been established by the petitioner that neither of the bullets of which fragments were found in the bodies of David Harvey Crewe and Jeannette Lenore Crewe could have been assembled with the cartridge case identified as exhibit number 350 in the course of the manufacture of a .22 rimfire round of ammunition?

2. If it is so established is such a finding inconsistent with the verdict of guilty, on both counts of murder, returned by the jury on the sixteenth day of April 1973 at the trial of Arthur Allan Thomas?

Five judges considered the evidence pertaining to the first question. Three of them, Chief Justice Sir Richard Wild, Mr Justice McCarthy and Mr Justice Richmond were the same men who had ordered a new trial and had subsequently rejected the second appeal. In view of this two other judges were added to the court: Mr Justice Macarthur and Mr Justice McMullin. This brought the total of judges who had direct involvement with the Thomas case to eleven.

During the nine-day hearing the court heard evidence from a variety of experts. The whole process of cartridge case manufacture was explored in great depth.

While the defence sought to demonstrate that the combination of Charles cartridge case with pattern 8 bullets had never existed, the Crown sought to establish that they had. Clearly the two points of view and the evidence called by either side were not reconcilable.

One of the weapons in the Crown's armoury was a bullet called 1964/2. Dr Donald Nelson had found this in his DSIR collection. He contended that he had obtained it from the Colonial Ammunition Company at some time between 24 January 1964 and 6 February 1964. It was also his contention that the cartridge case of this bullet was identical to the Charles case and although the bullet did not have a figure 8 on its base it was the Crown's view that the presence in New Zealand of such a case at such a time proved that cases identical to the Charles case could have been loaded with pattern 8 bullets. It was an attractive theory but the weight of evidence against such a view effectively demolished it. It was established that the cartridge case of 1964/2 was of a type using a wet priming method not used by the company before October 1965, at which date pattern 8 bullets had not been used for two years. What had been hailed by the Minister of Justice as a 'miraculous discovery' when Nelson had produced it in 1973, was dismissed by the five judges with: 'We have not been able to derive any assistance from Exhibit 1964/2.'

For the first and only time the curious events that had occurred on the final day of evidence in the second trial were subjected to judicial scrutiny. Had Dr Sprott made a mistake in his measurements of the imprints on the bases of the Charles and the Keith cartridges? Or had an error been made by Dr Nelson?

The alleged dumping by the police of both cartridges to a certain degree moved the discussion on those two questions to an academic level. Although photographs of the base of the Charles case exist no-one ever saw fit to photograph the Keith case, not even after it became such a contentious issue in the final stages of the second trial. That omission is an indictment of forensic science as is the shambles that passed for 'expert' testimony in the closing stages of the second trial. Dr Sprott's vital evidence and the manner in which it was presented is a further indictment, not only of forensic science but of the defence. Perry Mason tactics might be fine for the television; they have no place in a courtroom when a man is on trial and a life sentence is hanging over him. While the Crown and the defence and their respective experts played an ego game of one-upmanship the farmer from Pukekawa sat forgotten in the dock, the vortex in the whirlpool that swirled around him.

The events in the final days during which evidence was called in the second trial hold the key to much of the puzzle of this case. Two facts shine out like a beacon in the controversy over the Keith and the Charles cartridge cases: *the cartridge case that Dr Sprott examined on the assumption that it was the Keith case was not the Keith case. The cartridge case that Dr Nelson subsequently examined on the assumption that it was the Keith case was not the Keith case.*

At the Lower Court hearings, the first trial, the first referral, the second trial – at these four separate hearings Detective Stanley Keith's sworn testimony establishes beyond any doubt whatsoever that after he had discovered the complete bullet in the Thomas garage it was taken to the Otahuhu police station. It was dissected and the cartridge case was fired in a single shot .22 firearm to remove any traces of powder. Dr Nelson's sworn testimony at the Lower Court on this aspect was that he had received from Keith an unfired bullet and a *fired* cartridge case. The case that Sprott examined in the courtroom was *unfired*. The case that Nelson examined during the adjournment was *unfired*. Where had this unfired case come from? Did these two men examine the same unfired case?

Dr Nelson, while testifying in the Court of Appeal in January 1975, was closely questioned on this aspect by Peter Williams. He said that he could not remember exactly how he had described the cartridge case at the Lower Court hearing and suggested that a typing error might have been made by the court staff. If that be so one would have expected Nelson to pick it up when checking it through before signing his deposition. In fact the very line of his testimony that talks of receiving 'a fired shell case' bears his signature:

Nelson: At this stage I can only speculate as to what I said in court at depositions.

Yallop: Would you accept that you might be in error with regard to whether you received from Keith a fired or an unfired case? It is after all a basic fact that at that stage of the investigation the case was not of central importance.

Nelson: It's not recorded in my notes and when it was raised with me by the Crown prosecutor at the first trial I said: 'Oh, I don't know about a fired case. I haven't recorded that in my notes.' That's the best I can say about it.

Yallop: So basically when you received that case from Keith it could have been unfired or fired?

Nelson: Yes, that is so.

During my interviews with Dr Nelson and Rory Shanahan we discussed at some length the events that occurred on the last day evidence was heard during the second trial. Particularly the events after Dr Sprott had testified that the Charles and the Keith cartridge cases were different and the category that the Charles case came into did not contain pattern 8 bullets. Dr Donald Nelson:

'Well, first of all I wondered whether the sample of cartridge cases which had been examined was adequate for the conclusions which he drew. During the lunch adjournment I came down here to the DSIR and began to check through my stock of cartridges, particularly the old ones. I had just commenced work on these when I received a phone call from David Baragwanath who said: "Would you bring some equipment up to the court and measure these headstamps on the court exhibits?" I explained to him that any measurement done away from the lab would of necessity be crude but on the other hand to tell the difference between 1.2 and 1.5 mm should be the sort of thing that you can do with a hand lens, a pair of dividers, a steel rule and one or two other minor pieces of equipment. So I went up to the court armed with these items. David Baragwanath obtained permission from Mr Justice Perry and the exhibits were brought to the Crown robing room at the Supreme Court. Rory was assisting me. The court registrar, Ian Miller, brought the exhibits in. There were a number of other people in the room, Detective Keith, Bruce Hutton, Baragwanath. There were others who came and went. Then I measured them. As you are aware Dr Sprott's evidence had been that the letter C on the Keith case was approximately 1.2mm and the letter C on the Charles case was 1.5mm, both of those measurements referring to the respective heights. To my great surprise I could detect no difference between the heights of the letter C of these two exhibits. Very interestingly, although I was very surprised David Baragwanath was not. He had had the impression that a big bluff was being run on the Court and he was calling that bluff.

Yallop: But surely, demonstrably, if Jim Sprott is going to come out with this theory, the man is no fool, fundamentally he would know that there was going to be rebuttal evidence. That you would be given opportunity to examine those exhibits?

Nelson: No. No. No. Rebuttal is very rare.

Yallop: Oh, come on now. Not in a situation like this. This is a capital offence we are talking about.

Nelson/Shanahan: No. No. Rebuttal is very rare.

Very rare indeed. They had to go to judge's chambers to get this rebuttal.

Yallop: I cannot believe Sprott and for that matter Ryan did not consider that possibility. This was evidence that had not been put to you in cross-examination. It is obvious and it would have been obvious at the time to the defence, that the Crown would be given the opportunity to rebut.

Nelson: In that case, you have the other side of the argument. That Jim Sprott may have made a straight-out mistake.

Shanahan: So which will you choose?

Nelson: And this is the problem you have in writing a book about this case. It's a problem we have not got. We can give you the two alternatives but you have to choose.

Yallop: I can think of at least two other alternatives. One is that the exhibits were switched or exchanged either deliberately or accidentally. The other is that you deliberately examined a different cartridge case. Are you certain that you were examining the same exhibits that Sprott had previously examined?

Nelson: Well, they were handed to us by the court registrar, Ian Miller. You would have to go on his evidence not ours. At that stage we had no reason to doubt it. We just accepted the exhibits. They were in labelled containers, with the correct exhibit numbers on. We did not specifically examine the cartridge cases, the containers were the correct ones.

Although the two scientists took the position during this discussion that a switch either deliberate or accidental was not tenable, it clearly was. They accepted two containers in good faith. Dr Nelson merely checked that the exhibit numbers were correct. *He did not check against his previous examinations of the Keith and the Charles exhibits to ensure that what he compared in the robing room were the two original exhibits.* Add to this the fact that Miller at the time had only been No. 1 Court Registrar for about two or three months and had no previous experience in that capacity, and under cross-examination from Peter Williams during this referral admitted the possibility that from time to time during the course of trials exhibit labels became untied and separated from the actual exhibit. He was also clearly confused about when Dr Sprott had examined the Keith and the Charles exhibits. He was also clearly confused as to how he had initially obtained the various exhibits. He did not know whether he obtained them from witnesses or if he had obtained them prior to the commencement of the trial. He revealed that the exhibits still retained their numbers from the first trial and it was assumed that between the two trials, *a period of two years*, all the labels had remained intact on nearly 200 exhibits. He was unable to say for certain who had been present during the examination in the Crown robing room. It is a veritable hornet's nest of possibilities.

When one realizes that the exhibits were then up-lifted after permission had been obtained from Mr Justice Perry and removed to the DSIR and that no member of the defence was present at any stage of these examinations, it becomes apparent that there are many explanations as to why a fired case became an unfired case.

This is not idle nitpicking. It directly affected the verdict. *Foreman of the jury Bob Rock rationalized not only for himself but for the rest of the jury the difference between the base letters with his theory that the fact one of them was fired would spread the base letters and thereby cause a variation in the measurements. The issue of whether or not the Keith cartridge case was fired or unfired is therefore crucial.*

In October 1973 when the police were compiling their response to the Booth/Sprott submissions Detective Keith again confirmed to the assistant commissioner that the case had been fired. Inspector Hutton in his report took a different position. He declared that he was present when the bullet was dissected and that the cartridge case was not subsequently fired. If that be so why then did he as the police officer in charge of the investigation allow Detective Keith to appear to commit perjury on four separate occasions? I do not believe for one moment that Detective Keith did commit perjury on those occasions. I believe the testimony he gave on the firing of that cartridge case to be completely accurate. The Keith cartridge, this 'vital link' between the murder bullets and the accused because it established that on his farm was one round of a particular kind of .22 ammunition, lost all its credibility in the last week of the second trial. In the light of events that occurred in that week and Dr Nelson's admission to me this particular strand of rope that linked Thomas with the deaths of the Crewes is irretrievably cut. It was certainly dispatched to oblivion by those five appeal judges as they considered its relevance to the issue before them:

'In all the circumstances we do not think that on this referral we should place any reliance on Exhibit 343 (the Keith cartridge) and we have accordingly disregarded it when considering the probability of Exhibit 350 having derived from a hob earlier in date than the hobs "new" and "in current use".'

Significantly, although Inspector Hutton and Detective Keith were present in the Court of Appeal during Dr Nelson's evidence-in-chief and his cross-examination the Crown did not call either policeman to buttress the faltering memory of the man from the DSIR.

It will have been noted that the first of the two questions the Court of Appeal had been asked to answer put the onus of proof on Arthur Thomas. The very first words of this book make it abundantly clear that the onus or burden of proof in a criminal case is never upon the accused. It is always on the prosecution.

This is the fundamental concept of criminal law in this country. What happened in this referral was the five judges reasoned that the framing of that first question transferred the burden of proof to Arthur Thomas. They then applied to this question which dealt with a *criminal* matter the *civil* onus of proof of the balance of probabilities rather than the criminal burden of reasonable doubt. Part of their decision reads:

'On the probabilities we are therefore prepared to accept the submission made on behalf of Thomas that cartridge cases derived from these hobs could not have been manufactured and shipped to New Zealand in time to be assembled with pattern 8 bullets.'

The court in its judgment rejected virtually the entire case put forward by the Crown. Yet despite the fact that they acknowledged that no example of a cartridge case identical to the Charles case with a pattern 8 bullet had been discovered, despite the fact that none of the machinery necessary for such a combination had been discovered, they felt they could not exclude the reasonable possibility that such machinery had once existed. Their decision concluded with:

... We are unable to exclude the reasonable possibility that Exhibit 350 was produced in Australia at some time before October 1963 and therefore could have been loaded in New Zealand with a pattern 8 bullet.

In those circumstances our opinion is that Question 1 must be answered 'No'.

Conclusion:

The Court's answers to the questions are as follows:

Question 1. No.

Question 2. In view of the answer to Question 1 no answer to Question 2 is required. For that reason, and also because a determination on the applicant's petition is a matter for the Governor General-in-Council, the Court refrains from any discussion of the considerable body of evidence against Thomas, other than that relating to Exhibit 350, which was before the jury for their consideration in reaching their verdict.

Arthur Thomas had failed to prove a negative. The Crown had been given the benefit of the doubt, a benefit that is never given in a criminal trial. The man who had drafted the wording of those questions was Minister of Justice Dr Martyn Finlay. Talking to me about that court decision he said:

'I thought the evidence presented to the Court on behalf of Arthur Thomas was not only persuasive but virtually overwhelming. Yet the whole of the bench dismissed it. Much to my surprise. I would also add that the way they applied the burden of proof was not in accordance with my understanding of the law. I felt that they had put the burden of proof on Thomas rather than the Crown. I was astounded by the decision. But confronted by that unanimous decision from five judges I had to accept their conclusions.

'The decision to refer the matter to court rather than take it to the engineering faculty at Auckland University was mine. I thought at first that it was purely a scientific question and therefore the view of a scientist would be the best source of information. I still think that but then I decided that the determination of whether the evidence of the scientist was persuasive and acceptable ought not to be made by me but by an independent group, thinking of the Court of Appeal, and it was for that reason that I said this is still a scientific question but it should be determined, like any other question of fact, through the due legal process, a court of law.'

I asked Dr Finlay whether in all honesty he could say that those five judges were independent and reminded him that three of them had been deeply involved prior to this hearing with the Thomas case.

'Well, I had to assume they were. One assumes that

a judge can put aside any previous commitment to an issue and have a fresh mind.'

By the middle of 1976 Dr Sprott had examined over 25,000 rounds of .22 ammunition. He was attempting to find the combination of bullet and cartridge case that the Court of Appeal had considered a 'reasonable possibility'. He did not find one such specimen. He has still to find one such specimen.

In that same period of time Vivien Thomas stated publicly what she had privately wanted to state for a long time. Her marriage to Arthur Thomas was over and she announced that she was seeking a divorce on the grounds of four years' separation. It was a decision that Arthur Thomas locked in Paremoremo appeared to accept with stoical calm: 'I might have lost a wife but I have gained a great friend.' In fact he not only still deeply loves the woman who had fought so long and hard on his behalf, he still believes he and Vivien have a future together.

While Vivien's decision was greeted with sympathetic understanding, the continuing advertisements for .22 bullets upset a number of people including Sir Alfred North. He had been president of the Court of Appeal which had rejected Paul Temm's arguments to have the first trial verdict set aside. The 'fresh minds' that Dr Finlay hopes the five judges brought to the final referral were hopefully more detached than Sir Alfred's was in April 1975. He objected to the continued efforts that had been made on behalf of Thomas. He objected to Kevin Ryan stating that the British system of criminal trial upon which this country's system is based was weighted against the defendant. He said there was no justification for anyone to say that the dice were loaded against Thomas. The new trial had been granted on what he called 'flimsy evidence'. He considered that the Minister of Justice Dr Finlay had been induced 'absolutely wrongly' in his opinion to seek yet another ruling by the Court of Appeal. He objected to advertisements inviting people to contribute to a campaign fund for Thomas. Dr Sprott's suggestion that the technical evidence should once again be re-examined was, Sir Alfred declared, 'impudent'.

'It will be a sorry day for New Zealand if this sort of thing ever happens again.

'Incalculable harm has been done to our criminal judicial system by these events. The system would break down if it could be subjected to these continued allegations of unfairness.'

In late 1976 Pat Booth and Jim Sprott made allegations of far greater gravity than 'unfairness'. In yet another attempt to reverse the verdict a very large file was presented to the government. Another general election had taken place since the last referral, consequently the file went to Mr Muldoon's National Government.

The file contained not only detailed information on aspects of the Thomas trial that disturbed the two men. This time the ramifications were far wider and made allegations of corruption against a number of police officers. The corruption, Sprott and Booth asserted, had happened in a variety of cases totally unconnected with the Thomas trials. The one common denominator was that all of the police officers named had been involved in the police investigation of the Crewe murders. The central allegation concerned planting by police officers in these other criminal cases; the premise being that one, some, or all of these named men had been involved in planting the Charles case. The allegations also covered telephone tapping and conspiracy. The file was considered by Solicitor General R. C. Savage and the Secretary for Justice G. S. Orr. Their recommendation contained in a report to Cabinet that has yet to be made public was that no further action should be taken on the material they had considered. The Cabinet accepted that recommendation.

The charges of police malpractice were subsequently

investigated by two police officers. In late 1977 the two officers concluded there had been no police malpractice.

Also in 1977, the Arthur Thomas retrial committee announced a reward of $50,000 'for information relating to the Crewe murders and/or knowledge of any malpractice during the investigations and trials which would lead to the acquittal of Arthur Thomas'. The reward offer, which was open until 30 November 1977, closed with no takers.

In January 1978, Arthur Thomas's legal advisers announced they were going to take the case to the Privy Council in Great Britain. It is something that should have been done in 1971. It is something that again should have been done immediately after the last referral decision had been announced in February 1975. Perhaps if the case ever gets to Privy Council the law lords of Great Britain may be able to assist the defence in finding a solution to the question: How do you prove a negative?*

Dr Sprott has said to me many times that his prime concern is not Arthur Thomas but the quality of forensic science in New Zealand. I understand his point of view but it is not mine. My prime concern is for the flesh and blood of certain people. For Rochelle Crewe, orphaned tragically and horribly one winter's night in Pukekawa. I am acutely aware that this book may cause her distress. I hope one day when she has grown to womanhood she will understand why it has been written. Voltaire said: 'To the dead we owe nothing but the truth.' It is because of my acceptance of that philosophy that I undertook this task. And also because I believe that the living Rochelle deserves the truth.

For the Thomas family, particularly the parents of

*On 4 July 1978, the Privy Council's judicial committee announced they had no jurisdiction to hear the petition presented on behalf of Arthur Thomas.

Arthur Thomas, who for nearly eight years have attempted to cope with the uncopeable. Two people who should have been enjoying the autumn of their lives.

For Vivien Thomas, attempting now to build a new life with a new man. Here is a fragment from my last interview with Vivien Thomas:

Yallop: What would you say to people who said: 'Look, here is a man who has had two trials, two appeals, two referrals and a retired judge who conducted an inquiry. It has been considered at the highest level in the land including Cabinet meetings. Sir Alfred North put it that "no person, with regard to a criminal case, has ever been shown greater consideration in the history of this country".' Now if people made all those points to you and then said: 'Surely he must be guilty, why don't you accept the fact?' what would you say?

Vivien: My answer to those people would be: 'If it was your husband and you knew he had not done it, what would you do? Would you shut up? Would you fight and try and get him out of prison? There is no doubt in my mind at all. He is innocent. It would have been so easy to have left the whole thing alone. After all, look what it's done to the lives of all the people involved. It would have been easier if he had been guilty. I would have accepted that. His innocence and the knowledge of that innocence has meant so much suffering for so many. Physically. Mentally. Financially.'

And Arthur Thomas? He concerns me greatly. For many reasons but most of all because we are all potential Arthur Thomases. When I came to this country to research and write this book I had a totally objective view on the question of his guilt or innocence. Pat Booth wished to collaborate with me. I declined for only one reason. He was clearly subjective in his views and opinions on the case. He was already convinced that Thomas was innocent when we first spoke. I did not share that conviction. Indeed I was very aware that my research might bang the prison door more tightly on Arthur Thomas. I took nothing Booth, Sprott or anyone else said to me for granted. Everything was checked and double-checked. I now have a view and an opinion formulated not by others but by facts that I discovered for myself, about the strange and horrific nightmare that Arthur Thomas has been living for nearly eight years.

During my interviews with Arthur Thomas I tried hard to obtain from him a confession. The arguments I used were varied, including the fact that a penitent, self-confessed murderer was more likely to get paroled than a man defiantly still protesting his innocence. I talked to him of the damage the continuing fight to establish his innocence was having on the public's confidence in the police, the body politic, the legal system. I believe I tried harder than Bruce Hutton had tried to get that confession. I certainly tried for a longer period. He never broke. Never even wavered. I could quote many pages of his response. Perhaps the following few lines will suffice:

'Justice. The system. The judges. The police. They are all important. But above all of those is truth. Surely the whole of our society is based on that? If a person commits a crime then he must go through the courts and be punished. If a person is innocent and is found guilty then surely he has the right to appeal, to protest, to make moves, to put right what is wrong. That is the guts of our case now. It is not so much me. I'm stuffed. I've lost everything. The fight is to get this justice system put right. At the moment it has gone wrong. Very wrong. An innocent man is in prison. We have got to fight now. To make sure that it does not happen again. I'm thinking of the kids who are growing up. The kids of prison officers in here for example. This justice system is for them, isn't it?'

This man who still speaks today of his marriage as if it had a future has been permanently damaged by the past. We can never undo the wrong that has been done to him. The least we can do is acknowledge that wrong.

There is no doubt in my mind that a miscarriage of justice has occurred in the case of The Queen v. Arthur Allan Thomas. I believe that an innocent man is at present serving a life sentence for crimes he did not commit. New Zealand has a ten-million dollar man in Arthur Thomas, for that is the minimum it has cost to get him convicted and keep him convicted. It was a poor investment because while Thomas languishes in prison the guilty ones walk freely among you.

8

An Open Letter To The
Prime Minister of New Zealand

Dear Mr Muldoon,

Early in May 1977, you made several public statements about the Thomas case. When asked if you were satisfied about the outcome of the trials you are reported as saying:

'I don't think anyone who has studied this case closely, as I have, can be in any way satisfied because the verdict was based on circumstantial evidence.'

Many lawyers and judges would doubtless take issue with you on that remark and would extol the virtues of circumstantial evidence in general, while perhaps deploring the quality of circumstantial evidence brought against Arthur Thomas.

I believe that with regard to the case of The Queen v. Arthur Allan Thomas you were absolutely right to express dissatisfaction about the circumstantial evidence. The quality of the Crown's evidence was such that every essential ingredient of their case can be applied to another man. It is not my contention that this other man is in fact responsible for the deaths of Harvey and Jeannette Crewe but I believe the following illustration might usefully serve to demonstrate the possibility that a miscarriage of justice has occurred.

Based on sworn testimony and information that I have acquired, I believe the following case against Peter Thomas would convince any jury:

At the time Harvey and Jeannette Crewe died, 17 June 1970, Peter Thomas, a cousin, had been living with Arthur and Vivien Thomas on their Pukekawa farm for at least six months. He was employed by the Roose Shipping Company situated in nearby Mercer. His custom was to stay with Arthur and Vivien throughout the week and return to his family home some five miles away at weekends.

Access to Murder Weapon: The rifle that the Crown contended fired the fatal shots was kept in the bedroom of Peter Thomas. The ammunition was freely accessible whether from the kitchen or the garage.

Ability to use Murder Weapon: Peter Thomas confirmed to me when I interviewed him that prior to the deaths of the Crewes he was experienced at using a .22 rifle.

Access to Axle and Wire: The Crown contended that the wire found on the bodies of Harvey and Jeannette Crewe matched wire that the police removed from the Thomas farm. They further contended that an axle found on the bed of the Waikato river had been used to weight the body of Harvey Crewe and that this axle which had once been part of a trailer belonging to Arthur's father had been removed from the Thomas farm for the purpose of weighting one of the bodies. To support this contention they produced the stub axles that the police had allegedly found on the Thomas farm tip. The stub axles fitted the main axle. The Crown made much of the fact that this farm tip was hidden away at the bottom of a field and that even a close friend of Arthur Thomas's did not know of its existence. The premise behind that contention was that only Thomas could have removed the axle from his own farm and used it as a weight. Peter Thomas knew of the existence of the tip and admitted that on at least one occasion he had dumped rubbish there. He denied seeing the axle on the tip. If the axle came either from the tip or any other part of

413

the farm, clearly Peter Thomas had free access to it.

Knowledge of Local Area: Peter Thomas has lived in the area throughout his life. At the time of the Crewe deaths he was nearly eighteen years of age.

Knowledge of Crewe Farm: At the Lower Court hearing Peter Thomas said he did not know the Crewes but had been on their farm some years before when it had been managed by Mr Handcock. During the second trial he testified that he did know the Crewes and again stated he had visited the farm when Handcock was manager.

Transport: Peter Thomas had at the time of the Crewe deaths a blue Peugeot 403 car. If needed he also had access to the trailer belonging to Arthur Thomas. Testimony was given on behalf of Arthur Thomas that his car had a very distinctive whine and a neighbour whose farm Thomas would have had to pass to get to the Crewe farm did not hear the Arthur Thomas car that night. The blue Peugeot owned by Peter Thomas did not have any such markedly characteristic noises. During the first week of the police investigation they were advised that on the morning of 18 June, the morning after the murders were allegedly committed, a blue car had been seen. It was backed up to the Waikato river and a man was washing it out. The area where this sighting took place is only a few miles from where the bodies were subsequently found. It is equally only a few miles from where Peter Thomas worked. The sighting was at 10.30 a.m.

Alibi: Peter Thomas slept alone and by his own admission could easily get to the back door from his room. The Crown without actually specifying a time have always contended the Crewes were killed very late in the evening after television closedown at 11 p.m. Arthur's evidence that he never left the bed after retiring at between 9 p.m. and 9.30 p.m. is supported by Vivien Thomas. If Peter Thomas were to contend that he never left his bedroom there is no-one to support that contention.

Conflicting Statements from Suspect: The contradiction of not knowing the Crewes at the Lower Court hearing and then stating he knew them when testifying during the second trial has already been noted. Also at the Lower Court hearing he swore that he went to bed some thirty minutes after Arthur and Vivien then contradicted this during the second trial by saying that all three of them went to bed at the same time. At the Lower Court hearing Peter Thomas said: 'I was sleeping in the house on the night of 17 June in the same room as the gun was.' During cross-examination in the second trial he said when asked if the last time he could recall seeing the rifle it was in his room: 'Yeah, it was usually behind the door but I had moved to another room which was right in front of the house. I moved before 17 June.'

Motive: Neither trial judge accepted that the Crown had established a motive for Arthur Thomas. I know of no possible motive for Peter Thomas. Motive is not of course an essential element in a murder trial. It is not necessary for the Crown to prove motive before an accused can be convicted.

I have above outlined merely minimum details. If the police and the Crown had pursued Peter Thomas as ruthlessly as his cousin was pursued then assuredly more damaging circumstantial evidence could be and would be adduced against Peter Thomas.

As I said at the beginning of this illustration of the dangerous ambiguity of the case brought against Arthur Thomas, it is not my contention that his cousin Peter was responsible for the deaths of Harvey and Jeannette Crewe; but with a situation like the one I have just outlined how can anyone least of all you, Prime Minister, be sure that justice has been done in the case of The Queen v. Arthur Allan Thomas?

* * *

Peter Thomas, Mickey Eyre, Len Demler are just three of the people that a *prima facie* case could be established against. There are others. One of these others is the woman who fed Rochelle Crewe who is guilty of being an accessory after the fact of murder at the very least. I have sent you under separate cover information which identifies that woman together with certain recommendations. To ensure that those recommendations can be effected I have refrained from publicly naming the woman at this present time. I am confident that you will agree with me that now the identity of this woman has finally been established it is clear that in the case of The Queen v. Arthur Thomas an appalling miscarriage of justice has taken place and that Arthur Thomas should be freed from prison immediately and granted a free pardon. I ask you, Prime Minister, to directly intervene and order the immediate release of this innocent man and recommend to the Governor General that Arthur Thomas be granted a free pardon. Your advisers may argue that such steps are unprecedented in your country's history. They are not. I would refer your advisers to the Meikle Acquittal Bill of 1907. In the case of Arthur Thomas I do not ask lightly for these steps to be taken. Neither is the request made because I have discovered the identity of the woman who fed and tended Rochelle Crewe. Indeed if that facet is totally ignored, the argument for granting Arthur Thomas a free pardon is still totally overwhelming. I would ask you to consider the following facts which must surely lead you to the conclusion that a great wrong has been done to Arthur Thomas.

Suppressed Evidence: I have already within the body of this book cited various instances where evidence was suppressed during the trials and appeals and referrals. There is more evidence that has never been laid before a jury. Evidence of a crucial nature.

As mentioned earlier in this letter the Crown have

always contended that Harvey and Jeannette Crewe were murdered during the late evening of 17 June 1970. David Morris during his final speech on behalf of the Crown at the close of the second trial remarked: 'He (Harvey Crewe) was no doubt tired and relaxed when sitting with his wife in the lounge after their evening meal. The baby was bedded. Television was switched off.' Inspector Bruce Hutton was even more explicit during his testimony and talked of the murders having been committed after television closedown. The only so-called evidence to support this theory is the fact that five days later when the bloodstained farm was discovered the television set was unplugged! It was nonsensical 'evidence' of this nature that obtained a conviction. A later double murder was vital for the Crown's case. Arthur Thomas, Vivien Thomas and Peter Thomas all swore on oath that all three of them were on the Thomas farm that evening. That none of them went out. That after the evening meal and some television watching all three went to bed between 9 and 9.30 p.m. To weaken such a powerful alibi the police and the Crown contended that Arthur Thomas committed the murders after 11 p.m. Clearly, creating a picture of Thomas slipping from the marital bed and leaving the farm without disturbing his sleeping wife or cousin was a more credible proposition than asserting that all three were lying on oath and that consequently Vivien and Peter Thomas were at least accessories to murder. If the Crown had advanced this latter proposition they would have undoubtedly been torn to shreds by defence counsel asking: 'Why then have neither Vivien nor Peter Thomas been charged?' It may be argued that without any direct evidence it was perfectly proper for the police and the prosecution to play games and theorize about the actual time the murders were committed. If that argument is advanced, Prime Minister, it should be known that there is direct evidence as to the actual time Harvey and Jeannette Crewe died. Evidence that was made available to Inspector Hutton in August 1970. Evidence that was suppressed. Evidence that has never been heard by a jury.

The gate of the Crewe farm is, according to trial evidence, about a quarter of a mile from the gate to a farm owned by Owen Priest. On the night of 17 June 1970, Mrs Julie Priest retired to bed early, at about 8 p.m. The bedroom at the front of the house is in a direct diagonal line with the Crewe farmhouse. Between 8.15 p.m. and 8.45 p.m. Mrs Priest heard two shots. She was sure at the time and is sure today that those shots came from the Crewe farm. 'I would go into any courtroom and swear to this,' she told me. Tragically she was not asked to go into No. 1 Court in Auckland's Supreme Court during either of the trials and give this testimony. It should be noted that Mrs Priest is not and never has been part of the pro-Thomas faction that exists in Pukekawa. Her husband was a Crown witness and with regard to the Thomas case both are very pro-police and very anti-Thomas. In an odd way evidence that is favourable to Thomas from such a quarter carries a particular strength. As already recorded in this book no thought was given by the police or their pathologist to the possibility that the Crewes had been shot until Jeannette Crewe's body was recovered from the Waikato river on 16 August 1970. When Mrs Priest was advised of the discovery and of how Jeannette had died she immediately informed the police of the shots she had heard and the time she heard them. Inspector Hutton subsequently carried out a test. While he stood at the gate to the Priest farm one of his officers on the Crewe farm fired off a number of shots. Hutton was unable to hear them and assumed that Julie Priest was mistaken. This particular ballistic test has never been revealed before. What gun was used? What bullets fired? Where exactly were they fired from? Undoubtedly a .22 rifle was used; it would be pointless to use any other calibre. Which .22 rifle? This was not the only ballistic test to occur on the Crewe farm and remain secret. With regard to the test described above, Inspector Hutton advised Mrs Priest what had occurred. With regard to the second secret test he had no need to advise anyone. Owen Priest said to me:

'On this particular day I was standing over in much the same place where Julie had previously heard the shots on the evening of 17 June. I was in the garden over by the fowlhouse which is near the bedroom that Julie had been in that night. The fowls were kicking up quite a noise. Suddenly I heard these two shots. A short while later Bruce Hutton and Mike Charles came down the road from the direction of the Crewe farm. I stopped them and said: "You just fired two shots up at the Crewes'." Bruce Hutton was very startled. "How do you know that?" he asked. Quick as a flash I said: "I heard them." And I did. He said: "We never fired two shots." I said: "Yes, you did. They were from a .22 rifle, probably long range." '

Why, Prime Minister, did Inspector Hutton deny the firing? It should be noted that the cartridge case that Detective Charles subsequently found was .22 long range.

Even this is not an end to police firing tests that have remained secret until now. Mrs Priest told me of a third test. On this particular occasion she was aware that it was going to take place. 'I went into our bedroom and I heard them firing up at the Crewe farm. This was during the daytime.'

It should be noted that the police louvre firing reconstruction took place after dark on the night of 13 October 1970. It should also be noted that Detective Charles was not present during that test. Clearly there were at least three other occasions when the police were firing a .22 rifle on the Crewe property. Is it not possible that the cartridge case found by Detective Charles on 27 October 1970 in a flowerbed on the Crewe property had been fired during one of these tests? Massive

419

controversy has raged around that cartridge case. As will shortly become clear many people consider that it was deliberately planted to incriminate Arthur Thomas. It is possible that the explanation for its presence in that flowerbed is not police conspiracy but police stupidity, that the Charles case is a remnant from one of these secret tests. Such maladroit police behaviour would be in keeping with the entire investigation. To date there have been only two possible explanations. My investigations have established a third.

There are two curious postscripts to the two shots that Mrs Julie Priest heard between 8.15 p.m. and 8.45 p.m.

During my interview with Bruce Hutton he observed: 'It could have been more than two shots. There could have been more than one shot at Harvey.'

During my interview with David Morris he stated his belief that Harvey and Jeannette Crewe did not die 'after television had finished' but earlier in the evening. The timing he put on it was 'between 8.30 p.m. and 8.45 p.m.'

Clearly the man who led the police investigation and the man who led the prosecution of Arthur Thomas both believed Mrs Priest. If this evidence had been put before either jury and they had shared that belief the verdict would inevitably have been 'not guilty' in view of the fact that Thomas stood alone in the dock.

One more example of suppressed evidence out of the many that abound in this case will suffice. On Friday, 19 June, two days after the Crewes were last seen alive, Pukekawa farmer Ross Fleming was driving past the Crewe farm with his eight-year-old son Robert. At 7.30 p.m. the young boy saw sparks coming from the chimney on the Crewe farm. There can be little doubt that what the boy saw were fragments of partially burnt kapok from a cushion that was burning in the lounge fireplace. Someone had returned and was attempting to clean up the lounge and kitchen and also, if one accepts the opinions of Professor Elliot and Dr Fox, feed Rochelle Crewe. This sighting was only ten hours after Bruce Roddick had seen a tall fair-haired woman by the Crewe farmhouse, and eighteen hours prior to Queenie McConachie seeing a young child toddling about on the Crewe property.

At 7.30 p.m. on Friday, 19 June, Arthur and Vivien Thomas were attending a 21st birthday party at Pukekohe; they remained there until approximately 11.30 p.m.

The police were advised on Tuesday, 23 June 1970 by Ross Fleming of what his son had seen the previous Friday. Long before the first trial, indeed before the deposition stage the police were fully aware of exactly where Thomas and his wife were on that Friday evening. Clearly the facts were not compatible with the contention that Thomas was guilty. Like the statement from Julie Priest concerning the shots, the statement from Ross Fleming was suppressed.

The Charles Cartridge Case: This exhibit was rightly considered by the Crown during both trials to be 'absolutely crucial'. Curiously, Crown Solicitor David Morris now considers it to be less important in the case against Thomas than the axle. Perhaps his current position is not curious when one considers how thoroughly discredited the cartridge case has become. Here are the opinions of just a handful of the people I discussed this aspect of the Thomas case with:

'Oh, yes. There is not much doubt that the Charles case was planted. Someone put it there to be found.'

—Paul Temm, QC

'My instinct told me that the cartridge case had in fact been planted. I really believed that and I still do. I have never suggested that Charles planted it. I believe the a/b principle operated. A plants. B finds. I don't think it's a possibility. In my mind it's a certainty. That

421

cartridge case was planted. I know enough about police methods when searching to know they would not have missed that cartridge case first time around. I also know that Thomas is too intelligent not to have either got rid of his gun or to have radically altered it. Particularly after they returned his gun and he was advised that his gun might have fired the fatal bullets. Indeed the police did not say "might". At least three officers, and you know their names (Seaman, Parkes and Hutton) told him that it was definitely his gun that had fired the fatal bullets. That it was the murder weapon. They were, of course, lying but the important fact is he would have known that he had left a cartridge case up there on that farm which might be found at any moment. If, and I say if, Thomas carried out those homicides he was fitted up. The one thing happened that he would never believe could happen. A vital piece of evidence was deliberately manufactured by someone. He would not believe it could happen in this country. That's why his rifle did not disappear. That's why the firing pin was not tampered with. That is taking the Crown case at its highest. My view has always been that the cartridge case was planted.'

—Kevin Ryan, barrister .

'In my opinion, the shell case was planted. I think I've investigated this aspect as carefully as anybody because I conducted the second referral for Thomas in the Court of Appeal. I have no doubt in my mind that the shell case was planted.'

—Peter Williams, barrister

Prime Minister, it is possible that you may feel that the opinions of these three men may have been influenced by the fact that at varying times they were all defending Arthur Thomas. Here then are the opinions of others who do not fall into that category:

'There is a great deal of evidence that points to that case having been planted but there are other possibilities.'

> —Martyn Finlay, former Minister of Justice and Attorney General

'One cannot exclude the possibility that the cartridge case found in the Crewe garden was deliberately planted.'

> —Dr Donald Nelson and Rory Shanahan DSIR, Auckland. Both were expert witnesses for the Crown.

'It is of course quite possible that that cartridge case was indeed planted by an over-enthusiastic policeman but that is a long way from proving the innocence of Thomas.'

> —Sir Alfred North, former president of the Court of Appeal

'The cartridge case that was found in the Crewe garden may well have been planted. I do not think it was but one cannot rule out the reasonable possibility.'

> —Sir Trevor Henry, first trial judge

'I am aware that the present Deputy Commissioner of Police, R. J. Walton, carried out an investigation between the first and second trials into the possibility that the Charles case had been deliberately planted. I am equally aware that his conclusions were that there was no reason to doubt the validity of the find. All of the eminent men that I have just quoted were equally aware of this police inquiry into police behaviour. Clearly the above men and a great many others I have interviewed place as much faith in Walton's report as I do. As long as the police of your country are allowed to investigate themselves, observers will remain sceptical of conclusions deriving from such clearly vested interests.

When one realizes that forensic scientist Dr James Sprott, having examined over 25,000 rounds of .22 ammunition, has yet to find a single example that matches the Charles case with one of the fatal bullets; when one realizes that the police force and the DSIR have yet to produce a bullet and case of this particular category and this despite intense efforts; when one considers the opinion of I.C.I. executive Ian Cook who remarked on the likelihood of such a combination of bullet and cartridge case:

'It is about as probable as you and I both being struck and killed by meteors in the next second.' When Cook made this remark he was in Melbourne and the man he was talking to was in Wellington. When one realizes all of this together with all of the evidence contained in this book surely, Prime Minister, in the name of common sense one is driven to the inescapable conclusion that the Charles case was indeed planted. One question begs, indeed screams to be answered. Why was the .22 rifle belonging to Arthur Thomas *re-collected* by the police on 20 October 1970? Prime Minister, if you should ask that question yourself the answer you will get will depend on whom you are questioning. Based on their sworn testimony if you ask former Inspector Hutton (page 76 of 1st referral transcript refers) you will be told that it was re-collected because Detectives Parkes and Johnston found the stub axles on the Thomas farm dump that day. Stub axles that clearly came from the axle that had been recovered from the bed of the Waikato river close to the place where the body of Harvey Crewe was found. It seems a plausible explanation. If you ask Detective Parkes (page 148 1st trial transcript refers) you will be told that the rifle was re-collected on instructions the officers had been given *before* they went to the Thomas farm on 20 October. If you are told by anyone that the rifle was re-collected for further tests by the DSIR you should be aware that Dr Donald Nelson of the DSIR Auckland has told me that no request was made by the DSIR for a further examination of the Thomas rifle at this time. Seven days after it had been re-collected the Charles case was found in the Crewe garden. Why was Thomas's rifle re-collected by the police on 20 October 1970?

The more one examines the ballistic evidence in its entirety the more one is driven to the inescapable conclusion that justice has miscarried. The total contradiction in police evidence concerning why the Thomas rifle was re-collected has not been laid before a jury neither has the fact that despite dissecting a number of the unfired bullets taken from the Thomas farm police failed to find any pattern 8 bullets other than the solitary example found by Detective Keith. This fact was not passed on to the defence. It was suppressed by the police. Are we to believe that Thomas, hellbent on a double murder, disdained using ammunition from the supply that was in current use, went to his garage, hunted around, discovered three rounds that were of pattern 8 variety, took two of them and murdered, leaving the third round in the garage for the police to discover? It is a nonsense. Why did the police suppress the fact that none of Thomas's ammunition in current use was of the pattern 8 variety? Why the character assassination by the Crown on Graham Hewson? Why was Inspector Gaines instructed by Inspector Hutton to cease the search of the Waikato river for the murder weapon *before* the DSIR had irrefutably established that the Charles case had been fired from the Thomas rifle? He was given this instruction at about 2.30 p.m. on the afternoon of 28 October. Hutton had been advised by the DSIR about two hours earlier that the Charles case had been compared with three copper cartridge cases fired from the Thomas rifle and appeared to be from the same gun, but it was not until the following day that Rory Shanahan of the DSIR actually test-fired the Thomas rifle with brass cartridge cases for comparison purposes and confirmed that the Charles case had indeed beyond doubt come from the Thomas rifle. Calling off the search for the murder weapon at a time when the DSIR had given only a *qualified* opinion was surely a trifle hasty?

Why was a cartridge case that merited cleaning and mounting for display in the police museum after the first trial allegedly dumped on the Whitford tip after the second trial? Why dump a minute cartridge case and keep a large axle? Why does the foreman of the Whitford tip have no record of the police dumping exhibits on the day they allegedly dumped them?

Why were Dr Sprott and Dr Nelson given an unfired cartridge case to examine during the closing stages of the second trial? A cartridge case purporting to be the Keith case. Clearly the Keith case had been fired by the police prior to being entered as an exhibit. Doubtless you will have noted in this book that Dr Donald Nelson of the DSIR has now accepted the possibility that when the Keith case was handed to him in 1970 it was fired.

His acceptance of that possibility logically means that the Keith case was not the one he and Dr Sprott examined during the second trial. It means that the possibility that that particular exhibit was switched moves from a probability to a certainty.

The Watch: Believing that the facts contained within the body of this book clearly demonstrate the total irrelevance of the evidence of Eggleton the jeweller it had not been my intention to elaborate upon it in this open letter. That was my intention. Having read the views of your Cabinet colleague, Minister of Police Mr Allan McCready, further comment is imperative.

In the appendices you will find a copy of a letter written by Mr McCready to fellow Cabinet Minister Duncan MacIntyre.

I have already recounted in this book how the police and prosecution moved the watch that Thomas allegedly brought to Eggleton for repair from the arm of the living Arthur Thomas to the dead Harvey Crewe. I have also revealed for the first time that the watch that Eggleton allegedly accepted for repair in June 1970 was not Harvey Crewe's. In view of the fact that it has already been clearly established that Thomas never owned such a watch I find your Minister of Police's defence of police behaviour regarding this aspect deeply disturbing and a clear demonstration of the desire to maintain the conviction against Arthur Thomas at all costs including those of logic and common sense. I refer specifically to the extraordinary episode concerning the statement made to the police by one John Fisher of Feilding.

Eggleton, the eleventh-hour witness of the first trial whose evidence was so dubious that Sir Trevor Henry the trial judge would not have allowed it if the defence had raised objection, swore on oath that Thomas had brought a bloodstained mucus-covered watch into his shop for repair within a fortnight of the Crewe deaths. On 2 September 1971 (between the two trials) Fisher advised the police that he had taken a bloodstained mucus-covered watch into Eggleton's shop in late 1970. Subsequent examination of his watch established that it had in fact been repaired by Eggleton on 12 January 1971; a mere six weeks before Eggleton contacted the police.

The police duly suppressed Fisher's statement on the grounds that it was irrelevant to the Thomas trial, a decision that your Minister of Police quite clearly approves of. I was not aware that the police force of New Zealand and the Minister of Police had replaced the judges and juries of your country but clearly in this instance they have. If McCready and the police argue that because Fisher was mistaken with regard to the date that his watch was repaired by Eggleton and that a Fisher bloodstained mucus-covered watch repaired by Eggleton in 1970 is relevant but a Fisher bloodstained mucus-covered watch repaired by Eggleton in January 1971 is not, I would point out that the relevance is to the credibility of Eggleton as a witness and the relevance is initially for a judge and ultimately for a jury to decide, not the police force, not the Minister of Police. If we are to have McCready and the police functioning in this manner then let us dispense with the jury system, let us retire all the judges, put the legal profession on half pay and convert the courtrooms of New Zealand into medical centres for the treatment of megalomania.

Presumably Pukekohe is awash with men taking bloodstained mucus-covered watches into jeweller shops for repair? Two in a period of six months to the same jeweller? Both watches being rolled gold? Both watches with a damaged glass?

Your Minister of Police asserts: 'The Thomas retrial movement has attempted to make capital of a totally irrelevant issue.' I believe and so do many leading members of the legal profession of New Zealand that it is a highly relevant issue but then, unlike Mr McCready, we believe in the jury system.

Doubtless the fact that I have discovered another jeweller in Pukekohe who in February 1970 sold Arthur Thomas a stainless steel watch strap would also be considered 'irrelevant' by your Minister of Police? Doubtless he would also consider it irrelevant that the watch Eggleton alleges he received from Thomas in June 1970 had a leather strap? Presumably it would also be irrelevant to ask why Fisher had still not been told six years after he had contacted the police that his evidence was considered 'irrelevant'?

The Axle: 'The axle is the crucial piece of evidence. Take out the axle and the case against Arthur Thomas falls apart. One must acquit.'

—Sir Trevor Henry, interview with author, 1977

I am enclosing with the confidential dossier on the woman who fed Rochelle Crewe copies of five sworn affidavits concerning the axle known as Exhibit 293 in the two trials of Arthur Thomas. It is clear when these affidavits are studied that the axle, Exhibit 293, that was brought from the bed of the Waikato river to the Supreme Court in Auckland, has now been taken out of the case. It was removed from the Thomas farm by a group of young men in 1965, a year before Arthur Thomas leased the farm from his father. It is equally clear from these affidavits that the axle was subsequently dumped by the side of the road some miles from the Thomas farm. The owners of the farmland immediately next to the roadside where the young men dumped the axle are the Eyre family.

Conclusion: Sir Trevor Henry said to me: 'The axle is the crucial piece of evidence. Take out the axle and the case against Arthur Thomas falls apart. One must acquit.' Crown Prosecutor David Morris also considers the axle is the crucial piece of evidence. Demonstrably the affidavits that I am sending to you take the axle out of the case. What is left? The wire found on the bodies and the so-called motive that was dealt with so dismissively by both trial judges have, I believe, been more than adequately dealt with in this book. What then is left? I submit, Prime Minister, there is nothing left.

In May 1977, commenting on press reports that supporters of Thomas were going to take further steps to produce evidence, you observed:

'There is no reason why they should not do that. What they have to do is produce evidence that makes it clear that circumstantial evidence given at the trials – evidence of a substantial nature on which a jury may have based its verdict – was wrong and may be rebutted and that this rebuttal is of sufficient importance that it could have produced a different result had the jury been aware of those facts.'

Prime Minister, I believe this book fulfils that

requirement. If you had been a member of one of those juries and heard all the facts contained in this book what would your verdict have been? What is your verdict now? I am sure those who have struggled so hard to bring about the conviction of Thomas will be quick to dismiss the evidence contained in this book. Doubtless ex-Inspector Hutton will assert, for example, that Julie Priest and Robert Fleming were mistaken; that the former did not hear shots and the latter probably saw the lights of a nearby town. Are you prepared to countenance a situation where Hutton and others replace the jury?

To my mind there can be no question of another trial. Many of the exhibits have allegedly been destroyed by the police. Further, to find a jury of twelve good men and true who could put the events of the past seven years from their minds would be an impossibility. Clearly the second trial was a grotesque farce. Clearly all the evidence was not put before the jury in either trial. Clearly the interests of justice have, with regard to the Thomas case, been very badly served.

I have no wish for more secret reports from members of your Cabinet. I appeal directly to you, Prime Minister, and to you alone to take the one course of action that the evidence contained in this book demands. I ask you to free Arthur Thomas from prison immediately and grant him a free pardon.

I submit that if you personally consider all of the evidence contained within this book you will agree with me that not only has Arthur Allan Thomas not been found guilty beyond reasonable doubt. He has in fact been found innocent beyond reasonable doubt.

DAVID A. YALLOP
London,
May 1978

9

How Could Two Juries
Be Wrong?

'How could two juries be wrong?' It was the question most frequently asked of me by those who believe that Arthur Thomas is guilty of murdering Harvey and Jeannette Crewe. I believe that question has been overwhelmingly answered in this book. Contrary to a widely held view juries can 'be wrong'. They are not infallible. Leaving aside the extraordinary circumstances surrounding the selection of the jury in Thomas's second trial it is abundantly clear that neither jury heard all of the evidence. It may be some measure of comfort to the members of those two juries to know that others before them have sat in the jury box and brought in verdicts of guilty that were subsequently proved to be wrong and miscarriages of justice. I could cite a great many cases but feel the following three will suffice. A number of observers, writing of the Thomas case, have erroneously compared it with the Dreyfus affair. Though both men have suffered through a miscarriage of justice the comparison is limited. Dreyfus, unlike the following, was found guilty by a panel of court-martial judges, not by a jury.

TIMOTHY EVANS: Hanged in Pentonville prison in 1949 for the murder of his baby daughter Geraldine. Before his trial he had allegedly confessed to the police that he had murdered his daughter and his wife. The

431

confessions were contained in signed statements produced by the police at his trial. The main prosecution witness was John Christie, a special constable in the war reserve police force. The jury believed the evidence of a number of police officers and Christie to be true. It has now been established that the 'confessions' were false; that perjured evidence sent Evans to the gallows; that the police suppressed evidence favourable to Evans; that John Christie was responsible for the deaths of Geraldine and Beryl Evans; that John Christie murdered either twenty-one or twenty-two women, he was unsure of the precise number. Christie was hanged in Pentonville prison in 1953. On 18 October 1966, the then Home Secretary Mr Roy Jenkins, announced that Timothy Evans had been granted a posthumous pardon.

OSCAR SLATER: Found guilty in 1909 of the murder of Marion Gilchrist. Sentenced to death. Two days before his execution the sentence was commuted to life imprisonment. Despite continuous agitation by newspapers and writers including Conan Doyle, protesting that a miscarriage of justice had occurred, Slater served eighteen years in prison and was not released until 1927. The following year the sentence was quashed, he was pardoned and awarded £6,000 compensation. It was established that the police had suppressed evidence favourable to Slater; that perjured evidence obtained Slater's conviction; that the police had bribed key witnesses; that the procurator fiscal bribed a key witness. The real murderer, whose identity was known to the investigating police officers, was never prosecuted.

I have given the barest details of these two cases. It should not be thought that officialdom in the shape of the law or the body politic acted quickly to redress the wrong done to Evans and Slater. The fight to obtain natural justice for Timothy Evans took seventeen years and the 'pardon' was small comfort to the late Timothy

Evans. The fight to obtain 'justice' for Slater lasted nineteen years. In both cases the executive and the judiciary behaved disgracefully, again and again refusing to accept incontrovertible facts.

For a third and final example of how juries can be wrong there are, sadly, many cases that one could cite. Adolf Beck who served seven years' penal servitude for theft and fraud and after his release was again found guilty on similar charges only to be subsequently proved innocent on all counts and be awarded a 'free pardon' and £5,000. As with Arthur Thomas, Beck suffered injustice at the hands of two juries. George Edalji, who also received a seven-year prison sentence, in his case the crime was a series of atrocious cattle-maiming outrages. He was granted a free pardon. Kathryn Seaby, found guilty of throwing corrosive fluid into the face of a young woman. Subsequently granted a free pardon and £400 compensation which was increased to £700 after a public uproar. Rose Gooding, on two separate occasions found guilty of obscene libel by juries and sentenced to prison. Subsequently the actual culprit Edith Swan was charged and found 'not guilty' by a jury. Later Edith Swan was charged with further offences and found guilty. Mrs Seaby was granted a 'free pardon' and £250 compensation. This was a case where three juries and three appeal judges 'went wrong'. All of these miscarriages of justice occurred in Great Britain but an examination of any country on this planet would produce equally horrifying examples. Even a country like New Zealand, where the third example I have chosen occurred.

OLAF HALINEN AND ANDREW ANDERSON: Shortly before nine o'clock on the evening of 8 May 1908 Ernest Bourke was found dying in some horse stables in Westport. He had severe injuries to his face including a broken nose and jaw. There was also severe bruising to his chest.

433

Medical opinion at the inquest was that Bourke had been kicked by a horse and that there was nothing connected with the case to indicate foul play.

Two foreign seamen, Halinen and Anderson were arrested and charged with the murder of Bourke. At the resumed inquest, William Connelly, an eighteen-year-old sailor, testified that he had been present in the stables when Halinen and Anderson kicked Bourke to death and robbed him. Despite severe questioning from the jury Connelly adhered to his sworn testimony. His evidence was in part corroborated by another young sailor, William Murray. The jury's verdict was that Bourke had met his death by 'foul play' and that Connelly, Halinen and Anderson were all implicated.

With Connelly as the main prosecution witness, the Crown proceeded with the charge of murder against Halinen and Anderson.

At the magistrate's hearing a number of witnesses gave damning evidence against the two men. Their bosun testified that on the morning after Bourke's death both men had bloodstains on their clothing and Halinen had blood on his right boot.

It was established that Bourke had been attacked at 8.30 p.m. Both of the accused swore that at that time they had been in a local theatre, an alibi that was directly contradicted by a number of Crown witnesses. The magistrate, Mr Rawson, said it was his 'reluctant duty' to send both men for trial. 'I say reluctant because my own opinion is that Connelly alone is the murderer of Bourke.'

At the Supreme Court trial, prosecuting counsel told the jury that the accused had a powerful motive. 'Bourke had not accounted to the accused men for some contraband tobacco he had been given to sell.' He also told the jury that Connelly, 'who admitted to taking part in the crime to the extent of hitting the deceased, had no motive.'

Crown evidence established that after the dying man

had been discovered by a stable groom who raised the alarm, Connelly had appeared on the scene and done everything possible to aid the dying man who was described as being 'in the prime of life, a big man, some six feet tall and weighing fifteen stone'.

Forensic evidence was given that the clothes of both men at the time they were arrested were covered with blood. Crown witness hotelier Joseph Seward told the jury of seeing the dead man in the company of three men on the fatal evening and that later when Halinen bought him a drink he had noticed there were bloodstains on his clothes. Halinen had told him: 'I knocked my man out.' Two other witnesses gave identical testimony. All three refuted defence counsel's suggestion that the bloodstains had been caused when the two defendants restrained Connelly who was running amok in a nearby fish shop. It was established that Connelly had indeed attacked a woman in the fish shop and smashed the place up, cutting himself badly in the process. But the three Crown witnesses swore that Halinen and Anderson had blood on them *before* this incident.

A further three Crown witnesses testified that on the day after Bourke was murdered the accused men had appeared in another hotel and that Halinen had boasted of being in two fights the previous evening, one of them being with Bourke. Halinen had recounted in front of these three witnesses how he had punched Bourke in the face and then repeatedly kicked him as he lay on the ground. Anderson, according to these three witnesses, had stopped Halinen from telling more. One of the three witnesses was Police Constable Buttar. It transpired that because of their inability to speak English the accused, particularly Halinen, had described the 'fight' with Bourke largely in mime. Cross-examination established that another of the three Crown witnesses, hotelier Leonard Cockery, had recently left the police force. Cockery had telephoned

Buttar and told him to come to the hotel in plain clothes to listen to Halinen.

William Connelly, despite a five and a half hour ordeal in the witness box, continued to maintain that the two men had killed Bourke.

The jury, who were kept incommunicado throughout the trial, asked if they could sit late into the evenings 'as some of us are anxious to get back to our businesses'. Mr Justice Chapman advised them that regretfully he could not accede to their request.

For the defence, ship's steward Haakonson testified that he had been in the company of the two men throughout the evening that Bourke died. He swore that all three of them were at the local theatre between 8 and 10 p.m. and that neither man had blood on his clothes before Connelly wrecked the fish shop. This testimony was supported by nine other witnesses including six theatregoers and the ticket seller at the theatre.

After a retirement of four hours the jury returned a verdict that Halinen and Anderson were guilty of the manslaughter of Ernest Bourke. Both men protested their innocence as they were sentenced to seven years' hard labour. Mr Justice Chapman then complimented the police on the quality of their investigation. Verdict and sentence were on 1 July 1908.

Mr McDonald, who had been the defence solicitor, immediately brought a charge against Connelly alleging that he had murdered Bourke; subsequently a charge of perjury was added to the indictment and it was on this latter charge alone that Connelly was brought to trial. He was defended by the Crown Solicitor who was assisted by several senior police officers, a situation that gave rise to critical comment in Parliament.

Connelly's trial was presided over by Mr Justice Cooper, who throughout the proceedings showed himself to be favourably disposed towards Connelly. His summing up was virtually an instruction to the jury to acquit. After a retirement of four hours the jury returned a verdict that Connelly was guilty of perjury on eight counts. On 29 September 1908 he was sentenced to seven years' hard labour. A few hours after the sentence had been passed Connelly confessed to a chief detective that he and he alone had been responsible for the murder of Bourke. The motive had been robbery. In the attack he had lost his temper and had kicked Bourke to death. He had then concocted a story against two innocent men. The following day the government ordered the immediate release of Halinen and Anderson. Andrew Anderson who had been seriously ill since his arrest died two weeks after his release. Before his death both men had asked the government for compensation for wrongful arrest and imprisonment.

In December 1908 the government, who had stood so resolutely by the murderer and perjuror Connelly, announced that they 'were unable to recognize any claim to compensation or payment'.

Prime Minister Sir Joseph Ward observed: 'Naturally one has sympathy for anyone who has been placed in such a position, but it is not a question of sympathy, it is a question of doing what is right.'

In May 1909, Connelly stood trial charged with the murder of Ernest Bourke; he pleaded not guilty. In his opening speech to the jury the Crown Solicitor declared that 'there is strong overpowering circumstantial evidence that points to Connelly being the murderer'. One year earlier the Crown Solicitor had said precisely the same when Halinen and Anderson had stood trial.

The verdict of the jury was that Connelly had alone killed Bourke. He was sentenced to ten years' hard labour after being found guilty of manslaughter.

It will be clear to the reader that there are many similarities between the Thomas case and the Halinen–Anderson case. To cite just one, in both cases apparently strong circumstantial evidence was brought against the defendants. Two juries brought in the wrong verdict in the case of Halinen and Anderson. Two juries brought in the wrong verdict in the case of Arthur Thomas.

A few years before the two foreign seamen stood trial a treatise on the law of evidence was published. The writer was a distinguished British judge, Pitt Taylor. In the light of what transpired in New Zealand in 1908 and again during the two trials of Arthur Thomas, Mr Justice Pitt Taylor's comments on circumstantial evidence have a savagely ironic tone that can be heard loudly in 1978:

'In cases supported by circumstantial evidence, juries should remember that, although the number of facts drawn from apparently independent sources renders concerted perjury both highly improbable in itself, and easy of detection if attempted; yet, the witnesses in such cases are more likely to make unintentional mis-statements than those who give direct testimony. The truth of the facts they attest depends frequently on minute and careful observation, and experience teaches the danger of relying implicitly on the evidence of even the most conscientious witnesses, respecting dates, time, distances, footprints, handwriting, admissions, loose conversations, and questions of identity. Yet these in general are the links in the chain of circumstances, by which guilt is sought to be established. The number too of the witnesses, who must *all* speak the truth, or some link will be wanting, renders additional caution the more necessary. Besides, it must be remembered, that, in a case of circumstantial evidence, the facts are collected by *degrees*. Something occurs to raise suspicion against a particular party. Constables and police officers are immediately on the alert, and with professional zeal, ransack every place and paper, and examine into every circumstance which can tend to establish, not his innocence, but his guilt. Presuming him guilty from the first, they are apt to consider his acquittal as a tacit reflection on their discrimination or skill, and, with something like the feeling of a keen sportsman they determine, if possible to bag their game. Though both sportsmen and policemen alike would be horrified at anything unfair or "unsportsmanlike", yet, as both start with this object in view, it is easy to unintentionally misinterpret innocent actions, to misunderstand innocent words, *for men readily believe what they anxiously desire, and to be ever ready to construe the most harmless facts as preconceived opinions. These feelings are common alike to police, to counsel, engineers, surveyors, medical men, antiquarians, and philosophers; indeed, to all persons who first assume that a fact or system is true, and then seek for arguments to support and prove its truth.*'

The final italics are mine. This book is the result of an investigation that did not assume any fact or system to be true. The facts as I discovered them have led inexorably to an indisputable truth.

Arthur Thomas did not murder Harvey and Jeannette Crewe.

DAVID A. YALLOP .
London
1 May 1978

Epilogue

This book was first published in late October 1978 and was the product of an intensive investigation that had lasted over a year. During the hunt for the truth of what was always referred to as 'The Thomas Case' I learned a great deal not only about the case but also about New Zealand. After publication I learned about New Zealand media. It's a land where they cut down tall poppies – or try to.

TV reporters who attempted to have a trial by television, in this case removing Thomas from the dock and putting me into it, were followed by some interesting examples of journalistic objectivity, New Zealand style. 'David Yallop is no Emile Zola.' 'Author Yallop cashes in.' 'Englishman David Yallop is an opportunist.' There were also the odd passing references to a 'stirring Pommie bastard'.

On the 24th of October just before publication, I had a meeting with Prime Minister Robert Muldoon. Apart from giving him an advance copy of the book so that he could study the assembled evidence, I handed him a number of sworn affidavits concerning the axle that had been pulled from the Waikato river. In my view those affidavits removed the axle from the prosecution's case against Thomas. I also gave the Prime Minister a letter in which I named the woman who I was certain had fed Rochelle Crewe in those bizarre days immediately after her parents had been murdered. There was only one reason why I had not named her in the book. If named in so public a fashion how on earth could she then have a fair trial in New Zealand? Where could the judicial system find a jury of twelve who would not have heard my accusation and read the various details? Even an accomplice after the fact of murder is entitled to the full benefit of the law.

The day after our meeting Muldoon announced that he was asking a 'prominent lawyer' to investigate a number of my allegations.

The lawyer in question was an Auckland-based Q.C. named R.A. Adams-Smith. I waited. Others were busy. Very busy. One of the busiest was *Auckland Star* reporter Pat Booth.

As recorded within this book Booth first took an interest in 'The Thomas Case' during the second trial in 1973. It was an interest that remained undiminished for a number of years, but some time before my first visit to New Zealand, Booth had thrown the towel in and publicly declared he could do no more in the fight to obtain justice for Thomas and that he intended to get on with the rest of his life and its demands. I had been made aware of this involvement during that first visit and out of courtesy phoned the Auckland reporter before committing myself to an investigation of the case. I wanted to clear the ground and ensure that his active involvement had indeed ceased. He confirmed that it had and expressed delight that I might be conducting my own investigation.

'Can I run a story saying that you are investigating the case?'

'I'd rather you didn't. Even if I go ahead I prefer to do it very quietly. No publicity.'

'Fair enough.'

After I was back in England I received the story he had run the following day announcing my involvement. A small bell rang.

When I returned to begin the investigation proper Booth asked for a full scale interview with me. I declined, explaining that my style is to enter quietly. The noise can wait until the job is done. I then received a series of phone calls from Neil Robinson, my editor.

Booth was being insistent. Neil spoke of his earlier work on the case, urged me to make 'just this one exception. Pat says it will be very low key.' A journalist duly appeared. When I saw the two-inch headline to the interview I winced. It read, 'I want to interview the lot'. If anything was guaranteed to ensure that I did not get to interview 'the lot' it was that.

That was one side of Booth. I saw another as I began to investigate. If I needed a trial transcript I had only to ask the man at the *Auckland Star*, he was helpful at every turn, but from time to time small bells would ring. Deep into my investigation, I discussed with Kevin Ryan the fact that I had established through direct interviews that Ross Fleming's son had seen sparks coming from the Crewe chimney at 7.30 p.m. on Friday, the 19th of June. This was vital new evidence. Ryan lost little time in passing the information on to Booth. I was disturbed to read it under his byline the following day. I remonstrated with him, pointing out that it had been that very kind of piecemeal disclosure of evidence over the years more than any other single factor that had ensured that Thomas remained in prison. I thought he accepted the point. I was wrong.

At the time this book was first published Booth, along with the rest of New Zealand, wanted to know the identity of the woman I had named in my letter to the Prime Minister. The woman who I was convinced had fed Rochelle Crewe. I believed that if there was one man in the country that I could trust with that information it was Pat Booth. I was wrong.

During the course of my investigation I had for a number of reasons become convinced that I knew the identity of the woman that fed Rochelle Crewe. I believed it was imperative to show Roddick a photograph of this woman without indicating her identity and establish whether he could confirm my belief. I referred in the Introduction to this book to the advance I received for writing it. The amount had not even

443

covered our air fares back to New Zealand. Now, nine months later, deeply in debt and overdrawn, I lacked the financial resources to pay for an air ticket from Auckland to Melbourne where Roddick was living. I appealed to my editor, Neil Robinson, and to my publishers, Hodder & Stoughton, to advance the next tranche of money. It would only have been a few hundred dollars, but that was all I needed. They declined, reminding me that no more was due until the book was delivered. I pleaded with Robinson and told him why it was imperative that I made this journey. He understood, he was sympathetic, but they wouldn't oblige.

As luck would have it, one of the people I had interviewed for this book was at that time about to make a trip to Australia, with three friends. She agreed to act as a courier and interview Roddick on my behalf. The photograph of the suspected woman was placed with photographs of fifteen other different women in a folder. The suspect's photograph was marked number eleven.

When Roddick was shown the sixteen photographs of different women in his Melbourne home, by the four people acting on my behalf, he picked out two. One of the women was wearing clothing similar to that worn by the woman he had seen on that fateful morning outside the Crewe farm. That was interesting. But the other photograph he picked out produced more than an interesting response. He was certain. There was no doubt. 'That's her.' It was the woman he had seen at about 9 a.m. on the Crewe property on Friday, 19th of June, 1970. The photograph that Roddick had identified and which he then signed was number eleven. I had stressed to the persons showing these photographs to Roddick that at no time either before, during or afterwards were they to mention any names or give any identities of the sixteen women. They followed my instructions to the letter. For Roddick's evidence to be given the weight it deserved it was crucial that he remain ignorant of whom he had identified until questioned by the Prime Minister's representative.

Booth simply could not resist the lure of a big story. He flew to Australia, interviewed Roddick and during the course of his interview told Roddick who he had identified to my four representatives.

Confronted with the implications of that identity Roddick, precisely as I had predicted to Booth, began to back-track. In November 1977 he had according to the sworn affidavits of three of the people showing him the photographs on my behalf been certain. 'That's her' he had exclaimed. Asked to elaborate, he said:

'The lady on photograph eleven is the woman I saw outside the Crewe farm with a car behind her to the left and I am positive.'

Confronted now by the name and the identity of that woman, courtesy of Pat Booth, Roddick began to retreat.

'She is similar to the woman I saw, I can't go any further than that.'

And:

'I've never said for certain that that is the woman.'

For any journalist to do what Booth had done would have been grossly unethical. For a man who had himself given years of his life attempting to obtain justice for Arthur Thomas, to do what Booth had done showed self-interest at Olympic level and a stunning lack of morality.

Criminal history is full of instances of witnesses recanting or attempting to recant after becoming aware of the implication of what have been originally confidently asserted statements. Indeed Roddick was only one of a number who would deny saying to me or to my representatives what they had in fact said to me. If Roddick had not been interfered with as a clear vital witness in this manner I have no doubt that when Adams-Smith finally got around to talking to him two months later, and quite why it was two months later and not before axe-grinding journalists has never been explained, Roddick would have again picked without any hesitation the same woman.

Despite Pat Booth, the interim reports from the Q.C. appointed by the Prime Minister indicated the tide was turning. Confronted with Roddick's retraction and his highly significant reaction, 'When Booth told me her name, I wanted to crawl under the couch', Adams-Smith concluded that I had 'no proper basis' for asserting that I knew who fed Rochelle Crewe. And yet:

'I am satisfied that this woman for purposes of gain has before been prepared to break the law.'

Adams-Smith also accepted my contention that the baby had indeed been fed. In this interim report made public in January 1979 he suggested that further enquiries be made in three areas, one of these was to be with regard to the woman I had named to the Prime Minister. A second concerned the need for further investigation as to the precise time the Crewes had died. The third area that the Q.C. was going to enquire into was not specified.

Close on the heels of this interim report the New Zealand clobbering machine got to work again. Julie Priest was identified as one of the mysterious witnesses insisting I had seriously misquoted her. She wrote complaining to Prime Minister Muldoon who, without bothering to seek verification from me, gaily made her complaint public. The new evidence that I had obtained from Mr and Mrs Priest was in two areas crucial. It pinpointed the time of the murders. It powerfully established a strong probability that the police had planted a cartridge case as part of their conspiracy to frame an innocent man.

Because of the profound importance of this evidence I had gone back and re-interviewed Julie Priest a second time. When I allowed an independent lawyer to hear those particular tapes, he subsequently

446

confirmed publicly the accuracy of my version of the interview. Curious how the New Zealand clobbering machine works. The Prime Minister's disclosure of Julie Priest's complaint had been carried in every single New Zealand paper. My rebuttal was carried by one Wellington newspaper, *The Dominion*.

In late November 1979, Adams-Smith delivered his final report. The following month Prime Minister Robert Muldoon called a press conference on December 17th and announced that Arthur Thomas had been granted a Royal Pardon. The Q.C. had concluded:

'I have real doubt whether it can be properly contended that the case against Thomas has been proved beyond all reasonable doubt.'

Thomas was immediately released, a nation rejoiced and I experienced one of the sweetest moments of my life.

Inevitably the Auckland reporter reared his head again. Pat Booth had 'arranged' to spirit Arthur out of the prison to a relative's home for the night to ensure he had an exclusive story for the following evening's paper. It also ensured that after nine years imprisonment, Arthur spent one more night away from his home. Later Booth would be awarded an O.B.E. I remember the late Mike Bungay, then one of New Zealand's leading criminal lawyers, ringing me with this particular news.

'An O.B.E., David. The legal profession thinks that stands for Other Bugger's Efforts.'

Muldoon set up a Royal Commission of Inquiry into the circumstances that had led to the conviction of Thomas.

Of the 'affaire Roddick' it concluded:

'In our view it is clear that Roddick has retreated from an initially more positive identification than he gave before us. That having been said we are satisfied that there is insufficient evidence that the woman in the photograph named by Mr Yallop in his letter to the

447

Prime Minister is the woman seen on the Crewe property by Mr Roddick on 19th June 1970. We say that, not only on the basis of Mr Roddick's evidence, but also on the basis of certain other investigations which were carried out to determine whether the woman concerned could have been on the property that day. It is clear that it is not now possible to establish whether the woman named by Mr Yallop was the woman seen by Mr Roddick.

'Mr Yallop named the woman in his letter to the Prime Minister in good faith on the information available to him. There is, however, simply no means of justifying to an acceptable standard of proof his statement that the woman he named was the woman seen by Mr Roddick.'

In other areas my allegations met with greater success:

'We believe, for reasons already detailed earlier in this Report:

(a) That shellcase exhibit 350 was planted by the Police, and that this was known by Detective Inspector Hutton.

(b) The chances of the bullets which killed the Crewes having come from the Thomas rifle were significantly reduced by the factors omitted from Dr Nelson's evidence. Again, Detective Inspector Hutton knew of these matters, for he referred to them at a Police conference on 19th October 1970.'

'If we then leave to one side the evidence referred to in the preceding paragraph the only other evidence which the Police had then in their possession and would sustain the arrest and prosecution was as follows:

(a) **Motive** – We have already considered this in paragraphs 212–220. We reject entirely the notion that any of the evidence put forward in this respect established a motive by Arthur Allan Thomas to kill the Crewes.

448

(b) **Wire** – Again we have dealt with this in paragraphs 263–266. At best for the Prosecution, wire attached to the bodies was very similar to wire from the Thomas farm. No positive identification was made, and there was nothing placing the wire in Arthur Allan Thomas's hands.

(c) **The axle** – Recovered from the river with Harvey Crewe's body, matched stub axles found on the Thomas farm. The Police were at that stage justified in inferring that the axle had come from the father's trailer in former years. There was no evidence that Thomas knew of its existence, let alone had it in his physical possession at any time.'

There was much more. The final report runs to over one hundred pages. Having within its final conclusions torn a nation's beliefs in its judicial system in half, the Commission turned to the man who had for so many years stood at the heart of the storm. Arthur Thomas. It awarded him one million dollars compensation.

Now, fourteen years later, it is time to refer to this case by its correct name. The name it should always have been given. The name it must be given in the future. This is not 'The Thomas Case'. It is the murder of Harvey and Jeannette Crewe.

A miscarriage of justice is a double disaster. An obscenity perpetrated twice. As I wrote within the original text:

'There is no doubt in my mind that a miscarriage of justice has occurred in the case of The Queen v Arthur Allan Thomas. I believe that an innocent man is at present serving a life sentence for crimes he did not commit. New Zealand has a ten-million dollar man in Arthur Thomas, for that is the minimum it has cost to get him convicted and keep him convicted. It was a poor investment because while Thomas languishes in prison the guilty ones walk freely among you.'

So who then killed the Crewes?

I invite the reader to re-read Chapters One and Two, then to study the Appendices. All the clues to solve this case are contained within those pages. Consider:

Len Demler had since 1937 worked the land on his Pukekawa farm. It was extremely hard work but he was a hardworking man. He was also a good farmer. His daughters Jeannette and Heather inherit as young girls the farm adjoining the Demler property in 1950. Subsequently Heather sells her half of the farm to Jeannette's husband, Harvey Crewe. In August 1962 Demler is fined £10,000 for tax evasion. To avoid the calamity of selling the farm that he has sweated over for decades, Maisie makes over £9,500 available to him. Not as a gift, not as a loan, she takes by way of return half of her husband's farm. An action that I believe speaks volumes about the condition of their marriage. Demler later perjured himself during the second trial of Arthur Thomas by stating that he never received this money. The documentary proof is within the Appendices. Why would he lie? To cover a greater crime.

In July 1969, Maisie Demler, outraged that her daughter Heather had married a man that she for excellent reasons considered to be unsuitable, cut Heather out of her will and out of her life.

Len Demler retaliated by cutting Jeannette out of his will. Maisie died of a brain tumour on the 26th of February 1970.

Suddenly Demler was confronted with an unacceptable future. Half of the farm – *his* farm was now owned by a daughter he was hostile towards and a son-in-law he actively disliked. All of the rancour, all of the injustice, real or imagined by Demler, festered until June 16th when Demler as well as Jeannette discovered precisely how much she had inherited from her mother.

Determined to confront his unfavourite daughter and her overbearing husband, Demler visited them on the following evening. With a gun. What followed was not for financial gain. At issue was something as old as man. Land. Demler was not prepared to allow a situation to continue where for example his son-in-law would have a view, an opinion, about the older man moving stock off the land. 'Those are joint assets, Len. Half of them are Jeannette's.'

I believe Len Demler murdered first Harvey, then Jeannette Crewe. I believe he then prevailed upon a woman he totally trusted to feed Rochelle. A woman who in theory had a perfect alibi. She was officially in another country at the crucial time. There is but one flaw in this perfect alibi. Since my book was first published, many, not least Adams-Smith Q.C., the New Zealand police force and God knows how many hack reporters have tried to make that alibi stand up, have tried to demonstrate that I am wrong, have tried to find proof that this woman was indeed in another country. They have all failed. Therefore demonstrably the perfect alibi collapses. There is in truth no alibi at all for this woman, who is of course the woman that in November 1977 Bruce Roddick initially identified with such confidence and such certainty as the woman that he had seen standing by the Crewe farm on the 19th of June 1970.

To my mind, the solution of what occurred both prior to the murders of this young couple and in the days that immediately followed has been established beyond reasonable doubt.

DAVID YALLOP
March 1995

451

Appendices

APPENDIX 1

Memorandum of Transfer

LENARD WILLIAM DEMLER of Pukekawa, Farmer
being registered as proprietor of an estate in fee simple

(subject, however,
to such encumbrances, liens and interests as are notified by memoranda underwritten or endorsed
hereon,) IN all those pieces of land situated in the Provincial District of Auckland
containing FIRSTLY 423 acres 3 roods 35.5 perches

be the same a little more or less being part Section No. 2 Block XIII of the Maramarua..
Survey District and being the residue of the land comprised and described in ...
Certificate of Title Volume 242 Folio 176 (South) of the Register Books at .. ..
Auckland, SECONDLY 14 acres be the same a little more or less being Sections 4A..
and 4B Block XVI of the Onewhero Survey District and being the whole of the land.
comprised and described in Certificate of Title Volume 614 Folio 20 of the .. ..
Register Books aforesaid and THIRDLY 27 acres 1 rood 20 perches be the same a ..
little more or less being Lot 1 on a plan deposited in the Land Registry Office..
at Auckland under No. S.3657 and being the whole of the land comprised and .. ..
described in Certificate of Title Volume 1230 Folio 33 of the Register Books. ..
aforesaid SUBJECT to Section 59 of the Land Act 1948.

IN CONSIDERATION of the sum of NINE THOUSAND FIVE HUNDRED AND FORTY POUNDS .. ..
(£9,540. 0. 0.) (the receipt whereof is hereby acknowledged) paid to him by.. ..
CONSTANCE MAY DEMLER wife of the said Lenard William Demler
MAY CONSTANCE

DO HEREBY Transfer to the said May Constance Demler an undivided half share or
interest in the said land to the intent that the same shall henceforth be ..
held by them as tenants in common in equal shares.
all----------estate and interest in the said piece of land

In witness whereof I have hereunto subscribed my name this 24
day of August One thousand nine hundred and sixty-two.

Signed by the said
LENARD WILLIAM DEMLER
in the presence of

455

This is the written document now produced and shown to Lenard William Dealer of Pakepawa Farms and referred to in his affidavit to lead grant of probate to himself and Jannette Lenore Crawe of Pakepawa, Married Woman, as executors, sworn at Tuakau this 16th day of March 1970, before me :—

A. Solicitor of the Supreme Court of New Zealand

This is the last Will and Testament *of me*
MAY CONSTANCE DEALER *of Pakekawa Married Woman.*

1. I Revoke all former wills at any time heretofore made by me and declare this to be my last and only will.

2. I Appoint my husband Lenard William Dealer and my daughter Jannette Lenore Crawe hereinafter called "my trustees" which expression shall include the survivor of them or other trustee of this my will howsoever appointed) to be executors and trustees of this my will.

3. I Give and Bequeath to my daughter the said Jannette Lenore Crawe absolutely all my jewellery and silverware and articles of personal adornment.

4. I Give, Devise and Bequeath all the rest and remainder of my property both real and personal of whatsoever nature and wheresoever situate (hereinafter called my residuary estate) unto my trustees Upon Trust to allow my husband the said Lenard William Dealer the use and occupation thereof and the income arising therefrom during his lifetime and after his death to stand possessed of my said residuary estate upon the following Trusts:—

(a) as to the sum of Four hundred dollars ($400) for the Tuakau Vestry of the Anglican church to be used for the general purposes of the Tuakau church.

(b) as to the sum of Two thousand dollars ($2000) for my grand-daughter MICHELLE ROXANNE CRAWE for her own use absolutely upon her attaining the age of twenty-five (25) years.

(c) as to the balance of my said residuary estate for my daughter the said Jannette Lenore Crawe for her own use absolutely or if she should predecease me or die before attaining a vested interest hereunder for her issue and if more than one in equal shares for their own use absolutely upon their attaining the age of twenty-one years...

In Witness Whereof I have set my ... 16th ...

} M. C. Dealer.

APPENDIX 3

This is the last Will and Testament of me ....

JEANNETTE LENORE CREWE of Pukekawa Married Woman.

1.   I HEREBY REVOKE all former wills and testamentary dispositions.....
at any time heretofore made by me AND I DECLARE this to be my last and ..
only will.

2.   SUBJECT to him surviving me for a period of One (1) calendar month.
I APPOINT my husband DAVID HARVEY CREWE to be sole executor and trustee..
of this my will AND I GIVE DEVISE BEQUEATH AND APPOINT all my estate ....
both real and personal of whatsoever kind and wheresoever situate of which
I shall be possessed to which I shall be entitled or over which I shall .
have any power of disposition (including the proceeds of any policy or ..
policies of insurance) to my husband the said David Harvey Crewe for his.
own use absolutely.

3.   IN THE EVENT of my said husband failing to survive me as aforesaid
then I APPOINT my father LEONARD WILLIAM DEMLER and my mother MAY CONSTANCE
DEMLER (hereinafter called "my Trustees")which expression shall include..
the survivor of them or other the trustee or trustees of this my will ...
howsoever appointed) to be executors and trustees of this my will and ...
I GIVE DEVISE BEQUEATH AND APPOINT all my said estate to my trustees ....
UPON TRUST for my children and if more than one then in equal shares for.
their own use absolutely upon their attaining the age of Twenty-one (21).
years AND IN THE EVENT of no such child of mine attaining a vested ......
interest hereunder then UPON TRUST for the said LEONARD WILLIAM DEMLER ..
and MAY CONSTANCE DEMLER or the survivor of them in equal shares for their
own use absolutely.

4.   I EMPOWER my trustees:-

    (a)   TO SELL call in collect and convert into money all parts of ..
    my residuary estate not hereinbefore specifically devised or..
    bequeathed at such time or times and in such manner as he ....
    shall think fit and so that he shall have the fullest power...
    and discretion to postpone the sale calling in and conversion.
    of the whole or any part or parts of the said premises during.

    amalgamated company or reconstructed company.

IN WITNESS WHEREOF I have set my hand to this my will this 28th day.
of *August* One thousand nine hundred and sixty-seven.

SIGNED by the Testatrix the said   )
JEANNETTE LENORE CREWE as and ..)
for her last will and testament.)
in the sight and presence of us)   *J.L. Crewe.*
together present at the same ...)
tire who at her request in her..)
sight and presence and in the ..)
sight and presence of each other)
have hereunto subscribed our ...)
names as attesting witnesses:-)

457

APPENDIX 4

This is the last Will and Testament of me .....

DAVID HARVEY CREWE of Pukekawa Farmer.

1.   I HEREBY REVOKE all former wills and testamentary dispositions ....
at any time heretofore made by me AND I DECLARE this to be my last and only
will.

2.   SUBJECT to her surviving me for a period of One (1) calendar month.
I APPOINT my wife JEANNETTE LENORE CREWE to be sole executrix and trustee.
of this my will and I GIVE DEVISE BEQUEATH AND APPOINT all my estate both.
real and personal of whatsoever kind and wheresoever situate of which I ..
shall be possessed to which I shall be entitled or over which I shall have
any power of disposition (including the proceeds of any policy or policies
of insurance) to my wife the said JEANNETTE LENORE CREWE for her own use..
absolutely.

3.   IN THE EVENT of my said wife failing to survive me as aforesaid then
I APPOINT COLIN HARVEY of Mangakino Farmer (hereinafter called "my ......
trustee") to be the sole executor and trustee of this my will AND I GIVE ..
DEVISE BEQUEATH AND APPOINT all my said estate to my Trustee UPON TRUST ..
for my children and if more than one then in equal shares for their own...
use absolutely upon their attaining the age of Twenty-one (21) years .....
PROVIDED HOWEVER that if I should die leaving no children me surviving or.
if no such surviving children shall attain a vested interest hereunder ...
then I DIRECT my Trustee to hold my said estate UPON THE FURTHER FOLLOWING
TRUSTS:-

   (1)   AS to the sum of FIVE THOUSAND POUNDS (£5000.0.0) (the dollar
          equivalent being $10,000) to pay the same to my mother MARIE.
          LAL CREWE for her own use absolutely.

   (2)   AS to the residue of my estate to pay the same equally to ...
          LEONARD WILLIAM DEMLER and MAY CONSTANCE DEMLER or the ......
          survivor of them for their own use absolutely.

      I EMPOWER my Trustee:-

   (a)   TO SELL call in collect and convert into money all parts of..
          ~~my residuary estate not hereinbefore specifically excised or~~
          ~~thereof and my trustee shall be free from all responsibility.~~
          thereof and my trustee shall be free from all responsibility.
          and be fully indemnified out of my estate in respect of any...
          loss arising in relation thereto.

IN WITNESS WHEREOF I have set my hand to this my will this 24th day
of August One thousand nine hundred and sixty-seven.

SIGNED by the Testator the said
DAVID HARVEY CREWE as and for .
his last will and testament in.
the sight and presence of us ..
together present at the same ..
time who at his request in his.
sight and presence and in the..
sight and presence of each ....
other have hereunto subscribed.
our names as attesting ....
witnesses:-

D. H. Crewe

458

APPENDIX 5

Mr Justice Henry's Summing-up to First Trial Jury

In the final determination of this case you, as the jury, and I, as the Judge, now have separate parts to play. My task is to lay down for you such principles of law as are applicable in the deciding of this case. You are bound to follow and to apply the law as stated by me, but, so long as you do that, and within the framework of the law so laid down, it is for you and you alone to say whether you find the accused guilty or not guilty. That means that all questions of evidence, all questions of the value of evidence or any part of it, are solely matters for your determination. What faith, what trust, what credibility can be placed in any witness is for you. In short, you are the sole judges of all questions of fact and of the final result of this case.

It is important to remind you that you are really the true and final judges in the case because such a role requires you to bring clear, cool, calm and fair judgment on all the evidence that you have heard, and I stress to you upon all the evidence. There are two sides to every criminal trial. First of all it is in the public interest that persons who commit crimes should be convicted and punished, and, secondly, in the interests of justice that the person charged should not be convicted unless his guilt is proved according to law. You must hold the balance between the two, and, making a just and proper judgment, give a true verdict on the evidence as you judge it. You must not lean to one side or to the other unless and until all the evidence is fairly weighed and valued by you. That means, of course, that you must put entirely from your minds all previous notions, thoughts or judgments you may have entertained before you first entered this court room. This, I feel sure, you have done, and that the many hours you have been together concentrating on the case as it has been presented in this Court, will ensure that no outside considerations will intrude themselves into your consideration of this case. Sympathy for the accused or for his wife, or for anyone else, must be resolutely put to one side. So must all or any feelings of horror at the untimely deaths of Mr and Mrs Harvey Crewe. They are both now dead, and Rochelle is an orphan. You accept those things as fact and then proceed to a careful and unemotional appraisal of the evidence. The accused stands charged with the murder of both Jeannette and Harvey Crewe, charged as their killer. It is now your solemn duty, acting judicially, to say whether or not those charges have been proved. It is a matter of reasoning, of judgment, and of the fair and judicial assessment of the whole of the evidence you have heard, strictly applying the law as I lay it down for you, weighing all arguments, all comment you have heard already or may hear on that evidence, and then giving your final verdict on your individual and collective view of the true value of the whole of the evidence. It is perhaps unnecessary for me to say that any verdict, be it guilty or not guilty, must be one upon which you are unanimous. You cannot return any verdict until you reach that state, be it guilty or not guilty.

Now the only question in this case is, does the evidence, as you find on it, prove the guilt of the accused beyond reasonable doubt? If so, you convict him. If not, you acquit him. That is the situation in this case and that is the question even although evidence has been given by the defence. You are called upon to evaluate all the evidence and to give your verdict on your final view of all the evidence. If it proves guilt to your minds so that you are left in no reasonable doubt, then you ought to convict. If it does not bring that state of mind, that state of satisfaction, then you must acquit. There is no question of innocence or anything at all of that nature here. The sole issue is this: Has the guilt of the accused been proved beyond reasonable doubt? And your verdict will follow as to whether your answer is Yes or No to that question.

Now the case against the accused rests upon what is called circumstantial evidence. That simply means this. The prosecution seeks to prove certain facts upon which witnesses can give direct evidence because they say they have either seen or they have heard the particular matters to which they swear. If those facts be proved, then by a process of reasoning other facts may be inferred and so may be treated by a jury also as having been proved although no witness can be called as to the fact so inferred. This is a process of reasoning, as I have already told you, and it is a method widely used and widely accepted as proof of guilt in criminal cases. Most crimes, if premeditated, are committed by stealth or in secrecy, frequently with added attempts to destroy or hide any matter or thing which will disclose either the crime itself or the identity of the criminal. Therefore the law says that a jury may draw rational inferences from facts which it finds to have been proved, and a jury may ultimately find a verdict of guilty by this process of reasoning. I would suggest to you that you put to one side the analogy made by Mr Temm about the cricket ball. It is easy to state a set of circumstances be what it may, breaking windows or anything else, state them insufficiently, and state them with insufficient enquiry into the circumstances, and so they do not prove the happening that is in question. That is easily done. It is just as easy to state a number of circumstances that are sufficient, and to use an analogy, I suggest to you, is a dangerous method of proceeding, and although you may listen to the argument, you may give it weight, it is a matter for you. I suggest to you that what you are called upon here to deal with are not cricket balls and broken windows at all. Cricket balls and broken windows won't help you at all. You are here to deal with the evidence presented by the Crown concerning the deaths of these two persons and the evidence presented to you by the defence in that connection, and that is what you have to deal with.

Now whilst each piece of evidence must be carefully examined, because that is the accused's right and that is your duty, the case is not decided by a series of separate and exclusive judgments on each item or by asking what does that by itself prove, or does it prove guilt? That is not the process at all. It is the cumulative effect. It is a consideration of the totality of the circumstances that is important. One circumstance probably existing by itself may have but little effect. Other circumstances may make that circumstance more likely to be true, and also in combination to make those other circumstances themselves likely to be true or even true. Now that is the importance, as I see it, of circumstantial evidence. Whilst you examine each particular piece of it, its true worth, its true value cannot be ascertained until you look at it in the whole of the setting as you find that setting and say what you think about it. It is easy to say, of course, these bullets found in the heads could be fired by any rifle that has similar characteristics, and, as Mr Temm says, so what. But that is not the process by which you ought to – although it is a matter for you – approach this task. See what circumstances you have evidence of and then you see what other circumstances you have evidence of, and then you take the totality of them and then see what you think the weight is. That is what the process of reasoning is here, and that is the process by which circumstantial evidence is applied to the question of guilt. I will illustrate this to you as I proceed.

At the vital time when these two people died, you may think – except for this late suggestion about murder and suicide to which I shall make reference in a moment – that at least three people are involved. Harvey Crewe – he is dead – it is a matter for you and you may well think that he probably never knew anything of any untoward happening. Jeannette Crewe – she probably knew the identity of her killer – she was also shot and very soon died, and that leaves us with only one known person – it does not mean it must be the only one, but the killer. The bodies were disposed of by dumping into the Waikato river and no doubt the killer hoped that forever they were disposed of beyond recovery. That means that if that were so then the cause or the means used to cause the deaths could not be established unless and until they or one was recovered, and even the question of recovery, as we know here, delays very materially the question of detection. Indeed, unless both were recovered and, independently of what Mr Temm said, I was going to put to you, murder by one and possible suicide or disappearance of the other could be the case. That is only common sense, and I mention that because, as you will see, it would be a strange law that would not permit a jury to use circumstances, if sufficiently proved, to identify the killer, and our law allows just that, but it requires me to give you a careful direction on this matter of proof. I have tried to impress upon you, first

462

and foremost, it is a process of reasoning and not a matter of guessing or of conjecture. So you have to see what facts you find to be proved, and then you ask yourselves, is the proper conclusion from those facts, beyond reasonable doubt, that the accused was the killer? Or do those facts fail to give you that necessary degree of proof? I will enlarge upon that in a moment. The defence has called evidence here. The accused has categorically denied his guilt and he has given you an account of his movements on the night of the 17th June. His wife has also given evidence supporting what he says. This does not mean that he or the defence undertakes to prove he was not the killer. It does not alter the situation one iota. It is more evidence that you have to weigh. The question still is the one that I have posed to you, notwithstanding that that evidence has been given. Suggestions, by the way, have been made at other people who may be involved. Again, so far as the defence is concerned, the defence does not have to prove to you the possible guilt of any other person. That never falls to the defence. All the evidence, including all the evidence of the defence, must be considered and weighed by you, and at all times there is only one question, on your view of the whole of the evidence. Does it prove beyond reasonable doubt that the accused was the killer? If you judge that it does, then you convict. If you are left in reasonable doubt, you acquit.

In view of the way this case has proceeded, and in fact in similar cases, the situation is this: that proof beyond reasonable doubt means that you must be so satisfied of what I can divide into three separate things, that is on your view after considering the whole of the evidence. They are not altogether separate, because each one in the question of determination is bound up in the other, but you have got to have regard to each one, and the first is this. That you must be satisfied that you can safely reject the accused's denial of his guilt as being false, and that you can safely reject the evidence of his wife when she says that her husband, so far as she knew – and she is a light sleeper – never left their home that night. That is the first thing. The next is that the facts you find proved and the inferences you find that you can safely draw from these facts must point fairly to the accused as the killer; and, thirdly, they must be such that there is no reasonable explanation of those facts, that is the facts and the inferences, other than the fact that the deaths of these two people were at the hands of the accused. That is what is involved in this case in proof beyond reasonable doubt. That is a matter of law, and that is the direction I now give you. So, in short, the evidence on your judgment of it must satisfy you beyond reasonable doubt that there is no reasonable explanation of these two deaths except that they were caused by the accused, and that no-one else fired the two shots found in the heads of the bodies of Harvey and Jeannette Crewe. It must satisfy you of that so that you feel you can safely set aside as being false or incorrect the evidence given by the defence. I say no more than that. I define it for you and leave it there for you, but remind you that you must always keep in mind what proof beyond reasonable doubt as a matter of law arises on this case.

I have told you what the law is, and I have told you, I hope, and made it plain to you, how it applies to this case. I turn now to the evidence. It is my privilege to discuss the evidence with you, but I must tell you as emphatically as I can that what I say to you on the evidence is only comment or suggestion or discussion. What I say certainly has no greater, and may have very much less weight, than what Counsel may have said. If I appear to state a view or an opinion I do not suggest for one moment that you ought necessarily to accept it. Everything I say on the evidence is merely for your consideration, and if you disagree with anything I say you must follow your own judgment. I may not refer to some matters, and I do not propose to go over the whole of the situation which has been so capably put to you by both Counsel. If I do not refer to any particular matter, do not for one moment think that it is no less important because of that. I may dwell on some aspects of the evidence – again that does not mean that those aspects are necessarily important. What their importance is is a matter for you and not for me, and you are to judge the importance of them as you find and certainly not as you think that I might express some view, some opinion or some suggestion about them. In a nutshell, apply the law to this case as I have laid it down to you. Consider everything said to you on the evidence by Counsel, by myself, and come to your own conclusion, because it has been truly said, again and again, to a jury, the verdict must be yours. I again remind you of the evidence given for the defence. I remind you of the criticism of the evidence which the defence has developed before you concerning the prosecution's case. You weigh all those things. Weigh it against the evidence for the prosecution and the criticism by the prosecution of the defence evidence. Having done those things, does your judgment on all those things satisfy you beyond reasonable doubt that the defence denial is false, and that the only reasonable explanation of the evidence concerning these deaths is that the accused and no-one else caused them? Unless you answer that question Yes, you must acquit. If you answer it Yes, then you ought to convict him. That is a matter for you.

Now I suggest to you that you might start this case by considering whether there was any reasonable possibility that the killer was on the one hand a stranger to the Crewes, to the district, some passing burglar or a chance visitor, or, on the other hand, was he someone more familiar with the Crewe set-up. Although it is for you there is, I suggest to you, an ample basis for the conclusion that the killer was someone with a knowledge of the Crewes and of the district; and possibly of the Crewe household itself. Everyone who might be a source of enquiry, or, indeed of suspicion, comes into focus. Mr Demler came under strong suspicion, and so gradually did accused. He, in his turn, has suggested a Mr Booth might have something to do with the set-up, but that suggestion, you will remember, was quickly shown to be baseless. There seems to be no-one else except a report about a blue car being washed on a foggy morning by the river, and no doubt that has been safely laid to rest. You must, of course, always bear Mr Demler in mind, and he must be excluded before you can convict the accused and, as I have told you, so must every other reasonable possibility – reasonable, not possibility, reasonable possibility. Anything in this world may be possible, but what you deal with are possibilities in reason, reasonable possibilities.

The accused quite a long while ago was romantically interested in Jeannette Demler, later to become Mrs Harvey Crewe. It is said she did not return his interest and there was some difference about the evidence concerning dances. You may think that that has gone into the background and may be of little importance now. That is a matter for you. Accused married in November 1964. The Crewes married in June 1966, and settled in the Pukekawa district. The accused and his wife almost at the same time came to his father's farm which also was in the same district. The accused did not find financial success, and by last year he was having some financial difficulty – nothing very drastic. On the other hand, it is suggested that Mrs Crewe turned out to be a fairly valuable and desirable helpmate not only personally but also financially. This, so the Crown claims, is a background which is not unimportant in weighing later evidence. It has, I think, been called a motive. Motive for a murder is not a necessary part of proof. If one be proved it is only a piece of evidence to be weighed with all the rest of the evidence. That is only common sense, because a person may have a motive and not carry it out. However, so much for the question of motive. I myself, for the want of a better term, will call this early background. Although in the same district, it seems that the Crewes and the Thomases had no neighbourly association. You may think – it is a matter for you – that the accused has not always given consistent accounts on this. He told Detective Sergeant Hughes he had met Harvey Crewe, and that he, Harvey Crewe, appeared to be a decent type of chap. In his statement of the 15th October he says this: 'I spoke to Jeannette several times etc. I never saw her husband to speak to. The times I spoke to her she was alone.'

Only a small thing, but I just draw your attention to that. According to Inspector Hutton this was said to him:

'I then asked the accused, "How well do you know Harvey Crewe?" He replied, "I have never spoken to him although I knew him by sight." I pointed out to accused he had often met Jeannette in the streets and had been seen talking to her. He said, "Yes, that is right. I would run into her on her own and we would talk briefly about our farms and our lives." I said to him, "Why is it that you never approached Jeannette when she was with Harvey Crewe?" He said, "I just didn't bother." I then said to him . . .'

And he went on about the axle. So there you have that. You have a difference. First of all he said he had met Harvey Crewe, and then he says that he had not spoken to him, for

what it is worth, and then there seems to be an admission –
but it is a matter for you – of a number of meetings with
Jeannette. Now what did he say about it.

' "How long was it before her death that you last saw her?"
"Round about six months. It was in Tuakau at Arthur
Buckland's store . . . we stopped there for ten minutes or
quarter of an hour, that's all." '

And then further in cross-examination:

' "You saw her the final time in more recent years when
you were in Tuakau on occasions?" "I have seen her two or
three times in the street. Once to talk to."

' "Am I correct that since her wedding you only talked to
her once?" "That is right."

' "Was that the occasion you told Mr Temm about?" "That
is right."

' "Was that just no more than a casual meeting?" "That is
right."

' "Ever thought about her while you had not seen her?"
"Yes, on and off."

That, of course, may be something that you can take into
account. Now, is he being really frank about how much he
saw either Harvey Crewe or Mrs Jeannette Crewe? It is only
a small matter. He said to Detective Sergeant Hughes that
he had received no replies to his letters. That may be correct,
but we do know that at a later occasion he produces a letter
much later, and obviously the question of corresponding with
this lady in her earlier years was under discussion then. You
may think, it is a matter for you, that he made no mention
of gifts, and that it was only by further questioning that the
letter, the gift of the writing compendium, and the gift of the
brush and comb set came to light. Those are matters for you.
The implication of all this, including that statement I read
out from the accused himself, that he thought of her from
time to time, may well be – although it is a matter for you –
that he showed a continuing interest in Jeannette Crewe and
perhaps a desire not to disclose more than he thinks he ought
to at the particular time. He still kept a letter. He had in mind
some idea of what might have happened to the brush and
comb set, and I leave it there at the moment.

Now it is from this, you might think, rather vague background that subsequent events ought to be considered. It is

a setting or a backdrop. You have a man not altogether uninterested in the Crewes, and you have a man who has some knowledge of their home because he had been in it prior to their arrival there. I propose to turn to the events of June 17th and June 22nd.

It seems clear that someone, during the hours of darkness that night on Wednesday, 17 June, went to that place and – subject only to this question of murder and suicide to which I will refer in a moment – shot these two people through the head and killed them. The alarm was not given until Monday, the 22nd, when a bloodstained house and an abandoned and frightened child were reported to the police. I will not go over matters which have already been very fully discussed before you. You may be able to come to a clear conclusion on how the killer operated, and particularly, you may come to a clear conclusion as to where the shot was fired from and it may well help you in dealing with the rest of the evidence. Several things, you may think, are reasonably or fairly clear. The direction of the passage of the bullet through Harvey Crewe's head, left to right, on an incline. If there be a suggestion that he committed suicide, no question was ever put to the pathologist of the possibility of someone holding a rifle and firing that shot and what the situation was there. It is a matter for your consideration, but you may think it is fairly clear what direction the bullet took through his head, and you may find it clear that he was in his chair when he was bleeding, and you may conclude that the chair was somewhere near where it was found on the 22nd, or at least that is where it was when the blood seeped through. You see, as I understand it, there is no clear evidence that any blood went direct from his body to the floor. It may have, but the general idea seems to be a question of seepage, and whether it is necessary still to have his body in that chair whilst the seepage is taking place is a matter for you to consider, because if there is a large pool of blood it may take some considerable time before it finally seeps through, and then when one lines up that chair with the particular blood, then do we get answered anything more than where the chair was when the seepage took place? It is possible, I do not know, there is no evidence on it at all, that the body may have been removed from the chair by then. Can the chair remain in its place while removal of a body takes place? All those things are there for your consideration, and anyone jumping to a conclusion, I suggest to you – although it is a matter for you – that that chair must have been in the position where it was, exactly where it was found on the 22nd, may be jumping to a conclusion upon which there is no clear evidence, no evidence in fact other than that is when and where the seepage took place. Well, those are matters for you. I mention the three points: the direction of the bullet, the fact that he was in his chair when he was bleeding – we know that because of the blood – the fact that so far as seepage is concerned that can prove no more than where the chair was when the seepage took place, if it be seepage. If it be flow direct from his body, of course, it shows where the body might have been. The fourth matter, you may think, is that he seems to have had no real warning of his assailant, and even, you may think, Mrs Crewe did not get very far. You may come to the conclusion and it may help you to see the suddenness with which this thing took place. Of course there may be slow reaction. Many things might happen, but what I want to point out to you is this: it is all very well to reconstruct it, just look at it as a matter of common sense. No doubt the bullet is consistent with firing from the kitchen or from the louvres. No doubt at all that he was bleeding when he was in the chair, but there may be a source of error in stipulating that the chair must be in the very position in which it was found on the 22nd. That is where I suggest to you you have to be careful here and where you might use your common sense, because these very fine tests are assuming something, and it is a matter for you and not for me at all, you may think it is as exact as has been assumed, but you have the fact that he had no warning of his assailant and his wife did not get very far.

Apart from that, was Harvey Crewe shot from inside or from outside the house? If he did not commit suicide then, of course, he was shot from one place or the other, and that is quite common sense, is it not? It may be that both were possible. The Crown says that the fact that there was no sign of defence by Harvey Crewe, the proper inference for you to draw is that there was no entry to the house. Of course you will remember Mr Morris covered quite a number of other things, and you will consider those.

The defence has put demonstrations or reconstructions to you, which it claims would show – sometimes it seems to be impossible and other times you may think very difficult for this shot to go through Harvey Crewe's head if he were sitting in that chair in the exact position in which it was found on the 22nd June, and of course it means that he could not even do that much (demonstrates) if he suddenly got a start. Well, it is for you to decide those things. What do you think? What is the common sense of it? Where was the shot fired – was it from inside? What was the stance of the marksman if he were outside? We just don't know. We know, according to Dr Nelson, that he says that he could place himself in a position where he could execute the shot having the chair in the position in which it was found on the 22nd. I think Inspector Hutton said something about that too. On the other hand, of course, you have Mr MacKenzie, you have the other expert, in which they found grave difficulties in doing just that, and they, by drawing exact lines, suggested to you that Harvey Crewe could not have been shot from the louvre window. Well, you will weigh all these matters. It has been suggested to you by Mr Temm that the chair might have been around near the fire, in which case, of course, we get more complications than ever. Those are matters for you. That is where the chair was found on the 22nd. That is where, you may think, it was proved the blood had seeped, but is there any basis for ruling out that the shot was fired from the outside? It is a matter for you. Does common sense dictate that? If it does, on the facts as you find them, you can draw that inference. It is a matter for you. On the other hand you may think that the shot must have been fired from inside. Those are matters for you. See what conclusion you come to, but I do suggest to you that this is not a matter of fine reason because we have not got the set-up. We do not know exactly where Harvey Crewe was. We do not know exactly where the chair was, except for the fact that it was in a certain position when the blood dripped from it, and we do not know the stance of the marksman. We do not know a lot of things, but that is not to deter you if you think on a total consideration of this case the factors are relevant to it, that the shots were fired from outside, and in that, of course, you can take into account the finding of the bullet. Again, of course, it will require very careful consideration by you. You may agree with Mr Temm, I do not know, it is a matter for you, that the shot was not fired from there. So, having made that comment on it, I leave you to it.

Now I just want to deal very briefly with the night of June 17th. If there be no murder and suicide – which, of course, would involve I suppose, Harvey Crewe who shot his wife, the intervention of a third person to do the wrapping up and disposal of the bodies – then you have a double shooting some time during that night. Time is unknown. We have had evidence of the state of the meal. We have had evidence of the state of the table. We have had evidence of the situation found on the 22nd. There had been somebody in that house in the meantime even if it is murder and suicide. We have the situation of the state of this television set. We have the habits, the general habits of the Crewes as to the lateness of the meal and just how they usually acted on an ordinary night. Those are all matters that you can consider and it is by no means, you may think, right to say that the shooting must have taken place before the meeting of the farmers. The evidence would seem to suggest the contrary, but those are all matters for you. The time of the shooting, you may think, is in relation to the meal and what was found there, but that is as far as it can be taken, and therefore at some time during that night, if there be no murder and suicide, there was double shooting after the meal had reached that stage which you find about, and after this other evidence about the situation of the various chairs, the knitting, and things like that, and that, so it seems to me, is as far as you have that. It might be any time during that night but certainly before, of course, Mrs Crewe stirred herself to do the dishes, to do those things, but, so it seems to me, there is a fairly wide area of time there and one cannot say 7.30, 8.30 or anything else. I think there was some suggestion that they sometimes sat till 9 o'clock, something like that, before she moved to do the dishes. Well, there it is. It is a matter for you.

Now when that shooting took place, or before it, then someone got to that place, someone left that place and somebody took those bodies from that place wrapped in material got from that place. That all seems clear. Somebody did that. Now whoever did that was able to do it without detection because, despite the wide inquiries here, no-one has been found, no-one at all who can come forward and say that he saw any unusual movement of anything, any person, any car, or anything else that night, and so you then have the night of the 17th June. That, so it seems to me, is as far as that takes the matter. The next thing we know is the 19th June. Mr Roddick between 8.30 and 9.30 saw a lady in slacks. He said she had light brown hair, and you will remember the car he mentioned. That was a view 75 to 100 yards, so he estimated it. There was nothing then to excite his suspicion about anybody being there. He could not recognize Mrs Thomas at the police parade. She has darker hair than he said. You saw it. She denies, of course, that she was ever there. She says that was a normal day for her on the farm. Well, it is for you to weigh what you think of that view. You heard this man Roddick. He saw her at the time and there was no suspicion, and he is called upon later to give the description as best he can. It is some distance away. He seemed to have no particular reason to take notice. He does not tell us the colour of the slacks or anything else about the other clothing at all, but in his judgment for what it is worth, a man's judgement, she gave the appearance of having light brown hair. Well, you will weigh that. It is not for me to say any more than that about it. As I told you, Mrs Thomas, although she cannot give any detailed account – and there is nothing very remarkable about that – of what she did that day, she says she was not there.

On Saturday, June 20th, Mrs McConachie saw the child outside about 1.40 p.m. That was a day Mrs Thomas was in Auckland, but she had returned home before that time. She again said that she was not there quite positively, and she says that so far as her movements after returning home are concerned, which was well before 1.40 p.m., that it was the usual day on the farm. Now someone fed Rochelle. There seems to be no doubt about that, and according to the medical evidence the feeding might have been as far back as Friday, the 19th June, which was the day Roddick saw the woman, or he said 48 hours, which I think takes it back to the 20th June which was when Mrs McConachie said she saw the child. Well, that is as much as the police have been able to unearth about that, and I pass from it.

472

I pass to the evidence which the Crown claims points to the accused beyond reasonable doubt and as it must to the reasonable exclusion of anyone else as the killer, so that his denials of being in the area are false. As I told you, this evidence must be weighed against the evidence which the defence has called and in the light of the defence criticism of this evidence. Now according to accused he thought it was the night of 23rd June that he had discussions with his wife concerning his movements on the night of the 17th June, and Inspector Hutton's evidence about that I will just shortly read to you:

'I said to him, "How can you remember that particular night in preference to others?" He said, "Well, about a week later when the fact the Crewes were missing was known, Vivien and I discussed what we had been doing that night." I said to him, "What else did you do on the 17th June?" He said, "I think we both went to our dentist." '

He mentions a sick cow in the implement shed, and he was asked how he remembered that particular night and he said Vivien and he discussed what they had been doing that night.

That, of course, does not fix a date, but the accused was pressed on it here and he said he thought it was the night of the 23rd and a paper was produced to give a foundation for that. That is the night, according to the records, when the No. 4 cow was shot, and that was a time, as you will recollect from his evidence in answer to Mr Morris, that he had no difficulty in locating his rifle for that purpose. You may find that fact important, if you conclude that the rifle fired the fatal shots just six days earlier. It is a matter for you. It is natural for people to discuss a reported murder or disappearance of people from a bloodied house and the abandoned baby when those facts make headlines, but why at this stage, you may ask yourselves, should either the accused or his wife's movements be the subject of conversation? This is the 23rd. No-one has pointed a finger at them, and indeed you may think that then the matter was a complete mystery – the paper report no doubt shows that. Nevertheless, at this early stage, the day after the news broke according to the accused, and he fixed it as being that day, he is discussing with his wife the very essence of what is now put forward by the

473

defence in this case, the answer on his trial. It is a matter for you. I am not suggesting it is of any particular importance at all, but it is a circumstance and all the circumstances are important here, I will suggest to you in a moment. Mrs Thomas puts the first discussion as perhaps a week after the first broadcast and the discussion, of course, was concerning her and his movements. So she differs from him. He has come right forward, although being a little bit uncertain, but you may think he has come right forward to the 23rd immediately after the news broke, when he is on oath here and he has had time to think about it. So you have here, according to himself, a discussion as to his whereabouts on that occasion as early as that. She says it was about a week later. Well, so be it. Then we have Peter Thomas, the cousin, and he deposes to a discussion and he says that discussion resulted from inquiries they heard the police were making. Now of course you will see at once that that probably makes sense and it is understandable. According to him – it is a question of what faith you have in him – he said that Mrs Thomas said she wondered what they were doing that night. Now if Mrs Thomas was wondering at that stage – it is a matter for you and not for me at all – then of course this discussion on the night of the 23rd could not have solved anything, because there would be no wondering left, would there? They had the records of the cow, they had everything there. That is what he says. What value you place on it is purely a matter for you, but if that is what she said, that she was wondering what they were doing that night, that, you may think, may throw some light on this case. It is a matter for you and not for me. Anyhow, from these discussions, according to him, they went on about the sick cow in the shed. He is quite uncertain about the dates. Attempts were made to fix it and he fixed it with reference to when he was seen and when he was not seen, and I cannot make head or tail of that. But there you are, if you think that that conversation appears to be so much later than the two others deposed to by Mr and Mrs Thomas, if you have any faith in this cousin at all, then according to him they were wondering, and she wondered what they were doing that night. I simply mention these things. They only have the weight that you give them, but their circumstances are to be weighted and combined with and discussed, I suggest to you, with the other and more important things.

Now the next discussion given in evidence you may find of importance but that is a matter for you. Detective Johnston spoke to accused on the 13th October on a number of matters. The brush and comb set had then been found in an unwrapped state. The evidence on that is this:

'I asked the accused whether he knew Jeannette had used the brush and comb set that he had given her. He said he didn't know, it could still be wrapped up for all he knew.'

This was a gift made years ago and, according to him, never mentioned again, and it was in fact, you may consider, still wrapped up. Mrs Crewe senior said that the blanket recovered near her son's body was usually kept in the same room where the police say they found this unwrapped set. Now from that it is a matter that you can infer, if you wish, it is a matter for you, that the killer went into that room to get that blanket. It is a matter of inference, you may think it is worthless, but was that remark – and the accused did not really deny it – pure coincidence or does it point to the accused's probable knowledge of this unusual, you might think, keeping of an unwrapped gift? It is only a circumstance, but it is one which I am going to invite you to consider, as I think you must, in the totality of the circumstances.

Now the only other evidence of this nature that I wish to discuss with you is that of Detective Keith. He says:

'I could observe them through the cracks in the garage wall. Mrs Thomas said something to the accused. I could not hear what she said. He then replied "If they think I am guilty I am, and that's that."'

And you will appreciate it was put to him in cross-examination that he said on a previous occasion or agreed on a previous occasion that something more was added to that. Well, you will weigh it. This statement is under no circumstances to be treated by you as a possible confession. First of all, do you accept – and it is a matter for you – that it was said. Detective Keith – you heard him criticized – swears that it was, swears that he took a note of it. It is denied by the accused and his wife, although the accused does add what you might think a rather strange thing, it is a matter for you, because he says this:

' "Do you say no such conversation took place?" "I say that."

' "So that that detective is mistaken in that, you say?" "He only heard [part] of the sentence if he heard that sentence."

' "So he got it wrong?" "That is if I said that."

' "Did you say anything like that?" "Nothing like that at all."

' "Then he has got it entirely wrong then?" "Yes." '

Now if you do accept Detective Keith – and that is a matter for you – we do not know what the whole context of that discussion was, and without the context its true purport cannot be known, and that is why I warn you that under no circumstances are you to treat that as in any way being a confession or tending to a confession of guilt, but if they were talking like that, and if Mrs Thomas knew her husband's every movement on that night, and they had each satisfied the other that the accused could have no possible connection with the death of the Crewes, why should a discussion of that type take place? It is a matter for you. Why should they be talking in any context about that if, as he says, as early as the 23rd June they had worked out what they were doing? She knew what she was doing, and she knew up to a point what her husband was doing. You may consider that if you think that was said. You may consider that in the generality of the evidence. What its value is – it may be nothing at all – is for you.

I want now to turn to the really important items in the Crown case. Whilst you consider each separately to see what has been proved, in the end it is a matter of assessing the weight or value of all the circumstances proved and in the light of all the evidence. It is the combined weight of circumstances, their totality that in the end must be weighed by you against the claims of the defence.

Now when Harvey's body was recovered there was a blanket near it, and, according to Mrs Crewe senior, the bedspread – call it what you may – was usually in the spare bedroom, and I draw your attention back again to what I have already mentioned, that that was in a place in a room where the unwrapped gift was found. Is it possible that the accused has in some unguarded moment given himself away? By itself of course, this would carry little weight, but you ought to bear it in mind. We have a succession of other circumstances in evidence, and each has its importance and weight in conjunction with all others. In Harvey Crewe's head and in Jeannette Crewe's head there was lead from a bullet with No. 8 stamped on it. These bullets had been out of production for many years so not everybody would have them. Plenty of people would, there is no doubt about that, and in fact the accused did have them, and that is nothing unusual in itself. It only means that the accused had ammunition similar to that which killed the Crewes, and other people may also have similar ammunition.

The next step is that the Crown claims that fired leaden bullets leave land or rifle marks as a result of passing through the barrel of the rifle, and the evidence of Dr Nelson is important here. He says that they make distinctive markings, and it is for you to say whether you accept him. There seems to have been not much or any query on that. Dr Nelson claims he can eliminate all rifles except those which have a certain pattern of rifling. Now if you accept that evidence, then the person who fired those shots had No. 8. bullets, and he had a rifle with rifling similar to that of accused. Out of sixty-four rifles tested, [most] could be discarded. Two of those rifles could have been used and, of course, there may have been others. It is not an unusual pattern, but so far as we know the police net never disclosed any, but you may think that the classes of people who might be involved have now been narrowed to someone holding a rifle at the Crewes' home on the night of 17th June, with rifling and ammunition similar to that of the accused, because if you accept Dr Nelson that is the type of lead recovered from the dead bodies.

Now the next piece of evidence is, as you will realize, of the utmost importance in your considerations of the case, and I refer to the spent shell which Detective Charles said he found. The Crown claims it was found. It is a matter for you, of course, you know the length of time and so forth, but the Crown claims it was found in a position where it might well expect to fall after there was a reloading outside the louvre windows. Well, the question you have to ask yourselves is, was it fired by accused's rifle? And, if so, was it fired at the Crewes' home on that night? Of course, the final question is, who fired it? The two scientists, Dr Nelson and Mr Shanahan, swear that it was a shell fired by the accused's rifle. They have scientifically examined the test shell and the shell which Detective Charles said he found, and they say categorically that the same rifle fired both. They explain to you their method of examination and comparison. They explain to you what they saw under the microscope and how the various minute marks were produced in the test shell. In particular, I am speaking now of the minute marks seen under the microscope. It is, of course, for you to say whether or not you accept that evidence. No expert evidence was called to the contrary, and both these scientists have sworn to that. But it is still for you, as Mr Temm says, to say whether you accept their evidence.

Now photographs were produced so as to give you, as best a photograph can, some illustration of what some of the characteristics were, but the experts made it plain to you that their opinions are not based on photographs. Their methods are much more detailed and depend upon what they see under the microscope. Remember the magnifications and shifting back and forth and making the comparison. A photograph is in black and white or shades of those two colours. The shell itself has no white streaks such as those you see in the photograph. The scientists see the metal and not the flash of white that the camera will produce. I suggest to you that it is a matter for you when you are asked to discard this evidence merely on the photographs. Ridges and valleys, so the scientists say, are clear to them and are seen by them as three-dimensional objects and clearly magnified, whereas the photographs are only two-dimensional, black and white and shades of black and white, and do not show the comparative depths and, indeed, any of the fine detail made by the end of the firing-pin that the scientists speak of and upon which, as you will recollect the demonstration given to you, they so clearly rely. Now let us look at photograph 8 for a moment. Can you tell how deep that is, any idea at all? You look at it for a while, and you may start to wonder whether it is concave or convex, just how you get this light and shade, does it go in or does it lift up? What sort of a representation do you think that is when compared with looking at that shell – even with the naked eye for that matter, but particularly under the microscope? Look at photograph

478

7 – is that what you see under the microscope? You do not know what this material is over the '8', how deep it is, whether there on a flat, plane surface. What is the nature of the material, for instance, that is covering the portion of the '8'? What has happened to it? I suggest to you that it is completely impossible to tell that from the photograph, and that is something, I suggest to you, that you ought to keep in mind because photographs are to be used only as illustrations. They do not take the place of scientific examination where the object is seen properly in perspective, in its proper colour, and measurements can be compared, and things like that, and, of course, only yesterday we had some discussion here as to how far the rifle held by Mr MacKenzie was from the louvre, and I defy anyone to tell from the photograph whether it was two or three inches, and MacKenzie, I think, said it was right up alongside, touching or something of that nature. But that shows you how indecisive any question of a photograph is when you are looking at fine material, fine distinctions, measurements and things of that type, and particularly when the measurements go into the in and out valleys and ridges of the thing being examined, because it is only the extent to which light is reflected that you can get any appreciation of that at all. Well, that is a matter for you. As I say, it is for you to judge the expert evidence, to judge it in the light of all the criticism that has been made of it.

Now, if you are satisfied – and it is a matter for you – that the shell found by Detective Charles was fired by accused's rifle, then the question arises, as I have already told you, Was it fired at the home of the Crewes on that night, and, if so, who fired it? In the determination of those questions you must look at all the evidence, all the circumstances, and the evidence both for the Crown and for the defence. Is the only reasonable explanation on all the evidence that the accused fired that shell at the Crewes' place on that night? I have already drawn your attention to a number of matters, including the accused's remark about the unwrapped gift, in relation to the bedspread, in relation to the spare room, and it is at this stage, you may well think – although it is a matter for you – that its possible significance does arise in your minds as indeed – it is a matter for you – all the other matters which I have already mentioned to you. Now a claim has been made at some time that someone other than the accused, the suggestion was made, may have planted that shell. It did not come out very clear in the final address, you might think, but the claim was made because the accused himself said that someone was framing him. Now that would entail a visit to his farm and the search for and the finding of a spent shell to be planted by somebody of whom we do not know anything at all, and again, the shell will not involve the accused unless the bullets found in the heads of Jeannette and Harvey Crewe were No. 8, the same as his, and had the same rifling marks as would be made by his rifle. How would an unknown person know that his (accused's) rifle and spent ammunition from his farm would give that result? Because if the lead in the bodies did not match up with the lead found or fired from accused's rifle, then, of course, the spent shell is of no value at all, in implicating the accused, and this is the sort of thing, I suggest to you, you want to be on your guard about when suggestions were made this might have happened, and that might have happened. So it is only if his rifle or a rifle with a similar barrel, and the same ammunition with No. 8 on it, is used is it possible for any other person to involve the accused. I suggest that is important to you because he says, 'I have been framed. Somebody has cased the place', and claims like that are made. I suggest to you it is no use anyone picking up a shell from his place, putting it in the Crewes' place, unless that shell fired through the accused's rifle, or a similar rifle, can give the results of the lead found in the bodies of those two dead persons. Of course, if his rifle were used then the shell from the farm is not necessary. It woud produce its own shell, it would produce leaden bullets consistent with those fired from his rifle, and consistent with those found in the heads of these two dead people – consistent only – it goes not further than that. Please do not think I am suggesting it, but you may well think that any suggestion of the planting of a shell has little or no merit or validity. If you reject the claim made that the shell could have been planted, then, if you accept that it was fired by accused's rifle, you have his rifle being the one which fired the fatal shots, and you will ask yourselves, was it reasonably possible for someone, a stranger to the household, to obtain and return the rifle without the knowledge of the accused or his wife, and certainly return it so that he could get it with comfort on the day of the 23rd, whenever it was he shot the cow? It is a matter for you, but even if this was possible, you will ask yourselves, does the evidence as a whole exclude that possibility as being a reasonable one, and this leads at once, of course, to the other evidence which is relevant and which must be weighed by you on this topic, and, of course, you are entitled to and you ought to take into account all these matters that I have mentioned to you before, about the conversation, and any other matter that you think relevant.

[After the adjournment for lunch the summing-up continued.]

I was about to turn to the last topic I will be dealing with, subject to a little comment about it, to the question of the axle and the wire, and when I speak of wire I mean the wire found on the body of Harvey Crewe. Now first of all, of course, you have got to ask yourselves, did the axle come from the accused's farm? There is no evidence, of course, which can directly show to you that it was on the accused's farm but it is open for you to infer that it was. I will deal with this slightly in more detail in a moment. Rasmussen returned all the parts to, I think, someone called Richard after having done some work on the trailer, and there, so far as the axle itself is concerned, seems to be the end of it. Rasmussen was able to identify all the rest of the assembly. He identified the axle, and all the component or associated parts that were later found on accused's farm. Now there is just one aspect of this matter that I just want to turn your attention to before I deal with it a little bit more fully. The accused did not take part in the search for the bodies, although by then, in fact he says the 23rd, he was discussing his movements on the night that we are now concerned with. So, according to him, he is concerned with his movements but he does nothing to help in this search which people from far and wide apparently joined in. Well, he gives you his reasons for that and, of course, you must weigh them, and you must agree, of course, that they are fairly weighty reasons. He had just shot a cow, and apparently the other cows were coming in. But when the trailer, the axle and those things were advertised and the police were seeking for information concerning them, he does nothing again. You see, this is the second time, you might

481

think, that no move was made. He said when he was interviewed about it that he vaguely remembered his father's trailer and you may well think that it was well and truly in his mind because he was concerned about his movements, and had been getting those checked up, but he went on and said he thought his father would give the information. Well, you may well imagine at this stage that the police inquiries were intensive. You may well imagine that anyone at all who was concerning himself about his own movements and so forth, would realize the importance of any information that might come along at all. It was something, you may well come to the conclusion, that was well known in the district and – it is a matter for you – it may well be known to the accused, but there is no response from him, and no response from a man on whose property the rest of the assembly was ultimately found as a result of police tracking down of Rasmussen and tracking down various things and then going to his tip. Well, you again will remember what he said to you about that. I just mention it. You see, you have two occasions when he might help, one occasion about the search – he gives his reason for that – and the second occasion is the intensive enquiries that must have been made at this time both for this axle, when it was advertised, and for the trailer, and he left that on the basis he knew about it – that is quite obvious – but anyhow if there was any importance in it his father would report it to the police, and if the police had not been able to do some tracing, and father said nothing about it and he says nothing about it, then, of course, it comes to a dead stop. Now just what importance on that failure to move – I think it was only some few days – on the part of the accused is, is a matter for you, but I will pass now to deal with the axle.

Mr Temm claimed first of all that the evidence did not prove that the axle was attached to Harvey Crewe's body. Well, there was a very strong submission to you from the Crown that there were very good reasons for you to come to a conclusion that it was. Let us assume for a moment that the situation was as bad as Mr Temm claims, that this axle was found as stated by the police but that no-one knew anything about it until after the body had been recovered and the search was made in that area. Mr Temm puts it to you that that is pure chance that that would happen. Well, I am suggesting to you – although it is a matter for you – that it is perfectly competent for you or any jury to say that the chances of that were so long, so distant, that it could be ruled out as pure chance, and that a reasonable jury could come to the conclusion – because this body apparently had not been submitted to the air for a very considerable period – that the axle was in fact the weight so used. Now, if that is all there was, then there is still – despite that claim made by the defence – ample evidence from which a jury can make the inference, if it wanted to, that is if the case gets that far and you reject all the things Mr Morris said about the axle, so even on Counsel's argument and taking it at its worst state, it is still open for a jury to find it is such a long long shot that the axle should be in that part of the river, inaccessible as it was, in the precise area where Harvey Crewe's body was found. But, you see, this, as I suggest to you, is where this question of circumstantial evidence comes in, and where the various pieces ought to be weighed instead of just simply posing the issue – the axle is there, the body is there, no connection, pure chance, and out. The axle is part of an assembly and the wheels, the studs, the stub axle, all the rest of that assembly is found on accused's farm, and you will have no difficulty, I take it, in coming to the conclusion that it was his father's axle, and that it was more than likely to be on his father's farm at least at some time. So you have not just an axle, not just a question of pure chance, but you have got an axle, you may come to the conclusion, that has the rest of its component parts on the accused's farm, an axle belonging to his father, and an axle that you can well infer – not guess at all – must have got to the farm years ago which may well be when the rest of those articles got there.

Now that takes it so far, but you have not got only the axle there. You have got the body of Harvey Crewe, and in the body of Harvey Crewe, in his head, there is lead which according to Dr Nelson is No. 8 lead. According to him that lead has rifling similar to lead fired through the accused's rifle, not necessarily the same, but similar to it, consistent with it. So there you are, you have an axle, you have the component parts on the accused's property, and you have a dead body and in it – according to Dr Nelson, and it is a question what you say about that – lead which has the rifle markings and the No. 8 marking which one would expect to find from a bullet fired from the accused's rifle. Now that body also had on it some wire, and it is easy to say that there may have been tons and tons and tons of that type of wire produced anywhere at all. But, so far as the search is concerned, be it inconclusive or not, extensive or not, they did find and find only similar wire on the accused's farm. Remember the No. 1 and the No. 2 wires, and you will remember the evidence of Mr Todd, it was similar, the same component parts, and things like that. Of course nobody can say it was that wire. So you have the axle, you have the component parts on the accused's farm, you have a body and in it that No. 8 lead with rifling marks similar to those caused by firing through the accused's rifle, and, if you accept Mr Todd – and that is a matter for you – you have that body wire consistent with wire found on accused's property, and you see now that you have not just got an axle by pure chance, and nothing else in the area where Harvey Crewe's body is found. You have another body that is picked up further down the river, and it has similar lead in its head, as I understand the evidence. Again, of course, that depends upon what you think of Dr Nelson. Now that person had an unwrapped gift from the accused that she kept, and it was in the spare bedroom when the police visited the place, and Mrs Crewe says that in that bedroom the bedspread was kept, and that bedspread was found, as you will recollect, with some wire on it, fairly close to Harvey Crewe's body, and the wire on that bedspread, although it could not be positively identified, had some similarity, although not full similarity, with the wire samples. You have the remark of the accused, for what it is worth – and I suggest you ought to weigh it there – that for all he knew that parcel was still unwrapped, and it was. You go from there and consider the spent shell and see where it leads to. Now this, I suggest to you, shows the importance of what we call the totality of circumstances in coming to a conclusion. Each one by itself may not take the matter very far, but when you get this intermixing, this interchange, the fitting – if you may put it that way – the dovetailing and things like that, does not each one gather unto itself greater strength than when it was by itself? Does not the combination of all those things tell you something different from what Counsel put to you was pure chance that that axle could be there? Now that is the reason for circumstantial evidence, and that is why it is given, and it is a question of whether the circumstances mell when you look at them as you find them, so that these questions of pure chance, reasonable possibilities, can, as the result of the combined effect of the various circumstances, be ruled out so that you may come to a definite conclusion on it. I have spent a little bit of time on that, but I will not be any longer on it. It is important, I suggest to you, that when you deal with the axle, or deal with any part here, that you look at the other circumstances and see how they fit in, anything that was said by the accused, matters I have drawn your attention to, and you will see how facile it is to say that it is pure chance that the axle was there with the body. That is not what you have got at all. You have not got just the body, just the axle, you have got a body with lead in the head. You have got a body with a certain type of wire on it. You have got the rest of the assembly of that axle on the accused's farm. You have got bullet lead or bullet in the head that is consistent – no higher than that – with having been fired from the accused's rifle, and, as I say, you have got the dead man's wife further down the stream with similar lead in the head, and you have the coincidence – if you think it is, it is a matter for you – about this discussion about the unwrapped parcel. So that, I think, illustrates to you what I said before how important it is not to just take one and say 'I discard that,' and take another and say 'I discard that' or 'That takes me nowhere,' or, as Mr Temm says, 'So what.' You do not know, I suggest to you, the strength of any individual matter until you weigh it in all the circumstances, and you do not know the strength of the whole of the evidence until you put all the circumstances together as you find them and see what they spell out, and that is the process that you ought to go through. If you do this you will come to a particular judgment that you have got to make, if you do it properly. I am not suggesting to you for one moment how you should find it. Please do not think that at all. I am not expressing any opinion now. I want to stress again to you, as strongly as I can, these are matters for your consideration, and, having said that, I think I can close on this.

The defence claims that the accused never left his home

on the night of June 17th, that is at any time when these killings could happen. The defence claims that the Crown evidence in any event is not sufficient to prove guilt in the manner, of course, and to the extent which I have laid down for you. The Crown claims that when this evidence is properly evaluated and weighed it proves that the accused, despite what he and his wife say, did leave his home that night, and that it proves beyond reasonable doubt that it was the accused who fired the rifle at the Crewes' house on that night, and that it does enable you – it is a matter for you – to exclude the reasonable possibility that anyone else could have done it. Now that, as I have told you again and again, depends upon your evaluation of the whole of the evidence. It is for the Crown to prove its case, prove it to the extent that I have stated to you. It is no business of the defence to prove innocence or even prove a reasonable doubt. The defence, if it can show any weakness in the Crown case, if it can bring you to the stage where you have a reasonable doubt, then, of course, you ought to acquit, but that is only argument on the evidence. The burden of proof, as we call it, to prove the crime and to prove who was the criminal, rests and rests always upon the Crown, and it is now for you to come to your decision applying the principles of law I have laid down to you, and considering – as I am sure you will – all those matters that have been put to you by both Counsel, and considering – as I am sure you will – this circumstantial evidence on the basis I have put to you. You can do what you like about it. You are not bound to do that, but that is the method whereby circumstantial evidence is used and tested and considered, and you ought so to use it, you ought so to test it and so consider it, but what you shall do and how you shall do it, I have been at pains to tell you, is purely a matter for you, nothing to do with me at all. You observe the law as I have laid down to you, and within that, giving fair and careful consideration to everything, as I am sure you will, you will reach the verdict that you think proper. The matter now rests with you. Will you kindly retire to consider your verdict.

APPENDIX 6

Final Speech of Crown Solicitor David Morris to Second Trial Jury

The murders occurred on the eve of the Crewes' fourth wedding anniversary. Harvey Crewe was sitting in his armchair and Jeannette was knitting on the couch. As was his custom, Harvey was in stocking feet, resting after dinner before the wash-up. He had had a meal of fish and peas, had been at a stock sale during the day and may have had something to eat during the day.

He had had a full day. We know that he went to a farm at Glen Murray in the morning to inspect a bull, had morning tea at home with Mrs Pirrett and Jeannette, went to a stock sale in Bombay in the afternoon and in the late afternoon was working on a drain on his property.

He was no doubt tired and relaxed when sitting with his wife in the lounge after their evening meal. The baby was bedded. Television was switched off. It had been a wet day. Some of Harvey's clothes were drying in the drier.

It was a wet and windy night. The dogs were kennelled well away from the house. It was easy for the murderer to come on to the property unseen and unheard. At least one of the windows in the lounge was undraped, possibly others were not drawn. A murderer familiar with the house and the practice of leaving the kitchen sliding door open would know that he could see into the lounge through the kitchen windows from the region of the back steps.

The murderer has come armed to the property and fires the first shot through the louvre windows of the kitchen at Harvey Crewe, before Harvey – who had every reason to be alert to strange noises – had time to move.

Jeannette hears the shot and hurries to her feet as the

487

murderer enters the lounge through the kitchen and attacks her.

We fortunately do not know how long elapsed between the time Jeannette realized her husband was dying and her own death or just what happened in between.

We do know that at some stage she received a violent blow consistent with being from the butt of a rifle to her face; and that when she was finally shot, she was lying on the floor.

We also know that a long hearth mat and cushion were at some stage burned by the murderer; and also that the room was heavily bloodstained. Whether the burning of these items was like the use of two saucepans with a view to concealing the blood, or whether it was done to conceal other marks traceable to the killer or his treatment of Jeannette we do not know.

The murderer was impelled by some overwhelming motive, and that motive may have been more than merely to destroy Harvey, perhaps out of jealousy, and to silence the only other witness. The evidence is equally consistent with a desire to get to Jeannette, even if this entailed first killing her husband and later Jeannette herself.

Whether the murderer was impelled by a combination of these motives only he can say, but there is nothing to suggest any alternative.

It is common enough knowledge – and Thomas has said he well knew – that bullets in the head of the murdered person may be traced to the weapon which fired them. The murderer has therefore gone through the house to find wrappings to cover the bodies, both to conceal the flow of blood and to shield his load from view as he disposes of them.

The body wrappings show that the murderer has entered at least the main bedroom and the spare bedroom at the end of the corridor, and it is reasonable to infer that on his way from one to the other he has entered the middle bedroom; and in his search for wrappings where better to look than the wardrobe where the brush and comb set was subsequently found?

He drags the 16 stone of Harvey's body along the floor of the lounge and out the front door, where he uses the wheelbarrow to carry it to his vehicle. The lighter body of Jeannette he may well have carried – there is no similar trail of her blood. He returns the wheelbarrow to a point under the water tank where it was subsequently found – having apparently been washed out.

At some stage the murderer has realized that after his first shot through the window which killed Harvey, in a fit of passion he has reloaded his weapon, ejecting the fired shell case, before rushing in to Jeannette.

His search for this shell case and his cleaning of the barrow are both performed by the light above the back steps and in his haste, after failing to find the shell case, he locks the back door from the outside, leaving on the back light and leaving open the louvres through which the shot was fired.

Having wrapped the bodies he no doubt takes further precautions to ensure that their blood leaves no trace on his vehicle to link him with the murders. Black polythene of the type Thomas possessed and used for lining water troughs would be ideal for that purpose.

Realizing the significance of the lead in the heads, he wires to each body a weight and sinks them in the Waikato river: not to frame some other person, but so his connection with the killings escapes detection.

Thr murderer possessed or had access to a .22 rifle which left land markings of a distinctive nature. Its distinctiveness is shown by the random sampling provided by the police test firings, which showed that out of sixty-four rifles tested, only this and one other weapon could have made such markings.

Of the three .22 pump action Brownings included in the test weapons, only this could have fired the fatal shots.

The British Home Office report records that only four of the 268 .22 weapons held there could have left indistinguishable land markings.

His weapon will also leave a shell case bearing the firing pin, ejector and extractor marks which are repeated at each shot, and are unique to that weapon.

This man also had access to the axle, which matched exactly the stubs buried in Thomas's tip and was of the same model as the wheels found on Thomas's farm.

He must also have had access to the particular kinds of wire later found on the bodies.

In common no doubt with many others, he must have had access to No. 8 ammunition.

And again in common with many others, he must have had access to a vehicle – whether car and trailer or tractor – which could be used to dispose of the bodies.

He must also, again in common with others – have been a sufficiently good shot to kill Harvey with the single neat shot in his head which the pathologist Dr Cairns has described. In other words, no stranger to the use of a firearm at night and confident that he would strike his target with one shot, since any blunder would have had dire consequences from Harvey.

He would have also to know how he would dispose of the bodies successfully and without discovery, particularly since the river was in flood he would need extensive knowledge of where to get a vehicle sufficiently close to the river for his purpose.

Finally – and again of great importance, if difficult to discern – he must have had motivation for the murders.

This was not a case of murder for gain – there is no suggestion that anything of value was stolen. This is an un-provoked, premeditated, well-executed, coldblooded killing.

Except for its gravity, it is no different in these respects from the burglary of 30/7/67 when money was left untouched, the fire of 7/12/68 inside the end bedroom when Jeannette was in hospital after Rochelle's birth and again there is no evidence of any theft, and the barn fire of December 1969.

All four events result from a malicious and fierce desire to injure Harvey or Jeannette. It is reasonable to infer that all four are done not only for the same reason; but by the same person. This would indicate that the killer is no stranger to either the area or his victims.

Indeed the absence of other reasons for the killings must indicate a personal animosity of great depth, and if the other incidents are attributable to the same hand, of long standing.

Harvey was unknown in the area until his marriage four years before his death, and thereafter an incident occurred each year until the murders on the eve of their wedding anniversary. There was no evidence to suggest that Harvey had any enemy, and it is obvious that Jeannette was well liked by all with whom she came in contact.

What motive would account for the killing of this young couple?

Like the murderer, Thomas possessed a rifle .22 which

produced lead bullets indistinguishable in their markings from those in the heads of Harvey and Jeannette.

Like the murderer's weapon, Thomas's rifle makes distinctive firing pin, ejection and extractor marks on each shell case it fires. One of these, from this rifle, was found where it might reasonably be expected to have been thrown as the result of a hasty and violent reloading in the vicinity of the louvre windows and back steps.

Whereas the murderer had access to the car axle which weighted Harvey's body, Thomas had in his tip the two axle components – the stubs cut from that very axle.

These three parts of the old assembly taken from Rasmussen the man who altered a trailer for Thomas's father (and against his wishes in respect of the stubs) by Richard Thomas and returned to the farm.

It may reasonably be inferred that the axle would have been treated in the same way as the stubs each side of it, and at some stage have found its way with them on to Thomas's tip, where like the stubs, it remained unnoticed until the occasion arose for its use. This tip was, we know, visited by Thomas to dump cow 4 on 23/6/70: he was plainly in the habit of using it at about this time.

Thomas, like the murderer, had access to wire, and amongst the wire on his farm in six different places were five wires which were similar to the galvanized waist wire found on Harvey's body, and one wire which was similar to the chest wire. On the evidence of DSIR scientist Mr Todd, four of the five wires similar to the waist wire were in excellent agreement with it, and the fifth was in good agreement.

The sixth wire was in good agreement with the chest wire.

Of these wires, ten elements in all have been tested for – Mr Todd's original eight (of which four were tested for by defence) and two more to which Dr Devereux referred in cross-examination.

Mr Todd, with all his experience, is adamant that his opinion is correct, and you may think the undisputed facts would lead to an incredible coincidence if he were wrong.

His original results are now in respect of the chest wire supported by the work of Dr Devereux in respect of all the elements he tested with the exception of copper, where Drs Sprott and Devereux seize upon a minimal variation to justify

491

a complete rejection of Mr Todd's carefully considered opinion following two months' careful work within his own specialty – however reluctant the defence advisers were to acknowledge his pre-eminence in this sphere.

In judging the matter, you may, like Mr Todd, think it highly significant that nine of the ten elements separately tested for are indistinguishable, even stretching Dr Devereux's hypersensitive machine to its limits, and that Mr Todd is right in rejecting as overprecise the supposed copper differences.

And you may think it no less significant that a totally different wire – the galvanized waist wire – is indistinguishable in respect of eight elements on Dr Devereux's tests, and that his distinctions between the wires on the basis of the other two results are academic.

Is it not also significant that there should be such matching between two sets of quite different lots of wires: one set waist and farm, and one set chest and farm, whereas there is no such matching between any other two of the wires taken from fourteen farms.

Although the wires are in no way crucial to the Crown case, you may think that there is really no doubt about the connection and that it is singular indeed that Thomas is the only farmer of the fourteen whose wires match the body wires.

As to ammunition and transport, although by themselves counting for little, Thomas is a man having at least one No. 8 round his shed at the time of the police search: and he has both a car and trailer (which were not, as suggested, blocked in by Peter Thomas's car on the night of the killings) and a tractor with tray which was later used to take cow 4 to the tip.

Thomas was also a shooter – one who was accustomed to the difficult art of shooting opossums by torchlight, no doubt with no illumination of the foresight. And as a resident of Pukekawa for most of his life, he would know when and how he could get access to the river – whether by tractor down Mercer Ferry Road, or along another road, and where a vehicle could approach the river unobserved.

As to the final element to be looked for in a killer, Thomas had a motivation which was made very clear by the evidence. He had known Jeannette since primary school, and seen her go to boarding school and teachers college and then abroad while he worked in labouring jobs around the area. On her return home, she cut short her intended period of teaching at Mangatangi, and went south to Wanganui where she met and eventually married Harvey.

It is perfectly plain that even as a youth Thomas had what he described as a 'schoolboy crush' on Jeannette. Mrs Batkin's evidence establishes an unusually deep emotional involvement on his part even as a youth, and faced with the evidence of valuable gifts made by him to Jeannette, Thomas has admitted that his attitude deepened still further during 1960 at Maramurua.

He denies that his going to live there – a few miles from Jeannette four days after she took up residence – was more than coincidence, even though it meant throwing up the job he had had for five years, leaving home for the first time, and leaving there at about the stage when Jeannette must have been planning her overseas trip.

You may think it strange that a man so slow to be deterred should have seen the girl he was so attached to only twice at Maramarua. We have only his version of this. He is sufficiently interested to know she is going, to get her overseas address from her father, and to send her the pen set which is the subject of the letter he retained from February 1961 until after police inquiries had begun.

On her return from the UK he visits her with the brush and comb set, and is politely told she does not want to see any more of him. On his account, this is the end of the matter – he forgets her, marries in 1964 and that is all.

But the evidence proves otherwise. To her friends Mrs Willis and Mrs MacGee, Jeannette confided that she was pestered by Thomas – and she did not know Mrs MacGee until she had gone to Wanganui. And it is plain from her father's evidence that she complained to him about Thomas, and he was the reason for her leaving Mangatangi mid-year and travelling south – at a stage when Thomas says he thought nothing more about her.

Mr Liddell – whose evidence was uncontradicted – told the court of Thomas's wish to marry Jeannette and the visit to the fortuneteller, who apparently assured him that all would be well between him and her when she came back from down south and that he would be able to win her back from the other man.

From this time until the golf club dance between Jeannette's engagement at Easter 1966 and her marriage in June, there is no evidence of Thomas seeing her, and in the interim he had married Mrs Thomas in November 1964.

Whether this was a happy marriage is not a topic upon which I propose to address you. I would, however, remind you that Thomas obviously had a clear recollection of seeing Harvey and Jeannette together for the first time: you may think a significant recollection for one who had lost all interest in her in December 1962.

On his own admission his was not the normal attitude of a married man seeing an old girlfriend interested in some-one else: in cross-examination he agreed that 'no-one in Pukekawa had more reason than me to be jealous of Harvey Crewe'.

That you may think was a very significant piece of evidence. No doubt Harvey Crewe appeared prosperous and had a well-liked wife, and no doubt Thomas was having his troubles financially – along with other farmers in the area who had been hit by the drought.

But to think of Harvey Crewe in terms of such jealousy, particularly in his very cautious answers under cross-examination, is the plainest evidence that Thomas viewed Harvey differently from other apparently prosperous farmers in the neighbourhood.

Now Thomas agreed that he knew of no-one else in the district with a similar attitude towards Jeannette. This, to-gether with his acknowledged jealousy of Harvey, provide you may think, in the case of these two young people, the only kind of motivation there could possibly be for wanton destruction of their property, and the final tragic end to their lives.

No ordinary well-balanced person would behave in such a way.

But Thomas had a special attitude towards Jeannette; he had, he said, reason to be jealous of Harvey, and his own position was poor and with limited prospects.

Had he married Jeannette, as he had hoped to for so long, he would have been the master of the Chennell property, able to buy a new car and stock, and enjoy the fruits of a well-established farm.

Instead, he was the bare tenant of a leasehold interest in a poor farm, and under pressure from his bank and from creditors. He appears to have associated Jeannette with the relief of his money troubles – he said to Detective Johnston that if he needed money, Jeannette would lend him some.

Why should she have done so when she had never encouraged him, and on his own account, they had spoken only casually in the street on rare occasions since 1966?

You may think it highly impossible that she would have made such an offer; but what is significant is that Thomas thought she would.

Thomas is not on trial in respect of the incidents of burglary and arson. You may think, however, that his was the state of mind of a man motivated towards such acts. There is, of course, no direct evidence as to who was responsible for these. It should be remembered, however, that the burglar who left cash behind, took a brush and comb set, obviously being used by Jeannette; Thomas had given her another such set which was at the time no doubt wrapped up, unused, as it was at the time of the murders.

Now at the crucial time, the period up to 17/6/70, Thomas was under particular strain. In that month, he lost nine cows and two heifers; and on the very day of the murders, his wife prepared a reply to a letter of demand – and apparently made part payment.

Thomas and his wife – like Harvey and Jeannette Crewe – must have passed through Tuakau that day. We cannot know whether Thomas spoke to Harvey and asked for a loan which was refused, or whether he saw them in the car he could not afford with the girl he'd always wanted, or what precipitated the events of the evening.

Cow 4 may well have played a part – the prospect of the loss of another beast, and perhaps its calf as well, must certainly have weighed on his mind. He mentioned the sick cow to his dentist that day, and it was also mentioned to Mrs Rosemary Thomas, who rang about the ratepayers' meeting. The same day he had incurred a bill on his motor car.

It is plain that he was under substantial pressure, on the

evening of 17/6/70; he had reason to be jealous of Harvey; he had always aspired to Jeannette.

His is the only evidence of motivation for the killings, and you may think that the only type of motivation for these otherwise inexplicable murders.

Thomas and his wife have both claimed that he was home all that evening of 17 June. When his aunt called on the phone concerning the ratepayers' meeting at about 7.30, you will remember there was talk only of a sick cow, not of a problem with a calving.

Shortly after the news of the disappearance was made public on 22 or 23 June, they and Peter Thomas say they had a discussion to fix their movements for the nights of the previous week.

You may indeed think it remarkable that innocent people should have such a discussion rather than spontaneously recall 'that was the night of so and so'.

But more significant, according to both Thomas and his wife, it was in that discussion that they fixed the crucial Wednesday, the 17th, as the night when cow 4 calved.

Much later, in fact in October, Mrs Thomas produced Exhibit 351, in which she herself had written the alleged date of birth of cow 4's calf as proof of how they were able to remember their movements that evening.

Now, of course, the document proves nothing of the kind. It is only as good as the entries made upon it, and Detective Inspector Hutton was not contradicted in cross-examination by Thomas in evidence when he said that on 27/10/70 Mrs Thomas acknowledged agreeing that of the four shed sheets seen by Detective Sergent Tootill on 25/10/70, only that containing birth of cow 4 had been fully written up as 'I've been too busy'.

Mrs Thomas denied this in evidence, but to admit this would be to lose the whole basis relied upon as supporting her husband's alibi. The unusual form of the entries in the shed sheet which you have seen you may think also suggests a hurried writing up for the benefit of the police.

Nor is her later conduct consistent with the calf's having been born on 17/6/70. If shortly after 23/6/70 – the day of the television report and also the day cow 4 was shot – the Thomases really believed that cow 4 had calved six days before, Mrs Thomas could never have told Detective Johnston that the interval between birth and shooting was only two days – as she repeated twice. She must have done too much work in connection with the cow and its calf over the six days to have forgotten it.

And if they had fixed 17/6/70 by the birth of the calf, both Peter Thomas and accused would surely have remembered this – Peter when he gave evidence and accused when he was interviewed by Detective Senior Sergeant Hughes. Peter Thomas, in fact, gave a totally different account. He said that on the Wednesday he and Arthur were at the shed together before dinner and that Mrs Thomas was not present. He made no mention of calving, as one would expect, if it occurred only two days before the shooting on 23/6/70 – that is the Sunday when he was away from the farm.

Mrs Thomas in evidence of the 17th claimed to have fixed the cow in her mind by reference to the trip to the dentist.

This was quite contrary to what she had said in her written statement, and you may think was plainly an afterthought.

In truth, I would submit that whenever the calf was born, it was not the 17th; and the attempt to label it as born on 17th – the day of the notional birth date according to the Herd Improvement Association – has misfired.

Of course, in a way, despite the discussion of this matter at the trial, it is really a complete red herring.

This is because there is no reason at all why Thomas should not have performed the murders on the night of the day when the cow calved and after the calving. The real importance of this evidence is that it, with all the other evidence, shows that Mrs Thomas's evidence cannot be relied on when she denies that Thomas is the killer.

I have already mentioned the curious discussion in the week after the bodies were discovered. As to the intervening period, we know little except that on the Friday night Mrs Thomas came home early from a function, followed by her husband some time later, her explanation being that she had to attend a cat show next day.

Friday was the day when Mr Roddick, the farm labourer, working for Mr Chitty, claimed to have seen the lady inside the fence enclosure watching him feed out hay. In view of his account that the Crewe car was out of its garage and by the fence, and the woman made no attempt to conceal herself, you may think that Mr Roddick was right when he identified the woman as the bride in the exhibit photo 60 (Mrs Crewe) but he confused the dates.

It is unreal to suggest that from his distance in the glimpse he had, he could later assert that the woman in slacks was or was not a particular individual. It is difficult to visualize anyone driving the Crewe car out of the garage to the position suggested, standing in full public view, returning the keys to where they were later found inside the bloodstained house, and then locking up.

An honest person would have reported it; while an associate of the murderer would never have returned in broad daylight and acted in this way.

It is true that Mrs McConachie said that on the Saturday afternoon she had seen a child running about inside the road gate, and also a light-coloured car. On the Saturday, Mrs Thomas had returned from a cat show before midday; and she had travelled to and from it in her husband's *light*-coloured vehicle.

The same comments as to the improbable however apply; unless it was thought that with the whole community at the football, the coast would be clear to return (as Dr Fox considers happened) and do what could be done to alleviate the tragedy.

I wish to repeat, as I said in opening, and make it quite clear that the Crown has laid no charge against Mrs Thomas, and that the question of her involvement or lack of involvement is totally irrelevant, except insofar as it relates to that of her husband.

The Crown does not suggest that Mrs Thomas was in any way responsible for these horrible killings. It may be that she has no more than suspicions of her husband's involvement; or it may be that she has in some way attempted to act as a loyal wife and perhaps have tried to minimize the tragedy.

If you prefer Dr Fox's opinion that the baby was fed, you might think that the elaborate double napkin on the child, each folded differently, was the work of a woman rather than a man; and that the presence of soiled napkins in the bed and a dirty milk bottle in the kitchen indicates an agitated stranger rather than a mother.

On the other hand, you may feel that Dr Caughey's opinion is the preferable; and that any busy mother, through oversight, can leave soiled napkins about by mistake.

The Crown has called evidence on these topics so that you have full information before you.

It is in no way crucial to the Crown case against this accused to determine precisely what occurred over the period: the evidence against Thomas is consistent with either alternative and I do not press for acceptance of either of the doctor's opinions.

The next stage was, of course, the finding of the bloodstained house and the disappearance of Mr and Mrs Crewe. It is sufficient to observe that Thomas took no part in the search, unlike his near neighbours, Mr Cathcart and Mr Murray, and despite his former interest in Jeannette.

Nor did he take any steps to tell the police that he recognized the old trailer when he saw the photos in the *New Zealand Herald*.

When Detective Senior Sergeant Hughes interviewed him, his purpose was to ascertain from Thomas the extent of any relationship between the two of them as a result of certain information he had received. This information clearly placed Thomas amongst the prime category of suspects.

You may think that Thomas supplied to the police on this as on subsequent occasions no more information than he knew very well they would be likely already to possess. He gave a qualified answer to the suggestion that he had had some sort of passion for Jeannette replying: 'Well, sort of . . .'

Having seen him in the witness box, you may think that Thomas is very far from the guileless farm lad unable to comprehend the questions put to him by police officers. On this occasion he admitted only to telephoning Jeannette on a number of occasions – a statement which he has qualified in his evidence – and writing to her on a number of occasions both while she was here in New Zealand and overseas.

This answer also he has qualified in evidence. At no stage during this interview did he make mention of the visits to Jeannette about which we now know, or the presents he had given her.

Asked to account for his movements on the night of 17 June about which the police were particularly interested, he replied that he had been home every night of the week from 17 to 22 June and that he could not say why, but he would have been home with his wife.

At no stage did he refer to the calving of cow No. 4 as accounting for his movements on the night of 17 June. I need not remind you because it is no doubt still fresh in your minds, that Hughes claims that Thomas told him that whenever he had met Jeannette in either Tuakau or Pukekawa, they would stop merely to pass the time of day and he told Hughes that she showed him no encouragement whatsoever.

Hughes more importantly claims that Thomas told him that while he had been employed by an agricultural contractor some three or four years before the murders, he, Thomas, had actually worked on the Crewe farm and there seen Harvey; that he had had morning and afternoon teas in the house and that he had there met Harvey Crewe whom he described as a 'decent type of bloke'.

You may think it significant that Thomas now denies telling Hughes these things which would both involve a closer association with Harvey Crewe than he is now prepared to admit and also a continuing relation with both the farm and Jeannette, who was no doubt present on the farm at this particular time.

At this early stage in the inquiry, before the bodies, and so the means of death, were discovered, Hughes clearly had little information other than that received from Thomas, to attribute to him, and you may think it remarkable that Thomas finds it necessary to give the lie to this part of Hughes' evidence.

Thomas was subsequently seen by Detective Sergeant Parkes when he acknowledged in one way or another when shown a card, that he had written it to Jeannette and given it to her together with a brush and comb set.

He volunteered no further information on that occasion and it was not until the police investigation was well under way and he was seen by Parkes and Detective Sergeant Seaman on 7 September, that he gives them in any detail his true relationship and association with Jeannette.

At this stage, no doubt, this information was already in the hands of the police from other sources but it is particularly noteworthy that even then when being asked about his movements on 17 June, Thomas made no reference to the calving of cow no. 4. The only reference to a sick cow having trouble with calving was made with relation to his activities on the Tuesday night – i.e. 16 June.

Thomas, despite his inability to answer many of the questions put to him in cross-examination, claims to have a clear recollection that in these interviews with Parkes, he was told that the brush and comb set given by him to Jeannette in Christmas 1962 was found by the police still wrapped up.

If this is so, you may think it strange that at a subsequent interview with Detective Johnson, in answer to Johnson's query as to whether or not he knew whether Jeannette had used this gift, Thomas replied . . . 'It still may be wrapped up for all I know . . .'

If he was already aware of the fact that it was wrapped from information given to him by Parkes, he would have said what he knew about it.

His subsequent interviews really give nothing more away until on 28 October 1970, when interviewed by Detective Inspector Hutton at the stage where he was well aware of the evidence collated following the finding of both bodies, he made the significant remark that: '. . . I know that I am sitting on rocks; I have got to stick to what I have already told you otherwise I am a gonner.'

It was on this same occasion that when asked by the detective inspector why he had not told Detective Sergeant Parkes about the cow no. 4 calving, he replied: 'They did not mention it so I did not tell them.'

This you may think is indicative of his attitude throughout the whole inquiry.

A pointer you may think to his state of mind was the remark overheard by Detective Sergeant Keith on 21 October 1970 that 'If they think I am guilty I am and that's that'.

This remark which, in some contexts, could be innocently explained, assumes significance from both the fact that both Thomas and his wife deny that it was made and it presents another clash between the accused and his wife and another witness who noted the conversation in his notebook at the precise time that he heard it – namely at 11.42 that morning.

One other matter requires mention at this stage and that is the evidence from Mr Eggleton that in the week following the notification of Mr and Mrs Crewe, Thomas brought into his shop a watch covered with blood and mucus which had had its glass front pushed in. It was never suggested that Eggleton did not receive such a watch in that condition but Thomas claimed that he had been confused with his uncle William Gladstone Colin Thomas who had had dealings over a seamaster watch with Eggleton about this time.

You will recall that Eggleton identified Thomas as a result of seeing a photograph in a local magazine showing Thomas wearing a black singlet at a dance. Thomas concedes that, like other farmers, he possesses and wears such singlets but denies that he has ever done so when visiting Tuakau or Pukekohe.

Mrs Batkin who gave plain evidence that he had, in fact, done so on a number of occasions, was not challenged as to this and it must be plain to you that the suggestion that Eggleton has mistaken Arthur Thomas for his uncle is totally without foundation.

We know, having seen William Thomas and heard the evidence of him and his wife, that he had previously dealt with Eggleton over the proposed purchase of an expensive candelabra for the fine new home which you may recall having seen overlooking the new Mercer bridge at the end of Mercer Ferry Road.

You may think it inconceivable that such a distinctive and potentially valuable customer could ever have been confused with the accused.

A challenge to Eggleton's evidence was made on the grounds that he had told Mrs Maguire and subsequently her husband in December 1970 at or after the taking of the Lower Court depositions in this case, that he had never seen Thomas before.

Mr Eggleton candidly admitted that he had so told Mr and Mrs Maguire and gave as his reason that he had been threatened by her that his business would be affected were he to become involved.

The making of this threat and threats to Eggleton's children was confirmed by the police in their inquiries and again you may think it significant that although we have heard from Mr Maguire, his wife did not enter the witness box. The reason for such threats and for the non-appearance of Mrs Maguire

502

before you to deny them, are matters which you may think confirm Eggleton's account.

It will not have escaped your attention that the police found no wristlet watch belonging to Harvey – either on his body or in his house.

At different stages of the trial you may think, apart from his claim to have been at home on the night of the killings which I have already discussed with you, the accused has raised various, you may think, conflicting alternative defences.

The lead found in the heads of Harvey and Jeannette – it will be advanced on behalf of Thomas, I have no doubt, that the lead in the heads of the dead couple was fired either by Thomas's rifle without his knowledge or consent or by a different rifle which left identical land markings upon its bullet.

Thomas has never really denied that his rifle was at all material times in his house. According to Peter Thomas, it was in his bedroom behind the door of that room in June although exactly where it was on the 17th he was unable to tell us. On 17 August when Detective Sergeant Charles uplifted the rifle for the first time, Mrs Thomas admitted that it had come from the kitchen and from the well-kept appearance of the rifle it is evident that it was not left lying about. Clearly it has always been in the house either in a bedroom, in the kitchen or possibly in the wash-house. In any event, it is perfectly plain that no intruder could have entered the Thomas property at night, uplifted the rifle, committed the murder and returned it without alerting either the members of the household or the dogs who were nearby. This suggestion, you may think, is plainly to be rejected.

The alternative suggestion advanced by the defence was that the possessor of an identical rifle has committed these murders, and the finger has been pointed at John Michael Eyre whose mother gave evidence before you.

She told you that he was one of her two sons and would have been 28 years in June 1970. He was then living with both his parents – of whom Mr Eyre has since died – and a younger brother then aged 16 years, at Pukekawa about 1½ miles from the Crewe farm. She told you that John Michael was hard of hearing and had suffered from a speech impediment from birth and that not surprisingly, due to these impediments, he did not go out at night unless accompanied. You will also recall, I am sure, that she told you that he was at home with the other members of the family that night and he only possessed the rifle subsequently examined by the police because it had happened to be lent to them by the next-door neighbour.

To boost this attack upon him an allegation was made that he had on one occasion appeared with a rifle unheralded upon the verandah of the house of a Mr and Mrs Hooker, then living at Pukekawa. One can understand that these people were alarmed at seeing Eyre unannounced on their front verandah in possession of a weapon of some kind, however innocent his intention may have been, on account of the difficulty of communicating with him. Despite attempts to show a propensity for cruelty in Eyre, you have heard no evidence of any behaviour directed by him against another person and certainly nothing has emerged from the wide-spread inquiry into the deaths of the Crewes to suggest any involvement on the part of this man.

In what you may regard as a misleading attempt to develop a case against Eyre, the evidence was led from Mr and Mrs Hooker without reference to the date on which the events they describe took place. The impression must have been with you that this occurrence must have been at a time sufficiently approximate to the deaths of the Crewes to have been relevant to the inquiry. In fact, it emerged on cross-examination, that this had occurred some fourteen years before when Eyre would have been in his early teens. The possibility that Eyre was involved in any way with the deaths of the Crewes can safely be disregarded by you.

Attempts were also made to establish that the police search had not ranged sufficiently widely and evidence was led from Payne and from William Thomas that their rifles and one owned by Montgomery had not been collected and examined by the police and scientists. The reason for the limits of the police investigation were plainly described to you by Detective Sergeant Charles and supply the answer to that criticism. None of these men fell within the categories of those who might reasonably have been expected to be possibly involved – either as near neighbours of the Crewes, persons who had

had to do with them or having become involved in any other way in the inquiry.

At one stage, an attack was levelled at Mr Demler who was said to have had access to a firearm but this was shown to be equally unfounded when the weapon in question, originally owned by the Chennell Estate, was produced and found to be of substantially greater gauge and incapable of firing a .22 bullet.

Thomas, in cross-examination, as part of his claim to innocence, suggested, you may think somewhat ingenuously, that if he had done the homicide, the rifle would be well buried or in the river. You may think it plain that although he did, in fact, use the river as a means of disposing of the connection between himself and the killings, that he could not possibly have rid himself of the weapon which Peter Thomas and others knew to have been in his possession at the relevant time and it was registered in his name.

The defence were unable to challenge the Crown evidence that Thomas's rifle had fired the cartridge case, Exhibit 35, and there can be no doubt that this was, in fact, the truth. In order therefore, to deny his guilt in the face of such powerful and damning evidence, vehement attempts were made by the defence to establish that the shell case found in the enclosure garden by the back gate had been planted to provide false evidence against Thomas. The seriousness of this grave allegation cannot be overstated and I shall shortly make reference to this topic. Three separate attacks were mounted –

First, that contrary to all other evidence the area had been sieved so that any cartridge case must have been dishonestly planted after the date of the August search;

Secondly, it was claimed through Dr Sprott that the evidence of the appearance of the shell case when found was inconsistent with its having been in or under the ground for the four months from the date of the killing until Charles's discovery.

Finally, and you may think spectacularly, it was claimed that the particular shell case could never have been associated with either of the No. 8 bullets found in the heads of the deceased.

Now, as to Hewson's evidence, the following matters will

505

not have escaped your attention. Despite his claim to being virtually a member of the police party, it is plain that he had no idea of the theory underlying this particular search, namely that the murderer might have disposed of his shell cases out of windows in the house or as he removed the bodies by wheelbarrow after taking them out the front door. On this theory, the logical places for the most detailed searching were immediately around the house itself and in the garden on one side of the front path and the other gardens on each side of the front gate of the enclosure. It would have been illogical to reverse the pattern as Hewson claimed was the case by ignoring the kitchen garden which he thought had not been sieve-searched even though it immediately adjoined the house. His recollection was proved to be poor; one would expect a man who had taken a full part in the heavy work of sieve-searching in the month of August to have remembered the existence of the two gardens which he omitted and which were, indeed, amongst the first to have been searched and not to have known that the kitchen garden also had been sieved. He was plainly in error in asserting that a garden adjoined the front path on each side and admitted that after the mistakes he had made, he had to be careful and that he did not have a good memory.

He appeared to give the impression that contrary to the scheme underlying the search, the kitchen garden had merely been visually searched after the pulling out of certain growth, whereas, for no obvious reason, having elected not to sieve this area, the police had taken the trouble to search the entire length of the perimeter fence where the murderer would have no reason on that theory to have gone.

Hewson acknowledged that, as at August 1970, he was under considerable personal stress and that it was not until almost exactly a year later that he first tried to recollect where the sieving had occurred.

It may be that not comprehending the pattern underlying the search, Hewson has become confused. This submission is supported by all the other evidence available to the Court.

First, is the plan underlying that search which I have already discussed.

Secondly, there is the evidence of the four police officers engaged in it. Namely, Detective Sergeant Jeffries, the officer

506

in charge of the search, Detective Sergeant Gee, Detective Meurant and Constable Higgins. They had the responsibility for conducting this search, and bore the burden of the heavy physical work entailed whereas Hewson on his own admission was not there throughout the whole period.

It was suggested in cross-examination of Mr Chitty that the police were wrong when they claimed to have uplifted the mower used the following day and that Hewson's account of the whole matter was accordingly to be preferred. Mrs Chitty, however, volunteered before you that it was, in fact, Detective Meurant who had borrowed her mower and that it was on some other occasion that Hewson had called at her house.

In addition to these four police officers, evidence was given by Mr Handcock, the manager of the property, who unlike Hewson, had an active responsibility for the property at the time of this sieve search.

He, a farmer and latterly a nurseryman by occupation, gave clear evidence that the sieve-search had not extended over the area claimed by Hewson and he confirmed the police account that the kitchen garden had been sieved. You will recall the description he gave in each case.

Further, you heard the evidence of Detective Sergeant Charles as to the condition of the bed as at the date of his search in October and of the work entailed in performing the sieve search which he and Detective Sergeant Parkes attempted to carry out.

Charles's evidence was confirmed by Handcock and neither was cross-examined on this topic nor, indeed, were any of the four police officers involved in the search given the opportunity of commenting on the account which Hewson subsequently gave.

Most fortunately and by pure chance, it happens that photographs taken for another reason show the condition of the gardens and illustrate the accuracy of the account given by the police officers and Hewson.

One shows the condition of the enclosure garden at the time of the original search in June and you can see in the background the remains of plants which were left in the ground at that stage.

Another photograph taken at the time of Charles's

discovery, shows that same plant having propagated – something which could not have happened had the bed been sieved as claimed by Hewson.

In truth, the reason for the final search by Charles was the admission of Jeffries that his party had not sieved this particular spot and this coupled with the suggestion of Johnston of the explanation for the open louvre windows and the back light being on led to the reconstruction about which Dr Nelson has spoken. There can be no reason for Jeffries to have said that the garden had not been sieved if, in fact, it had and it is submitted that Hewson is simply wrong in the evidence he has given.

In anticipation of the attack by Dr Sprott, evidence was called from Mr Shanahan, Mr Braithwaite and Mr Matson to establish that the appearance of Exhibit 350 as described in the evidence was entirely consistent with its having been in or under the soil for the appropriate period.

Mr Shanahan conducted a survey of a type which Dr Sprott, in giving evidence in the Court of Appeal, accepted as appropriate, although before you, he endeavoured to reject as misguided. I invite you to accept his earlier evidence on this topic as the more reliable. The survey carried out over an appropriate period in many places provided us with a broad spectrum of samples and in the opinion of Mr Braithwaite, an expert of the greatest possible experience in the field of metal corrosion, abundantly supported and confirmed Mr Shanahan's opinion that Exhibit 350 could well have been in or under the ground for the requisite period.

Mr Metson, the soil expert, gave confirmatory evidence and was not contradicted by any defence witness having appropriate experience in matters of soil chemistry.

It was the plain effect of the evidence on this topic that the behaviour of brass shell cases buried in or under soil for a period of four months is quite unpredictable and that a wide variety of results is to be expected.

An attempt was made to show that Exhibit 350 was insufficiently corroded around its radius to be consistent with the history asserted by the Crown but Mr Shanahan's evidence of its 30 per cent corrosion and of the other shell cases which were relatively uncorroded in this area refuted this claim. It is, you may think, highly significant that Professor

Titchener who inspected the case on behalf of the defence prior to the first trial, apparently found nothing strange about its appear- ance in the light of its history nor did the British Home Office whose report you have. On Dr Sprott's own evidence, the description of the shell case given by Detective Sergeant Charles who found the shell, is what he would have expected in a shell case buried for the time in question and if his evidence is acceptable to you, that is the end of the matter.

You will also recall the evidence of Detective Sergeant Parkes and of Detective Inspector Hutton who inspected this shell and which are consistent with even Dr Sprott's require- ments. It is true that there are variations among these descrip- tions but it must be remembered that their main interest was in the firing pin impression and that the allegation of plant was raised at a very late stage. It may be observed that if they had wished to give false evidence, a carefully dovetailed account would presumably have appeared.

It is of particular significance that Detective Inspector Hutton was the officer responsible for the retention of this exhibit through which an attack is now levelled against him and the party of police officers whom he headed throughout this inquiry.

I make this latter observation particularly because any allegation of planting must necessarily affect these men. I need not repeat the gravity of this allegation which is so easily made. For such a serious and sinister allegation to be open for acceptance, a police officer or officers – particularly those who have given evidence – must have been involved. But the sequence of events within the police party – commencing with the return of Thomas's rifle on 8 September 1970 to Johnston's reconstruction of the reason for the open louvre window and the light being on at the stage when he joined the search in September resulting in the reconstruc- tion and the decision to have the bed sieved – follows logically and reasonably. Nothing in this affords any support to this vehement attempt by the defence to break this powerful and damning piece of evidence which even by itself would justify your convicting Thomas.

If it is said to be planted, one must consider when and by whom. Plainly it must have been by a police officer as a planting by an outsider would be purposeless unless he knew that a fresh police search was to be mounted. In fact, however, as Charles says, the police took extreme care to keep knowledge of this fact within their ranks.

Now prior to the return of Thomas's rifle on 8 September 1970, there could have been no reason to retain a fired case for subsequent planting; of the three shells fired, all were retained by Dr Nelson and they were of course not brass but copper. Thomas's rifle was uplifted for the second time on 20 October 1970 by Johnston and Parkes together, who thereupon gave it to Detective Sergeant Keith who from then until the day after Exhibit 350 was found by Charles, had exclusive possession of the Exhibit rifle and kept it in a locked cabinet inside a locked room to which he had the only keys.

Yet it was never put to Keith that he had been involved in the planting. It is plain that the suggestion leading to the new search came from Johnston but no allegation of plant was directed at him. No other officer could have had access to the rifle and so the other members of the squad including Parkes who is the only one to whom the allegation was put, could have been responsible unless at least Johnston and Keith are party to a conspiracy of the most terrible kind.

The fact that the shell case escaped the initial search when the theory was that a blunt instrument had been used and also the visual search in August when other gardens were sieved, is accounted for by the evidence of Vesey who, called for the defence, acknowledged that search failed to reveal the existence of one of the six shell cases known to have been placed in an area covered by the diameter of the stub axle.

The final ground on which planting was alleged by the defence was that the Number 8 bullets found in the heads of the deceased were inconsistent with the type of bullets to be expected from a shell case of the kind of Exhibit 350. This was the purpose of Dr Sprott's diagram and evidence. No part of this evidence was put to any Crown witness including Mr Aitken of the C.A.C., who had given evidence that the composition of shell cases had not altered over recent years and that the No. 8 was stamped into bullets made over the period from 1949 until 1963. Nor was any hint of this defence made to the Crown's ballistic experts Dr Nelson and Mr

Shanahan. That is why leave was given to call the rebuttal evidence of Mr Shea and Dr Nelson.

Mr Vesey, who, we were told, was the organizer of the Thomas retrial committee, made no reference in his evidence to supplying Dr Sprott with some samples of cartridges so that the validity of his sampling might have been explored on cross-examination. The defence evidence-in-chief was left on the basis that apparently proper inquiry and sampling had led to the conclusion both that the Keith shell found in Thomas's shed and bearing the No. 8 on its lead was quite dissimilar to the Charles shell and of crucial importance, the Charles shell could never have contained a No. 8 bullet.

As a result, however, of urgent inquiries and the leave given to call Mr Shea and to recall Dr Nelson, a very different picture emerged. It is now plain beyond any doubt that Dr Sprott's 3 and 4 are, in fact, indistinguishable; that the Charles shell and the Keith shell are indistinguishable; and that disregarding all the other evidence in the case, there is no reason whatever why the Charles shell should not have contained the bullet of Harvey or Jeannette.

The axle, like the shell case, although quite independent of it, would by itself justify Thomas's conviction on the present charges. For the axle which had weighted Harvey's body to have come from the matching stub axles on the accused's tip, the existence of which was not known to his best friend and next-door neighbour Cathcart, is of most enormous probative value against Thomas. For this reason, no doubt, strenuous efforts were made to break the link both between the body and the axle and between the axle and Thomas.

Much cross-examination was directed to the police photographer present at the retrieval of Harvey's body, plainly directed to showing that the axle was not connected to the body at the material time. For this reason, the body photos have been put in evidence and these together with the accounts of Inspector Gaines, Detective Inspector Hutton and the police divers establish beyond any doubt that Harvey's body had wired to it the axle which broke as a diver exerted pressure on the body cradle and caused Inspector Hutton to lose his grip upon it, following which it was retrieved from directly under the body by a diver and was brought to the surface bearing the rust marks from wires which have been shown to you.

It is altogether inconceivable that that axle should have found its way by coincidence from its company with the stub axles from the Thomas farm to this remote spot, well down stream from the Tuakau Bridge and inaccessible except by boat, to the very place where Harvey's body happened to end up.

Rejecting this challenge to the connection, I pass to the claims that the axle either never reached the farm or having reached it disappeared from it and by strange coincidence, happened to reach the body containing a bullet consistent with having been fired by Thomas's rifle. Evidence was called as to the presence of scavengers and vintage car enthusiasts on the Thomas farm who might have taken an axle from it. It was also said by one Lee Martin, that Bruce Richard Eyre (who it is not suggested was a member of the family of Mickey Eyre) had removed some kind of axle from the farm when he took away a car on which he had been working. The true position is, however, that all the other original components of the trailer remained on the tip or farm despite the presence of the searchers and if these remained untouched, one would reasonably expect a similar history for the axle until such time as a heavy portable weight came to be required for the purpose of which we know.

The challenge to Rasmussen's account that all the replaced components were taken back to the Thomas farm against his wishes can be briefly dismissed. Although it was put forcefully to Rasmussen that his evidence on this topic was wrong, it is now quite plain from the evidence of Mr Thomas snr, taken with Mr Rasmussen's, that the accused's brother Richard who was not called by the defence, both brought the trailer to Rasmussen and later returned it with all the components to the farm at the Mercer Ferry Road. The argument that it would have been uneconomic for Rasmussen to have done this work for the price he mentioned, was effectively answered by him and there can be no doubt that the axle with all the other components, found its way back to the Thomas farm and was used by the accused as the body weight for Harvey Crewe.

512

There can, on the whole of the evidence called, be no reasonable doubt that Arthur Allan Thomas on the 17th day of June 1970 at Pukekawa murdered Harvey and Jeannette Crewe.

APPENDIX 7

Letter from Minister of Police the Hon. A. McCready
to the Hon. D. MacIntyre

19th September 1977

The Prime Minister, the Rt. Hon. R. D. Muldoon, has referred
your letter of 15 July concerning your discussions with Mr A.
Thomas Snr, father of Arthur Allan Thomas, to me for reply.

You will recall that, with your letter to the Prime Minister,
you enclosed the letter which was addressed to you by Mr
Chris Birt of P.O. Box 648, Tauranga, who commented on
the evidence given at the Arthur Allan Thomas trial pertaining to the statement of John Fisher of Feilding.

I have discussed the matter with the Deputy Commissioner
of Police who advised that, in a statement supplied to Birt,
John Fisher of Feilding related how in September or October
1970, when he had been working in the Pukekohe area, he
had slaughtered some pigs and in so doing he had damaged
his gold watch. Being unable to wash the blood off the
watch because of the broken glass he had taken it in
to Eggleton's shop for repairs. Birt's contention was that
Eggleton had confused Fisher with Thomas and had given
incorrect evidence.

The fact Fisher had a watch repaired by Eggleton first came
to the notice of the police on 2 September 1971, when Fisher
spoke to Constable C. W. Bell at Feilding. On 9 November
1971, a detailed statement was obtained from Fisher and his
watch taken to a jeweller for examination to determine
if there were any jeweller's repair marks inscribed inside
the back. Examination of the watch by G. Brandt, jeweller
of Feilding, revealed one mark of significance. This was
B10678E over 12/1/71.

This mark was known to be that used by William Eggleton,
jeweller of Pukekohe, and the date 12/1/71 was the date of

514

repair. It was then apparent that Fisher's watch was not of any relevance to the Thomas trial.

Eggleton had given evidence that on Thursday, 24 June 1970, Arthur Allan Thomas had taken a blood-stained gold watch to him for repairs. He first reported this matter to the police on 23 February 1971, during the first trial from 15 February 1971 to 2 March 1971. Although this was eight months after the incident he was certain of the date and the fact that it was Thomas who had brought the watch to him. Fisher's watch was repaired on 12 January 1971, about six weeks before Eggleton came to the police. He is adamant that he was aware of the significance of the Thomas watch incident a long time before he informed the police and is in no doubt about any confusion arising from the Fisher watch. Eggleton has viewed a photograph of Fisher and verified that he was not the man about whose watch he gave evidence. He was and still is positive about his identification of Thomas.

The police did not call Fisher as a witness in the second trial of Thomas or inform the defence of his claim because it had been clearly established that the repairs to his watch had no relevance to the matter before the Court. Fisher may have made an honest mistake about the date on which his watch was repaired, September/October 1970, whereas it was actually January 1971, but those actively interested in the Thomas re-trial movement have attempted to make capital of a totally irrelevant issue.

Fisher was not informed the result of police inquiries. As you are aware, the Thomas affair has been something of a saga and police members involved in the investigation were kept busy on the case from mid-1971 until some years later because of new trials, appeals and referrals to the Court of Appeal. Apparently the matter of informing Fisher was overlooked. This has now been rectified.

A further aspect of the evidence in relation to wristlet watches raised during the passage of the Thomas case through the judicial system should be brought to your notice. Evidence was given by William Gladstone Colin Thomas, an uncle of Arthur Allan Thomas, that he had had a silver-coloured watch delivered to Eggleton for repair during the early part of 1970. He had called on Eggleton in June of that year to see how the repairs were progressing. As a defence witness his evidence was thoroughly tested and presented to the jury along with that of Eggleton, who had told the Court that he remembered his dealings with William Thomas quite distinctly from those involving Arthur Allan Thomas.

Eggleton is quite certain that his transactions with Arthur Thomas, William Thomas and Fisher were unrelated in time and did not result in any confused state of mind on his part.

The evidence given by Eggleton was included in the police case heard by a jury on two trials and been subject to review by a judge or judges on five other occasions. Despite the critical and frequent testing of the evidence, Thomas remains convicted of the murders of Jeannette and Harvey Crewe.

Bibliography

LEGAL DOCUMENTS

First Trial Transcript: February 1971 to March 1971

Fifty-seven sworn affidavits dated variously 1971 to 1978

Final Speech of Crown Solicitor, David Morris, to second trial jury: April 1973

Five affidavits concerning the removal of an axle from the Thomas farm in 1965: November 1977

Initial statements made by a number of people to the police: Between 22 July 1971 and 26 February 1972

Lower Court Depositions taken in December 1970

Memorandum of Land Transfer from L. W. Demler to M. C. Demler: August 1962

New Zealand Law Reports: 1955, 1956, 1972, 1973

Report of Assistant Commissioner of Police to Commissioner of Police: 27 October 1973

Report of Detective Inspector Bruce Hutton to the Assistant Commissioner of Police plus a number of attached sworn affidavits: 24 October 1973

Second Trial Transcript: March 1973 to April 1973

Transcript of Appeal hearing and Appeal Court's judgment: June 1971

Transcript of Appeal hearing and Court's judgment: July 1973

Transcript of Mr Justice (now Sir Trevor) Henry's summing-up to first trial jury: March 1971

Transcript of Mr Justice (now Sir Clifford) Perry's summing-up to second trial jury: April 1973

Transcript of referral hearing December 1972 to January 1973, and transcript of Court's judgment.

Transcript of Sir George McGregor's report to the Minister of Justice: February 1972

NEWSPAPERS PERIODICALS
New Zealand newspapers and magazines: 1970 to 1978
Los Angeles *Examiner*: 1969
San Francisco *Examiner*: 1969
The *Nelson Colonist*: 1908–1909
The *Grey River Argus*: 1908–1909
The *Press*: 1908–1909
Parliamentary Reports for 1908–1909
Inangahua Times: 1908–1909
The *Buller Miner*: 1908–1909
The *Wairarapa Daily Times*: 1908–1909
Westport morning and evening newspapers: 1908–1909
Rolling Stone: 10 May 1973
Documentation and technical data from I.C.I. and IMI Australia and CAC Auckland: 1955 to 1975
Technical data from Roeszler & Sons Ltd Melbourne: 1965 to 1975

BOOKS, PERSONAL DIARIES, PRIVATE CORRESPONDENCE, SPECIAL REPORTS
BAILEY, Earl. *Quash the Verdicts – The Thomas Affair* and *All In The Public Interest*. Auckland, 1976
SWAIN, Evan. *The Crewe Murders*, Auckland, 1971
SPROTT, Jim and BOOTH, Pat. *A.B.C. of Injustice*. Wellington, 1976
BOOTH, Pat. *Trial by Ambush*. Wellington, 1975
KIND, Stuart and OVERMAN, Michael. *Science Against Crime*. London, 1972
YALLOP, David A. *To Encourage the Others*. London, 1971
TAYLOR, Judge Pitt. *A Treatise on the Law of Evidence*. Tenth edition. London, 1906
MATTHEWS, Ella. *Yesterdays in Golden Buller*. New Zealand, 1957

PEARSON, Hesketh. *Conan Doyle, His Life and Art*. London

DU CANN, G. G. L. *Miscarriages of Justice*. London, 1960

KENNEDY, Ludovic. *Ten Rillington Place*, London, 1961

BELL, Terry. *Bitter Hill*, Auckland, 1972

Private diaries of Mrs Dorothy Cathcart: 1954 to 1960

Private diaries of Mrs Margaret Smith: 1969 to 1975

Private correspondence of Arthur Thomas, Allan Thomas, Vivien Thomas, Margaret Smith, and many others

CHAPMAN, Guy. *The Dreyfus Case*. London, 1963

Citizens of Pukekawa. *Pukekawa Profile:* A Jubilee Book privately published 1970

ELLIOT, Robert, Professor of Paediatrics, School of Medicine, Auckland. *Report on Rochelle Crewe*: 1970

FOX, Thomas, children's physician to Auckland Hospital Board. *Report on Rochelle Crewe*: 1970

Various scientific papers, kindly supplied by their authors Dr Donald Nelson and Rory Shanahan of the DSIR.

DSIR Chemistry Division booklet. New Zealand, 1976.

INDEX

535

536

541

A SELECTION OF RELATED TITLES
AVAILABLE FROM CORGI BOOKS

THE PRICES SHOWN BELOW WERE CORRECT AT THE TIME OF GOING TO PRESS. HOWEVER TRANSWORLD PUBLISHERS RESERVE THE RIGHT TO SHOW NEW RETAIL PRICES ON COVERS WHICH MAY DIFFER FROM THOSE PREVIOUSLY ADVERTISED IN THE TEXT OR ELSEWHERE.